Female Stars of British Cin

Female Stars of British Cinema
The Women in Question

Melanie Williams

EDINBURGH
University Press

In memory of my mum, Mary Jean Williams (1955–2008):
a star in her own right.

Edinburgh University Press is one of the leading university presses in the UK. We publish academic books and journals in our selected subject areas across the humanities and social sciences, combining cutting-edge scholarship with high editorial and production values to produce academic works of lasting importance. For more information visit our website: edinburghuniversitypress.com

Edinburgh University Press Ltd
The Tun – Holyrood Road
12 (2f) Jackson's Entry
Edinburgh EH8 8PJ

Typeset in Monotype Ehrhardt by
Servis Filmsetting Ltd, Stockport, Cheshire,
and printed and bound in Great Britain by
CPI Group (UK) Ltd, Croydon CR0 4YY

A CIP record for this book is available from the British Library

ISBN 978 1 4744 0563 8 (hardback)
ISBN 978 1 4744 0564 5 (paperback)
ISBN 978 1 4744 0565 2 (webready PDF)
ISBN 978 1 4744 0566 9 (epub)

Contents

List of Figures   vi
Acknowledgements   vii

1. Introduction: Questions of Female Stardom in British Cinema   1
2. 'A Girl Appears in Camiknickers': Jean Kent's Austerity Stardom   36
3. 'Blonde Glamour Machine': Diana Dors in the 1950s and Beyond   59
4. British New Waif: Rita Tushingham and Sixties Female Stardom   88
5. 'A Constant Threat': Glenda Jackson and the Challenges of Seventies Stardom   111
6. 'From Schoolgirl to Stardom': The Discovery and Development of Helena Bonham Carter and Emily Lloyd in the 1980s and 1990s   133
7. National Treasure: Judi Dench and Older Female Stardom into the 2000s   173
8. Conclusion: The Unbearable Whiteness of Being (a Female British Star)   194

Bibliography   209
Index   235

Figures

1.1 Kate Winslet, Elizabeth Hurley and Emma Thompson on the cover of *Radio Times* 7
1.2 Signed photograph of Ann Todd 9
1.3 Helena Bonham Carter versus the Kardashians 25
2.1 Jean Kent dances the Zambra as Rosal in *Caravan* 43
2.2 Jean Kent as bedraggled Astra in *The Woman in Question* 50
3.1 Diana Dors as happy-go-lucky showgirl Pearl in *As Long as They're Happy* 69
3.2 Diana Dors as condemned woman Mary Hilton in *Yield to the Night* 69
3.3 Diana Dors as wicked housekeeper Mrs Wickens in *The Amazing Mr. Blunden* 77
4.1 Rita Tushingham playing Kate in *Girl with Green Eyes* 94
4.2 Rita Tushingham as Nancy in *The Knack . . . and How to Get It* 101
5.1 Glenda Jackson as Gudrun in *Women in Love* 117
5.2 Glenda Jackson as Vicky in *A Touch of Class* 122
6.1 Helena Bonham Carter as Lucy Honeychurch in *A Room with a View* 143
6.2 Helena Bonham Carter playing bohemian Cora in modern-day Edinburgh in *Women Talking Dirty* 150
6.3 Emily Lloyd as Lynda in *Wish You Were Here* 152
6.4 Emily Lloyd as wannabe gangster's moll Betty in *Chicago Joe and the Showgirl* 159
7.1 Judi Dench as Ursula in *Ladies in Lavender* 179
7.2 Judi Dench as Evelyn Greenslade in *The Best Exotic Marigold Hotel* 187
8.1 Parminder Nagra and Keira Knightley in *Bend It Like Beckham* 200
8.2 Naomie Harris as 'Bond woman' Eve Moneypenny in *Skyfall* 202

Acknowledgements

I would like to thank everyone at Edinburgh University Press, but particularly Gillian Leslie and Richard Strachan, for their enthusiasm, encouragement, efficiency, and infinite patience throughout the process of getting this project off the ground and then moving it through the various stages of production. Thanks also to Laura Booth for her stalwart editorial work.

The research for this book has brought together material that I've been thinking about and working on for many years, and has therefore drawn on many different libraries and collections. However, the British Film Institute's (BFI's) library and its Special Collections have been absolutely invaluable and instrumental to the project, for which I would like to say a particular thank you. I have made particular use of the library's press cuttings files, which are hugely useful sources but that do not always contain author, title, or page number information – hence their absence in some of the references to follow (as indicated).

Neil Sinyard and Su Holmes have read sections of this book in draft form and it was hugely helpful to have their perceptive advice on a range of issues, so my heartfelt thanks go to them. My colleagues at the University of East Anglia (UEA) continue to be wonderfully sympathetic and intellectually stimulating company; extra special thanks go to Eylem Atakav, Richard Famer, Mark Fryers, Sarah Godfrey, Sarah Hill, Su Holmes again, Sarah Ralph, and Tim Snelson for enabling me to talk, sometimes at great length, about different aspects of this book and always being interested, or at least feigning interest very plausibly. The same goes for all the other friends and colleagues further afield who've done likewise over the years. Special thanks also to my work neighbours Rayna Denison and Mark Rimmer for putting up with my intermittent swearing. The University of East Anglia allowed this book to come into being by granting me a period of leave and offering other forms of support for the research and writing, for which much thanks, particularly to Keith Johnston and Mark Jancovich as Research Director and Head of School during the period in question. Thanks also to Sheldon Hall for doing some very helpful scanning from his extensive periodical collection.

Some elements of Chapter 5 first appeared in 'Staccato and wrenchingly modern: Reflections on the 1970s stardom of Glenda Jackson', in Paul Newland (ed.), *Don't Look Now: British Cinema in the 1970s* (Bristol: Intellect Press, 2010). Elements of chapter seven appeared in 'The best exotic graceful ager: Dame Judi Dench and older female celebrity', in Deborah Jermyn and Su Holmes (eds), *Women, Celebrity and Cultures of Ageing: Freeze Frame* (London: Palgrave Macmillan, 2015). I'm grateful to be able to draw on that work here.

The final piece of the jigsaw was Chapter 4 on Rita Tushingham and the 1960s, research for which was supported by the Arts and Humanities Research Council and constitutes part of 'Transformation and Tradition in Sixties British Cinema: Production Cultures, Cross Media Relations and National Branding', a research project based at the Universities of York and East Anglia (grant number AH/L014793/1).

Finally, on to the most important acknowledgements of all. Matthew Bailey, my husband, has been his usual amazing self: encouraging and supportive, endlessly thoughtful, providing me with those most precious commodities of all: time and space. It couldn't have been done without him, not least because he read the whole thing and helped me make sense of it. And although it's been great fun spending time with Jean, Diana, Rita, Glenda, Helena, Emily, Judi, and all the other remarkable women covered in this book, they have kept me at work late on numerous occasions and it's always been good to get back home to my own little star Lara Bailey. My final thanks must go to both Matthew and Lara for their love, kindness, and fun, all of which kept me going.

CHAPTER 1

Introduction: Questions of Female Stardom in British Cinema

This book presents a diachronic study of female stardom in British cinema from the 1940s to the present day, examining its discursive construction by means of detailed case studies of seven specific stars whose careers collectively span the period: Jean Kent, Diana Dors, Rita Tushingham, Glenda Jackson, Helena Bonham Carter, Emily Lloyd, and Judi Dench. As the book's subtitle suggests, these stars figure as its central 'women in question', borrowing the phrase from the film *The Woman in Question* (1950) that presented five different versions of the same woman (all played by Jean Kent) as seen through the eyes of five different people. Here the careers and personae of seven different women are used to provide multiple perspectives on the single, but multivalent, phenomenon of British female stardom.

Founding star studies scholar Richard Dyer claimed that stars function as 'embodiments of the social categories in which people are placed and through which they have to make sense of their lives . . . all of these typical, common ideas, that have the feeling of being the air that you breathe, just the way things are'.[1] Two examples of these 'common-sense' social categories described by Dyer are gender and nationality, and these are the two identity groupings that form this book's investigative parameters. It focuses on stars who are both British and female, and what it means when those two identities intersect in a star persona (while also engaging with their interaction with numerous other social categorisations, including ethnicity, class, regional identity, sexuality, and age).

In undertaking this particular project, I build upon previous academic scholarship on British stardom, most notably Bruce Babington's excellent essay collection *British Stars and Stardom: From Alma Taylor to Sean Connery* and Geoffrey Macnab's insightful monograph *Searching for Stars: Screen Acting and Stardom in British Cinema*, both of which paid equal attention to female and male stars, with Babington's book covering the entire twentieth century while Macnab focused more specifically on the British film industry's initial sixty years of existence.[2] Both books did essential groundwork in setting out the ways in which British modes of stardom may differ from, and indeed define themselves against, Hollywood's modus operandi.[3] In addition, Sue Harper's indefatigable overview *Women in British Cinema: Mad, Bad and Dangerous to Know* has also been an essential reference point for my work here, particularly the first section of Harper's book that explores the full range of women's screen representation in British cinema from the 1930s to the 1980s, including its female stars (Andrew Spicer's book *Typical Men: The Representation of Masculinity in Popular British Cinema* performs a parallel function in providing a history of male typology).[4]

What I am doing in this book both complements and supplements these previous analyses of British stardom and intervenes in debates on British film stardom in three specific ways. First, by focusing exclusively on the operations of female film stardom in the British context, I show both its centrality to the national film culture and examine its gendered specificities and how it operates in slightly different ways from the construction of British male stardom. Second, I extend the analysis of female stardom beyond the 1990s into the present day, thus making an important contribution to understanding of contemporary British film stardom. Third, rather than present an overview, I have chosen to base my study on very detailed analyses of a selected number of stars, finding in the microcosms of their individual careers a macrocosm of how British cinema stardom has functioned in relation to women. Although this book has seven 'women in question' rather than being a 'single-star case study', I hope that it possesses some of the virtues of that single-star approach that, as Lisa Downing and Sue Harris suggest (writing on Catherine Deneuve), provides a really good model for understanding in detail 'the developments, breaks and lines of continuity that constitute [the star's] image over the course of a career'.[5]

In the course of its contextualising introduction, six case study chapters and a conclusion that deals with the issue of whiteness and British female stardom, this book will explore and investigate the variety of British star femininities that have captured the public imagination over the last seventy-five years or so, while also acknowledging and interrogating some of the omissions and absences from that firmament.

British Film Stars 'Female, Assorted, Innumerable': Contexts and Parameters

BUT IS THERE *NO* STAR MATERIAL IN ENGLAND? WHERE IS *OUR* STAR – OUR VERY OWN STAR? DOES SHE RUN A LIFT LIKE DOROTHY LAMOUR USED TO – THEN SHE SHOULD GO AND PESTER A FILM PRODUCER RIGHT AWAY IF SHE'S AS DYNAMIC. HAS A TALENT SCOUT MISSED THE PARTICULAR REP COMPANY SHE IS IN? BUT WHERE IS SHE? – WE OUGHT TO TRY AND FIND HER.[6]

It seems that female stardom has always presented problems for British cinema: finding stars, knowing what to do with them, keeping them. As this impassioned closing plea from an article in *Picturegoer* in 1945 quoted above — made more so by being printed entirely in uppercase lettering – makes clear, the impulse to identify 'our very own [female] star' has at times been seen as a matter of utmost urgency, even desperation. The idea conveyed in this article that there may be a perfect star out there whose discovery can galvanise an ailing industry is a powerful and recurring one, as we shall see. But while this article suggested that British cinema just needed 'to find a star' (the title of the article), other commentators implied that the problem was not a lack of star potential among British actresses but rather with the domestic cinema's inability to make proper use of the female talent at its disposal. Nothing illustrates that more effectively than Sue Harper's discovery that when the Associated British Picture Corporation (ABPC) had Audrey Hepburn under contract in the early 1950s, they seriously considered a Gracie Fields biopic to be a suitable potential vehicle for her, completely misreading what she had to offer as a star.[7] William Wyler and Paramount laboured under no such delusion, knew that she was a princess-in-waiting rather than a galumphing music hall entertainer, cast her in *Roman Holiday* (1953), and the rest was (Hollywood) history.

This Hepburn anecdote seems to bear out what Christine Geraghty has also noted, which is how 'British cinema even in its most successful or innovative periods has often been seen as a difficult place for an actress'.[8] One actress, Anne Crawford, even went so far as to describe the domestic industry as 'afraid of women' in 1949, and actively hostile to them whatever they did: 'If they find one with a mind of her own they label her "temperamental". When we try the big-eyed, clinging vine technique they call us "dumb". They get embarrassed if we wear something sensational.'[9] This discomfort with the feminine is inextricably linked to a sense that British cinema is far more at ease with masculine stories and imagery. Kenneth Tynan's observation on Ealing's post-war output being all about 'men at work, men engrossed in a crisis, men who communicate with their women mainly by postcard' has a far wider applicability to British cinema than that period or studio alone.[10] From *The Dam Busters* (1955) to *Zulu* (1964), *Withnail and I* (1987) to *Lock, Stock and Two Smoking Barrels* (1998), to name just a few generically diverse examples, British cinema's recurrent recourse to male-dominated homosocial narratives throughout its history is striking. And what has been its knock-on effect for British female stars? According to Raymond Durgnat, it has resulted in a climate in which 'starlets, female, assorted, innumerable' have experienced 'extraordinary difficulty' in forging star careers.[11] Sometimes they have been accused of underperforming: 'Why British girls fail to – Our men famous, but women disappoint', reported the *Daily Mirror* in 1934, which surmised that 'the non-success of the English girl' in films was because she was 'afraid to "let herself go"'.[12] Alternatively they have been burdened with impossibly high expectations, as when starlet Anne Heywood was placed on the *Daily Express*'s 'star-o-meter' in 1957 to see whether she could match the 'sex appeal' of Marilyn Monroe, 'personality' of Audrey Hepburn, 'acting ability' of Carroll Baker, 'determination' of Diana Dors, 'poise' of Grace Kelly, 'experience' of Susan Hayward *and* 'intelligence' of Deborah Kerr – not asking too much of her then.[13]

Arguably, the problem in developing female stars was not solely determined by gender but had more to do with a deep-seated antipathy towards the whole business of movie stardom – a certain incompatibility between 'British' and 'stardom', to adapt Truffaut's famous phrase, noted by both Macnab and Babington. While 1909 saw the emergence of the 'picture personality' in America, later to become upgraded to the Hollywood film star, in Britain the story developed along different lines.[14] Theatrical prowess was understood as the true marker of performative skill, and cinema both borrowed and was cowed by its prestige: Jon Burrows notes the 'overdetermined fashion' in which theatre stars dominated early cinema.[15] Of course, the convenience of proximity had a lot to do with British theatre and film's especially intimate interconnectivity, with Macnab pointing out that while Hollywood and Broadway are 'a little over 3000 miles' apart from 'Pinewood or Elstree to London's West End is only half an hour's travel by car or train'.[16] But beyond simple geographical fact, deeper prejudices and snobberies about a newer medium were also at work and endured for a long time thereafter. Even as late as 1995, journalist John Heilpurn noted how 'sooner or later in Britain, everything comes back to theatre . . . The British are stage actors first, and last.'[17] The theatre was also seen as a better bet for maintaining actorly range, something prized far higher than building a consistent movie-star image, with pioneering British director

Maurice Elvey even suggesting in 1920 that the very 'process of starring' was also 'the process of cramping' an actor's development.[18] Furthermore, film stardom was seen to entail an undue amount of self-disclosure that went against the grain of a national culture uneasy with the 'vulgarity of self-display'.[19] This fatally inhibited the development of an effective publicity machine to make nascent stars knowable as off-screen personalities as well as on-screen performers: emblematic here is Celia Johnson's insistence on personal modesty, quoted by Babington: 'One doesn't talk about oneself, does one?'[20]

The abiding impression of British cinema's relationship with stardom is one of deep ambivalence. There is a perfect demonstration of this in two articles, both published in 1943 in *Picturegoer* and both authored by Lionel Collier. The first, from February of that year, asks, 'Must we have stars?' and goes on to express disdain for Hollywood's garish display: 'Well, do we really want to follow the American star system? Commercially, no doubt, it has been a great success. It is amazing what tripe you can put an accepted star in and get away with it.'[21] But the second, from October, represents a total volte-face as Collier asks, 'Are we making our own stars at last?', delighting in the fact that 'real strides are being made to further hitherto little-known talent'.[22] Collier's completely self-contradictory position on stardom sums up what Sarah Street later described as Britain's 'fascination and admiration for Hollywood's success in building stars' being counterbalanced by its equally 'profound desire to distance itself from the concomitant dangers of industrial commodification' that Hollywood's star system represented.[23]

This sense of contradiction is evident at the very heart of British constructions of stardom. On the one hand, a distinctive 'anti-star inflection' often manifests itself. Babington senses it in the self-effacing, impersonatory, un-starry performances of male actors such as Alec Guinness, Peter Sellers, and Gary Oldman (and one can add to his list the more recent example of Michael Sheen).[24] Christine Geraghty discerns something similar in the attempts made by a range of British actresses to slough off or deny stardom, from Margaret Lockwood making clear her preference for 'acting as opposed to starring in' a film to Julie Christie describing her battle against 'the whole apparatus' of stardom.[25] But, on the other hand, the institutions of British cinema have never simply rejected stardom and all its works and it has been ardently longed for as much as it has been repudiated. There has always been a deep-seated longing for 'home-grown stars' who, as Sarah Street points out, can be 'invested with a patriotic imperative as bearers of British national culture'.[26] This longing for British stars of world-beating brilliance goes back a long way: back in

1917, one film magazine's question, 'Is there an English Mary Pickford?', instigated a year-long debate on its letters page about who might be worthy of being spoken of in the same breath as the colossally popular American star and perhaps even able to rival her.[27] The same kind of discourses were still in full effect on the cover of the *Radio Times* on 11 May 1996, which was devoted to a composite image of Kate Winslet, Liz Hurley, and Emma Thompson, and was accompanied by an inside story on 'Our girls in Hollywood' and whether they were now challenging American stars for supremacy. The British public are especially encouraged to invest and revel in home-grown stars' international award successes, particular Oscar wins, something that Babington reads as symptomatic of the deeply held 'desire for British primacy' in film.[28]

While Emma Thompson and Kate Winslet may have been amenable to being co-opted into an award-winning British actorly tradition, someone like Liz Hurley was slightly harder to place on that continuum, being known far more for her alluring appearance than her acting abilities. Hurley's incongruity in that company points to British cinema's frequent difficulty in accommodating glamour, which obviously overlaps with its overall ambivalence to movie stardom (which was seen to promote glamour at the expense of talent) and this has had particular consequences for the place of female stars in British cinema. Glamour is a competitive arena in which Hollywood's female stars have generally been deemed to 'win', as Geraghty puts it.[29] Jack Davies noted in the 1950s that while British screenwriters were 'splendid' at 'funny old ladies' or 'comedy school-mistresses', their typewriters 'seem[ed] to develop mechanical trouble' whenever they tried to create 'smart, sophisticated women'.[30] But another writer made a case for actress Margaret Leighton as an exemplar of a very British form of glamour, rather more classy than the gaudy norm: 'The word glamour may not seem entirely appropriate to describe Miss Leighton's kind of attraction, but that is because the word has been vulgarised by its attachment to bobbysoxers' idols.'[31] A slight variation on this position of simultaneous boastfulness and defensiveness is to suggest that British actresses represent 'natural' beauty rather than the derogated currency of 'artificial' glamour, that 'British girls, it seems, have still got something everyone wants – even if it isn't the canned stuff that has been dished up to us as "glamour"'.[32] This line of argument stretches all the way from the dismissal of Mae West's 'extravagant make-up' and 'conventional, stiff waves' back in 1934 in favour of 'English beauty' right through to the comparison of Sharon Stone's 'brassiness' with the 'fine-boned delicacy' of Julia Ormond in 1996.[33]

If one sought a good example of how some of the tensions around

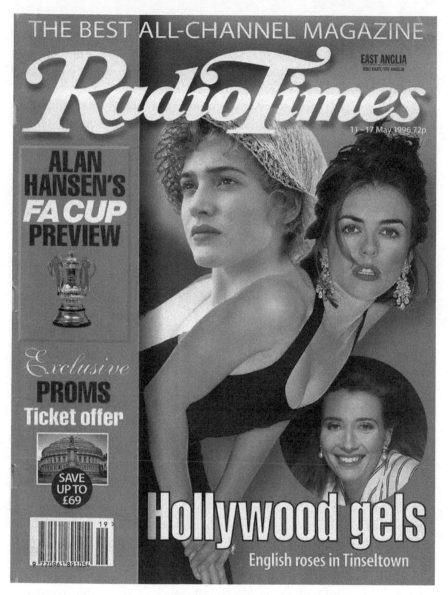

THE BEST ALL-CHANNEL MAGAZINE

EAST ANGLIA
BBC EAST/ITV ANGLIA

RadioTimes

11–17 May 1996 72p

ALAN HANSEN'S **FA CUP** PREVIEW

Exclusive **PROMS** Ticket offer

SAVE UP TO £69

Hollywood gels
English roses in Tinseltown

Figure 1.1 'English roses in Tinseltown': Kate Winslet, Elizabeth Hurley, and Emma Thompson on the cover of *Radio Times*, 11 May 1996.

stardom and glamour and British femininity coalesced then one could hardly improve on the moment of British star Ann Todd's entry into Hollywood in the late 1940s. Todd had gained an international profile through the huge success of her film *The Seventh Veil* (1945), and her coolly enigmatic allure seemed to answer the need voiced by one reader of *Pictureoger* for 'glamour and lots of it' in British films, because for 'an austerity-sick audience, it is very welcome'.[34] It looked like she may be able to crack America too, which, as *Picture Post* argued, would be a real fillip to Britain's overseas profile: in order to combat that fact that Britain 'export[ed] some ninety million precious dollars yearly to pay for the pleasure of seeing American feature pictures alone' while 'our returns on the showing of British pictures in the dollar regions are derisory', we needed to build up and export more 'lovely, melting stars' like Todd.[35] The actress duly went to Hollywood and appeared as a cool blonde in Hitchcock's *The Paradine Case* (1947) and a Victorian femme fatale in *So Evil My Love* (1948) and described how her regal reception upon arrival differed significantly from the diffident treatment she was used to: 'Over there you're Miss Todd, the new British star, and you're made to feel as if you're the only star, the only person who matters, a queen arriving to meet her subjects.'[36] But Todd also argued that British restrictions on overseas currency prevented her from doing her job properly:

> Our limited allowance is not enough for British stars to live on as they should live, in a place where things are judged by their face value and personal prestige means so much. The British industry is looked down upon because of this . . . as a visiting poor relation, whereas we should be ambassadors, said Miss Todd.[37]

She hammered home the point by wearing an ermine fur borrowed from Hollywood star Loretta Young to a film premiere in April 1947, and admitting as much: 'It's sad but we haven't the dollars to buy furs here. They were shocked that any star could say such a thing', commented Todd to a reporter, conveying the issue of British penury but also a certain amount of inverted snobbery in flouting the usual American star proprieties. [38] Todd's borrowed fur was worn over a silk evening gown, which she said was 'made from the parachute my husband used on D-Day'.[39] Her choice of dress for the premiere connoted both impecuniousness, as a recycled piece of clothing made from repurposed military equipment, but also a powerful sense of national pride, with not only thrift but indomitable British courage and victory in war literally written across the star's body, and then displayed within the Hollywood heartlands on Britain's behalf. Ann Todd's reported utterances and her eloquent outfit seem symptomatic of some of the contradictions at the heart of British female stardom – a compromised but proud glamour, a rejection of stardom's excesses combined with an enjoyment of its prestige.

Richard Dyer defined the power of stars in terms of their ability not only to represent different social categories but to 'speak to dominant

Figure 1.2 A 'lovely, melting star': signed photograph of Ann Todd from a book of British and Hollywood star portraits, published by D. McKenzie, Glasgow, circa 1948.

contradictions in social life – experienced as conflicting demands, contrary expectations, irreconcilable but equally held values – in such a way as to appear to reconcile them'.[40] In the persona of Ann Todd and many other British female stars, one can see how the ideological work of effecting 'the dissolution of contraries, the embrace of wildly opposing terms' is fully in evidence.[41]

Despite the high hopes pinned on someone like Todd, women stars have often been seen as of lesser importance in British cinema's history and development. This can be seen in *Films and Filming* critic Richard Whitehall's claim in 1963 that hardly any women had 'ever counted for much at the box-office', while those who had enjoyed significant success like Jessie Matthews, Phyllis Calvert, and Anna Neagle were dismissed as anodyne: 'much of a muchness, all spiritually at home in South Kensington'.[42] Inadvertently echoing this position decades later, albeit from a completely different direction, Jackie Stacey's work on women's memories of cinema-going in 1940s and 1950s Britain completely erased any mention of British female stars except as the (unspoken) binary opposite to Hollywood glamour.[43] But this absence seems particularly strange given the huge box-office popularity of British stars during that time, with Anna Neagle, Phyllis Calvert, and Margaret Lockwood proving extraordinarily popular with British audiences, often more so than US stars, according to various popularity polls from the period run by trade journals such as *Motion Picture Herald* and *Kinematograph Weekly*.[44] So powerful was their impact, images from their films even reverberated in the dreams of some spectators, with visions of Lockwood in *The Man in Grey* (1943) and Calvert in *Madonna of the Seven Moons* (1944) being cited in J. P. Mayer's sociological research.[45]

Although a definite heyday for female British stars, the 1940s were by no means an isolated period in generating on-screen women that the British public admired. Decades earlier, silent star Alma Taylor had beaten the global megastar Charlie Chaplin into second place in a magazine poll to find the most popular British-born film actor in 1915.[46] Cockney spitfire Betty Balfour, alliteratively dubbed 'beautiful, British and best' by *Picture Show* magazine in 1928, was a major box-office attraction of her era.[47] And while Richard Whitehall mentioned in passing the very popular 'dancing divinity' of 1930s musicals, Jessie Matthews, he neglected to mention Gracie Fields as a very different but equally successful major musical star of the decade. Fields frequently outperformed her seductive foreign competitors in the domestic market, summed up in the statement of one Sunderland cinema proprietor: 'Gracie was always a bigger draw than Garbo.'[48] Gracie's attractions may have more to do with gusto than glamour, but British stars could also be figures of aspiration as well as homely familiarity. Margaret Lockwood was chosen to advertise beauty products like Lux soap and Drene shampoo to British female consumers on the basis of her huge fan following, while her beauty spot was imitated by women who drew them on with eyeliner pencil, according to some tes- timonies.[49] Even today, certain British female stars are strongly coded as aspirational beauties, with Keira Knightley, Kate Winslet, Rachel Weisz, Emily Blunt, Helen Mirren, Emma Watson, and Gemma Arterton all fronting advertising campaigns for major cosmetics, skincare, fragrance, or fashion brands.[50]

British female stars have not only been very domestically popular at times, they have also enjoyed significant international success. Flying in the face of accusations that they lack star quality, they have often exerted a powerful allure for Hollywood producers and casting directors who have assigned them plum roles over their US competitors, from Vivien Leigh as Scarlett O'Hara in *Gone with the Wind* (1939) right through to Daisy Ridley as Rey in *Star Wars: Episode VII – The Force Awakens* (2015).[51] Clearly there is another story to be told about British female stars, which is not about their inadequacy or marginality or absence but about their remark- able appeal and their notable box-office success in the face of a national film culture that has often regarded them and the feminine-focused stories in which they sometimes feature as 'an unwelcome cuckoo-in-the-nest'.[52] Rather than being negligible or 'much of a muchness', female British stars have been and still are a crucial component of the national film culture and of popular culture more broadly. Indeed, if we follow Raymond Durgnat in believing that 'the social history of a nation can be written in terms of its film stars', then their inclusion in the construction of that social history is vital for the insights they offer into women's place in the national imagi- nary and the acutely gendered nature of Britain's narrative of itself.[53]

The expectation that female British film stars will represent the nation and embody certain national and gendered virtues slots into a much longer cultural tradition of women being used to embody the nation. From Mother Russia or Britannia, to Marianne, the spirit of revolutionary France (whose statue was directly modelled on both Bardot and Deneuve in turn in the twentieth century, indicating just how closely yoked film stardom and national mythology can be), nation itself is often conceptual- ised as a feminine entity, as Susan Hayward points out:

> The woman's body is closely aligned/identified with nationalist discourses. We fight and die for our mother-nation; the colonised referred to the colonising country as mother-country. When 'she' is invaded by the enemy, she is raped.[54]

But despite nationhood often being strongly gendered as feminine, the national status of actual women has conversely been much less clearly defined than men's. As Alice Jane Mackay and Pat Thane point out in their work on the construction of the identity of the Englishwoman, women '*had* no fixed nationality. They were made to adopt that of their husband; on marriage to a foreigner they lost their English status': it was no mere rhetorical flourish when Virginia Woolf announced that 'as a woman I have no country' in her 1938 work *Three Guineas*.[55] Despite this, women were not exempted from patriotism but they were urged to express their allegiance to their country in an appropriately feminine fashion: Mackay and Thane contrast the *Boy's Own Paper* telling its readership in 1879 that 'your future efforts, boys' would forge 'a nation's destiny' with the contemporaneous equivalent publication for young women, the *Girl's Own Paper*, counselling its readers that 'the essence of girlhood is in spiritual qualities rather than in actions', and that their primary role should be supporting men.[56] By comparison, British imperialism, so crucial a component of national self-image throughout the nineteenth century and early twentieth, was predicated on masculinity to such an extent that the 'core of the curriculum' at the public schools that acted as the empire's incubator '*was* masculinity' itself.[57]

While ideas of national identity remained 'pre-eminently masculine before the First World War', according to the historian Alison Light, beyond this point there occurred a profound shift in which 'the treacherous instability of former models of masculine power' were revealed.[58] Therefore, Light argues, the 1920s and 1930s 'saw a move away from formerly heroic and officially masculine public rhetorics of national destiny . . . to an Englishness at once less imperial and more inward-looking, more domestic and more private', in which 'woman and the home' were suddenly placed 'at the centre of national life'.[59] For all the abstract symbolic power of a Boadicea, Gloriana, or Queen Victoria, up to this point, the Englishwoman had been an ill-defined and 'surprisingly illusive' figure, according to Mackay and Thane, particularly in comparison with the much more clearly delineated Englishman.[60] But in the interwar years, this previously inchoate female counterpart came into her own. One example of this was the 'crisp commonsense' femininity of Mrs Miniver, created in the late 1930s and then memorably rendered on film by Greer Garson in MGM's morale-boosting 1942 film.[61] Another was Laura Jesson as played by Celia Johnson in *Brief Encounter* (1945). For Light, the fact that Jesson, this 'ordinary' suburban middle-class married woman, could be read as a perfect exemplar of Englishness provided a powerful indication of just how far national mythology and imagery had shifted: as she suggests, the notion of finding its quintessence in 'a housewife changing her library books and buying a new toothbrush would have seemed bizarre in 1914 and inconceivable in 1850'.[62]

This book's chronological focus begins just at this point in British history when women were being granted a new representational significance in relation to nation, further intensified in propaganda encouraging their full participation in the war effort.[63] The decision to span the seventy-five year period from 1940 to 2015 in this book's analysis was partly a matter of editorial expediency but also because those years presented themselves as a discrete historical entity in which major change had occurred in British society, especially for women. From the upheaval of the Second World War and the long shadow it cast over the years that followed, to the renewed emphasis on domesticity in the fifties, from the advent of sixties 'youthquake' and seventies 'Women's Lib' through to the first women Prime Minister at the end of that decade and the advent of post-feminist 'girl power' in the nineties, it is apparent how women's social roles have been in a state of ongoing metamorphosis, even while certain elements of feminine identity seem to have remained stubbornly unchanged.[64] While there has been a broadening acceptance of women's lives not having to be defined exclusively by home and (heteronormative) family, these are still often presented, even now, as women's highest and most noble callings. While avoiding any naïve sense that cinema straightforwardly 'reflects' reality, it is possible to trace those wider social and cultural developments through changing patterns of female stardom that mediated, responded to, and sometimes anticipated shifting expectations and ideals of femininity. Clearly film stars are not 'typical' women – indeed, their status as stars necessitates being singled out as 'special' – but they are still subject to the same kind of patriarchal strictures as their non-famous peers, and in fact those strictures are often amplified and intensified by the scrutiny that fame entails. This is abundantly clear from many of the misogynistic commentaries on female stars that I quote from in the chapters that follow. My admiration for the courage of these women in the face of the ideological obloquy to which they have been subjected, often but not always by a male commentariat, remains undimmed throughout this study. Their very particular stories, placed end to end, provide a 'refracted' view of the history of women in Britain from the 1940s to now, as seen through the 'prism' of film stardom.[65]

It is worth adding that the book's periodisation also covers immense changes in the cultural position of cinema itself, from its mid-1940s peak as the primary medium of audio-visual entertainment and an essential leisure activity for a large proportion of the populace through a long process of decline and redevelopment before reaching its current position as an enduringly popular form of entertainment, but just one among many. Film stardom has also changed shape in accordance with this process of transformation, as we shall see. Contemporary British film stars, more than ever before, take their place in a complex intermedial celebrity landscape and, as Barry King argues, are compelled to be entrepreneurial and develop an 'elastic' persona to 'cover all contingencies'.[66] Indeed, their main platform in most cases is no longer their film work but a much more holistic idea of the self as multi-media 'brand', with social media playing an increasingly indispensable role in star labour. If one thing has intensified over the seventy-year period covered by this book, it is the level of scrutiny to which stars are subjected. While they had always been the object of gossip and debate, the advent of round-the-clock digital media coverage has upped the ante considerably. This not only entails being talked about and photographed but demands that the star (or their publicist) deftly manage their own online identity, and the analyses that follow attempt to take into account the effects of the changing shape of celebrity mediation over the decades.

Two further essential points on the scope of this book and its case studies must be made. The first is the correlation of Englishness and Britishness in much of what has already been said and much of what follows. That 'caps lock' clamouring for a star quoted at the outset of this chapter says that it's trying to find a star somewhere in 'England' but I think its scope is actually British and this is a typical oversight rather than a deliberate exclusion of Welsh, Scottish, or Northern Irish candidates. Rather, this kind of slippage reflects what Colls and Dodd describe as the problematic 'Anglo-British tradition', which makes Englishness the hegemonic identity of Britishness while confining other national identities within it to a 'Celtic fringe'.[67] Unsurprisingly, the same kind of Anglo-British hegemony has also operated within a British cinema industry 'overwhelmingly English in its centres of production and ideological emphases' and populated by what Babington refers to as mainly 'anglicised' stars.[68] However, gender is a factor in this: although male stars such as Richard Burton, Stanley Baker, or Sean Connery have successfully forged images built on their Welsh or Scottish distinctiveness, it is difficult to think of female equivalents who have done the same, with Catherine Zeta-Jones and Kelly MacDonald perhaps coming closest (although they arguably achieved their international success through being able to disguise their accents when required – something Sean Connery's never had to do).[69] Likewise, it is interesting to note how Deborah Kerr's Scottish origins were seldom emphasised and were overwritten instead with the hegemonic national identity of 'English

Rose'.[70] The dominance of Englishness in the construction of British star femininity is reflected in this book by the fact that, without deliberate premeditation, all seven stars selected for analysis have ended up being English-British.

The other common factor that links all seven of them is their shared whiteness. In addition, most of them are also either red-headed or blonde, the latter being 'the most unambiguously white you can get' in Richard Dyer's estimation.[71] British film stardom, both male and female, has always been overwhelmingly white in its constitution and still remains so, a problem that runs far deeper than a mere lack of opportunities for Black, Asian, and Minority Ethnic (BAME) actors in British films, although this is certainly a factor. Rather it seems that whiteness is 'hard-wired' into many of British cinema's ontological structures. In the case of BAME female representation, the strictures placed upon what kinds of femininity are prized and seen as worthy of elevation to star status appears to be crucial, and the 'English rose' category in which so many British female stars have been placed has traditionally been an ethnically exclusionary one. In addressing this issue, my concluding chapter moves beyond its star case studies to reflect instead on the grounds upon which it is decided who is a candidate for stardom in British cinema and who isn't – in short, its longstanding and ongoing 'unbearable whiteness of being'. While this chapter looks back over British cinema's past, it also fixes its gaze on the prospect of a more ethnically diverse future for British female stardom in which BAME actresses can finally be accorded their rightful place.

Sources and Methods

In my quest 'to find a way of understanding the social significance of stars which fully respects the way they function as media texts', the methods employed for my star analysis in this book follow the models pioneered by Richard Dyer which, as Sean Redmond and Su Holmes state:

> offered ambitious methodological tools for the analysis of stardom: an integrated model for mining the cultural significance of a star that involved textual and bio-graphical analysis (assessing the 'on- and off- screen', 'public and private', 'mediated and authentic' life of the star); questions of pleasure and identification; and ideological and historical specificity. This synthetic approach enabled the meaning of the star to emerge out of the cultural world in which they signified.[72]

On that latter point, I am aware that, as Martin Shingler points out, analyses of how 'a film star embodies or incarnates a particular set of social values or a specific and identifiable period within a culture's history are invariably open to charges of reductionism and over-simplification'.[73] I have attempted to avoid these limitations by offering analyses of my chosen stars' personae that are fully attentive to their nuances and contradictions and envisaging each star as a refraction rather than simple reflection of their society's mores and codes.[74]

I plan to delicately sidestep some of the complexities, deftly outlined by Shingler, of descriptive nomenclature within star studies, which has variously deployed 'personality', 'persona', and 'image' as interlocking and sometimes contradictory definitional terms.[75] I will primarily use Dyer's coinage of persona to cover the star's total discursive production, encompassing on-screen characters and typology as well as the off-screen personality constructed through media coverage and fan talk of various kinds (the 'real' person who definitely exists or existed, and whose inner truth much of this material tantalisingly promises to disclose and reveal, ultimately remains unknowable). However, I also reserve the right to use terms such as 'image' or 'type' in my analysis wherever they feel appropriate and helpful. Another descriptive label carrying significant baggage is 'celebrity', and despite its often derogated status in opposition to 'stardom' (seen as more elevated and impressive), this concept is a vital point of orientation for this study. Alongside frameworks derived from star studies, I have also made use of ideas and approaches derived from the more methodologically interdisciplinary field of celebrity studies that draws on 'media, television and cultural studies (as well as sports studies, popular music studies, work on digital culture and beyond)' in order to take into account the broader permutations of what it means to be famous.[76] I therefore conceptualise the fame of my chosen stars on a continuum of British celebrity femininity that goes beyond film stars to also encompass members of the royal family (whose entire purpose is to act as national figureheads), pop stars, sportswomen, stage or television actors, businesswomen, comediennes, politicians, television presenters, models, authors, YouTube stars, and others. Christine Gledhill's suggestion in 1991 that 'cinema still provides the ultimate confirmation of stardom' no longer rings true in the 2010s, if indeed it ever did; most of the stars discussed in the chapters that follow worked in arenas beyond film, sometimes very extensively, on stage or on television or as recording artistes or writers or television presenters (or all five in the case of Diana Dors).[77] My analysis accommodates their broader intermedial celebrity even if the common factor that draws them all together in this particular book is the fact that they have all been understood as British *film* stars at one point.

The book's primary research sources are magazine and newspaper coverage of stars, film reviews, trade press coverage, publicity, press books, posters and other promotional materials, biographies, advertising campaigns for products endorsed by stars, sources generated by fan activities, and, since the 1990s, ever-accelerating online versions of all of the above. These have been read not only for the direct information they provide about particular stars but also for the indirect information they can offer on what Diane Negra calls the 'broader, more nebulous patterns of popular feeling' during any given period that feed into a star's image and its reception, and that suggest possible reasons for their popularity at that particular moment in time.[78] I have found some of the richest material for my study in newspaper coverage of stars, something that completely transformed as the British press became progressively more tabloidised, with the rise of 'personality-based news' by journalists like Donald Zec and Peter Evans and later Lynn Barber vital to this process.[79] Film-focused magazines like *Picturegoer, Photoplay, Empire*, and *Premiere*, have also all been great sources of intense 'star talk'. So too have more general interest men's and women's magazines, TV magazines, and the fashion and music presses. The discursive work around stars contained in all these publications, sometimes respectful in tone but sometimes more scurrilous and gossipy, continually plays with the idea of seeing 'the real person' behind the roles, adhering to the series of defining star oppositions set out by Dyer: public/private, on-screen/off-screen, mediated/authentic. Sometimes it appears that we hear the star's voice verbatim, coming through in interview or other kinds of reported speech, but it is important to treat this as another element of their discursive construction rather than uniquely privileged access to the 'true self' (even though it may be presented as such). These are not necessarily the star's thoughts, although it is how their thoughts were being presented at a given moment. But at the same time I do not want to disregard totally what P. David Marshall calls 'the work of active human agency' that can be glimpsed in these utterances, and how stars' confessions and disclosures, however circumscribed, can speak eloquently of their struggles for autonomy.[80] These expressions of agency are arguably all the more important in thinking about stardom through the lens of gender, with female celebrities of various kinds often seen as particularly subject to commodification and manipulation, and being spoken for rather than being at liberty to speak for themselves.

As I hope should become obvious from the chapters that follow, while I am primarily engaged in examining (from the standpoint of gender) how 'a star image is made out of media texts', to use Dyer's phrase, I am also interested in what Barry King refers to as 'stardom as a form of working', and have been keen to uncover traces of star labour that are discernible from sources such as general and trade press coverage (*Kine Weekly*,

Motion Picture Herald, and *Variety* have been crucial in that respect), publicity and marketing materials, and biographies.[81] In the Hollywood context, Paul McDonald has made salient recommendations that star studies scholars should take a closer look at the talent agencies, personal managers, and publicists who 'make, manage and control the capital of stardom'.[82] That has been beyond the scope of my study here, except in passing references, but it is certainly the case that a thoroughgoing systematic account of British star practices covering the industrial mechanisms of how stars have been 'discovered, developed, deployed, presented and evaluated within the film industry' in Britain, mapping the contributions made by agents, publicists, and managers, would be a very welcome addition to existing scholarship on British cinema.[83] In the meantime, this study aims to frame its stars as both 'symbolic and economic entities' and remain cognisant throughout of how they 'operate as sources of capital for the film business' – not merely textual constructions but industrial players and notional guarantors of profits.[84]

Material on audience and fan responses to British female stars has also been built into the chapters wherever available, from contemporaneous surveys, questionnaires, and polls, or letters to magazines and newspapers, to fan-club material if extant, and a more recent proliferation of material online in the shape of fansites and social media activity (although we cannot always infer a more general response to a particular star or film or performance from the views of a self-selected vocal minority, as is the case with all ardent fan-texts, whether digital or analogue).

Finally, the films in which the stars appear are also an indispensable primary source for this study, providing examples of the star in action and motion, sometimes demonstrating what all the critics were raving about (or disapproving of) at the time, and offering an essential third dimension to any thoroughgoing consideration of film stardom. If stars can be understood as textual constructs, then one of the most important categories of text that contribute to that process of construction is the films, which are identified as their primary star output and expression. However, I must add that this book does not offer meticulously detailed scene-by-scene analysis of screen performance of the kind undertaken in other studies, not because it sees such work as unimportant but rather because to do it properly would require the word length of another book.[85] While I agree that acting and other forms of screen performance have traditionally been neglected in Film Studies and sympathise with the attempts to remedy this with the turn towards probing micro-analysis of frames and sequences, it lies outside my remit here. The chapters that follow will occasionally alight upon a particularly telling moment of screen performance – a gesture, a look, or the way a particular line of dialogue is delivered – but their primary concern is with star personae as broader entities that incorporate but are not fully determined by what happens in the star's films.

Finally, although physical embodiment is crucial to star representation, this should not obscure the importance of sonic as well as visual dimensions in constructing a persona, a word that, as Shingler points out, actually means 'through sound'.[86] This all began with the transition to sound, which claimed victims in Britain just as it had in Hollywood. Mabel Poulton's Cockney accent doomed her to oblivion but over-elocuted voices could prove just as problematic, as evident from the occasional hostility towards Jessie Matthews (born in Soho to a working-class family) on grounds of her bogus hyper-posh tones in the 1930s.[87] Any account of British traditions of stardom is as much a story of voices as it is of faces and bodies. The speaking voices of British actresses have often been their primary national identifier and sometimes their most distinctive feature, from Joan Greenwood's sexy, parodically plummy tones to the celebrated 'sob-catch' at the heart of Judi Dench's voice, or the bell-like clarity of Anna Neagle's voice, evoked in David Thomson's anecdote about hearing 'a sweet voice boom "This is Anna Neagle speaking"' on a crossed telephone line and being 'unnerved by such melody emitting from the technological maelstrom'.[88] Despite the turn away from Received Pronunciation in the 1960s in favour of more diverse styles of speaking, the crucial association of class and voice never really went away. It was on account of her 'brittle, upper-class, honeyed and moneyed tones' even more than her 'English rose' looks that Helena Bonham Carter was judged 'British, sir. British to the sweet little core' when she first found fame in 1986.[89]

Choosing the Women in Question

In making my selection of star case studies, it was important to focus on figures who had not been extensively written about before but who deserved further scrutiny. In connection with that, I wanted to avoid writing about stars who had already been covered in academic work: one reason why there are no chapters on the aforementioned Lockwood, Neagle, or Calvert (in spite of their popularity), or Googie Withers, Virginia McKenna, Kay Kendall, Julie Christie, Ingrid Pitt, Mary Millington, Helen Mirren, Kate Winslet, or Tilda Swinton, despite each of them representing fascinating tendencies or moments in British cinema's history from the 1940s to the present day.[90] My inclusion of Diana Dors is the exception to this general rule, because she had already been written about by several scholars, but she seemed too perfectly emblematic of the tensions around femininity, Britishness, and stardom to ignore in a book of this kind.[91]

I was keen to explore figures who were in some way representative of or of central relevance to particular moments in British film history: forties melodrama (Jean Kent), the sex-symbol craze of the fifties (Diana Dors), the British New Wave and 'swinging London' in the sixties (Rita Tushingham), seventies crisis and nostalgia (Glenda Jackson), eighties heritage film and nineties post-feminism and laddism (Helena Bonham Carter and Emily Lloyd), and the rise of the older protagonist in the noughties (Judi Dench). But, at the same time, it was important to avoid the pitfall that Richard Dyer identifies of undertaking an over-determined analysis in which the star is made to 'simply reflect some aspect of social reality that the analyst cared to name'.[92] Each of the stars discussed herein signifies much more than their epitomising of any one trend and I have tried to ensure that my analysis provides adequate breathing space for the full polysemy of their personae to emerge.

While some of the stars I have chosen to focus on were major figures of their particular eras and often went on to sustain careers of remarkable longevity, the stardom of others proved more minor or ephemeral, as with the comet-like intensity but sudden burnout of Emily Lloyd's career or the long slog towards and then rapid waning of Jean Kent's stardom. Some of the stars I discuss may fall short of the more stringent selection criteria for stardom put forward by film scholar Paul McDonald but, as Babington points out, that approach may have limited applicability beyond the Hollywood industry anyway, particularly so 'within the British context, in which the various criteria of stardom are often underplayed'.[93] In any case, merely looking at the very uppermost tiers of stardom, as Sue Harper points out, offers 'something of a blunt instrument' for understanding the intricacies of any given film culture, in which lesser or auxiliary stars are an equally important part of the ecosystem.[94] However, it is worth adding that I have chosen to avoid focusing on anyone who may be primarily understood as a character actress, despite acknowledging the vitality of that acting tradition in British cinema and recognising the greater degree of permeability between the categories of star and character player in British films than is perhaps the case in other national film cultures. Margaret Rutherford – the best example of a female 'character star' in British cinema – has already been written about extensively elsewhere by Sarah Street and Claire Mortimer, and while other character actresses from Edith Evans to Brenda Blethyn may have 'starred' in films, they seem to have been less subject to the paratextual discussion that usually surrounds a star, and that has been so central to my research methodology on this project.[95]

Nor does this book include case studies of British actresses whose film careers have been wholly or predominantly or most successfully conducted in Hollywood productions, such as Dorothy Mackaill, Ida Lupino, Greer Garson, Julie Andrews, Kate Beckinsale, or even the English-born archetypal Hollywood megastar Elizabeth Taylor. Ditto someone like Barbara Steele who found her place as a star in European horror that, as Raymond Durgnat noted, seemed to know how to exploit her 'strange, spiky, whiplash strength' much more effectively than any British production, or contemporary British actress Amy Jackson who has found fame in the Indian cinema.[96] While acknowledging the transnational framework for the vast majority of British film production from the 1960s onwards, my primary engagement in this study is with those female stars who are understood as British stars and whose careers have tended to remain more tightly tethered, whether willingly or not, to the British industry in all its compromised alterity and occasional glory.

Each of the six chapters that follow focus primarily on a particular decade in which the chosen star (or stars in the case of Chapter 6) had the greatest impact or in which their persona was formed. So Chapter 2 emphasises the 1940s, Chapter 3 the 1950s, and so on. At the same time, the complexity and longevity of most of the star careers detailed are impossible to reduce to a single discrete ten-year period and so I have allowed the analysis to encompass the fuller range of their activities over time; this is particularly useful with someone like Diana Dors who periodically reinvented herself as a means of preserving her public profile.

The six chapters also cluster conveniently into pairs. Chapters 2 and 3, dealing with Jean Kent and Diana Dors, have a shared concern with British stars who were constructed as 'bad girls', sexy antitheses to a presumed feminine norm of English/British niceness and modesty. Kent seemed happy to be one rung down from Lockwood and Calvert at Gainsborough Studios in the 1940s: their resident 'girl in camiknickers' to be brought in if a bit of extra sexual piquancy was required. She did a lot with fairly meagre and marginal parts until she got better and bigger chances in the late 1940s and finally became a star in her own right, even hailed as a British equivalent to pin-up girl Betty Grable at one point, with 'everything that the sultry stars of Hollywood have got. And in the right places!'[97] Unlike many of her contemporaries, Kent also appeared to relish being famous: 'Life is grand fun. Stardom is a great thrill' she was reported as saying in 1947 and it was 'exciting to have one's name in enormous letters outside cinemas' – sentiments that seem to fly in the face of the usual British tendency to view stardom somewhat suspiciously.[98] However, doing several films in quick succession in which she played characters older than her own age, including her multiple versions of one woman in *The Woman in Question*, had an unfortunate effect on Kent's star career, making her prematurely aged in casting terms. Kent described herself as being 'too old for young parts, too young for older ones' when she was in her mid-thirties, stranded between categories.[99] As she observed in the mid-1950s: 'People are always telling me "My dear, you'll be wonderful when you're older." But I *am* older. I'm getting older all the time. Jolly soon I'll be *too* old.'[100] This mid-life drought was not unique to Kent. Eileen Atkins observed a similar phenomenon in her own career and described it as 'like being an athlete who has been running races for years and is suddenly told, when he is at his peak, that there is nothing to run anymore'.[101] The problems posed by ageing while trying to sustain a star career reverberate throughout many of these case studies, reflecting a wider sense of cultural anxiety around women's ageing.

While Jean Kent was struggling to sustain a career in the 1950s, Diana Dors picked up the bad-girl baton and ran with it. She luxuriated in the trappings of stardom – furs, gowns, cars, swimming pools – and represented like no one else the promise (and perils) of consumerism for a society negotiating its way from austerity to affluence. So notorious was her lifestyle and image at this time that she became a byword for luxury and/or profligacy, which sometimes cropped up in the oddest places: when Salford City Council increased their expenditure rather than making budgetary cuts in 1957, they were accused of playing with 'fancy Diana Dors figures'.[102] Part of Dors' game-plan was to conquer Hollywood, an objective that was very nearly fulfilled when she was offered a contract with RKO in 1956 and went off to the States to great fanfare. But events conspired against her and she never achieved the levels of success that had briefly, tantalisingly, seemed possible. More of a tall poppy than an English rose perhaps, she was chopped down to size and returned to Britain while, ironically, it was the more rosily inflected British female stars Deborah Kerr and Jean Simmons who ended up forging the more durable US careers around that time, fulfilling rather than confounding cultural expectations of English femininity. But Dors showed admirable grit and staying power by converting herself into a kind of British folk heroine, 'a symbol of all that is ripe and robust in British entertainment' according to television interviewer Russell Harty in 1977.[103]

While Kent and Dors encountered problems in advancing their careers in the 1940s and 1950s due to their status as British bad girls, female star typology began to change in the 1960s as it responded to and mediated broader social change. Moving into this decade, Chapters 4 and 5 look at two stars who found fame at opposite ends of the sixties, Rita Tushingham and Glenda Jackson. Both were seen as epitomising a sense of newness and change, particularly in the way that they departed significantly from previous models of British female stardom. As commentators were quick to point out, neither would have been picked for the Rank Charm School due to their 'unconventional' looks and both suffered in the press as a result, with Tushingham labelled an ugly duckling and Jackson likened to a gargoyle. Their backgrounds differed from the norm too, both being from the Merseyside region and not taking the trouble to disguise the fact, and as Northern-girls-made-good they seemed exemplary of the era's social mobility. In truth, in that respect they were exceptions to the general rule for actresses of this period, even those associated with new kinds of cinema. Julie Christie, Vanessa Redgrave, and Susannah York, for instance, were all securely middle class in background and the class breakthrough achieved by the British New Wave and its aftermath seems in retrospect to have been more to the benefit of working-class male actors, among them Albert Finney, Tom Courtenay, Michael Caine, and Sean Connery. But Rita Tushingham's debut in *A Taste of Honey* (1961) added an important new female presence to the social-realist pantheon, and 'Tush' then managed to reposition herself as the perfect quirky ingénue to sum up the new questing spirit of the sixties: a 'little female elf with big wide eyes'.[104]

The 1970s proved more challenging territory for Tushingham, as an actress so firmly associated with the previous decade and its youthful joie de vivre. In any case, this period saw the bottom fall out of British production as a result of withdrawal of US finance, a situation that had 'dire consequences for the representation of women', according to Sue Harper, and saw actresses generally having 'to be content with slim pickings'.[105] However, one female star who did flourish in the 1970s, and indeed enjoyed her greatest period of success during those years, was Glenda Jackson. Her flintier and more combative model of femininity was seen to match the period's harsher mood, and she was frequently associated with the contemporaneous rise of the women's liberation movement. While Jackson's aura of sexual challenge was very modern in many respects, particularly her frequent appearance in explicit nude scenes, in other ways her persona harked back nostalgically to older Hollywood models of stardom, with Katharine Hepburn and Bette Davis evoked as reference points for Jackson's updated take on the smart, spiky heroine.

After the social and aesthetic challenges posed by new kinds of stars in the 1960s and 1970s, the 1980s saw a partial retrenchment in gender typology. The English rose returned with a vengeance in the cycle of period drama subsequently labelled heritage film, exemplified by the emergent young star Helena Bonham Carter. Like her frequent employer Merchant

Ivory, her name became synonymous with a certain kind of genteel roman-
ticism about the past, and she was loved and criticised in equal measure for
her ability to play the Edwardian ingénue so convincingly. Bonham Carter
is one of two young actresses examined in Chapter 6, alongside Emily
Lloyd who represented a rather different model of British female stardom
that emerged around the same time. There were obvious semiotic differences between the early roles that defined them: the aestheticised sexual
awakening of Helena Bonham Carter's Lucy, kissing in a poppy-strewn
field accompanied by Puccini in *A Room with a View* (1985) contrasts
sharply with the sordid parlour groping from a seedy older man and sex in
a garden shed experienced by Emily Lloyd's Lynda in *Wish You Were Here*
(1987). But both were teenage discoveries presented as 'the next big thing'
when they made their divergent film debuts, and looking at them together
offers some interesting insights into British cinema's strategies for developing and showcasing young female talent around this time. While Lloyd
was presented as a modern girl, an ordinary London teenager who just
happened to be extraordinarily talented, Bonham Carter found herself
mired in the past not just in the majority of her screen roles but in her
overall image as an old-fashioned 'little English rosebud', forever laced
up in corsets.[106] In the long run, Bonham Carter was able to complicate
and diversify that original image to build a more complex career while the
initially more promising Lloyd, far more hotly pursued by Hollywood at
the time, struggled with mental health issues and industry machinations,
eventually dropping out of making films altogether. She is one of the
great 'what ifs' of this book, representing a good many other charismatic
and brilliant British actresses who have not been able to realise their full
potential, for whatever reason.

Still in her teens, Emily Lloyd was being described as a 'national treasure', somewhat surprisingly since this is a label more readily applied to
older stars like Dame Judi Dench, the subject of this book's final case
study chapter.[107] In comparison with Chapter 6's teen discoveries, Chapter
7 examines the unusual case of someone who found fame as a film star
much later in life. Suddenly becoming an Oscar-winner with real bankability while in her sixties, Dench seems to confound the usual narratives
of female ageing that inevitably see it in terms of deterioration and decline.
While venerated as an immensely skilled actress, she is also admired as a
fun-loving celebrity as well as a role model for age-appropriate elegance.
With the current prominence of older female British stars like Dench,
Helen Mirren, Maggie Smith, and Charlotte Rampling, it does appear that
things have moved on since the days when journalists were able to claim
with confidence 'no one loves a film star who looks forty' or, heaven forbid,

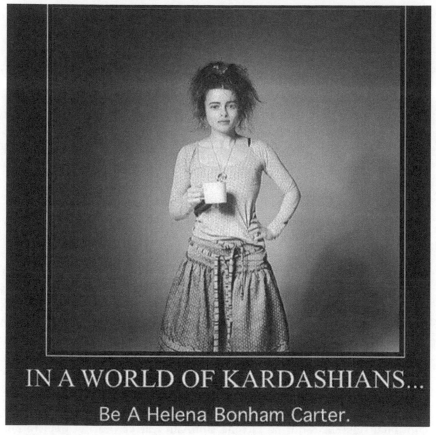

IN A WORLD OF KARDASHIANS...
Be A Helena Bonham Carter.

Figure 1.3 Helena Bonham Carter versus the Kardashians: a British female star in meme culture (reproduced from http://knowyourmeme.com/memes/in-a-world-of-kardashians).

older.[108] But as some barriers to stardom are broken down, others prove much harder to dismantle, as will be explored in this book's conclusion.

British female film stars have always been part of a much wider celebrity landscape and that has only been intensified by contemporary digital intermediality. But despite heightened competition for attention, the femininities they embody still seem to offer something distinctive and desirable. In early 2016, an online meme began to circulate that was captioned 'In a world of Kardashians, be a Helena Bonham Carter' over a characteristically quirky image of the British star. Just one version of a whole string of memes that compare the Kardashians, or sometimes specifically Kim Kardashian, unfavourably to other famous women who are perceived as having greater elegance or individuality, Princess Diana, Audrey Hepburn, Lucille Ball, and Janis Joplin among them, the Bonham Carter variant gained greater notoriety when it was posted and then removed from fellow actress Anne Hathaway's Instagram account on the grounds of having unintentionally 'thrown shade' (criticised Kardashian by implication).[109] As Holmes and Negra argue, female celebrities are continually pitted against each other in ways that suggest how disproportionately judgemental our culture is towards women, and indeed these kinds of memes are often repudiated on those grounds.[110] But how interesting that in this case a *British* female star should be deployed as the diametric opposite of the devalued and derogated reality television and Internet celebrity represented by Kim Kardashian and her family. Some of the entrenched privileges around *film* stardom as opposed to other kinds of celebrity are in operation around this elevation of Bonham Carter, but so too are ideas of class and nationality, with the supposedly more admirable, authentic, and independent-minded stardom of Bonham Carter imbricated with her upper-class Englishness. If this kind of 'classiness' is often seen as the 'unique selling point' of the British actress, then it is a highly problematic way of carving out a niche in the celebrity universe, depending as it does on the derogation of other kinds of femininity by comparison.

However, it's certainly not a new way for British female stars to claim 'special' status. One can see exactly the same kind of snob appeal at work in the construction of Alma Taylor's image back in the 1910s and 1920s. For example, the emphasis placed on Taylor's plush upbringing in a country house once lived in (supposedly) by Anne Boleyn feels very similar to the continual references during Helena Bonham Carter's early career to her illustrious ancestors, with both stars' publicity materials being animated by the same 'conservative emphasis on lineage and social distinctions' that has been central to certain British formations of stardom.[111] There are also uncanny similarities in the ways in which Alma Taylor's and Helena Bonham Carter's styles of dress were talked about, with Bonham Carter's love of 'vintage' in the 1980s ('her grandfather's brown waistcoat, her father's grey socks . . . her own baggy trousers and braces') sounding very similar to Taylor's rejection of film-star finery back in the 1920s ('I'm not frightfully fond of clothes. At home, I enjoy myself in the oldest things I can find'), even down to the way both women's fondness for masculine footwear was used to characterise them, with Taylor described as striding out in 'a pair of brogues that claim no connection with "fashion"' while decades later Bonham Carter was summarised as describing her as an 'unusual girl plodding steadfastly into the future in her Doc Martens'.[112] As the proverb goes, there is nothing new under the sun. Indeed, researching this book has often felt like repeatedly peering down a kaleidoscope in which the view appears to change while always being comprised of the same basic elements just slightly agitated and rearranged. But I hope to provide a full examination of those component parts in what follows and convey something of the special character of British stardom when it has been mediated through female personae, to suggest models of analysis applicable to other national cinemas and media contexts, and to generate new knowledge of the intricate interactions of stardom, celebrity, gender, and national identity.

Notes

1. Richard Dyer, *Heavenly Bodies: Film Stars and Society* (Basingstoke: Macmillan, 1986), p. 19.
2. Bruce Babington (ed.), *British Stars and Stardom: From Alma Taylor to Sean Connery* (Manchester: Manchester University Press, 2001); Geoffrey Macnab, *Searching for Stars: Screen Acting and Stardom in British Cinema* (London: Cassell, 2000).
3. As Ginette Vincendeau has pointed out in the context of her work on French stardom, for the majority of people "'stars' means 'Hollywood stars'", something also evident in formative works of star studies from Dyer onwards, which have tended to focus predominantly on Hollywood examples. Ginette Vincendeau, *Stars and Stardom in French Cinema* (London: Continuum, 2000), p. vii.
4. Sue Harper, *Women in British Cinema: Mad, Bad and Dangerous to Know* (London: Continuum, 2000); Andrew Spicer, *Typical Men: The Representation of Masculinity in Popular British Cinema* (London: I. B. Tauris, 2001).
5. Lisa Downing and Sue Harris (eds), *From Perversion to Purity: The Stardom of Catherine Deneuve* (Manchester: Manchester University Press, 2007), p. 8. It is interesting to note that while a number of key female French stars have had academic single-star-study treatment, with Susan Hayward, *Simone Signoret: The Star as Cultural Sign* (London: Continuum, 2004) and Ginette Vincendeau, *Brigitte Bardot* (London: BFI Palgrave, 2013) as well as the Downing and Harris book, that method has taken longer to be applied to British female stars, with scholarly studies now forthcoming in BFI Palgrave's Film Stars series on Julie Christie (by Melanie Bell) and Deborah Kerr (by Sarah Street). However, there have already been two academic books focused on specific male British stars, Gill Plain's *John Mills and British Cinema: Masculinity, Identity and Nation* (Edinburgh: Edinburgh University Press, 2006) and Michael Williams's *Ivor Novello: Screen Idol* (London: BFI, 2003).
   Books undertaking similarly structured analyses of multiple female film stars include Antje Ascheid, *Hitler's Heroines: Stardom and Womanhood in Nazi Germany* (Philadelphia: Temple University Press, 2003); Neepa

Majumdar, *Wanted Cultured Ladies Only! Female Stardom and Cinema in India, 1930s–1950s* (Chicago: University of Illinois Press, 2009); Mia Mask, *Divas on Screen: Black Women in American Film* (Chicago: University of Illinois Press, 2009); and Diane Negra, *Off-White Hollywood: American Culture and Ethnic Female Stardom* (London: Routledge, 2001).

6. P. J. Dyer, 'To find a star', *Picturegoer*, 21 July 1945, p. 7.

7. Harper, *Women in British Cinema*, p. 81.

8. Christine Geraghty, 'Crossing over: Performing as a lady and a dame', *Screen*, Vol. 43, No. 1, spring 2002, p. 42.

9. Anne Crawford, 'Of course British stars can be glamorous!', *Picturegoer*, 29 January 1949, p. 9.

10. Tynan's comments are quoted in Charles Barr, *Ealing Studios*, third edition (Berkeley: University of California Press, 1998), p. 77.

11. Raymond Durgnat, *A Mirror for England: British Movies from Austerity to Affluence* (London: Faber & Faber, 1971), p. 184. He diagnosed the root cause as 'the fog of British reserve – a fog blackened, it must be said, by the smutty anger of British misogyny, puritanism and shyness' (p. 185).

12. Reg Whitley, 'Why British girls fail to – our men famous, but women disappoint', *Daily Mirror*, 13 April 1934, p. 20. Thanks to Adrian Garvey for the reference.

13. John Lambert, 'How's your starometer rating?', *Daily Express*, 19 September 1957, p. 8.

14. Richard DeCordova, *Picture Personalities: The Emergence of the Star System in America* (Urbana: University of Illinois Press, 1990).

15. Jon Burrows, *Legitimate Cinema: Theatre Stars in Silent British Films, 1908–1918* (Exeter: Exeter University Press, 2003), p. 225.

16. Macnab, *Searching for Stars*, p. 59.

17. John Heilpurn, 'Empire of the stage', *Vanity Fair*, November 1995, p. 166.

18. Elvey quoted in Christine Gledhill, *Reframing British Cinema 1918–1928* (London: BFI, 2003), p. 77.

19. Babington, 'Introduction', in *British Stars and Stardom*, p. 13.

20. Johnson cited in Ibid.

21. Lionel Collier, 'Must we have stars?', *Picturegoer*, 6 February 1943, p. 6.

22. Lionel Collier, 'Are we making our own stars at last?', *Picturegoer*, 16 October 1943, p. 5.

23. Sarah Street, *British Cinema in Documents* (London: Routledge, 2000), p. 89. For more on Rank's Company of Youth, popularly known as the Charm School, see Chapter 5 in Geoffrey Macnab, *J. Arthur Rank and the British Film Industry* (London: Routledge, 1993), and Macnab, *Searching for Stars*, pp. 177–83. There is a very interesting article detailing the initiative's achievements two years into its existence: John K. Newnham, 'Progress report on the Charm School', *Picturegoer*, 25 September 1948, pp. 6–7.

24. Babington, 'Introduction', in *British Stars and Stardom*, p. 20.

25. Geraghty, 'Crossing over: Performing as a lady and a dame', p. 43.

26. Sarah Street, *British National Cinema* (London: Routledge, 1997), p. 119.
27. Burrows, *Legitimate Cinema*, p. 8.
28. *Radio Times*, 11–17 May 1996. Babington, 'Introduction', in *British Stars and Stardom*, p. 9.
29. Geraghty, 'Crossing over: Performing as a lady and a dame', p. 41.
30. Jack Davies, 'I'll take the mink and the glamour', *Picturegoer*, 11 December 1954, p. 23.
31. Duncan Blair, 'Glamour as you like it', *Picturegoer*, 25 March 1950, p. 11.
32. Crawford, 'Of course British stars can be glamorous!', p. 9.
33. 'Letters from our readers: English beauty v. Hollywood glamour', *Picturegoer*, 28 July 1934, p. 30. Alison Graham, 'Our girls in Hollywood', *Radio Times*, 11 May 1996, p. 18.
34. Anonymous, 'Letters from our readers: More glamour', *Picturegoer*, 31 August 1946, p. 14.
35. Anonymous, 'A new star made in Britain', *Picture Post*, 24 November 1945, pp. 26–8.
36. Ernest Betts, 'Ann Todd: I borrowed clothes . . . shocking!', *Daily Express*, 8 April 1947, p. 3.
37. Unlabelled article, *Daily Mail*, 25 March 1947. Press cuttings file on Ann Todd, BFI Library.
38. Betts, 'Ann Todd': I borrowed clothes . . . shocking!', p. 3.
39. Ibid.
40. Richard Dyer, 'Four films of Lana Turner', in *Only Entertainment* (London: Routledge, 1992), p. 80.
41. Judith Mayne, *Cinema and Spectatorship* (London: Routledge, 1993), p. 138.
42. Richard Whitehall, 'DD', *Films and Filming*, January 1963, p. 22.
43. Jackie Stacey, *Star Gazing: Hollywood Cinema and Female Spectatorship* (London: Routledge, 1994). Babington examines its absenting of British stars in more detail in his introduction to *British Stars and Stardom*, culminating in his *cri de coeur* of disbelief, 'Surely *someone* mentioned Margaret Lockwood!' (p. 4). Certainly, in Janet Thumin, *Celluloid Sisters: Women and Popular Cinema* (London: Macmillan, 1992), which also uses women's memories of films from the same period as a research resource, British stars figure more prominently as aspirational or glamorous figures worthy of imitation and adoration.
44. There is more detailed discussion of this in Chapter 2, which covers the 1940s period.
45. J. P. Mayer's 1946 study *Sociology of Film* is cited in Sue Harper, 'Historical pleasures: Gainsborough costume melodrama', in Christine Gledhill (ed.), *Home Is Where the Heart Is: Studies in Melodrama and the Woman's Film* (London: BFI, 1987), pp. 189–90.
46. Jon Burrows, 'Our English Mary Pickford: Alma Taylor and ambivalent British stardom in the 1910s', in Babington (ed.), *British Stars and Stardom*, p. 30.

47. *Picture Show* on Balfour quoted in Macnab, *Searching for Stars*, p. 54. For more on stars of the teens and twenties, see Jon Burrows, 'Girls on film: The musical matrices of film stardom in early British cinema', *Screen*, Vol. 44, No. 3, 2003, pp. 314–25; Christine Gledhill, 'Reframing women in 1920s British cinema: The case of Violet Hopson and Dinah Shurey', *Journal of British Cinema and Television*, Vol. 4, No. 1, 2008, pp. 1–17; and relevant sections in Matthew Sweet, *Shepperton Babylon: The Lost Worlds of British Cinema* (London: Faber & Faber, 2005).

48. Alf Black cited in Reg Whitley, 'Who are the stars of 1952?', *Daily Mirror*, 20 December 1951, p. 2. Fields signed a contract to make films for Twentieth Century Fox for an unprecedentedly high fee, suggesting how her appeal was not seen as solely parochial. For an account of the transatlantic adventures of a number of female stars of the 1930s including Fields, Cicely Courtneidge, Madeleine Carroll, Jessie Matthews, Vivien Leigh, Constance Bennett, and Merle Oberon, see Sarah Street, 'Star trading: The British in 1930s and 1940s Hollywood', in Alastair Philips and Ginette Vincendeau (eds), *Journeys of Desire: European Actors in Hollywood* (London: BFI, 2006), pp. 61–70. For more on female stars of the 1930s, also see John Sedgwick, *Popular Filmgoing in 1930s Britain: A Choice of Pleasures* (Exeter: Exeter University Press, 2000) and relevant sections on Fields and Matthews in Jeffrey Richards, *The Age of the Dream Palace: Cinema and Society in Britain 1930–1939* (London: Routledge and Kegan Paul, 1984).

49. Cited in Thumim, *Celluloid Sisters*, p. 167. This also includes testimony from a woman who remembered imitating Ann Todd's dirndl skirts from *The Seventh Veil* and even learning to play the piano in imitation of the film's heroine.

50. Keira Knightley for Chanel, Kate Winslet for Lancome, Rachel Weisz for Burberry, Emily Blunt for Yves Saint Laurent, Helen Mirren for L'Oreal, Emma Watson for Burberry, and Gemma Arterton for Avon and Neutrogena.

51. Although it is equally salutary to remember the 1932 suicide of British actress Peg Entwhistle, whose despair about her failed film career led her to jump off the then-recently erected 'Hollywood' sign; she was the first person to take her life is this way but sadly not the last.

52. The phrase originally comes from Justine King's essay 'Crossing thresholds: The contemporary British woman's film', in Andrew Higson (ed.), *Dissolving Views: Key Writings on British Cinema* (London: Cassell, 1996), and was used as a touchstone in the editors' introduction, 'The hour of the cuckoo: Reclaiming the British woman's film', in Melanie Bell and Melanie Williams (eds), *British Women's Cinema* (London: Routledge, 2009), pp. 1–18.

53. Raymond Durgnat, *Films and Feelings* (London: Faber & Faber, 1967), p. 137.

54. Susan Hayward, 'Framing national cinemas', in Mette Hjort and Scott

MacKenzie (eds), *Cinema and Nation* (London: Routledge, 2000), p. 97.

55. Alice Jane Mackay and Pat Thane, 'The Englishwoman', in Robert Colls and Philip Dodd (eds), *Englishness: Politics and Culture 1880–1920*, second edition (London: Bloomsbury, 2014), p. 218. Virginia Woolf, *A Room of One's Own and Three Guineas* (London: Penguin, 1993), p. 234; emphasis in original.

56. Mackay and Thane, 'The Englishwoman', p. 222.

57. Philip Dodd, 'Englishness and the national culture', in Robert Colls and Philip Dodd (eds), *Englishness: Politics and Culture 1880–1920*, second edition (London: Bloomsbury, 2014), p. 29; emphasis in original.

58. Alison Light, *Forever England: Femininity, Literature and Conservatism between the Wars* (London: Routledge, 1991), p. 211, p. 8.

59. Ibid., pp. 8–10. Women's acquisition of the vote and just the demographic fact of their abundance, many of them spinsters or war widows, were also factors in this new public prominence of the feminine.

60. Mackay and Thane, 'The Englishwoman', p. 217.

61. Light, *Forever England*, p. 118.

62. Ibid., p. 208.

63. For more on representations of British femininity during wartime, see Christine Gledhill and Gillian Swanson (eds), *Nationalising Femininity: Culture, Sexuality and Cinema in World War Two Britain* (Manchester: Manchester University Press, 1996) and Antonia Lant, *Blackout: Reinventing Women for Wartime British Cinema* (Princeton: Princeton University Press, 1991).

64. Useful summaries of women in twentieth-century Britain include Sue Bruley, *Women in Britain since 1900* (London: Palgrave, 1999); Jane Lewis, *Women in Britain since 1945* (Oxford: Wiley-Blackwell, 1992); Annette Mayer, *Women in Britain, 1900–2000* (London: Hodder, 2002); Ina Zweininger-Bargielowska (ed.), *Women in Twentieth Century Britain* (London: Routledge, 2001).

65. The concepts of film as prism and refraction rather than reflection being a model for film's relationship to social reality are indebted to Sue Harper, 'The British women's picture: Methodology, agency and performance in the 1970s', in Melanie Bell and Melanie Williams (eds), *British Women's Cinema* (London: Routledge, 2009), p. 127.

66. Barry King, 'Embodying the elastic self: The parametrics of contemporary stardom', in Thomas Austin and Martin Barker (eds), *Contemporary Hollywood Stardom* (London: Arnold, 2003), p. 60.

67. Robert Colls and Philip Dodd (eds), *Englishness: Politics and Culture 1880–1920*, second edition (London: Bloomsbury, 2014), p. 6. In relation to the formation of an 'Anglo-British' cultural identity, Arthur Aughey also talks about how this is seen to combine the 'Englishness that appealed to liberties and rights derived from the past' with 'the Britishness of industry,

empire and moral improvement'. Arthur Aughey, *The Politics of Englishness* (Manchester: Manchester University Press, 2007), p. 28.

68. Babington, 'Introduction' in *British Stars and Stardom*, p. 5.
69. Others who may be considered as clearly identifiable as Welsh or Scottish include Rachel Roberts and Shirley Henderson, although in both cases these performers may not be seen as full stars.
70. Celestino Deleyto, 'The nun's story: Femininity and Englishness in the films of Deborah Kerr', in Babington (ed.), *British Stars and Stardom*, pp. 120–31.
71. Richard Dyer, *Heavenly Bodies*, p. 139.
72. Ibid., p. ix. Sean Redmond and Su Holmes (eds), 'Introduction', in *Stardom and Celebrity: A Reader* (London: Sage, 2007), p. 7. See also Su Holmes, 'Starring Dyer?: Revisiting star studies and contemporary celebrity culture', *Westminster Papers in Communication and Culture*, Vol. 2, No. 2, 2005, pp. 6–21.
73. Martin Shingler, *Star Studies: A Critical Guide* (London: BFI Palgrave, 2012), p. 174.
74. Harper, 'The British women's picture', p. 127.
75. Shingler, *Star Studies*, pp. 122–6.
76. Diane Negra and Su Holmes (eds), *In the Limelight and under the Microscope: Forms and Functions of Female Celebrity* (London: Continuum, 2011), p. 11.
77. Christine Gledhill (ed.), 'Introduction', in *Stardom: Industry of Desire* (London: Routledge, 1991), p. xiii. This is not merely film studies being partisan. As late as 1997, celebrity studies scholar P. David Marshall was arguing that film stars represented the 'pinnacle of the celebrity hierarchy'. P. David Marshall, *Celebrity and Power: Fame in Contemporary Culture* (Minneapolis: University of Minnesota Press, 1997), p. 226.
78. Negra, *Off-White Hollywood*, p. 7.
79. Babington, 'Introduction', in *British Stars and Stardom*, p. 18.
80. Marshall, *Celebrity and Power*, p. 242.
81. Richard Dyer, *Stars*, second edition (London: BFI, 1998), p. 60. King quoted in Paul McDonald, *Hollywood Stardom* (Oxford: Wiley-Blackwell, 2013), p. 5.
82. Paul McDonald, 'The star system: The production of Hollywood stardom in the post-studio era', in Paul McDonald and Janet Wasko (eds), *The Contemporary Hollywood Film Industry* (Oxford: Blackwell, 2008), p. 180. This is echoed in celebrity studies by Graeme Turner, who argued a similar case in 'Approaching celebrity studies', *Celebrity Studies*, Vol. 1, No. 1, 2010, pp. 11–20.
83. Shingler, *Star Studies*, p. 92.
84. McDonald, *Hollywood Stardom*, pp. 4–5.
85. Notable examples of this approach include James Naremore, *Acting in the Cinema* (Berkeley: University of California Press, 1990) and Andrew Klevan, *Film Performance: From Achievement to Appreciation* (London: Wallflower Press, 2005).

86. Shingler, *Star Studies*, p. 80.
87. Macnab, *Searching for Stars*, pp. 52–3. Annette Kuhn, 'Film stars in 1930s Britain: A cast study in modernity and femininity', in Tytti Soila (ed.), *Stellar Encounters: Stardom in Popular European Cinema* (New Barnet: John Libbey, 2009), p. 186.
88. David Thomson, *A Biographical Dictionary of Film* (London: André Deutsch, 1995), p. 536.
89. William Marshall, 'I can be loud-mouthed, even cocky but I'm not a little madam', *Daily Mirror*, 14 April 1986, p. 9.
90. Bruce Babington, 'Queen of British hearts: Margaret Lockwood revisited' in Babington (ed.), *British Stars and Stardom*, pp. 94–107. Sarah Street, 'A place of one's own? Margaret Lockwood and British film stardom in the 1940s', in Ulrike Sieglohr (ed.), *Heroines without Heroes: Reconstructing Female and National Identities in European Cinema, 1945–51* (London: Cassell, 2000), pp. 33–46. Josephine Dolan and Sarah Street, 'Twenty million people can't be wrong: Anna Neagle and popular British stardom', in Bell and Williams (eds), *British Women's Cinema*, pp. 34–48. Brian McFarlane, 'Ingénues, lovers, wives and mothers: The 1940s career trajectories of Googie Withers and Phyllis Calvert', in Bell and Williams (eds), *British Women's Cinema*, pp. 62–76. McKenna and Kendall are covered in Christine Geraghty, 'Femininity in the fifties: The new woman and the problem of the female star', in *British Cinema in the Fifties: Gender, Genre and the 'New Look'* (London: Routledge, 2000), pp. 155–74; Melanie Bell, *Julie Christie* (London: BFI Palgrave, forthcoming); Kate Egan, 'A *real* horror star: Articulating the extreme authenticity of Ingrid Pitt', in Kate Egan and Sarah Thomas (eds), *Cult Film Stardom* (London: Palgrave, 2013), pp. 212–25; Julian Petley, 'There's something about Mary . . .', in Babington (ed.), *British Stars and Stardom*, pp. 205–17; Kirsty Fairclough-Isaacs, 'Mature Meryl and Hot Helen: Hollywood, gossip and the "appropriately" ageing actress', in Imelda Whelehan and Joel Gwynne (eds), *Ageing, Popular Culture and Contemporary Feminism: Harleys and Hormones* (London: Palgrave, 2014), pp. 140–54; Sadie Wearing, 'Exemplary or exceptional embodiment? Discourses of aging in the case of Helen Mirren and *Calendar Girls*', in Josie Dolan and Estella Tincknell (eds), *Aging Femininities: Troubling Representations* (Cambridge: Cambridge Scholars Press, 2012), pp. 145–60; Sean Redmond, 'The whiteness of stars: Looking at Kate Winslet's unruly white body', in Sean Redmond and Su Holmes (eds), *Stardom and Celebrity: A Reader* (London: Sage, 2007), p. 265; Jackie Stacey, 'Crossing over with Tilda Swinton – the mistress of "flat affect"', *International Journal of Politics, Culture, and Society*, Vol. 28, No. 3, 2015, pp. 243–71.
91. Key academic writings on Dors are Christine Geraghty, 'Diana Dors', in Charles Barr (ed.), *All Our Yesterdays: 90 Years of British Cinema* (London: BFI, 1986), pp. 341–5, and Pam Cook, 'The trouble with sex: Diana Dors and the blonde bombshell phenomenon', in Bruce Babington (ed.), *British*

Stars and Stardom (Manchester: Manchester University Press, 2001), pp. 167–78. She is also dealt with in Harper, *Women in British Cinema*, p. 98.

92. Dyer, *Heavenly Bodies*, p. ix.

93. Paul McDonald, 'Star studies', in Joanne Hollows and Mark Jancovich (eds), *Approaches to Popular Film* (Manchester: Manchester University Press, 1995), p. 80. Babington, 'Introduction' in *British Stars and Stardom*, p. 6. For Babington, the question of who is a star and who is 'a significant performer' lies much more in the eye of the beholder and 'is less theoretically resolvable than is sometimes thought.' (p. 8). McDonald later provided a very nuanced outline of the full 'food chain' of contemporary Hollywood stardom encompassing everything from 'fireproof' A-listers through 'stars' and then 'names' down to 'working actors' and what lies beneath in *Hollywood Stardom*, pp. 19–24, and it would be interesting to apply a similar hierarchy to the operation of stardom in British film and television.

94. Sue Harper, 'Thinking forward and up: The British films of Conrad Veidt', in Jeffrey Richards (ed.), *The Unknown 1930s* (London: I. B. Tauris, 1998), p. 121. This also corresponds with the line of argument espoused by Bruce Babington that some British performers 'remain local stars – but no less meaningful for that'. Babington, 'Introduction', in *British Stars and Stardom*, p. 10.

95. Sarah Street, 'Margaret Rutherford and comic performance', in I. Q. Hunter and Laraine Porter (eds), *British Comedy Cinema* (London: Routledge, 2012), pp. 89–99. Claire Mortimer, 'Mrs. John Bull: The later life stardom of Margaret Rutherford', in Lucy Bolton and Julie Lobalzo Wright (eds), *Lasting Screen Stars* (London: Palgrave, forthcoming). For more on the specificities of female 'character stars' in British cinema, see Andrew Higson, 'Britain's finest contribution to the screen: Flora Robson and character acting' in Babington (ed.), *British Stars and Stardom*, pp. 68–79; Estella Tincknell, 'The nation's matron: Hattie Jacques and British postwar popular culture', *Journal of British Cinema and Television*, Vol. 12, No. 1, 2015, pp. 6–24. This general area is also discussed in Melanie Williams, 'Entering the paradise of anomalies: Studying female character acting in British cinema', *Screen*, Vol. 52, No. 1, spring 2011, pp. 97–104.

96. Durgnat, *A Mirror for England*, p. 184. Dawn Collinson, 'Liverpool teen Amy Jackson on her new life in Mumbai and becoming an in-demand Bollywood leading lady', *Liverpool Echo*, 25 January 2012. http://www.liverpoolecho.co.uk/news/liverpool-news/liverpool-teen-amy-jackson-new-3355952. I have also not included overseas stars who spent significant moments of their career making British films but worked across various national industries, such as Anna May Wong, Elisabeth Bergner, Lili Palmer, Mai Zetterling, or Ursula Andress, while still recognising their significance to the star landscapes of British cinema during their respective periods of popularity.

97. John Harvey, 'She's becoming our top dollar earner', *Reynolds News*, 21 August 1949. Press cuttings file on Jean Kent, BFI Library.

98 'Britain's bad girl', undated press release for *The Loves of Joanna Godden* (1947). BFI Library press cuttings file for Jean Kent.

99. *Daily Mail*, 4 September 1959. Kent felt that this was a huge waste of potential: 'Forty is the most awakening age in a woman's life. Who cares about a few wrinkles, the odd grey hair or the inch or so more around the waist.' *Sunday Graphic*, 20 September 1959. Both taken from press cuttings file on Jean Kent, BFI Library.

100. Jean Kent, 'They make me too old', *Picturegoer*, 13 November 1954, p. 23; emphasis in the original.

101. Cited in Clare Colvin, 'Mystery moves', *The Times*, 23 May 1983, p. 17.

102. Anonymous, 'News of the north-west', *Manchester Guardian*, 21 March 1957, p. 14.

103. Russell Harty,, 'Works outing', *The Observer*, 14 August 1977, p. 26.

104. Anonymous, 'The padded waif', *Time*, 8 June 1962. Press cuttings file on Rita Tushingham, BFI Library.

105. Harper, *Women in British Cinema*, pp. 137–8.

106. Lynn Barber, 'Couldn't she just wear a babygro?', *The Observer Magazine*, 20 April 1997, p. 5.

107. 'In Britain, she's already being perceived as a national treasure, but her film future may be in Hollywood'. Ivor Davis, 'Sign please! Hollywood's in a fizz for Emily', *Sunday Express*, 4 September 1988, p. 19.

108. Robert Ottaway, 'No one loves a film star who looks forty', *Sunday Graphic*, 3 October 1954. Press cuttings file for Jean Kent, BFI Library.

109. See http://knowyourmeme.com/memes/in-a-world-of-kardashians.

110. Holmes and Negra (eds), 'Introduction' in *In the Limelight and under the Microscope*, pp. 1–16.

111. Burrows, 'Our English Mary Pickford: Alma Taylor and ambivalent British stardom in the 1910s', p. 30.

112. Gill Martin, 'Fame is a pain in the neck for Lady Jane Grey', *Daily Express*, 25 January 1985, p. 13; Burrows, "Our English Mary Pickford', p. 36; Katharine Hadley, 'Queen Helena's keeping her head', *Daily Express*, 22 May 1986, p. 28.

CHAPTER 2

'A Girl Appears in Camiknickers': Jean Kent's Austerity Stardom

During the peak years of British cinema attendance in the 1940s, which reached an all-time high of more than 1.6 billion admissions in 1946, British female stars flourished in abundance.[1] This was the decade in which Anna Neagle's London films, with titles traversing the posher parts of the capital – from *I Live in Grosvenor Square* (1945), *Piccadilly Incident* (1946), and *The Courtneys of Curzon Street* (1947) to *Spring in Park Lane* (1948) and *Maytime in Mayfair* (1949) – were among the biggest box-office attractions of their age (or indeed any other), as revealed by their high position in the BFI's 2005 compilation of the most successful films in the UK.[2] *Spring in Park Lane* came out as top British film and the fifth most popular film of all from the advent of sound through to 2004, ranking far higher than more canonical British offerings such as *The Third Man* (1949), which only attained twenty-sixth place in the same list. Wooden she may appear to modern eyes but Neagle, as Josephine Dolan and Sarah Street point out, 'was a star they paid to see again, again and again' in Britain in the 1940s, consolidating the star status initially established back in the 1930s with her adroit move from Cochrane chorus girl to Queen Victoria in *Victoria the Great* (1937) and *Sixty Glorious Years* (1938).[3]

The appearance of *The Wicked Lady* (1945) at number nine in the same BFI list indicates the significance of Gainsborough Studios as purveyors of popular entertainment during the 1940s. Another major female star, Margaret Lockwood, played its titular role opposite James Mason as her highwayman lover, sealing both their positions as the most popular stars of the era. In Lockwood's case, this was further proven by her victory in the *Daily Mail*'s National Film Actress Award in 1946 (synoptically looking back over all the war years), in 1947 and also in 1948, as well as the fact that she topped or ranked very highly in polls conducted by *Motion Picture Herald* and *Kinematograph Weekly*, the Bernstein questionnaire (a survey conducted by a particular chain of exhibitors), and in the *Picturegoer* awards over those same years.[4] As with Neagle, Lockwood's star image had been initially established in the 1930s but then modified to meet newly emerging audience needs and generic contexts, taking on full-blooded melodramatic (and sometimes unashamedly conniving) roles from *The Man in Grey* (1943) onwards.

Neagle and Lockwood were probably the two biggest female stars of the era but their success was complemented by that enjoyed by a profusion of other British actresses who also featured strongly in these same surveys and popularity polls. They included Lockwood's Gainsborough peers Phyllis Calvert and Patricia Roc, Ann Todd, Celia Johnson, Rosamund John, Deborah Kerr, Anne Crawford, Valerie Hobson, Googie Withers, and Jean Simmons, to name a few – all prized for their variations on the theme of British femininity.[5] Yet another star who featured very strongly in surveys from this period was Jean Kent, another Gainsborough alumna but one who was well aware of her lowlier position in that studio's feminine hierarchy, which according to Kent ran 'Margaret [Lockwood], then Pat [Roc] and Phyllis [Calvert], then me. I was the odds-and-sods girl. I used to mop up the parts that other people didn't want.'[6] But even in odds-and-sods parts, she was getting noticed by audiences; the top name listed in response to Bernstein's 1947 enquiry, 'Which film actors or actresses whom you have seen in comparatively small parts would you like to see in star roles?'[7] Off the back of a greater number of starring roles towards the tail end of the 1940s, she would enter the select company of *Motion Picture Herald*'s annual list of the top ten British stars (both male and female) in 1950 and 1951.[8] Kent may never have quite attained the elevated poll-topping status of a Neagle, a Lockwood, or even a Calvert, but she was an important British star of the post-war period nonetheless, one whose fan-club newsletter at one time rivalled the circulation of a more high-brow publication such as *The Spectator*.[9] And thanks to the British Film Institute's special collection of materials on Jean Kent, we have rare access to that fan-club ephemera. These archival materials provide fascinating insights into Kent's interactions with her legions of followers and a sense of what they saw in her that they particularly liked and admired.

Perhaps it was the fact that Kent offered something special within the taxonomy of wartime and post-war British female stardom, as 'Britain's no. 1 bad girl', according to one studio press release, who 'attracted the most attention when being wicked'.[10] In one of her first films, *Bees in Paradise* (1944), she led a predatory dance number in which she made the animalistic boast that her lineage was 'wolf on my mother's side'. More than a decade later, playing a music-hall performer in *Grip of the Strangler* (1958), she sang with gusto, 'I'm big, I'm bad, I'm bold!' Unlike many of her contemporaries, she seemed comfortable with playing sexy women (sexy usually being synonymous with bad) and was one of the few British stars convincingly aligned with a pin-up girl tradition more readily associated with US culture in the 1940s. As Kent herself later reflected on her slightly risqué image, 'if they opened a script and saw "A girl appears in camiknickers", they used to send for me'.[11] It's difficult to think of many other British female stars of the time being able to deliver with the same brazen conviction the line that her character has to say in *The Rake's Progress* (1945): 'I know what you think I am' – Googie Withers or Greta Gynt perhaps, Margaret Lockwood on occasion, but Jean Kent was still in very select company in being able to play a plausible British femme fatale. As the chorus girl who's more than happy to be an aristocrat's mistress in *Fanny by Gaslight* (1944) – 'something for nothing, that's my motto' – or as the younger sister who selfishly craves 'nice things', including her sister's boyfriend, in *The Loves of Joanna Godden* (1947), Jean Kent was a star whose screen persona ran counter to officially sanctioned discourses of self-denial and moral probity during wartime and post-war austerity. Even those camiknickers could have got Kent into trouble if they had roses and butterflies embroidered on them, like the pair that one West End seamstress found herself in court for having unnecessarily decorated, flouting government regulations. As Harry Hopkins noted of the case, 'this was the time when a jungle of petty restrictions reminiscent of the medieval sumptuary laws positively invited evasion'.[12] In such a context, it wasn't hard to see how the moderately rebellious girl who desires 'nice things' may have been a figure with whom many young women (and men) could sympathise and identify.

Making the Grade at Gainsborough

Like many British stars, Jean Kent had a stage background but not in the legitimate theatre; rather, her lineage was in vaudeville and variety, concert parties, and music halls. These more demotic theatrical connections would continue to reverberate throughout her film career, as she frequently played performers from that world and brought the earthy good humour of its habitus to many of her roles. She was talked about as a 'trooper' and a 'hard worker', and unlike some of her Gainsborough peers, she didn't blanch at touring round to make personal appearances (always bringing a spare bouquet with which to be presented, she said, 'in case they didn't have one').[13] She was an obvious choice to star in a pantomime put on by cinema owners in 1947 to 'eke out dwindling stocks of Hollywood films' during the American trade embargo, being entirely at home with pantomime's lively interactivity and outright populism, and stating in a 1946 interview: 'I enjoy anything in the entertainment line.'[14]

Born into a theatrical family in 1921 and an enthusiastic and talented dancer from childhood, Jean Kent's professional career began very young, taking off when the teenager took over a stage role to replace her indisposed mother, suggesting her prodigious maturity as a performer. At the age of only thirteen (using a borrowed birth certificate to lie about her age and adopting the professional name Jean Carr), she landed a job as a chorus girl at the Windmill Theatre, famous for its nude tableaux (although Kent never appeared in them).[15] She then stooged for famous comedians Ernie Lotinga and Max Miller in stage revue before being signed by Gainsborough to do similar supportive work for Tommy Handley in the radio spin-off *It's That Man Again* (1943) and for Arthur Askey in *Miss London Ltd.* (1943) and *Bees in Paradise* (1944). As well as being a smart soubrette in her formative film appearances, Kent also slotted very comfortably into the role of pin-up around this time, featuring as 'girl of the month' in *Soldier* magazine and in a Navy, Army and Air Force Institutes (NAAFI) free issue 'pin up news sheet'. Described around the time of her appearance in *It's That Man Again!* as 'fond of swing, swimming and svelte sweaters', Kent was being built up as a sexy fun-loving modern girl, an image that gained her plenty of 'ardent soldier fans'.[16]

The years 1944–6 at Gainsborough marked a slight change of direction as Kent partook fully in the studio's costume-drama boom, playing scene-stealing supporting roles as the feckless showgirl Lucy in *Fanny By Gaslight* (1944), Stewart Granger's jealous lover in *Madonna of the Seven Moons* (1944), a tiny uncredited role as highwayman's doxy in *The Wicked Lady* (1945), and second fiddle – pardon the pun – to Phyllis Calvert, again competing for Granger's attention, in the Paganini biopic *The Magic Bow* (1946). She also appeared in the more contemporary settings of *Waterloo Road* (1945) and *The Rake's Progress* (1945), once again as women of questionable virtue, but perhaps her most interesting modern role around this time pitted her against Phyllis Calvert again, as inmates in a French internment camp in *Two Thousand Women* (1944). Kent plays Bridie, a striptease artiste 'whose narcissism is signalled by the pinups of herself performing on the walls of her room' and who attracts the animus of Calvert's brisk journalist Freda.[17] Completely unpatriotic, Bridie is willing to flirt shamelessly with the Nazi commandant in order to get a private room, perching on his desk all the better to show off her legs while warning him, as she playfully traces a fingertip on the desktop, that the amatory sweet nothings she murmurs in her sleep would disturb a roommate: 'I'm not thinking of myself – it's the girl I'd have to share with.' Bridie's amoral sexuality is posed as a threat to the successful integration of this all-female community, especially when they try to mobilise an escape plan for some British soldiers and suspect that she may be the treacherous weak link.

Divisive bad girl she may be, especially in comparison with the team-players played by Calvert and Patricia Roc in the film, but Jean Kent's playing of Bridie was undertaken with unusual assurance for a British star, prompting Babington's later reflection that she was 'surely the most potently erotic of all British actresses of the period, a Susan Hayward in a cinema unable quite to find a sustained place for her'.[18] His comments, which position Kent as a star whose outright sex appeal seemed much closer to Hollywood than British models, echo those made in *Picturegoer* magazine at the end of the 1940s:

> Seven years ago, British films discovered a lovely redhead with the combined roman-tic potentialities of Rita Hayworth and Ginger Rogers, changed her professional name from Jean Carr to Jean Kent – and have only occasionally done right by the gal ever since . . . to date, Miss Kent's career has been handled with the cheerful incon-sequentiality of a village beauty contest . . . Out of this raw material could have been shaped a colossus, a great international star as bright as [Marlene] Dietrich, [Joan] Crawford, Bette Davis, and as glamorous as Doris Day.[19]

It is difficult to imagine higher praise than to be placed in the legend-ary company of Hayworth, Rogers, Dietrich, Crawford, Davis, and Day, even if it was to make the point about Jean Kent's *unrealised* colossal star potential, misunderstood and squandered by a national film industry that verged on the amateur when it came to creating female stars. The refer-ence points for Kent are all Hollywood actresses, suggesting a lack of any ready British analogies for her kind of stardom. Whereas a British star like Deborah Kerr evoked 'sweet virgin' spirituality, and even Margaret Lockwood skilfully held wickedness and goodness in equilibrium through alternating 'white queen' and 'black queen' roles, it seemed that Jean Kent's destiny was to be British cinema's 'not-quite-nice' girl and while that gave her a definable persona, it also caused her some problems.[20] 'Being a bad girl has led her to movie stardom', trumpeted one press release from 1947, which also quoted Kent as saying that her roles in *Two Thousand Women*, *Madonna of the Seven Moons*, and *The Rake's Progress* 'have all given me grand opportunities. With humdrum, conventional parts I might not have got the chance to reach stardom.'[21] But this created a problem with typecasting, as journalist Ruth Miller had noted in 1946: 'some people want her to be a young harpy forever'.[22] In fact, her very ease in adopting a sexy 'not-quite-nice' persona – the girl in camiknick-ers – seemed to militate against her being able to truly flourish in British cinema around this time. As Charles Hamblett observed in 1950, 'having discovered a natural hoydenish beauty, it almost seemed that her sponsors were slightly afraid of the consequences'.[23]

This sense of ambivalence towards the kind of glamorous quasi-American film stardom Jean Kent had the potential to develop was of a piece with broader anti-glamour tendencies in British stardom (see Introduction) but the way it was inflected in the 1940s spoke of some specificities to that historical moment. During the war, British films had been seen as gaining a new maturity and confidence through their deployment of documentary-style realism, so that, in the words of critic of the time Richard Winnington, they began to 'possess a craftsmanship and freshness above that of the regular flow from Hollywood', making them 'miracles of taste and intelligence'.[24] This spurred what Charles Barr describes as a state of 'post-war critical euphoria that saw British cinema, after its important wartime development, as being ready to challenge the world commercially and artistically', an optimistic belief in all-conquering prestige British cinema, definitively anatomised by John Ellis in his work on 'the quality film adventure'.[25] But while a number of British films gaining large audiences had met the critics' 'quality control' requirements, like *This Happy Breed* (1944), *The Way to the Stars* (1945), or *Great Expectations* (1946), the most popular examples of indigenous filmmaking at this time were in fact the critically derogated melodramas seen as the very antithesis of any aspirations towards prestige. Gainsborough's output in particular attracted opprobrium for its fast-and-loose approach to period accuracy and its revelling in often sadistic sexual psychodrama. Its stars, the aforementioned Mason, Lockwood, Calvert, and Granger, were managing to outrank Hollywood stars in popularity for the first time ever in Britain and while on some levels this should have been cause for patriotic celebration, the fact that it was happening through the auspices of films regarded as lowest-common-denominator potboilers, no better than Hollywood, made it a bittersweet British success story. This entailed some serious soul-searching about what British stars should be and do , and whether they should reject the kind of stardom that had previously only been within the grasp of Hollywood stars or actively embrace their star status: the 'must we have stars?'/'are we making our own stars at last?' dyad discussed in the introduction. And if this was true of male stars then it was doubly applicable to their female counterparts who seemed to shoulder an even greater representational burden. In November 1945, John Y. Stapleton's article in *Picturegoer* 'Ladies or dames?' bifurcated different star femininities along national lines, with the demure British 'lady', exemplified by Phyllis Calvert, juxtaposed with the glamorous Hollywood 'dame', typified by Betty Grable.[26] Letters to the magazine earlier that year had emphasised the 'charm and natural refreshing beauty' of British actresses as opposed to the 'tinsel and painted "angels" of Hollywood' swathed in 'a cloak of glamour'.[27] Then, alongside the discussion of glamour (imbricated with questions of good taste and national identity), came a parallel consideration of female morality via the attractions of the wicked heroines played by some female British stars, Googie Withers, Margaret Lockwood, and Jean Kent among them. In August 1946, one reader spoke up in favour of 'naughty wenches' ('men want to meet them and women like to be them'), while another piece from October of the same year in *Picturegoer* stated, in slightly self-contradictory terms, that 'good girls will always be welcome, but so will bad girls be, as long as they keep within the tenets of good taste'.[28] An aspiring star of the time like Jean Kent, forging her film career and star persona at precisely this moment of intense discussion about how British women stars should present themselves, what kind of roles they should play, and how they could stay within the boundaries of 'good taste', would be very much caught up in these debates and have her career partly determined by its frames of reference.

Kent herself expressed a certain impatience with the strictures imposed by ideals of national character, espousing a different model of behaviour in which passionate self-expression should be 'given more free rein':

> I think English girls have some temperament, but they aren't encouraged to show it. You see it at cocktail parties and in films. English boys and girls all have this ridiculous desire to be 'ladies' and 'gentlemen' and suppress their temperament.[29]

It was around this time that Kent got her best opportunity to showcase her own 'temperament' by playing Rosal, the foot-stamping, shawl-swishing, fan-snapping Spanish gypsy dancer in *Caravan* (1946) who even gets to ask (of Anne Crawford), 'What do you know of love with your cold English ways?' Crawford and Kent both love the same man – Stewart Granger's Richard/Ricardo – and although ladylike Crawford ultimately gets him, it is Jean Kent who gets to enjoy the connubial idyll with him, its primitivism indicated by taking place in caves lit by open fires. Kent also gets a noble (not to mention beautifully lit) deathbed scene after she's taken a bullet for the hero, in the self-sacrificing manner of Frenchy in *Destry Rides Again* (1939). Kent's Rosal was a more sympathetic version of the discarded gypsy lover she'd played opposite Granger in *Madonna of the Seven Moons* a few years earlier, but this time occupying far greater screen time and featuring more prominently in publicity materials. Kent not only gets a nude swimming scene in *Caravan*, she also gets several striking dance numbers (the 'Zambra' and the 'Farruka', according to the film's press book) that foreground her sinuous movements and svelte physique, shown

Figure 2.1 'Sexual energy and power': Jean Kent dances the Zambra as Rosal in *Caravan* (1946).

off to great advantage via Elizabeth Haffenden's sparkling and revealing costumes. As Pam Cook notes of the 'exquisite' costuming for Rosal: 'Her rustling skirts, the shiny pieces of glittering metal with which they are decorated and the tinkling bells of her tambourine all transmit sexual energy and power.'[30]

Caravan got her some international interest too, with *Motion Picture Herald* calling her a 'phenomenon lately revealed in the Gainsborough setup': 'Miss Kent, doubtless, is a new one on Hollywood. She makes the grade herein with an assuredness which must inevitably attract the attention of that band of American prospectors now in Britain.'[31] In fact, the previous year, Kent had been specifically named in the US trade press, along with Patricia Roc, James Mason, and Margaret Lockwood, as one of the cohort of British stars that J. Arthur Rank planned to 'build up internationally' using 'Hollywood publicity methods', part of his attempt to gain greater traction and power in the American market.[32] With *Caravan* she was starting to make an impact as a British female star with potential transatlantic appeal. In *Motion Picture Herald*'s 'What the picture did for us' section, in which exhibitors reported back on what was doing well – or not – in their cinemas, *Caravan* was deemed a hit, largely on the strength of Kent's performance alongside Granger: 'Jean Kent as the gypsy girl was outstanding. Our patrons enjoyed this. Well worth playing time. Above average crowd turned out.'[33] Continuing on a period-drama tack, Kent had another full-bloodied melodramatic role, this time in Technicolor, in the Sydney and Muriel Box Graham Greene adaptation, *The Man Within* (1947). As the wanton woman who tries to seduce Richard Attenborough's innocent into testifying against the smugglers, her 'come hither' look was judged 'worth the price of admission alone' by one reviewer, while another thought she 'put the sex in Sussex'.[34] But translating the picture to the US could prove tricky, suggested one American reviewer, precisely because Kent's scene of sexual enticement was so 'sensuous' that it was 'likely to be cut by American censors'.[35] But otherwise the film's blend of 'adventure, action, suspense and sex', packed with 'situations and dialogue considerably more daring than one usually finds' was felt by another reviewer in the American trade paper *Film Bulletin* to guarantee it 'better box-office returns here than most English films'.[36] This seems borne out from trade ads from 1948 that boasted of the 'great business' done by *The Smugglers* across the US: 'Ask the theatermen who played it in Los Angeles, New York, Cleveland, Newark, Denver, Indianapolis, Salt Lake City, Washington, Oakland, Springfield, Mass., Oklahoma City and all the other great engagements across the board, big and small!'[37] Kent's image, in full-on 'come hither' mode, chemise slipping from her shoulder, was a prominent feature of the film's marketing campaign (along with a sado-masochistic image of maritime punishment). Here was a British lady who had the potential to come across as a 'dame' of the US vernacular kind.

Films, Farming and Fandom: Kent at her Peak

As well as marking Jean Kent's entry into top-billed stardom, *Caravan* marked a personal watershed for the star, as the production on which she met her husband Yusuf Ramart, who'd been working as Stewart Granger's stand-in (the couple would get married in 1946 and remain so until his death in 1989). Publicity material on the star's private life would henceforth emphasise the couple's happy rural existence on their Sussex farm, as with the 1948 article 'Down on the farm with Jean Kent', which talks about the actress 'cooking, decorating, looking after the poultry, helping her husband in the fields and being completely happy':

> [T]here's such a lot to talk about, so many plans to make and execute. How are the tomato pots in the big glasshouse? Is the tractor running sweetly today? Some of the trees in the orchard need to be pruned and transplanted while twenty pigs are on

their way to occupy the renovated sties. 'I'm going to learn how to home-cure bacon', Jean announces.[38]

But while Kent was establishing the farm – a piquant contrast with her flighty younger sister desperate to get away from the family homestead in *The Loves of Joanna Godden* (1947) – many of her most prominent screen roles at this time were more urban in flavour, from international secret agent (glamorous but disappointingly marginal) in *Sleeping Car to Trieste* (1948), to fashion house mannequin in the portmanteau *Bond Street* (1948), and, most successfully, as the beleaguered young heroine Gwen in Sydney Box's controversial *Good-Time Girl* (1948). Once again she played a girl undone by her love of 'nice things' but this time the reasons for her downfall are presented as environmental and external rather than inherent in the girl's poor character. As Sue Harper suggests, Muriel Box's script 'carefully locates social deprivation as the source of Gwen's problems'.[39] The press book does likewise, describing Gwen as 'just an ordinary poor teen age girl who likes pretty things and a good time. Her home life is bad.' This young girl is victim rather than simply villain, betrayed and abused by parents, employers ('Give me a little kiss and we'll forget about the brooch, shall we?'), lovers, and state institutions alike. Her story may still be a cautionary tale of 'how a girl who likes dressing up may come to a sticky end' via the 'whisky-strewn path to penal servitude', as one reviewer put it, but her downward trajectory is presented with a good deal of sympathy and insight.[40] Gwen succumbs to the appeal of black sequins and nightclub cocktails and gets herself embroiled in corrupt criminality but, with her hair in plaits and wearing a borrowed dressing gown after being taken in by kind club pianist Dennis Price, the little-girl-lost desperate for affection is all too evident through the grown-up gloss.

Good-Time Girl and her next star vehicle, *Trottie True* (1949), probably represented the apex of Jean Kent's stardom. Both performed well at the box-office, and both enabled her to showcase her talents at length, no longer being consigned to the margins of films in sparkling but under-developed supporting roles but unambiguously taking centre stage. Back in 1944, Kent had first made her mark in the minor role of a nineteenth-century chorus girl in *Fanny by Gaslight* and she returned to that milieu five years later in *Trottie True*; but this time photographed in colour and featured as the film's star. Beautiful and talented soubrette Trottie is an inherent populist who cannot abandon her old music-hall practices even when she climbs the ladder into more refined venues, still enthusiastically urging her audience to join in with the song. When she moves to the Gaiety Theatre and begins consorting with aristocratic 'stage door

Johnnies' and finally gets married to one, Lord Digby Landon (James Donald), it looks as though a class-system clash may be on the cards between Trottie and her in-laws. Instead, Trottie's effortless ability to traverse and bring together different social classes are celebrated, as with the Christmas dance below stairs in which she leads the singing and dancing. 'You are a born Duchess,' her mother-in-law tells her. 'You are never afraid of doing something that others might consider wrong, or in bad taste, and subsequently you are an aristocrat and entirely free of vulgarity.' Although temporarily wrong-footed by unspoken aristocratic behavioural codes surrounding husbands and mistresses, ultimately Trottie is not just true but triumphant, rewarded with a happy marriage as well as material wealth: a potent fantasy of cross-class consensus and social mobility that seems to speak to the ambitions of late-1940s Britain. Moreover, Trottie's plain-speaking unpretentiousness corresponded perfectly with Kent's off-screen image as the girl 'immune to flattery', able to turn on the glamour when required but happiest of all on the farm with her husband, pickling, baking, and tending to the livestock.[41]

This down-to-earth image was also foregrounded in the communications of Jean Kent's fan club, run by the star herself and at one point numbering more than 20,000 members. An assortment of fan-club ephemera – pocket calendars, membership cards, signed photos, and newsletters – is held by BFI Special Collections, and this archive provides a rare and fascinating glimpse not only into Kent's fandom but more broadly into the operation of fan culture in the late 1940s and early 1950s. Decades before the 'unmediated' communication of a star to her Instagram or Twitter followers, the Jean Kent international fan-club newsletter offered the thrill of direct communiques such as 'Kent's candid column' and 'Jean's letter to you', detailing her life in the studios and on location but also at home on the farm with her husband. The newsletters include intimate insights into the star through items such as recipes, handicrafts (a 'Jean Kent knitting book' for fans), beauty tips (including her revelation 'I have never worn false fingernails'), and special fashion promotions, such as 'priority attention from the stockist' of the Jean Kent range of shoes created by S. A. Squirrel and Co. 'on presenting proof of membership' at participating stores in 'about one hundred of the more important provincial towns and cities'.[42] Similar kinds of activity could be accessed through more general film magazines like *Picturegoer* or *Picture Show* but the newsletter's difference from those kinds of fan texts is in its strikingly bespoke and detailed attention to the activities of individual members. The fan-club newsletter includes numerous personalised messages in response to specific fan letters, congratulating fans on their success in swimming galas, in teaching their dog to do tricks, or fundraising for charity: 'Member 9004. Bravo, Dilys! You have done well to raise £50 for the hospital.'[43]

Kent made a special point of cherishing her fans, and at one point was described as not only having 'one of the largest fan clubs in Britain' but also 'mak[ing] a business of attending to it herself'.[44] We may take with a large pinch of salt the suggestion that all the letters (reported in 1949 as reaching 17,000 a week) were answered by Kent and her mother alone with no other secretarial support but sometimes some of its administrative intricacies and hiccups do suggest an amateur operation rather than a slick studio-run machine.[45] There's a cumbersome request for renewals for members 9,102 to 11,726 inclusive, apologies to one particular member for failing to respond to previous correspondence ('sorry your last letter went astray'), and blanket apologies for the late arrival of a previous newsletter due to an underestimated print run. But what was probably more crucial in sustaining her fan club was that Kent strongly and publicly aligned herself with her fans' tastes and preferences as she made clear in an interview with *Picturegoer* in 1947:

> Jean Kent more than any other film star believes in her fans; believes in their essential rightness of view about everything in the cinema . . . The fans form a mirror for a star's work, if she chooses to study the reflection. 'They never make a mistake, such as people in the trade make, and that is why I think they deserve more attention from producers than they receive.'[46]

In a sense, the fans often had to make do with thin gruel in terms of the on-screen appearances of their idol, with the exception of a few star show-cases. But their fandom was clearly kept alive through the dynamism and scale of the star's fan club. However, it is important to note that sometimes Jean Kent fandom seemed to act merely as a pretext for a broader kind of engagement with cinema culture or general sociability. Kent was happy to field questions not only about herself but also about other film stars ('What is James Mason's shoe size?'), to enable fans to swap materials, especially photos, books, and magazines, about a whole range of screen, radio, and stage stars, to set up an essay-writing competition about film music, and to run a pen-pal section that even resulted in two fan club members getting engaged to each other. One wonders what riches may lurk in the fan-club documentation of other contemporaneous stars but much of it, sadly, is lost to the dustbin of history.[47] Or perhaps Jean Kent was a special case in having an especially vibrant and personalised fan culture, a compensation for the fact that she was never able to ascend to the top tier of British stardom like Neagle or Lockwood. Perhaps her most significant impact on post-war culture was not in the films she appeared in but in her apparent ability to elicit weekly fan mail in the thousands from 'the customers in the one-and-three-penny seats' who, according to journalist John Harvey in 1949, 'clamoured for advice on ways and means of being slightly naughty and yet nice'.[48]

From 'Darling of Today' to 'the Star that Films Forgot': Jean Kent's Accelerated Ageing

One of the things that Kent's fans wished for most fervently was a film to show off her skills as a dancer and singer as well as actress, and the aforementioned *Trottie True* was one of the few films to enable this. As well as fitting in with the forties fad for Victorian music hall in British films such as *Champagne Charlie* (1944), *I'll Be Your Sweetheart* (1945), and *Gaiety George* (1946), *Trottie True* can also be seen as an attempt to mimic Hollywood's colourful musicals set in the 'gay nineties', especially those featuring pin-up girl Betty Grable, such as the hugely popular *Coney Island* (1943), *Sweet Rosie O'Grady* (1943) – which has its heroine marry an English duke, just as Trottie does – and *Mother Wore Tights* (1947).[49] At a point when J. Arthur Rank was continuing to do his level best to get British films making profit in the US, albeit with limited success, Kent seemed like a good bet to build up, combining the glamour and chutzpah of the Hollywood pin-up girl with something more recognisably English in its cultural roots. In a newspaper article from 1949 entitled 'She's becoming our top dollar earner', Kent is specifically named as 'the screen star on whom Rank is now gambling thousands of pounds as Britain's first real dollar-earning "pin-up"' with Rank 'seriously grooming Jean to be a serious rival to the Grables and Hayworths of Hollywood'. The article patriotically concludes that 'Jean Kent seems to have got everything that the sultry stars of Hollywood have got. And in the right places', endorsing her attempt on the US market on its own terms.[50] Although John Y. Stapleton asked in 1945, 'Where is the British Lamour? Where is our Grable, our Montez, our Mae West? You will search in vain, for these types are alien to the British', it seems that by the decade's close, Jean Kent was being offered as a partial answer to those questions.[51] 'We gotta Grable!' announced the *Daily Mirror* in its review of *Trottie True* while the *Sunday Dispatch* concurred that Jean Kent had been 'Grable-ised . . . you will find her in sequins, frilly lace, and smoky nylon tights; the kind of tights Betty Grable would never be seen in films without'.[52] *Trottie True*'s press book proudly announced Kent as both 'The Idol of the Nineties – the Darling of Today, saying her name is the key to your publicity', and the film's British poster was dominated by a Grable-esque image of Kent's legs mid-Can Can.

But even then, there were indications that the kind of lavish 'musi-colour' star vehicles that 20th Century Fox so lovingly and skilfully crafted for Betty Grable would be hard to replicate in the context of a British film industry that was still smarting from the failure of its big colour musical *London Town* (1946), and that moreover seemed to have trouble with pre-senting musical numbers so as to facilitate star power, as Kent herself observed:

> They weren't good with the music. I had a battle with that . . . I wanted to prevent them, while I was actually singing the number, from cutting away too much, which they used to be very fond of, in British films. The whole point of somebody singing the song is for the audience in the cinema, not the people in the movie. So I had to devise ways to keep moving all the time so they couldn't get the scissors in.[53]

Just like her character Trottie, Jean Kent's firm grasp of public taste enabled her to see what needed to be done, even if this only made it into the final film in truncated form in the shape of a few short musical numbers. Despite the film's box-office success, *Trottie True* didn't lead to a run of musical rom-com vehicles for Kent. Her starring role in one the few Georgette Heyer film adaptations *The Reluctant Widow* (1950) got lost in its somewhat indifferent (although eventful) diegesis, and a farce made in Italy, *Her Favourite Husband* (also known as *The Taming of Dorothy*) (1950), didn't really prosper, despite the comic talents of Gordon Harker and Margaret Rutherford being enlisted.

Kent's career then took a turn for the darkly dramatic in her next notable film, Anthony Asquith's *The Woman in Question*. In the same year as the Japanese classic *Rashomon* (1950), this British film took a similar approach to the subjectivity of truth by presenting the events leading up to a woman's death through the different perceptions of five characters who remembered her in very different ways. Jean Kent played 'the woman in question', a down-at-heel fortune teller called Astra. Although the film offered great opportunities to demonstrate her versatility as an actress and she rose brilliantly to the challenge, several of Astra's iterations were far from glamorous, and involved her donning smeary make-up, a tatty satin kimono, and what Kent would call 'a scrubby old wig'.[54] After convincingly playing a teenager just a few years before in *Good-Time Girl*, Kent was now playing a woman several years older than herself, and one who often appeared 'hideously deglamourised' to boot: the *Daily Express* confidently claimed that 'no other British film beauty has ever before allowed a charac-ter make-up to libel her looks quite so harshly as this'.[55] Despite the valiant attempts at feminine-angled promotional tie-ups ('when it's a question of woman's beauty, Blogg's beauty parlour has the answer . . . cosmetics,

Figure 2.2 'Libelling her looks': Jean Kent as bedraggled Astra in *The Woman in Question* (1950).

hairstyles, clothes, jewellery, shoes are among the subjects which might be suitable for this treatment'), the absence of aspirational feminine allure from *The Woman in Question* was absolute.[56]

The reviews for *The Woman in Question* spoke positively of Jean Kent's performance(s) even if the consensus was that the structural conceit hadn't quite come off. She also received glowing reviews in another film for Asquith the following year, the Terence Rattigan adaptation *The Browning Version* (1951). Again, she played a character considerably older than her actual age, the frustrated middle-aged wife of the downtrodden classics master Andrew Crocker-Harris (Michael Redgrave) who has an affair with her husband's more popular colleague, science teacher Hunter (Nigel Patrick). No longer a mere 'bad girl', Jean Kent's Millie Crocker-Harris is a bad woman, contributing to her husband's downfall through her callous cruelty. As Raymond Durgnat suggests of the film, although the incompatible marriage of the Crocker-Harrises could be viewed as 'reciprocally tragic' we are encouraged to sympathise much more with the male partner 'and condemn the female one'; for 'his rebellion is admirable, but hers is treachery!'[57] Kent plays Millie without sentimentality, not stinting on the character's harder edges, but perhaps played it too well to benefit her career. It was a hard-bitten mature role and coming so soon after the similarly dark and jaded *The Woman in Question* it only accelerated the problem of age and ageing already making its presence felt in Kent's career trajectory even though she was only just into her thirties in 1951. Nonetheless she had reached a familiar female impasse that she described as being 'one of the in-betweens. Around thirty, a girl is too old to be romantic, and too young to be the older woman.'[58]

Kent had spoken earlier in her career about the importance of age-appropriate casting, stating: 'Youth is impossible to imitate – it's embarrassing or simply silly to try. I want to make the switch-over to the sophisticated women at about 30. Bette Davis and Joan Crawford *have* given up being young and gay in time, and stay top-rank. But I know a lot of 35s who are going down because they're trying to be 20.'[59] But now she faced a different problem, having played several much older roles in quick succession. In an article entitled 'No one loves a film star who looks forty', journalist Robert Ottaway suggested that the actress had inadvertently offered a 'lesson for all British glamour girls. Don't do as Jean Kent did . . . and scrape away your beauty treatment in order to look old enough for the part. She's been suffering for that: no one believed she could be young.'[60] 'Whether producers ever stop to remember that she's a still young thirty-three is doubtful', reported Margaret Hinxman in 1954, but 'what they do remember is that her biggest screen success was as a hard, slightly cruel middle-aged wife'.[61] That same year, she was playing the mother of an actress only five years her real-life junior in *Before I Wake* (1954), and wearing dowdy clothes and her hair up in an unbecoming bun. One commentator felt that she was 'edging herself into the character actress class years before her time.'[62] But it appeared that her options were limited if she wanted to carry on making films.

But larger changes in British cinema were afoot too, and Kent was just one of a number of female stars, including her Gainsborough peers Lockwood and Patricia Roc, as well as Anna Neagle, who found their prominent position in the British star hierarchy usurped as the 1950s progressed and male stars began to dominate popularity polls, among them Alec Guinness, Jack Hawkins, Richard Todd, Norman Wisdom, Kenneth More, Dirk Bogarde, and John Mills, all repeatedly ranked highly in *Motion Picture Herald*'s top-ten British stars list from 1952 onwards. By 1954, only a few years after making the top ten herself and being hailed as Britain's answer to Betty Grable, Kent was instead labelled 'the star that films forgot', and returned to the stage as her main mode of performance.[63] The fan-club publications also appear to have ceased by this point. But there was some recognition that British cinema's inability to find a place for a star of Kent's calibre spoke of its deeper 'woman trouble'. Reviewing one of her stage performances in *Daily Film Renter* in 1956, Frank Jackson commented that Kent looked 'radiantly lovely – a mature, gracious woman who could be a tremendous asset to the British screen if we did not insist on dividing female stars into flappers or frumps'.[64] Likewise, in 1957 Robert Robinson noted in the *Sunday Graphic*:

> Jean Kent gives off a giant, orchidaceous femininity which properly used might make British films famous for something a little more attractive than Mr Jack Hawkins playing coppers. And so you will ask what the Dickens she is doing ornamenting Minehead's weekly rep.[65]

But such comments were to no avail. Her mooted musical number in *The Prince and the Showgirl* (1957), as the Trottie-esque star of the show in which Marilyn Monroe's chorus girl performs (and catches a royal eye) was cut in favour of a protracted coronation scene that did nothing to liven up an already turgid film. Blink and you'd miss her very minor supporting role in *Bonjour Tristesse* (1958). Her desire to play the seductive older woman Alice Aisgill in *Room at the Top* (1959) went unfulfilled, and the role (and the camiknickers) went to Simone Signoret instead. As Kent later reflected: 'It was this old English thing that only foreigners have sex appeal. They'd forgotten me by that time, you see.'[66]

As with many female stars, her strong association with a certain type of femininity and a particular era precluded more diverse casting, as she reflected in the mid-1950s: 'I was always wicked in those pictures. Perhaps I look wicked. But do you know what I'd like to play now? Suffragettes. Or Lady Doctors. I wouldn't mind playing Amy Johnson or I'd love to play Jane Austen.'[67] Most of these ambitions went unfulfilled but Kent did get to play Queen Elizabeth in the popular British television series *Sir Francis Drake* (1961–2), taking on the kind of regal role that she had never been allowed to essay on film. Television offered her new opportunities, and she appeared in the popular drama series *Emergency-Ward 10* from 1963 to 1965 and *United!* from 1966 to 1967. She was also striking in the BBC 'Wednesday Play' *A Night with Mrs Da Tanka* (1968) as a heavy-drinking, outspoken older woman, 'sparing neither herself nor her audience with a full blooded performance which went right to the heart of the woman she was portraying', according to Eric Braun.[68] For Kent's Gainsborough and non-Gainsborough peers, 1970s television drama offered an opportunity to reprise their strong women personae in a new medium: Margaret Lockwood played a commanding star barrister in *Justice* (1971–4), Googie Withers was a prisoner governor in *Within These Walls* (1974–5), Phyllis Calvert a magazine columnist in *Kate* (1970–2) while Kent had a major role in a drama of industry, *Tycoon* (1978). Soap opera also offered a haven for actresses of a certain age, and Kent was even mooted to replace Noele Gordon as the matriarchal motel boss in the hugely popular *Crossroads* in 1981 but viewers' ongoing uproar at the supposed killing-off of Gordon's Meg to make way for fresh talent meant that Kent's role remained a briefer guest appearance.[69]

Conclusion: Staying Local

Tracking Jean Kent's somewhat meandering pathway to starring roles, having slogged away in supporting parts (as *Picturegoer* said in 1949, 'No actress in British studios has worked harder than she for the success she has now achieved'), and then the swift curtailment of her stardom through being prematurely aged and slotted into supporting roles once more, it's hard to avoid the feeling that she was just one more victim of a much broader tendency in post-war British cinema: an automatic discomfort around sex and glamour. Given Jean Kent's stated admiration for Claire Trevor, the 'gutsy, worldy-wise' moll of Hollywood gangster films, one wonders how she might have fared in similar roles in Hollywood: if she, instead of her Gainsborough peer Phyllis Calvert, had appeared in a film directed by noir master Robert Siodmak.[70] Or if she, instead of fellow Brit Peggy Cummins, had been talent-spotted by Daryl F. Zanuck to play the lead in *Forever Amber* (1947), ultimately played by Linda Darnell – after all, Kent had once been described as 'a cross between the Wicked Lady, Forever Amber and the barmaid at the local'.[71] She might have followed the same pathway as another South London woman, born less than two miles away into a similarly theatrical family who, coincidentally, had also replaced her mother on the stage when she was indisposed: Ida Lupino, the hard-boiled, plausibly Americanised dame of *They Drive by Night* (1940), *High Sierra* (1941), and *The Hard Way* (1943). But that kind of Atlantic crossing didn't come to pass for Kent, for personal reasons as much as professional ones it must be said, and she remained working at the level of 'the local' in more ways than one. Her final television appearance was on a local news report on the occasion of her ninetieth birthday in 2011, presented as a forgotten star from long ago enjoying a secluded retirement in Suffolk, the elegant and humorous old woman contrasting with the clips of the flashing-eyed vamp doing the Zambra in *Caravan*.[72]

Capable of mixing 'the appeal of a pin-up girl with the dignity of a duchess', suturing the gap between 'lady' and 'dame' like no-one else (and able to nurture a strong fan following), Jean Kent's austerity-era stardom not only speaks eloquently of that period's dreams and aspirations but also of some of the roads not taken in British film culture at this pivotal moment, and some of the feminine qualities it was ultimately unable or unwilling to accommodate fully.[73]

Notes

1. Cited John Spraos, *The Decline of the Cinema* (London: Allen & Unwin, 1962), p. 14.
2. The high placing of several of these films is recorded in Ryan Gilbey (ed.), *The Ultimate Film* (London: BFI, 2005). For more on Anna Neagle as a key female star from the 1930s onwards, see Dolan and Street, 'Twenty million people can't be wrong: Anna Neagle and popular British stardom', pp. 34–48.
3. Ibid., p. 48. Neagle appears as the sixth most popular British star for the period 1932–7 in John Sedgwick's POPSTAT calculations, using box-office data. See Sedgwick, 'Cinema-going preferences in Britain in the 1930s', in Richards (ed.), *The Unknown 1930s*, p. 18.
4. Jeffrey Truby (ed.), *Daily Mail Film Award Annual: British Films of 1947* (London: Winchester Publications, 1948); Jeffrey Truby (ed.), *The British Film Annual 1949* (London: Winchester Publications, 1949). Anonymous, 'The stars you pay to see!', *Picturegoer*, 17 January 1948, p. 3. The Bernstein report, 1947, M/0 FR 2464, Mass Observation Archive, Sussex. For further information on Lockwood's popularity, see the section on the star in Street, *British Cinema in Documents*, pp. 77–107; Street, 'A place of one's own?', pp. 33–46; and Babington, 'Queen of British hearts: Margaret Lockwood revisited', pp. 94–107.
5. For more on Calvert and Withers as key stars of the era, see McFarlane, 'Ingénues, lovers, wives and mothers: The 1940s career trajectories of Googie Withers and Phyllis Calvert', pp. 62–76. On Kerr, see Deleyto, 'The nun's story: Femininity and Englishness in the films of Deborah Kerr', pp. 120–31.
6. Quoted in Sweet, *Shepperton Babylon*, p. 203.
7. Reported in *Kine Weekly*, 17 April 1947, p. 6.
8. Reported in 'Success of British Films', *The Times*, 29 December 1950, p. 4, and 'Stars who fill the cinemas: Anna Neagle's distinction', *Manchester Guardian*, 28 December 1951, p. 6.
9. Cited in Paul Swann, *The Hollywood Feature Film in Postwar Britain* (Kent: Croom Helm, 1987), p. 42.
10. 'Britain's bad girl', undated press release for *The Loves of Joanna Godden* (1947). Press cuttings file for Jean Kent, BFI Library.
11. Brian McFarlane, *Autobiography of British Cinema* (London: Methuen/BFI, 1997), p. 340.
12. Harry Hopkins, *The New Look: A Social History of the Forties and Fifties* (London: Secker and Warburg, 1964), p. 97. For more on women and British cinema in relation to post-war austerity, see Christine Geraghty, 'Post-war

choices and feminine possibilities' in Ulrike Sieglohr (ed.), *Heroines without Heroes: Reconstructing Female and National Identities in European Cinema, 1945–51* (London: Cassell, 2000), pp. 15–32.

13. John K. Newnham, 'Jean enjoys her fame', *Picturegoer*, 23 November 1946, p. 12. Sweet, *Shepperton Babylon*, p. 207.
14. Cecil Wilson, 'Panto will fill the cinema', *Daily Mail*, 26 September 1947. For more on the UK tax of US films and the subsequent US film embargo, see Swann, *The Hollywood Feature Film in Postwar Britain*, pp. 81–104. Newnham, 'Jean enjoys her fame', p. 12.
15. Never one of the Windmill's famous nudes, she was nonetheless once surprised in a state of undress by the Lord Chamberlain making an impromptu appearance to the girls' dressing room, led in there by the theatre's owner Laura Henderson. See 'Behind the scenes at the Windmill', *Sunday Dispatch*, 6 January 1957. Press cutting in scrapbook, box 3, Jean Kent Collection, BFI Special Collections.
16. Undated press cutting in scrapbook, box 3, Jean Kent Collection, BFI Special Collections.
17. Bruce Babington, *Launder and Gilliat* (Manchester: Manchester University Press, 2002), p. 77.
18. Ibid., p. 78.
19. Charles Hamblett, 'Kent's heading for a crisis!', *Picturegoer*, 28 October 1950, pp. 12–13.
20. 'Britain's bad girl', undated press release for *The Loves of Joanna Godden* (1947). Press cuttings file for Jean Kent, BFI Library.
21. Ibid.
22. Ruth Miller, 'Jean Kent has something to say', *Leader*, 15 June 1946, p. 18.
23. Hamblett, 'Kent's heading for a crisis!', p. 12.
24. Winnington quoted in Charles Drazin, *The Finest Years: British Cinema of the 1940s* (London: I. B. Tauris, 1998), p. 11.
25. Charles Barr, 'Introduction: amnesia and schizophrenia', in Charles Barr (ed.), *All Our Yesterdays: 90 Years of British Cinema* (London: BFI, 1986), p. 6. John Ellis, 'The quality film adventure: British critics and the cinema 1942–1948', in Andrew Higson (ed.), *Dissolving Views: Key Writings on British Cinema* (London: Continuum, 1996), pp. 66–93.
26. John Y. Stapleton, 'Ladies or dames?', *Picturegoer*, 10 November 1945, p. 11.
27. Shelia Coxhill, 'Letters from our readers: Stay as you are!', *Picturegoer*, 17 March 1945, p. 3.
28. *Picturegoer*, 3 August 1946 and 26 October 1946, quoted in Sue Harper, *Picturing the Past: The Rise and Fall of the British Costume Film* (London: BFI, 1994), p. 145.
29. Miller, 'Jean Kent has something to say', p. 18.
30. Pam Cook, *Fashioning the Nation: Costume and Identity in British Cinema* (London: BFI, 1996), p. 99.

31. Anonymous, 'Caravan', *Motion Picture Herald* (product digest section), 4 May 1946, p. 2,971.

32. Peter Burnup, 'Rank states design to be distributor in America', *Motion Picture Herald*, 28 July 1945, p. 20. Another trade press article went into further detail on Rank's interests and how they 'have realized for a long time that it will be necessary to make their stars known all over the world as part of their fundamental commercial program. The first campaign of its kind has now been launched by Gainsborough Pictures under the leadership of Maurice Ostrer', with 'bus and subway cards, each of which carries a plug for a particular star'. Anonymous, 'Star campaigns being launched in London', *Showmen's Trade Review*, 7 July 1945, p. 17.

    For detailed accounts of Rank's strategies for expansion into the US, see Robert Murphy, 'Rank's attempt to the American market, 1944–9', in James Curran and Vincent Porter (eds), *British Cinema History* (London: Weidenfeld and Nicolson, 1983), pp. 164–78, and Macnab, *J. Arthur Rank and the British Film Industry*.

33. From a 'small town and rural patronage' cinema, in Anonymous, 'What the picture did for us', *Motion Picture Herald*, 15 February 1947, p. 52. A later item on *Caravan* from an Arkansas cinema owner presented a similar story: 'Jean Kent was well liked. Better than average draw'. Anonymous, 'What the picture did for us', *Motion Picture Herald*, 24 January 1948, p. 38.

34. Jympson Harman, *Evening News*, 7 April 1947. Press cuttings file on *The Man Within*, BFI Library. The 'sex in Sussex' quote is cited in Alan Strachan, *Secret Dreams: A Biography of Michael Redgrave* (London: Weidenfeld and Nicholson, 2004), p. 287.

35. Anonymous, 'The man within', *Showman's Trade Review*, 12 April 1947, p. 19.

36. Anonymous, 'British technicolor drama will appeal', *Film Bulletin*, 2 February 1948, p. 8.

37. Advertisement for *The Smugglers* (US title for *The Man Within*), *Showman's Trade Review*, July September 1948, p. 2.

38. Ruth Grimstead, 'Down on the farm with Jean Kent', *Picturegoer*, 6 November 1948, p. 6. She's similarly hailed as 'career girl, wife and farmer' in Leonard Mosley, 'One girl – three lives', *Daily Express*, 11 August 1950, p. 4.

39. Harper, *Women in British Cinema*, p. 180.

40. *Daily Mail*, 30 April 1948; *Sunday Chronicle*, 2 May 1948. Press cuttings file on Jean Kent, BFI Library.

41. Typical here are Miller, 'Jean Kent has something to say', Grimstead, 'Down on the farm with Jean Kent', and Newnham, 'Jean enjoys her fame'.

42. Referred to in the press book for *Good Time Girl*, BFI Library. For more on British stars' involvement with promotional campaigns of this kind, again using the example of shoe retailer tie-ins, see Felice McDowell, 'Clarks "star" advertisements of the 1940s: Classificatory terms and practices of historical interpretation', *Film, Fashion and Consumption*, Vol. 3, No. 3, December 2014, pp. 241–58.

43. Jean Kent International Fan Club newsletter, October 1949. Jean Kent Collection, box 4, BFI Special Collections.
44. John Ware, 'Hard time girl', *Picturegoer*, 20 December 1947, p. 8.
45. Harvey, 'She's becoming our top dollar earner'.
46. Ware, 'Hard time girl', p. 8.
47. In his discussion of Margaret Lockwood, Babington notes that one example of a similar fan club newsletter for Kent's Gainsborough colleague, Patricia Roc, is available as part of the press clippings file on the star in the BFI Library's holdings, so at least there is one accessible comparable document.
48. Harvey, 'She's becoming our top dollar earner'.
49. For more on Grable's popularity in Britain, see Melanie Williams and Ellen Wright, 'Betty Grable: An American icon in wartime Britain', *Historical Journal of Film, Radio and Television*, Vol. 31, No. 4, Dec 2011, pp. 543–59.
50. Harvey, 'She's becoming our top dollar earner'.
51. Stapleton, 'Ladies or dames?', p. 11.
52. *Daily Mirror*, 12 August 1949; *Sunday Dispatch*, 14 August 1949. Press cuttings file on *Trottie True*, BFI Library.
53. McFarlane, *Autobiography of British Cinema*, p. 341.
54. *Daily Graphic*, 5 October 1950. Press cuttings file on *The Woman in Question*, BFI Library. There is a fascinating account in a press release included in the file on how costume designer Yvonne Caffin offered subtle variations on the same clothes to suggest different perceptions of Astra: 'For Susan Shaw's version of the story the dressing gown was made of home-dyed utility satin, specially treated with floor polish, nail varnish, margarine, brown dye, lipstick and cigarette burns. The feather trimming was dipped in egg to give it an extra scruffy appearance . . . For Charles Victor and Hermione Baddeley the dressing gown was made of non-utility cyclamen satin, cut in extremely good taste. The full sleeves were edged with hand-made feather trimming and the result was extremely pretty. When Dirk Bogarde and John McCallum describe Astra, the gown was badly ironed and thinner feather trimming was tacked on to the gown. This made it appear to be a much worn garment.'
55. Unlabelled review, *Daily Express*, 4 September 1950. Press cuttings file on *The Woman in Question*, BFI Library.
56. *The Woman in Question* press book, BFI Library.
57. Durgnat, *A Mirror for England*, p. 191.
58. Ottaway, 'No one loves a film star who looks forty', *Sunday Graphic*, 3 October 1954.
59. Kent cited in Miller, 'Jean Kent has something to say', p. 18.
60. Kent cited in Ottaway, 'No one loves a film star who looks forty'; emphasis in the original.
61. Margaret Hinxman, 'They make me too old, says Jean Kent', *Picturegoer*, 13 November 1954, p. 23.
62. Anonymous, 'It took courage to look like this', *Picturegoer*, 26 March 1955, p. 14.

63. *Daily Sketch*, 6 January 1954. Press cuttings file on Jean Kent, BFI Library.
64. *Daily Film Renter*, 7 February 1956. Theatre press cuttings, Jean Kent collection, box 1a, BFI Special Collections.
65. Robert Robinson, 'Now Jean is out of the doldrums', *Sunday Graphic*, 11 August 1957. Theatre press cuttings, Jean Kent collection, box 1a, BFI Special Collections.
66. Kent cited in McFarlane, *Autobiography of British Cinema*, p. 342.
67. Kent cited in Robinson, 'Now Jean is out of the doldrums'.
68. Eric Braun, 'Rank's young generation', *Films and Filming*, October 1973, p. 36.
69. On Jean Kent and *Crossroads* see *Sunday People*, 8 November 1981, and *TV Times*, 26 September 1986. Press cuttings scrapbook, Jean Kent collection, box 3, BFI Special Collections.
70. McFarlane, *Autobiography of British Cinema*, p. 339. The background on this fraught Universal production, *Time Out of Mind* (1947), is sketched in by Sweet, *Shepperton Babylon*, p. 210.
71. Unlabelled review, *Daily Express*, 28 April 1950. Press cuttings file on *The Reluctant Widow*, BFI Library.
72. *Anglia News*, 1 July 2011. Report archived on YouTube: https://www.youtube.com/watch?v=KSqh31eDEuU
73. Unlabelled article, *Daily Mail*, 4 January 1955. Press cuttings file on Jean Kent, BFI Library.

CHAPTER 3

'Blonde Glamour Machine':
Diana Dors in the 1950s and Beyond

In the Jean Kent film *Good-Time Girl*, her story is framed as a cautionary tale told by a social worker to a young delinquent called Lyla about to
make the same mistakes. But having heard this dire warning, Lyla resolves
to lead a blameless life henceforth. The irony is that Lyla was played by
Diana Dors, the star who not only took on Jean Kent's mantle as 'Britain's
number one bad girl' and accepted roles Kent had rejected, like the saloon-
bar entertainer in *Diamond City* (1949), but also took the bad-girl persona
to new and unprecedented levels of public visibility and infamy. Kent may
have been slinkily suggestive on-screen (and glamorously polished for all
her personal appearances) but, as we have seen, was presented as a devoted
bucolic housewife when off duty, happiest pig-keeping and pickling. Her
cocktail-party tip of using food colourant to create multi-coloured ice
cubes speaks of the very modest aspirations towards glamour in austerity-
era Britain.[1] By contrast, Diana Dors' reputation as a star, even in its
formative years, was founded upon scandal and controversy. Before she
was twenty-five, she had been hired and 'let go' by the Rank Organisation;
made several court appearances accused variously of non-payment of rent,
house-breaking and larceny; had become registered as a limited company
to protect her property investments; had all her financial affairs queried
not only by the Inland Revenue and the House of Commons but also
mentioned on the BBC News; and she had even been accused of involvement in an obscene publication (the stereoscopic pin-up book *Diana Dors
in 3-D*). All of this was reported with great glee by the popular press who
frequently featured her latest antics on their front pages.[2] As one writer
surmised in the early 1960s, turning back to the foundational elements
of the star's image, 'whenever people see the name Dors they still auto-
matically say to themselves – mink, blonde bombshell, policemen, arrests,
controversial, etc.'.[3]

This made her a very different prospect from many of her immedi-
ate female peers in British cinema. 'Was there ever a British girl quite

like Diana?' asked *Picturegoer* in 1955, emphasising her newness within the landscape of that particular national cinema.[4] Rather than fitting into the standard English rose typology, Dors famously proclaimed herself 'the only sex symbol Britain has produced since Lady Godiva', whose aspirations to glamour went far beyond coloured ice cubes, and spiralled into lavish furs and gowns, expensive properties, luxurious cars and even a self-piloted private plane at one point.[5] She laughed off the suggestion by US interviewer Mike Wallace that she should cut her hair and wear something 'tweedier' in order to appear more of a 'lady'.[6] Being ladylike and tasteful would never garner as much attention as stepping out of a Venetian hotel wearing a mink bikini and then riding a gondola down the Grand Canal, as Dors did in 1955 – a film festival publicity stunt that even inspired a successful 1956 stage musical, *Grab Me a Gondola*. Through this relentless promotional activity and presentation of herself as a sex symbol, Dors became what she later described as a 'blonde glamour machine', churning out a bright shiny performance of celebrity along Fordist lines.[7] But her pouty performance of sexiness was always leavened by 'a sense of self-mockery' and she was frequently characterised as a star who managed to combine her glitz with humour and 'a reassuringly home-grown air of down-to-earth matiness'.[8] As Christine Geraghty suggests, in the class-ridden and often snobbish landscape of the 1950s, 'she was 'one of "us"', not one of "them"'; for all the glamour, still a woman of the people, or 'Our Di', as Durgnat puts it.[9]

Her sense of the ridiculous would serve her well as her career navigated the highs and lows of post-war British popular culture as well as a much-hyped sojourn in Hollywood to take up a contract with RKO that ultimately did not work out as planned. By the time she died of cancer in 1984, Dors had become an icon of light entertainment and tabloid anecdotage. But even in her early years, there had been a certain bathetic mismatch between the glamorous (American?) aspirations of her persona and the more quotidian (British?) realities that underpinned them. She grabbed headlines for supposedly piloting her plane while wearing full evening dress to her film premiere, but the destination was Stockport and the film was the decidedly un-glamorous low-budget Northern comedy *My Wife's Lodger* (1952).[10] The infamous mink bikini was actually made from rather-more-affordable rabbit fur. A half-baked entrepreneurial scheme that Dors mentions in her first autobiography *Swingin' Dors* around the marketing of a soft drink called 'Diana Juice, the drink that Dors adores' – actually a batch of welfare-state orange juice that had been over-sulphurated, acquired from the Ministry of Food at a knock-down price by a 'businessman' of dubious legality– speaks so eloquently of a country and a culture in transition, with star-inspired consumerism beginning to usurp older notions of thrift and deference. [11] Diana Dors was at the very centre of this watershed moment in modern British history and, as Pam Cook suggests, 'was emblematic of conflicting forces of social change in a way no other British star was able to achieve'.[12] This chapter explores how the woman described by *Tit-Bits* magazine as 'Britain's Princess of Glamour' navigated the challenges of female stardom during the shift from austerity to affluence, and eventually managed to acquire the status of a national heroine – 'Britannia herself' according to pop impresario Simon Napier-Bell.[13]

Becoming a Star

Looking back from the vantage point of middle age, Diana Dors recalled her childhood self as 'a fiercely ambitious young girl, spurred on by Hollywood films watched breathlessly from the darkness of the cinema stalls'.[14] When I asked to write an English composition at primary school entitled 'What I want to be when I grow up', the young Diana Fluck, as she was then, elected to be 'a film star with a cream telephone and a swimming pool' – all of which she achieved in adulthood.[15] Her mother encouraged her ambitions, perhaps vicariously expressing her own thwarted dreams of stardom as a singer, and her father took her along with him when he entertained billeted troops in nearby army camps, letting her sing 'Ma, I Miss Your Apple Pie' in the style of Shirley Temple. However, the tween-age Diana was an early physical developer and she had soon outgrown Shirley Temple in favour of more grown-up role models like Betty Grable and Veronica Lake. On holiday with her parents, she entered and won a beauty competition at Weston-super-Mare's lido, lying about her age (only thirteen but pretending to be seventeen) to meet the entry requirements. The prize was to be featured as a pin-up in *Soldier* magazine (where Jean Kent had also been a pin-up), and Diana Fluck's success in this endeavour seems to have acted as a catalyst for taking her nascent ambitions of being an actress to the next stage of development.

Still only fifteen, she applied to and was accepted into the prestigious London stage school London Academy of Music and Dramatic Art (LAMDA), and studied there while living in a World Young Women's Christian Association (YWCA) hostel, picking up silver and bronze medals for her elocution and performance skills. It was at this time that she changed her name from the dangerously close-to-obscene Fluck to the more pleasingly alliterative Dors, her maternal grandmother's name. Striving to make good her childhood dreams of film stardom, the fifteen-year-old actress was delighted when she was offered her first film role, as a blackmailer's girlfriend in *The Shop at Sly Corner* (1946), and was able to return to Swindon for its premiere and receive a hero's welcome (her home town would not always offer such a warm reception in the years to come).

Spotted and then signed by Rank's 'Company of Youth', known popularly as its 'Charm School', an initiative designed to foster future British stars, the initial excitement that Diana Dors felt at receiving a regular salary and a shot at the big time quickly turned to disappointment at its limited opportunities and typecasting. As she detailed in a remarkably candid article she wrote for *Picturegoer* in 1950 after being released from her contract:

> It is little wonder that graduates from the Charm School look back on those days with relief and amusement rather than affection. For we were all madly keen and ambitious – and therefore rather frustrated . . . It was not long before I realised that unless something drastic happened, or I could make something drastic happen, I was going to be Rank's stock 'bad girl' . . . the flighty, sexy little thing who pops in and out of the story whenever a little light relief seems to be called for. In most of the films I made under my contract, I appeared to do a good deal more than my fair share of popping in and out.[16]

This shrewd diagnosis certainly applied to many of her early film parts for Rank, especially her recurring role as vampish cousin Di, jitterbugging, chewing gum, or painting her nails in the *Huggetts* films. In addition, Dors felt that while under contract to Rank, there had been 'little linking of publicity from picture to picture, no planned, steady intensive campaigns such as Hollywood starlets enjoy'.[17] Even if 'one had given a promising performance, there was no rapid follow up', Dors complained: for instance, her widely commended performance as the obsequious young housemaid in *Oliver Twist* (1948) led to nothing else of that calibre.[18]

After being released from Rank's rather diffident approach to star-making, Dors and her first husband Dennis Hamilton masterminded and implemented their own intensive publicity campaign to make Diana Dors the top British star. Associating her with luxury was an important plank of their strategy, as a statement of self-value and high ambition. This meant splashing out on big flash cars or fancy apartments even if the couple had not 'the slightest notion of how we were going to keep up the monthly payments'; but this was immaterial because 'only the rich can afford to look poor'.[19] Being the youngest ever owner of a Rolls-Royce or owning a plane got her press coverage, which was crucial to the plan as retrospectively outlined by Dors in 1954: 'First thing was to get my name known. I run a Rolls, pilot my own plane, and let everyone know when I have a good time' (and as the impressed journalist interviewing her commented, Dors 'knows what she is doing. Always has').[20] The starlet's ever blonder hair and ever skimpier and/or clingier outfits also helped to grab attention and column inches, as when her scenes in bikini and underwear had to be re-shot for the more prudish US in *Lady Godiva Rides Again* (1951) and *Is Your Honeymoon Really Necessary?* (1953).[21] For Dennis Hamilton, there truly was no such thing as bad publicity and he told his wife that his aim was to turn her 'into a female Errol Flynn, someone who's always in trouble, only the trouble will make you more publicised than anyone else in the country. It will turn you into a character' rather than 'the dreary little girl next door'.[22] This tactic certainly seemed to yield results, as when Dors was in court – again – for alleged house-breaking in 1953 (a practical joke gone wrong was her defence). The story made the front page of the two UK newspapers with the highest circulation at that time, the *Daily Express* (on both 22 July and 28 July), and the *Daily Mirror* (on 25 July and 28 July), and certainly helped to make sure that her name was on the lips of everyone in the country. Her unconventional courtroom outfit of 'tight-fitting black cocktail trousers, a white wrapover sweater, gold sandals, and big, gipsy earrings' was pored over by the papers, who also made a point of observing that the star 'was hatless', finding such informality combined with opulence mesmerising.[23]

Hamilton and Dors also knew when to play the British card, stage-managing Dors' refusal of a Hollywood contract in 1952 because, as Hamilton advised his wife: 'You'll go down on record as being the only British film star ever to turn down a Hollywood contract, and that'll make you more headlines than if you accepted, like all the rest.'[24] His hunch was proven right with the press then praising the young star's patriotic loyalty.[25] Hamilton may have been intermittently thuggish and utterly untrustworthy but if Dors' account is to be believed, he also had a shrewd sense of how media manipulation worked. So too did Dors, whose aura of business-like agency and control could elicit a slightly fearful reaction, as we can see in critic Derek Hill's response to the star: 'Diana Dors, it is generally accepted, has her head firmly screwed on; and her other attributes are equally well assembled. The first thing one studies on seeing her in the flesh is the floor. It seems safest.'[26]

Although Dors' aim was to become known as a film star, what is equally notable about her career around this time, and indeed for the majority of its thirty-five-year duration, is that making films was very far from being her predominant occupation, and instead variety and revue were much closer to being the star's core business. This was partly determined by what paid more, with the grand objective of mega-stardom counterbalanced by the impulse to make as much money as possible in the short term, often motivated by the need to pay off angry creditors. As an agent had put it to Dors in the early 1950s, she had to decide what she wanted from her career: 'Do you want to make big money and live off the fat of the land or do you want to do all this for art's sake, and live on your press notices?'[27] For the time being, the decision was to go for the former rather than the latter. To that end, Dors tried her hand at variety, enduring the fieriest baptism possible by debuting her act at the notorious Glasgow Empire Theatre where she met with a deeply unenthusiastic reception (although as the stage manager assured her, if the audience didn't actually throw improvised missiles, you could regard it as a success).

Her autobiography *Swingin' Dors* provides a good sense of the mixed portfolio of work that constituted her career during the first half of the 1950s, with film roles interspersed with appearances in the TV-derived stage show *Life with the Lyons* (1953) in Blackpool, and in the West End revue *Rendezvous* (1952), performing the title role in the pantomime *Aladdin* (1954) in Bournemouth, releasing a record 'A Kiss and a Cuddle and Kind Word from You' (1954), and starring in the television drama series *Douglas Fairbanks Jr Presents* (1954; run 1953–7) as well as the Terry-Thomas sitcom *How Do You View?* (1951; run 1949–53) in addition to honing her variety act (1952 onwards) at venues across the country. Indeed, as *Picturegoer* pointed out in 1954, working in variety was 'so good to La Dors (she earns an appetizing £300 a week) that acting in films means loss of revenue'.[28] But letting money determine her career choices had other unseen costs. Dors had complained about the 'flighty, sexy little thing' roles she felt she'd been confined to while under contract with Rank but she seemed to be picking similarly trifling roles of her own volition now. While the American blonde bombshell Marilyn Monroe was making a name for herself in Hollywood spectaculars like *Niagara* (1953) and *Gentlemen Prefer Blondes* (1953), Dors was guesting in Frank Randle's decidedly unglamorous broad Lancastrian comedy *It's a Grand Life* (1953) because it paid very handsomely for a relatively short-term engagement. Building a profile through being prolific was one thing (and making money was undoubtedly important too) but the longer-term vision of making Diana Dors into a major movie star seemed to be getting slightly lost in the pursuit of short-term gains.

Pink Caviar and Prison Uniform: Peak Dors

Fascination at a physical appearance always perceived as excessive continued to figure throughout Dors' career but it had a particular force at the point when British society had 'never had it so good' and began to embrace consumerism in the mid-1950s, a social revolution that sparked concerns about good taste entangled with issues of class and gender. The challenge was to buy the right thing, to consume classily, but Dors transgressed these unspoken boundaries of tastefulness in the way she furnished her home, the cars she drove, and the outfits she wore. As the *Daily Mail* pointed out in 1956, 'the Dors concept of dressing up has everything to make the average Englishman cringe . . . [her] approach to clothes is not a question of good taste or bad; it is beyond the realm of taste altogether'.[29] But the star's vulgarity may be interpreted along the word's original etymology 'of the people', as Richard Whitehall suggested in his profile of Dors.[30] In fact for all that she was 'more neon-strip as opposed to clogs and shawl' and therefore possibly not 'Richard Hoggart's favourite pin-up', according to Whitehall, she actually provided a perfect demonstration of Hoggart's evocation of working-class popular culture as 'highly-ornamental, rococo extravagance. It loves the cornucopia, all that is generous and sprawling, that suggests splendour and wealth by sheer abundance and lavishness of colour.'[31] Taste is immaterial in this realm and Donald Zec's 1954 description of Dors in domestic repose seems to exemplify rococo sprawl (as well as parodying Enobarbus' description of Cleopatra in her pomp):

> She sat on an antique chair stroking the stuffed head of a glass-eyed lion . . . Her full, moist lips were painted ('Pink Caviar') and her long nails were tinted ('Fatal Apple') . . . Diana unwound out of the chair, stepped over the lion's head, across a leopard skin rug (past the TV set with the 5ft screen) to put on a Lanza record of 'Ave Maria'.[32]

This potent blend of déclassé consumer goods, from animal rugs to pink lipsticks to widescreen televisions, are all entangled with derogated notions of female glamour. The tacky religious recording and misplaced antique furniture embody the 'failed seriousness' that Sontag defined as the source of camp.[33] No wonder John Waters once cited Dors along with Elizabeth Taylor as the stars he most ardently wished he could have worked with, while Dors herself stated how proud she was of her gay icon status in 1978 (using the vocabulary of that time): 'poufs and drag artists like me [because] I am extreme and outrageous'.[34] But in an era often classified as dully monochrome, the 'colourful' existence of Diana Dors – in all the term's connotations – was seen as adding to the gaiety of this particular nation, whether driving her famed powder blue Cadillac with zebra-print upholstery and 'DD' embossed in silver on the door, or her bespoke blue Delahaye 'with solid gold fittings and a crystal steering wheel', or sporting a pair of 'tangerine shorts' or 'peacock-blue pyjamas, a lot of diamonds, and Perspex and diamanté-strapped shoes', or just showing off her 'saffron' hair and eyes as green as 'parts of the sea off some of the Caribbean islands' as she posed in 'a lustrous little silver bathing suit'.[35] As well as appearing in vivid colour, Dors' glamour also entered the third dimension through the publication in 1952 of *Diana Dors in 3-D* (complete with 3-D glasses) that featured the star in mildly titillating poses captured by photographer Horace Roye, and that gained new momentum in 1954 when it was alleged to be obscene. Pam Cook describes this contretemps as 'a camp precursor of the *Lady Chatterley's Lover* obscenity trial in 1960', with the offending book in this case likewise exonerated, while Dors protested that she didn't know 'what all the fuss was about'.[36]

As Cook suggests, Dors represented a new kind of figure in the British cultural landscape 'unashamedly putting libido and conspicuous consumption on display'.[37] She fused her sexual and financial candour in the way she presented herself as a 'blonde goldmine' (the phrase used on a *Daily Mirror* front page in 1956), a commodity for sale: 'What merchandise! And boy, how it sells', she was quoted as saying in a 1955 article entitled 'Visible export' (more mercantile metaphors), adding 'I might as well cash in on my sex now while I've got it. It can't last forever, can it?'[38] Although in some quarters she was criticised for chasing 'money, more money, and yet more money', the sell-by date of the sex-symbol identity meant that she had, in her own estimation, 'only seven or ten years at the outside in which to make money', offering this sense of urgency in expiation at her alleged avarice.[39] She had her defenders. One letter in the *Daily Mirror* defended Dors' supposed audacity in asking for a fee to appear on BBC's cinema show *Picture Parade*: 'When stars wane, fees wane. Now's the time to gather diamonds to her bosom.'[40]

Unlike someone like Lady Docker, the industrialist's wife infamous in the fifties for her mink coats and gold-plated Daimler on expenses, Dors' apparent extravagance could at least be legitimated as necessary for the upkeep of her professional façade. As she said of her expenditure to the *Manchester Guardian* and *Picturegoer* in turn in 1954:

> My secretary and fan mail cost me £25 a week; my car costs me about £10 a week in petrol because I do a lot of traveling; clothes and hairdressing – well you can use your imagination about them. You cannot be photographed in the same thing twice . . . How you can compete with American stars when you have to pay 19s 6d in the pound income tax is beyond me.[41]
>
> A girl has to be impeccably turned out – the nylons I get through! You never see any American stars photographed more than once in the same outfit, do you? I need clothes for personal appearances, garden parties, opening bazaars, dances, business auditions.[42]

Dors' candour sprang partly from her hand being forced by the scrutiny of her financial affairs by the Inland Revenue but it also corresponded with her image as a very self-reflexive and frank film star, refreshingly eager to let in light on the magic of how her glamour was practically achieved, how it was part of her work as a star, and what kind of expenditure it all entailed.

Ironically, she didn't have to spend much money on the outfit that she wore for her most notable publicity stunt, that 1955 gondola trip in the mock-mink bikini at the Venice Film Festival, which earned her front-page coverage across Europe. The British press expressed a sense of national pride in Dors and her compatriots winning the 'Venice Battle of Glamour', with the *Daily Mirror*'s reporter enthusing: 'Never before have I seen Continental film fans mobbing stars. And never did I expect to see these stars knocking Continental rivals for six – and sex.'[43] Although Dors had been warned by journalist Paul Holt back in 1949 that she had to choose between cultivating her sexiness as 'a full-blown vamp' or doing 'what Mae West did and make fun of the whole thing', the mink bikini stunt suggested that she could hold these supposed opposites in equilibrium and simultaneously embody *and* send up the absurdities of being a sex object.[44] As Kenneth Tynan suggested in a review of one of her early stage performances, Dors was an 'unabashed parodist of desire'.[45] But she also managed to be a sought-after pin-up girl, with her pictures described lasciviously in 1956 as 'a standard piece of Navy, Army and Air Force equipment', straightforwardly catering to heterosexual male desire as well as satirising it.[46]

The years 1955–6 probably represented the apex of Diana Dors' film stardom. At the end-of-year *Motion Picture Herald* exhibitors' poll to determine who had been 1955's top British stars, she was the only woman to make an appearance, at number nine. Dirk Bogarde topped the poll, followed by John Mills, Norman Wisdom, Alastair Sim, Kenneth More, Jack Hawkins, Richard Todd and Michael Redgrave – this all-male parade indicating how far the 'hegemony of the tweed jacket' reigned supreme at this time, and how exceptional a figure Dors cut against such a stolidly masculine backdrop.[47] She had made the list on the strength of her appearances in the hit colour comedies *An Alligator Named Daisy* (1955), *As Long as They're Happy* (1955) and *Value for Money* (1955), and a more dramatic role, also in colour, in Carol Reed's urban fable *A Kid for Two Farthings* (1955). Each of these performances played with extratextual knowledge about Dors' image, casting her as glamour girl and featuring her in tight dresses, skimpy lingerie, or déshabillé bathroom scenes similar to those featured in her pin-up photographs. Even in the humbler East End setting of *A Kid for Two Farthings*, her character Sonia cut a particularly dazzling figure as a young woman desperate to get married to her hunky wrestler fiancé. As if to acknowledge this potential incongruity, the film's dialogue mentions Sonia's decision to 'go blonde' and her worries that it looks brassy, and even refers to 'an epidemic of Marilyn Monroe in the neighbourhood', directly invoking Dors' most famous rival in the sex-symbol stakes.

In a serendipitous moment of cultural exchange in 1956, Dors travelled over to America just as Monroe arrived in Britain to film *The Prince and the Showgirl* (1957). The *Daily Mirror* used the occasion to stage a 'Battle of the two High-Explosive Blondes' on their front cover in July 1956, with Dors judged the ultimate victor ('Diana steals front page from Marilyn'), which was an impressive achievement even allowing for the paper's patriotic allegiance to a home-grown star.[48] One British teenager interviewed by Anthony Sampson that same year also thought that Dors was Marilyn's superior: 'The Americans got no one like Diana Dors. She's gorgeous. I don't like that Marilyn girl – she's covered in make-up.'[49] Obviously these two sex symbols ended up occupying very different positions in popular memory, with Monroe enshrined as legend while Dors became a funny footnote, an unlikely 'what might have been'. This is summed up by a sketch in the comedy show *Psychobitches* (2012–14) – premised on famous women from history visiting an analyst to cure their various neuroses – which presented 'Diana Dors', as played by comedienne Katie Brand, as a coarse, gluttonous country bumpkin who is gripped by the (ridiculous) delusion that she is actually Marilyn Monroe, even though she thinks 'pork pies' rather than diamonds are a girl's best friend. Faced with the shimmering dainty apparition that is the 'real' Monroe (played by Samantha Spiro), she has to concede defeat. It's a funny sketch that speaks to several aspects of Dors' persona, particularly her humour and ability to mobilise the 'common touch', but it underestimates just how close the real Dors came to making good on that promise of international stardom glimpsed briefly in the 1950s. Dors was a genuine contender, and worthy competitor for Monroe. Under the headline 'See! I dunnit!', the *Daily Express* celebrated the star's 'triumphant "told you so" smile' as she was pictured 'storming into America's filmland on the wings of a legend of high class wisecracks and low cut dresses' and discussing 'a five-year contract that may bring her £214,000 a year' in the summer of 1956.[50]

The star's final film to be released in Britain before she departed for Hollywood was *Yield to the Night* (1956). Pam Cook draws an interesting parallel between Dors and Brigitte Bardot as stars whose individual films were secondary components in their stardom, both primarily famous for

Figure 3.1 Looking down the lens, part one. Diana Dors as happy–go–lucky showgirl Pearl, singing the 'Hokey Pokey Polka' in *As Long as They're Happy* (1955).

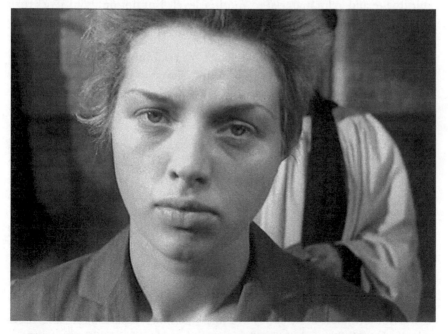

Figure 3.2 Looking down the lens, part two. The pitiful final moments of Dors as condemned woman Mary Hilton in *Yield to the Night* (1956).

'being a film star'.[51] However, Bardot's one really well-known film *Et Dieu . . . Créa la Femme* (And God . . . Created Woman) (1956) epitomised her sex-kitten image whereas the best-known title from Dors' career, *Yield to the Night*, confounded rather than consolidated that star's sex-symbol image. Playing an ordinary working-class woman called Mary Hilton awaiting execution for murder, the star's immaculate platinum hair was grown out to reveal dark greasy roots, and her sequined gowns and stiletto heels exchanged for plain prison uniform and flat frumpy slippers. She had to convince as woman experiencing the agony of waiting for her execution by hanging, hoping in vain for a reprieve, and suffering sleepless nights under the glare of a light that never goes out, while she revisits the events leading up to her crime. She had looked down the lens before, like when she began her vampy musical number 'The Hokey Pokey Polka' in *As Long as They're Happy*, but her direct look to camera at the end of *Yield to the Night* was completely different. Here it was the devastating conclusion of a harrowing, claustrophobic drama that offered its heroine no reprieve and ended on her final walk to the scaffold.[52]

If the casting of Diana Dors as an East End milliner's assistant in *A Kid for Two Farthings* had seemed slightly unlikely, then her role in such an uncompromising protest film as this took the disjunction between glitzy star image and grim material to another level. But not only did Dors turn in a performance of total conviction and emotive power, *Yield to the Night* also cleverly harnessed its star's resonant extratextual image to its advantage. Teaming a notorious star with controversial subject matter formed an effective strategy for marketing a film that vowed to 'set the whole country talking'. While the studio publicity material encouraged cinemas to stage debates about the rights and wrongs of capital punishment, it also went in for more traditional ballyhoo as well, suggesting a 'contest to find the girl who most resembles Miss Dors in face and figure. Prize: a washing machine!'[53] Despite the doubts that she wouldn't be capable of taking on such a demanding dramatic role, Diana Dors won the applause of the critics at home and abroad, including cheers and a standing ovation when the film was screened at Cannes. The film's premiere, Dors later reflected, was the best night of her life: 'my hour of triumph – all I had worked and prayed for'.[54]

Hollywood and After

It was not long after her Cannes triumph that Dors departed for America to take up her Hollywood contract with great expectations of future success. At this point, she seemed all set to relocate permanently, with the US magazine *Screenland* guessing that this newly arrived Brit would be 'with us for four pictures and possibly a lifetime'.[55] But after the initial fanfare of her arrival, with parties given in her honour and exciting roles lined up, things very quickly began to turn slightly sour. Dors realised that her husband's slightly spivvy brand of charm that operated quite well for him (and her) in Britain didn't translate well stateside, with gossip columnist Hedda Hopper's cold rebuke to his obsequious attentions ('Okay Hamilton. Don't overdo it') providing an early warning of things to come.[56] Also, as in any homespun fable, Dors came to realise that her dreams of wealth and fame were hollow ones:

> One evening I sat alone in the pool-house among the orchids and the orange trees, gazing up at the big, floodlit white mansion. Coloured lights adorned exotic flowers, and the sky-blue swimming pool, my dream since childhood, stretched before me illuminated in the dark. What happens now? I thought, with almost a touch of panic. This is all I ever wanted; I've achieved a life-long ambition. But where do I go from here?[57]

Downwards, came the answer to Dors' question, and the swimming pool would provide the setting for the moment of reckoning with Hollywood. During a party at their home, Dors, her husband, and a number of their colleagues, were pushed into the pool fully clothed while photographers captured the scene. Hamilton, always violent and volatile, attacked the individual he believed to be responsible for pushing them in – to the horror of onlookers – kicking and punching him until he lost consciousness. The fallout from this incident was widespread disgust at his behaviour, with his wife deemed guilty by association (and in some lurid versions of events, even accused of joining in the violence), all summed up by the *New York Enquirer* front-page headline: 'Go home, Diana! – and take Mr Dors with you!'[58] Later that year, RKO used the morality clause in her contract to revoke it, on the grounds of an affair with her married co-star in *The Unholy Wife* (1957), Rod Steiger, but the underlying financial reality was that the ailing RKO were trying to divest themselves of any expensive overheads by any means necessary.[59] Although a number of the films she made during her period in Hollywood would be released in the ensuing years and her cabaret turns in Las Vegas and Palm Springs were well received, it was clear that Diana Dors' sojourn in the states had not gone as gloriously as she had hoped. The initially feverish press speculation about whether or not she would take on American citizenship and permanently relocate there began to die down, although there was still plenty of front-page discussion of her marital troubles and subsequent split from Dennis Hamilton. Just as the contemporaneous Suez crisis would reveal Britain's assumptions of being a major player on the world stage to be misguided, and prove that the 'Special relationship' with the US didn't necessarily equate to unconditional support for all British ventures, similar transatlantic tensions were mediated in Diana Dors' attempt to take Hollywood by storm, with her big ideas and grand ambitions being swatted back into their place at the hands of a hostile US press machine.

The Suez parallel is a pertinent one, since Diana Dors figured unexpectedly prominently in the debates around the military action. She was mentioned by name in the infamous *Times'* August 1956 leader making the case for the invasion among a number of bogus causes for national pride that paled in comparison with re-achieving imperial might:

> Doubtless it is good to have a flourishing tourist trade, to win test matches and to be regaled by photographs of Miss Diana Dors . . . But nations do not live by circuses alone. The people, in their silent way, know this better than the critics. They still want Britain great.[60]

Dors actually had a strategic function in the Middle East: earlier that year, it had been reported on the front page of the *Daily Express* that her pin-up pictures were being deployed for propaganda purposes by the government, 'used as bait to sell the British way of life to the Communist-wooed people of the Middle East. They appear in the magazine *Al Alaam*, circulation 70,000, inspired by the British Foreign Office . . . printed in Arabic, with photographs and articles supplied by the Central Office of Information.'[61] In this context, Dors was presented not as a circus distraction but as an ideal of the British way of life, her comely pin-up girl identity used to exemplify its freedoms and pleasures. And yet what she represented, in the shape of a feminised, consumer society, was simultaneously being repudiated as a distraction from the rightful path of national greatness. 'Look at the *Daily Mirror* or any other large circulation newspaper', fulminated Woodrow Wyatt in July 1956. 'It is the curves of Diana Dors that matter, not the down curves of British motor-car exports.'[62] On the one hand, what she sold could be seen as a legitimate commodity for export. Cartoonist Cummings was only half-joking when he placed Dors and Monroe in the import and export columns of Harold Macmillan's ledger that same month.[63] The *Daily Mail* thought she was doing for the British bust what Rolls-Royce, Dunhill, Savile Row and a few other hallowed names have 'done to uphold the prestige of British workmanship and quality in other fields'.[64] But on the other hand, relying upon celebrity culture for our sense of national pride and identity was a terrifying prospect at this point in Britain's history when it had lost an Empire but not yet found a role. It would embrace the soft power of popular culture far more wholeheartedly in the following decade with the export of the 'swinging London' phenomenon.

While Dors had been working in the US during 1956–7, her reputation had suffered at home (not helped by obstacles to the release of her Hollywood films in the UK) and by the time of *Motion Picture Herald*'s 1956 poll, Dors had now lost her top-ten star position, with Virginia McKenna now replacing her as the only woman in the list of British stars, and in attaining fourth place McKenna had even surpassed Dors' ninth position the previous year.[65] McKenna had won her place largely on the strength of *A Town Like Alice* (1956), the box-office hit in which she turned in a remarkable performance as an 'English rose' under extreme duress during wartime.[66] Diana Dors' equally fine performance as another suffering blonde in *Yield to the Night* seemed not to have registered as strongly. Her accomplishments in that film made no difference to the kind of roles she was offered when she finally came back home from Hollywood, which reverted to the pouting sexpot stereotype in *The Long Haul* (1957), *Tread Softly Stranger* (1958), and *Passport to Shame* (1958), with a brief Italian stopover for *La Ragazza Del Palio / The Girl Who Rode in the Palio / The Love Specialist* (1957). In 1959 she even declared that she had 'called a halt to making films because I have enough self-respect not to want to be in any more stinkers'.[67]

Once again Dors returned to the warm (and lucrative) embrace of live cabaret, with a glitzy extravaganza that played successfully on both sides of the Atlantic and that traded on her celebrity status, as this review from *The Times* suggests:

> Outside the theatre her name is emblazoned in gigantic letters; her act is introduced with a stridently sycophantic chorus in her honour, and at its climax a downstage curtain parts to disclose the object of these elaborate attentions shimmering coyly in a resplendently hideous garment.[68]

Diana Dors, the reviewer continued, had become one of those stars whose fate 'is to be overtaken by their own celebrity; whatever talent they had is progressively masked and stifled by the habit of maintaining the personality the public expect to see'.[69] Interestingly, the more middlebrow *Daily Express*'s reviewer enjoyed the show much more, describing Dors as 'a delight. Her appearance seems a huge joke at the expense of the cutie type. She wriggles with animation and fun.'[70] Dors' live act had always referred to her status as film star but now it could draw on a whole raft of new insider tales about the Hollywood hierarchy. She had always been a star who revealed the inner workings of stardom; now it had become her core business.

Separated from an increasingly volatile Dennis Hamilton and planning a divorce so she could marry aspiring comedian Dickie Dawson, Dors was shocked and seriously affected by Hamilton's sudden death in 1959 (from the effects of tertiary syphilis it was later alleged), not only emotionally but also financially as the creditor for his enormous debts. This was a major factor in her decision to sell her life story to the *News of the World* in 1960 for £35,000 (much more than Anthony Eden got for his war memoirs, Dors was proud to claim), an absolutely necessary injection of income for someone facing dire financial straits. The paper's newly hired editor Stafford Somerfield had identified kiss-and-tell stories involving famous people as the best way to revive its falling circulation figures, and Dors was once again at the vanguard of a new development in celebrity culture, paving the way for the government-slaying revelations of Christine Keeler and Mandy Rice-Davies in the same paper just a few years later.[71] However, the luridly ghost-written revelations about her private life, paying particular attention to her late husband's voyeuristic peccadilloes, and his use of two-way mirrors and hidden tape recorders at sex parties in their country mansion, and Dors' willing collusion with his games, had unfortunate side effects. They made her, once again, the most talked about woman in Britain, but the talk was not always complimentary. She was denounced from the pulpit as 'a wanton hussy' by the Archbishop of Canterbury, while Labour Shadow Minister Barbara Castle held her up as symbol of the parlous state of the contemporary media (fixated solely on 'unwholesome, grossly lewd and salacious' elements, according to the Press Council): 'You only have to open a Sunday newspaper to read the unedifying life of Diana Dors to wonder if we have got an educated democracy in this country.'[72] Others passed judgement on Dors' ability to be a good mother (she had given birth to her first child, Mark, in February 1960), with Baroness Mary Stokes on the panel of the BBC Radio programme *Any Questions?* advising that the best thing she could do for her child was get him adopted as soon as possible.[73]

The Long Haul's director, Ken Hughes, allegedly asked Diana to play herself in a film to be entitled *The Diana Dors Story*, based on her memoirs, but this moment of highly self-reflexive (self-devouring?) celebrification did not come to pass.[74] Instead it seemed that the law of diminishing returns was in operation around Dors' invocation of film-star glamour. In the space of a few years, she had gone from doing highly paid cabaret engagements at the Dunes Hotel in Las Vegas and the Chi Chi Club in Palm Springs to playing the working-men's club circuit in the UK – and not just bigger venues like the Dolce Vita in Newcastle or the Cavendish Club in Sheffield but places as tiny as the Glazebrook Club, in a village *near*

Warrington.[75] This marked quite a vertiginous descent from the heights of international fame that had seemed possible in 1956.

The changes wrought by age, which would define Dors' career over the next twenty years, also began to make their presence felt, even though the star was at this point still only in her early thirties. Praising her 1962 cabaret show and stating that 'D. D. is still the best home-grown sex symbol we've got', the *Daily Express*'s reviewer nonetheless noted: 'Her face is not as copybook as it was. There are tell-tale prints of time round the eyes, and the cheeks are rather fleshier than they should be. But probably all that has happened is that the brassy blonde bombshell look has given way to the softer, rounder, less strident expression of motherhood.'[76] Dors becoming a mother, first to Mark, and then another son Gary in 1962, certainly added new and surprising elements to her star persona, as one journalist suggested: 'wearing a pink flannel nightgown' having not long given birth to her first child, it seemed that 'Diana, one time goddess of the Chase and the Ooh-la-la!' had been 'transformed in motherhood'.[77] Some commentators were venomously hostile to this sexualised working mother (the main breadwinner in her family) out peddling glitzy allure while her infant son suffered the fate of 'cabaret orphan', as expressed by the comments of Baroness Stokes quoted earlier. Others simply found the combination of motherhood and knowing sexuality 'difficult to reconcile', finding dissonance between 'the two images – one of the vampish, affected, diamond-hunting, gold-digging, pool-jumping, hell-raising Dors, the femme fatale. And the more recent one of the relaxed, contented, home-loving Dors, the fond mother.'[78] As she played the 'mature' role of faded party girl in *West 11* (1963) or the housekeeper grateful for a bit of Richard Johnson's attention in *Danger Route* (1967), it became clear that age and motherhood, and the physical and personal changes that these were seen to entail, meant that the Dors image required appropriate modification.

The mood of the times had changed, and in the 1960s different things were required from film stars. As Dors pointed out in 1966, 'one has to play it cool to be fashionable. The Julie Christie kooky dolly look is all the rage now . . . The luxury and glamour that was once part and parcel of being a film star is now passé', concluding that 'no matter how hard I try, I guess I'll never be able to look like Rita Tushingham'.[79] In 1968, she noted how cinema's new sexual explicitness had left her old image looking out-moded: 'I don't kid myself . . . what sold ten years ago they'd laugh at now. Remember me in the bubble baths?'[80] At that point, she had attempted a pop career, both as manager of Troy Dante and as a singer in her own right, and had filmed some episodes of a modish big-budget detective series for Associated-Rediffusion in 1965 called *The Unusual Miss Mulberry* that had been intended to rival *The Avengers* but was never shown, for reasons unspecified.[81] But her most prominent popular culture appearance around this time was ironically in archetypal fifties sexpot mode, in waxwork form, on the cover of The Beatles' *Sgt. Pepper's Lonely Hearts Club Band* album. However, her marriage to actor Alan Lake in 1968, after only a few weeks' acquaintance, would help put her back in the headlines, as would her ongoing financial woes that saw her filing for bankruptcy the same year (and exiting the hearing to find a £2 parking ticket on her car).[82]

Ripe and Robust: Dors, Ageing and Celebrity

In terms of her film and television career, Dors appeared sanguine about her movement towards character roles, unblinkingly taking on the role of dowdy counterpart to Goldie Hawn's fashionable kook in *There's a Girl in My Soup* (1970), although *Films and Filming*'s Eric Braun felt 'the part was not really good enough to justify the mess she had to make herself look'.[83] She went even further in Jerzy Skolimowski's *Deep End* (1970), in which she played a violently lustful overweight older woman visiting the public baths who forces the teenage male attendant to collude with her frenzied masturbatory fantasies of the footballer George Best ('he just pushed it in, just glided it in, slowly, just inside the post. Oh no, you can't keep Georgie out') until she reaches orgasm and then unceremoniously shoves him away.[84] The grotty municipal swimming pool that provided *Deep End*'s setting was a far cry from her Hollywood pool, the one that she had dreamed of since her school essay, or even the lido where she'd first been discovered, just as the Dors of the early 1970s differed significantly from her former incarnation as blonde glamour machine.

The shift had its upside: 'I've got a chance of varied roles at my age, now that I'm not tied down to sex and glamour and vacuous romantic leads', she claimed in 1970.[85] She delivered on this promise in what the *The Observer* called her 'astonishingly masterful character performance' in the 1970 Royal Court production *Three Months Gone*, as well as her grotesque warty 'evil gin-swigging old tart of 60' (her own description) in the children's fantasy *The Amazing Mr. Blunden* (1972).[86] But just as in her early career, Dors was faced once again with a choice between money and good notices, although she now had a sharper awareness of the longer-term implications of plumping merely for the latter:

> I now have to be choosy if I'm not to undermine the good that was done by *Three Months Gone* [1970], which brought about some wonderful offers and a new recognition of the fact that I could act. People soon forget, and if one accepts too many

Figure 3.3 Playing an 'evil gin-swigging old tart of 60': Dors embraces character roles as wicked housekeeper Mrs Wickens in *The Amazing Mr. Blunden* (1972).

crappy parts, it becomes a case of 'Wasn't she in a good play – once?' On the other hand you have to strike a balance; art all too seldom equals box office.[87]

The attempts to maintain that balance between art and commerce sometimes resulted in bewildering juxtapositions, such as her appearance as Jocasta in Sophocles' *Oedipus* at the Chichester Festival in 1974 coming shortly after filming a pilot for a pet-focused chat show *Paws for Dors* that had Dudley Moore, Zsa Zsa Gabor, and the Marquess of Bath as its guests.[88] In the 1970s, Dors took minor parts in numerous sexploitation and horror films, the mainstays of British production at the time, and regularly guested on game shows ('God knows how they cram me into my little box' she said of her appearances on *Celebrity Squares*) and on chat shows, never wracked by the self-loathing that afflicted Kenneth Williams at having to earn money this way.[89] Her eventful personal life made her just as much a tabloid fixture as she had ever been, with the papers following the misadventures of her husband who was frequently in trouble with the law for drunk and disorderly behaviour and other forms of affray. They also covered Dors' multiple serious illnesses, including near-fatal meningitis in 1974 and the recurrent cancer that would eventually kill her.

Having had her third son, Jason, in 1969, Dors also began to cut an increasingly domesticated figure in the press from the 1970s onwards, providing her recipe for fruitcake to the *Daily Express* around Christmas 1973, for example.[90] Her lead roles in the television sitcoms *Queenie's Castle* (1970–2) and *All Our Saturdays* (1973) were as blousily glam, bossy

Northern matriarchs, which seemed to tally with the way that her image had developed: 'all backless, strappy white high heels, fingers creaking under enough shiners to furnish a Bond Street jewellers – and eyelashes long enough to stir a Manhattan'.[91] For columnist Jean Rook in 1976, Dors had become a sort of light-entertainment Mother Earth, 'ripely and plentifully overflowing'; 'what you mean is I'm beginning to look like some marvellous Hogarthian whore' was Dors' riposte.[92] Praise for Diana Dors often took an architectural turn in its metaphors, although she certainly didn't physically correspond with what Pevsner saw as the keynote of English architecture: its 'negation of the swelling rotundity of the body'.[93] Her body was a celebration of swelling rotundity. The star was compared to impressive British structures of various kinds from the Albert Hall ('she remains something of a British institution – like the Albert Hall, an edifice she'd be the first to tell you she now solidly resembles') to Big Ben ('Diana Dors, like Big Ben, symbolises Britain's greatness'), although even back in the 1950s Kenneth Tynan had been describing her as a great British landmark and suggested that 'the National Trust already have their eyes on her'.[94] Taking a slightly different tack, *The Times*' parliamentary sketch writer used a battleship metaphor to exemplify Dors' status as 'a figure out of Britain's past greatness' when she visited the House of Commons in 1983: 'As she sailed majestically into her seat, it was clear she was in magnificent condition – like a warship with a turbulent history of battle now rendered obsolete by faster craft, but still doing sterling service as a training vessel.'[95] Imbuing her with monumental qualities was a way of expressing a sense of chauvinistic pride in Dors as a national asset, a Britannia as 'resolutely British as Shrove Tuesday and Brighton Rock'.[96] Dors herself stated that she was a 'twentieth-century Boadicea', a new warrior queen for the nation, adding: 'The people *need* me. In the fifties, when I was Britain's answer to Marilyn Monroe and it was all those tiger skins and waterfalls, I knew it was fake but they lapped it up – austerity days, you see? Now we're going through a depression and they need Diana Dors again.'[97] She was the perfect choice to play the fairy godmother in the video for Adam and the Ants' (1981) pop single 'Prince Charming', dispensing glittery magic with a wave of her wand, a New Romantic *avant la lettre*. Given such intimations of female authority and leadership within her persona, it was unusually astute casting that had Dors play the powder-blue uniformed generalissima of a female dictatorship in 'The Worm that Turned' comedy serial in *The Two Ronnies* in 1980.[98] And it was perhaps inevitable that Dors should also be compared to the country's recently elected Prime Minister Margaret Thatcher who had been similarly lionised as a

Britannia/Boadicea figure. The parliamentary sketch writer from 1983 drew a direct connection between the two, wondering what Dors thought 'of the woman at the government dispatch box who had succeeded her in the newspapers as Britain's wildest blonde?'[99] A similar connection was made back in the late 1970s by Oswald Mosley, former leader of the British Union of Fascists, who told *The Sunday Times* that he had 'just become an admirer of Diana Dors, whom he recently saw on the Russell Harty show. He refers to her in the same breath as Margaret Thatcher, whom he describes as "all things bright and beautiful."'[100] It is clear that both Thatcher and Dors transcended their mere professional statuses to become feminine figureheads in popular culture, symbolised by achieving the rare British honour of becoming bingo calls, 'number ten, Maggie's den' and 'all the fours, Diana Dors'.[101]

Leading from the front again, Dors headed up the 'dieting dozen', twelve volunteers from the general public who were trying to lose weight along with her, in a slot for the ailing ITV breakfast television provider TVAM in 1983. Concocting recipes like 'Apricot Chiffon' (a dessert made from tinned apricots, lemon jelly, and yoghurt) and appearing to lose weight but secretly just removing an item of jewellery at each weigh-in, the flamboyant Dors was as instrumental in the programme's revival as the puppet Roland Rat, with *The Times* noting that 'Diana Dors' slimming classes just before 9 am on Fridays are also breaking the million viewer barrier'.[102] Dors' struggles with her weight in middle age, caused partly by her sweet tooth ('The dessert trolley arrives and her eyes light up. "Do you think they have any meringues?"', reported one journalist in 1978) and her simultaneous fight against and embrace of her ample figure ('Plump and happy, that's me', ran one typical headline) made her someone with whom many viewers could identify.[103]

Her appeal to women built upon aspects of female camaraderie in her image from much earlier in her career: back in *Lady Godiva Rides Again*, the beauty-contest veteran she played kindly mentored the inexperienced heroine and manipulated the contest in the novice's favour, and in *The Weak and the Wicked* her character Betty developed a deep friendship with her fellow prisoner, Jean (Glynis Johns), while in *Value for Money*, Dors' showgirl Ruthine selflessly cooperated with the hero's childhood sweetheart so that the 'correct' couple could be reunited at the end, rather than taking advantage of his infatuation with her showgirl charms. She could be a 'brick' as well as a bombshell and, in 1960, she wrote proudly of her female following: 'It pleases me that 90 per cent of my fan mail comes from middle-aged housewives who admired me.'[104] Her very last film role, in Joseph Losey's final film *Steaming* (1985), provided a nice continuity with that element of her image as she presided wisely and kindly over the all-female community attending the steam baths at which she is manageress.

In her final years, while suffering with the recurring cancer that would kill her, the primary quality with which her star image was associated was, ironically, survival, consolidating the persona she had acquired since the 1960s of being 'never-say-Di'.[105] In spite of the career lows and the personal tribulations, she still had her pride and she still had a swimming pool, featured on the cover of her 1984 book *Diana Dors' A–Z of Men* and in a special 1981 Russell Harty chat show in her honour, at which she sang Peggy Lee's 'Where did they go?', a song all about the ephemerality of youthful pleasures.[106] Not dying young, like her fellow blonde bombshells Jean Harlow or Marilyn Monroe, meant that Dors had been forced to change and adapt her image to fit the changing times and her changing appearance as she aged – and doing so by embracing a glamour that had always verged on vulgarity, the tackiness of 'tiger skins and waterfalls', as she put it.[107]

Conclusion and a Coda on Coding

One may feel regretful that towards the end of her life she was best known for tabloid kitsch, such as covering the plaster cast on her broken ankle with a gold rhinestone-studded sock donated by her friend Liberace, or one of her final public engagements being to open the doors to a new shop devoted to selling 'nothing but doors, door handles and door locks' in Redhill (sadly not Dorking).[108] One may wish that she had had more and better chances to demonstrate the acting skill that was only demanded of her on occasion. But wishing that she had been spared some of her tackier moments would feel like wishing away a core element of her persona. A version of Diana Dors in good taste would be a contradiction in terms. There are more than enough demure English roses growing on the peaks and lower foothills of British cinema, but there are all too few stars who manage to do what Dors did, and leap from suburban Swindon to Hollywood stardom and back again, navigating all those peaks, troughs, and chicanes in her careers with self-reliant good humour. The disappointment and lost causes are part of the myth, as Morrissey so wisely recognised when he elevated Dors into his pantheon of yearning post-war misfits. Her appearance on the cover of The Smiths' 1995 *Singles* compilation suggested her ongoing cultural resonance, even more than a decade after her death. Unflattering though their approach may have been, the writers of the comedy *Psychobitches* felt that it was Diana Dors who merited sketch treatment, not the vastly more contemporaneously popular Anna Neagle or Margaret Lockwood. Her image lives on in a way theirs do not.

Dors has been the subject of a biographical miniseries, *The Blonde Bombshell* (1999), as well as several television documentaries that have unearthed new aspects of her life and career. The most surprising and intriguing was *Who Got Diana Dors's Millions?* (2003), which revealed how the star had employed masonic secret codes dating back to the sixteenth century in order to keep secret accounts and avoid full disclosure of her financial affairs to Her Majesty's Revenues and Customs. Such activities were nefarious but also impressively cerebral for someone whose public persona did not suggest expertise in cryptology. But as the documentary went on to show, Dors' adventures in coding were ultimately fruitless, given that the documents that completed the full code had long since disappeared and so all the money she so meticulously squirrelled away in numerous bank accounts set up in false names would remain unclaimed until eventually going back to the taxman anyway. As an audacious plan ultimately doomed to ignominious failure, it provides a neat metaphor for Dors' ambitions of international stardom, undone by bad luck, bad behaviour, and being in the wrong place at the wrong time. But it was Dors' bigger triumph to keep the wheels of the blonde glamour machine turning for so long, from the 1950s right into the 1980s, and to do it with such brassy bravado.

Notes

1. Anne Edwards, 'Woman's point of view', *Daily Express*, 17 October 1949, p. 3.
2. Anonymous, 'Artistes (Income Tax)', *Hansard*, 28 October 1954, vol. 531, cc 2124–6.
3. Robin Douglas–Home, 'DD', *Daily Express*, 8 January 1962, p. 4.
4. Margaret Hinxman, 'The remarkable diary of Diana Dors', *Picturegoer*, 7 May 1955, p. 14.
5. Quoted in David Beresford, 'Diana Dors dies at 52', *The Guardian*, 5 May 1984, pp. 1–2.
6. Diana Dors on *The Mike Wallace Interview*, 9 November 1957. https://www.youtube.com/watch?v=bSr-kHg32j4
7. Diana Dors, *Dors by Diana* (London: Queen Anne, Macdonald Futura, 1981), p. 127.
8. Eric Braun, 'Diana Dors: In her own terms', *Films and Filming*, February 1973, pp. 28–30. Beresford, 'Diana Dors dies at 52', p. 2.
9. Geraghty, 'Diana Dors', p. 345. Durgnat, *A Mirror for England*, p. 55.
10. Diana Dors, *Swingin' Dors* (London: World, 1960), p. 63. The *Daily Express* devoted space to detail Dors' 'favourite flying outfit: black silk kerchief

knotted at the side of her neck, white open-necked sports shirt, black tailored slacks' accessorised with a 'broad leather belt'. Robb, 'The things they do', *Daily Express*, 10 October 1952, p. 3.

11. Dors, *Swingin' Dors*, p. 111.
12. Cook, 'The trouble with sex', pp. 174–5.
13. Napier-Bell cited in Advertisement for *Tit-Bits* in *Daily Mirror*, 20 October 1953, p. 12. Clive Limpkin, 'A Boadicea for the 20th century', *The Sunday Times*, 17 January 1982, p. 15.
14. Dors, *Dors by Diana*, p. 310.
15. Ibid., p. 21.
16. Diana Dors, 'They made me a Good Time Girl', *Picturegoer*, 7 October 1950, p. 8.
17. Ibid., p. 9. She did get a chance to advertise Goya lipstick and Pin-Up Perms ('all the loveliest young stars now have Pin-Up Perms') under contract though. See advertisements in *Daily Express*, 20 September 1949, p. 4, and *Daily Express*, 17 November 1949, p. 3.
18. Dors, 'They made me a Good Time Girl', p. 9.
19. Dors, *Swingin' Dors*, pp. 43–4.
20. David Lewin, 'Diana dares', *Daily Express*, 14 July 1954, p. 3.
21. Reg Whitley, 'Why Diana is banned again', *Daily Mirror*, 31 January 1952, p. 4.
22. Dors, *Swingin' Dors*, p. 62.
23. Anonymous, 'Golden Slipper Diana Dors goes to court in a Rolls', *Daily Express*, 25 July 1953, p. 5.
24. Dors, *Swingin' Dors*, p. 50. But this was not before Dors had provisionally agreed to the contract, according to reportage in *Picturegoer*, 8 December 1951, p. 5.
25. Dors, *Swingin' Dors*, p. 51.
26. Derek Hill, 'A window on Dors', *Films and Filming*, April 1955, p. 10.
27. Dors, *Swingin' Dors*, pp. 57–8.
28. Ken Sherry, 'I bet this shook the boys', *Picturegoer*, 25 September 1954, p. 12.
29. Unlabelled article, *Daily Mail*, 9 May 1956. Press cuttings file on Diana Dors, BFI Library.
30. Whitehall, 'DD', p. 22.
31. Ibid.
32. Donald Zec, 'At home – with Miss Dors', *Daily Mirror*, 31 May 1954, p. 2.
33. Susan Sontag, 'Notes on camp', *Against Interpretation and Other Essays* (New York: Picador, 1966), p. 281.
34. Judy Rumbold, 'The mullah of Mondo Trasho', *The Guardian*, 10 July 1990, p. 37. Suzanne Lowry, 'Diana, opening new doors', *The Observer*, 12 February 1978, p. 24. Even in recent decades, Dors figures as a gay icon: Dors lookalike Naomi Polley states that her most frequent gigs are gay weddings. Naomi Polley, 'My life as Swindon's Diana Dors', BBC Wiltshire, 16

December 2009. http://news.bbc.co.uk/local/wiltshire/hi/people_and_places/newsid_8416000/8416029.stm

35. Dors, *Swingin' Dors*, p. 118. John Weaver, 'A flying fan drops in on Dors', *Daily Express*, 21 April 1958, p. 4. Pendennis, 'Table talk', *The Observer*, 10 February 1957, p. 6. Rene MacColl, 'Why Diana Dors can blossom like a rose in the desert – this place IS a desert, even if SHE'S no rose!', *Daily Express*, 5 September 1956, p. 6.

36. Cook, 'The trouble with sex', p. 172. 'Halifax magistrates yesterday ruled that "Diana Dors in 3-D", a half-crown picture publication with red and green spectacles supplied, was not obscene'. Anonymous, '3-D book found not obscene', *Manchester Guardian*, 5 October 1954, p. 3.

37. Cook, 'The trouble with sex', p. 174.

38. Front page headline of *Daily Mirror*, 21 May 1956. Anonymous, 'Visible export', *Time*, 10 October 1955. Press cuttings file on Diana Dors, BFI Library.

39. Candidus, 'Close that Dors!', *Daily Sketch*, 20 July 1956. Press cuttings file on Diana Dors, BFI Library. Anonymous, '"It's not true" says Miss Dors', *Manchester Guardian*, 29 October 1954, p. 1.

40. Anonymous, 'Letters: Don't slam Dors', *Daily Mirror*, 14 June 1956, p. 2.

41. Anonymous, '"It's not true" says Miss Dors', p. 1.

42. Ernie Player, 'Where does your money go?', *Picturegoer*, 27 November 1954, p. 18. Elsewhere she responded disingenuously to accusations: 'Fiddle the income tax? Why, I'm still saving up for my first mink coat.' Anonymous, 'How does Diana Dors draw £50 a week tax free?', *Daily Express*, 29 October 1954, p. 5. This issue had long been a matter of concern for the star and even back in 1950, Dors was making similar points about how far her £10 contract salary had to stretch each week: 'In the first place, there's the percentage to one's agent. Then there is rent for the kind of living accommodation considered appropriate . . . the starlet has to supply her own clothes, which must obviously be of a certain standard of good taste and quality: shoes, accessories, make-up and hairdressing.' Dors, 'They made me a Good Time Girl', p. 8.

43. Reg Whitley, 'Success!', *Daily Mirror*, 8 September 1955, p. 1.

44. Paul Holt, 'Looking at the rushes', *Picturegoer*, 9 July 1949, p. 5.

45. Tynan reviewing *Rendezvous* in *Evening Standard*, quoted in David Bret, *Hurricane in Mink* (London: JR Books, 2010), p. 46.

46. Unlabelled article, *Daily Mail*, 9 May 1956. Press cuttings file on Diana Dors, BFI Library.

47. Anonymous, '3 Ds are the tops!', *Daily Mirror*, 29 December 1955, p. 9. Andy Medhurst, 'Can chaps be pin-ups? The British male film star in the 1950s', *Ten 8*, 17, 1985, p. 3. To underline how marginal any female presence was in the star hierarchy of this time, Doris Day was the only other woman listed anywhere, coming in at number four in the list of top international box-office draws.

48. Anonymous, 'Diana steals front page from Marilyn', *Daily Mirror*, 17 July 1956, p. 1.
49. Quoted Antony Sampson, 'Dig that crazy jive, man!', *The Observer*, 16 September 1956, p. 11.
50. Anonymous, 'See! I dunnit . . .!', *Daily Express*, 18 July 1956, p. 3.
51. See Cook, 'The trouble with sex', p. 169.
52. I have discussed *Yield to the Night* at greater length elsewhere, including in 'Twilight women of 1950s British cinema', in Robert Murphy (ed.), *The British Cinema Book*, third edition (London: BFI, 2009), pp. 286–95, and in *Prisoners of Gender: Women in the Films of J. Lee Thompson* (Berlin: VDM, 2009).
53. *Yield to the Night* pressbook, BFI Library.
54. Dors, *Swingin' Dors*, p. 143. There's another interesting parallel here with Monroe who also changed critical perceptions of her acting abilities in her film of the same year, *Bus Stop* (1956).
55. Hopper cited in John Maynard, 'Diana Dors: Girl with three dimensions', *Screenland*, March 1957, p. 67.
56. Dors, *Dors by Diana*, p. 153.
57. Ibid., p. 156.
58. 'Go home, Diana! – and take Mr Dors with you!', *New York Enquirer*, 1 September 1956, p. 1. The *Express's* 'picture-analysis desk' offered a blow-by-blow reconstruction of events with witness statements and minutely detailed photographic scrutiny in an article entitled 'Well? WAS she pushed – OR did she fall?', *Daily Express*, 21 August 1956, p. 3.
59. Indeed, Dors took RKO to court in December 1958, on the charge of defamation of character. She alleged she had 'become an object of disgrace, ill-will and ridicule' at RKO's hands because the company didn't want to fulfil its contract with her. She settled with them out of court in 1960 for $200,000. *Variety*, 18 February 1959, p. 10, and *Variety*, 13 July 1960, p. 8.
60. Anonymous, 'Escapers club', *The Times*, 27 August 1956, p. 9.
61. Anonymous, 'Diana – propaganda pin-up', *Daily Express*, 27 February 1956, p. 1.
62. Woodrow Wyatt, 'Wake up!', *Daily Mirror*, 4 July 1956, p. 11.
63. *Daily Express*, 18 July 1956, p. 6.
64. Unlabelled article, *Daily Mail*, 9 May 1956. Press cuttings file on Diana Dors, BFI Library.
65. John Lambert, 'The star-meter', *Daily Express*, 7 December 1956, p. 3.
66. For more on McKenna, see Geraghty, 'Femininity in the fifties: The new woman and the problem of the female star', pp. 155–74. McKenna rejected the label of English rose most emphatically: see Tom Hutchinson, 'The rose shows her thorns', *Picturegoer*, 12 November 1955, p. 13.
67. Diana Dors, 'My blonde blunder', *Daily Express*, 13 May 1959, p. 10. This resolve did not hold and further stinkers ensued, including a quite literal stinker, the Smell-O-Vision production, *Scent of Mystery* (1960).

68. Anonymous, 'Miss Diana Dors at Finsbury Park: Upholding celebrity's mask', *The Times*, 7 October 1958.
69. Ibid.
70. John Barber, 'Miss Dors razzles', *Daily Express*, 7 October 1958, p. 7.
71. Documentary-maker Adam Curtis's 2013 blogpost 'What the Fluck!: The point at which journalism fails and modern power begins' sees Dors' serialised memoirs as a watershed moment in inaugurating a new approach to privacy. http://www.bbc.co.uk/blogs/adamcurtis/entries/441 22901-c2e8-34f5-93e0-d4402c163966
72. Anonymous, 'Government supports press bill', *The Guardian*, 6 February 1960, p. 2.
73. Bret, *Hurricane in Mink*, p. 155.
74. Ibid., p. 158.
75. See Fiona McCarthy, 'Sweet Lives', *The Guardian*, 7 June 1967, p. 6, and Harry Whewell, 'Time to kill a few myths', *The Guardian*, 22 January 1966, p. 14.
76. Douglas–Home, 'DD', p. 4.
77. Nancy Spain, 'Diana Dors – that well-known mother', *Daily Express*, 10 February 1960, p. 9. One interesting newspaper article asked the same set of questions of both Dors and Brigitte Bardot as expectant mothers and sex symbols. Peter Evans, 'To Bardot and Dors: The same questions on going to be a mother', *Daily Express*, 28 November 1959, p. 6.
78. Douglas–Home, 'DD', p. 4.
79. Dors cited in Clive Hirschhorn, 'I'm out in the cold now, says Diana Dors', *Sunday Express*, 15 September 1966, p. 22.
80. Donald Zec, 'The old firm', *Daily Mirror*, 3 May 1968, p. 9. Her brief cameo in *Baby Love* (1968) as the teenage heroine's mother who we see slashing her wrists in a very unglamorous-looking bathtub seemed a deliberate desecration of the star's prior association with luxurious bubble baths.
81. See Damon Wise, *Come by Sunday: The Fabulous Ruined Life of Diana Dors* (London: Sidgwick and Jackson, 1998), p. 230.
82. George Fallows, 'Diana's new £2 ticket – on top of her £49,000 debt', *Daily Mirror*, 6 December 1968, p. 27.
83. Braun, 'Diana Dors: In her own terms', p. 28.
84. By strange coincidence, Dors claimed in the 1970s that 'her old Madame Tussauds waxwork had been melted down in favour of George Best. They must have had some wax left over.' *Evening Standard*, 28 June 1974. Press cuttings file on Diana Dors, BFI Library.
85. John Hall, 'Dianamite yet', *The Guardian*, 18 March 1970, p. 9.
86. Ronald Bryden, 'The genius of Genet', *The Observer*, 1 February 1970, p. 28. Braun, 'Diana Dors: In her own terms', p. 28.
87. Ibid.
88. Wise, *Come by Sunday*, p. 256.
89. Jean Rook, 'Larger than life Diana – billowing into a new golden age', *Daily*

Express, 12 November 1976, p. 15. For more on Dors as television celebrity, see David Lusted, 'The glut of personality', in Christine Gledhill (ed.), *Stardom: Industry of Desire* (London: Routledge, 1991), pp. 251–8. Russell Davies (ed.), *The Kenneth Williams Diaries* (London: HarperCollins, 1994).

90. Shelia Hutchins, 'Some fruity advice from a domestic Diana Dors', *Daily Express*, 20 December 1973, p. 14.

91. Raymond Gardner, 'Powder blue bankrupt', *The Guardian*, 10 February 1978, p. 8.

92. Rook, 'Larger than life Diana', p. 15.

93. Nikolaus Pevsner, *The Englishness of English Art* (London: Architectural Press, 1956), p. 133.

94. Clive Hirschhorn, 'Men were my downfall – says Miss Dors', *Sunday Express*, 17 September 1978, p. 23. Rosalie Horner, 'Dors doing it in style', *Daily Express*, 30 June 1981, p. 23. Tynan quoted in Bret, *Hurricane in Mink*, p. 46.

95. Frank Johnson, 'Miss Dors listens in on the other wild blonde', *The Times*, 28 January 1983, p. 28.

96. Dors cited in Whitehall, 'DD', p. 23; emphasis in the original.

97. Limpkin, 'A Boadicea for the 20th century', p. 15.

98. Dors had felt that the Women's Liberation movement was unsympathetic to glamour girls: 'They don't approve of me, darling and I don't think they ever will [but] if I burned my bra, I'd be knock-kneed.' Diana Dors, 'I have never been very wise about men', *TV Story*, April 1974, p. 19.

99. Johnson, 'Miss Dors listens in on the other wild blonde', p. 28. Dors wrote to Johnson to clarify the fact that, despite being the guest of Labour MP Joe Ashton on that occasion, 'like my father before me, I am a staunch Tory'. Frank Johnson, 'Now we know why he is called the Speaker', *The Times*, 4 February 1983, p. 26.

100. Anthony Holden, 'Mitfords and Mosleys', *The Sunday Times*, 3 April 1977, p. 32.

101. Ann Clwyd, 'The family shiftworkers', *The Guardian*, 22 October 1973, p. 9.

102. Kenneth Gosling, 'TV-am viewers top million mark', *The Times*, 15 August 1983, p. 3.

103. Lowry, 'Diana, opening new doors', p. 24. Patricia Boxall, 'Plump and happy, that's me, says Diana Dors', *People*, 19 April 1970. Press cuttings file on Diana Dors, BFI Library.

104. Dors, *Swingin' Dors*, p. 121.

105. Anonymous, 'Diana Dors: My stories of the stars – as only I can tell them', *Daily Mirror*, 6 December 1977, p. 1.

106. In talking about the recurrent swimming-pool trope in Diana Dors' career, it is important also to acknowledge its seedier connotations. According to her son Jason, and other witnesses/participants, her pool and the manor house to which it was attached, was the site of numerous 'adult' events or swinging parties, not dissimilar to the ones she had co-hosted with Dennis Hamilton

in the 1950s. Niema Ash with Jason Dors-Lake, *Connecting Dors: The Legacy of Diana Dors* (London: Purple INC Press, 2011).

107. On the topic of ageing as a female star, what a pity Dors never got the chance to take up the Bette Davis role in a West End stage version of *Whatever Happened to Baby Jane?* she was offered, scheduled to open January 1984. Noele Gordon, of *Crossroads* fame, was to play the Joan Crawford role, but in the event both actresses were already too ill with the cancers that would kill them to take up the engagement. Bret, *Hurricane in Mink*, p. 222.

108. Anonymous, 'Diana shows off her all-star cast', *Daily Express*, 25 November 1981, p. 15. Anonymous, 'Diary', *The Times*, 20 January 1984, p. 10.

CHAPTER 4

British New Waif: Rita Tushingham and Sixties Female Stardom

Young British women made a huge impact, both nationally and internationally, across a range of media in the 1960s. The fashion models Jean Shrimpton and Twiggy exemplified the period's fashionably slender-framed new look and became significant celebrities. Female pop stars such as Cilla Black, Sandie Shaw, Dusty Springfield, Marianne Faithfull, and Lulu enjoyed high profiles and topped the pop charts, sometimes on both sides of the Atlantic. If they happened to appear on the television show *Ready, Steady, Go*, they would be introduced by television presenter and 'queen of the mods' Cathy McGowan, usually dressed in an outfit by young female designers (Marion) Foale and (Sally) Tuffin or Barbara Hulanicki of Biba (another female designer, Mary Quant, had already made her mark on women's fashion, with her diffusion range sold throughout America via the J. C. Penney chain). Elsewhere on television, cat-suited Diana Rigg became the action heroine par excellence Emma Peel in *The Avengers* in 1965, following on from Honor Blackman's pioneering Cathy Gale, while a more realist type of TV heroine, played by Carol White, was central to the influential dramas of social critique *Up the Junction* (1965) and *Cathy Come Home* (1966). In film, Hayley Mills began the decade as Disney's top girl and one of the most popular international stars of the era before embracing more adult roles after *The Family Way* (1966), while Julie Andrews conquered the world via her blockbuster success in *Mary Poppins* (1964) and *The Sound of Music* (1965). Indeed, such was the appeal of young British actresses around this time that in 1966 *Photoplay* magazine proclaimed 'the fall of the Hollywood love goddess' in favour of 'the rise of the British actress':

> Time was when the English rose bloomed to blush unscreened . . . But no longer. The Day of the Rose has come. The British Rambler has become a Climber, with the movie moguls of Hollywood on their knees to plant and water them with dollars. The British actress has risen to international acceptance at last![1]

The same article lists Samantha Eggar, Susan Hampshire, Sarah Miles, Vanessa Redgrave, and Susannah York as among the beneficiaries of the new trend for casting British actresses in big international productions, but the most significant exponent of the trend was probably Julie Christie, who came to represent the presiding female spirit of the age: the 'embodiment of the independent, swinging, short-skirted, knee-booted young English female' of the 1960s, according to historian Arthur Marwick.[2] Christie made her first major impression as Liz in *Billy Liar* (1963), the girl who caught the train down south to London and left the faint-hearted hero behind, and then won an Oscar for her performance as the self-centred girl-about-town in *Darling* (1965). Her growing international fame was then consolidated by her role as Lara in David Lean's epic blockbuster *Doctor Zhivago* (1965), one of the most successful films of the 1960s. But Christie still maintained a casual bohemian image, as this publicity material for her film *Fahrenheit 451* (1966) suggests:

> Primarily attached to her independence, she likes dancing until the early hours, living in her kitchen, reading lying on the floor, dressing as she pleases – sweater, short Courreges-style skirt, white socks, flat-heeled shoes and absolutely no make-up – going to see old films in the London art cinemas, disappearing when she feels like it and with whom she wants – in short, living the way she likes.[3]

Clichéd it may be but this evocation of liberated autonomous femininity was very different from the ideal of even a few years before, when marriage and domestic contentment were generally presented as the dominant goals for young women.

Christie and her peers, the climbing English roses, were able to ascend to unprecedented levels of international popularity due to the new admiration for all things British, made possible by the vanguard of Beatlemania. As director Ralph Thomas observed, it had become 'fashionable to follow British trends. It is chic to wear British clothes, you are one up on your neighbour if you drive a British car, so logically it is also in vogue to use British actresses and to enthuse over British films'.[4] Clearly, the climate for a British star of either sex trying to 'crack' America had changed dramatically since the somewhat more ambivalent welcome offered to Diana Dors in the 1950s, and many British actors were now reaping the rewards of a renewed Anglophilia that envisaged Britain as the site of all that was cool and innovative.

Alongside Julie Christie in the cast of *Doctor Zhivago*, but playing a smaller role confined to its framing narrative, was Rita Tushingham, another highly significant female presence in British cinema of that period – an 'indelible face of the Sixties' just like Christie.[5] In many ways

Tushingham may be considered a more convincing emblem than Christie for the cultural and aesthetic revolution said to have taken place during the 1960s, for if Julie Christie had the kind of golden-haired radiance that arguably would have made her a star in any period, then Tushingham represented a very different mode of femininity that arguably could not have risen to leading-lady prominence in any previous decade. In US *Vogue*, Tushingham was characterised as an off-kilter version of female stardom, 'what might have resulted if a star-making machine had been fed a card chewed at random by field mice', although they added that 'she crossed all the usual wires and came out the winner'.[6] Once memorably described as looking like the 'product of an unlikely coupling between Audrey Hepburn and Pinocchio', Tushingham's looks combined large-eyed gamine beauty with more angular features that had not traditionally been the province of the female film star.[7] In this respect she epitomised British cinema's innovative developments during the 1960s, and became closely associated with a new kind of filmmaking (which demanded a new kind of look), first rising to fame on the crest of the British new wave in *A Taste of Honey* (1961). She then shifted into playing the idiosyncratic ingénue of a number of 'swinging London' films, including *The Knack* (1965) and *Smashing Time* (1967), as forthright Northern girls who cast a sceptical eye on metropolitan cant. As Christine Geraghty suggests, Tushingham's debut role as Jo in *A Taste of Honey* represented the first of a new 'unconventional and quirky' female type in British film whose youth is 'associated with transparency of purpose, a refusal to compromise or pretend', pre-empting the quixotic young women Julie Christie would later play in *Billy Liar* and *Darling*.[8] For writer Sally Vincent, Tushingham embodied the emergent youthful zeitgeist of the 1960s and the new kinds of womanhood it enabled:

> It was as though she owned, tapped into and made visible the gravity, humour and wishes of a generation too long land-locked by the timidity of its cultural heritage. At all events, it was suddenly all right to be a girl without being slavish about it, without teetering precariously between childhood and middle-age.[9]

The actress was still a teenager when she made her film debut, itself written by nineteen-year-old playwright Shelagh Delaney, and one of Tushingham's first significant awards (in 1961) was the Variety Club's Most Promising Newcomer accolade that she shared with fifteen-year-old pop singer Helen Shapiro, indicating how youthful tastes and teenage stars were taking over the British entertainment establishment, a trend that would only accelerate as the decade progressed. Youth was absolutely central to Tushingham's persona in the 1960s, as it was to popular culture more generally during the period, and Alexander Chancellor's retrospective characterisation of Tushingham's star image as one of 'childlike innocence, curiosity and enthusiasm' not only sums up her appeal but also seems to speak more broadly to the positive qualities of youth venerated in the 1960s.[10]

Lovely Rita: The Tushingham Look

The fact that Rita Tushingham suggested a new model of film stardom that departed from previous expectations was perhaps most clearly evident from the extensive press coverage on her looks. According to *The Sunday Times* in 1961, Tushingham had 'the scribes riffling their word boards' for suitable adjectives to describe 'her face – "unusual". Various astigmats have even called her ugly.'[11] Questions around beauty and ugliness defined Tushingham's career before it had barely begun. Seeking to cast an unknown as the teenage heroine in the film version of *A Taste of Honey*, Woodfall's co-conspirators Tony Richardson and John Osborne made it known in the national press that they were looking for 'an ugly girl' and invited photographs with covering letters so that they could begin auditioning.[12] Eighteen-year-old Rita, an aspiring actress working in the lowly role of trainee assistant stage manager at the Liverpool Playhouse at the time, had been teased by her brothers that she fitted the bill perfectly. Recognising the opportunity it presented, she thought she may as well have a go, but never expected to hear anything back.[13] Her subsequent call for audition in London, followed by a screen test, followed by finally being cast in the film meant that she was catapulted very rapidly from total obscurity into the intense glare of the media spotlight, with very little preparation for what that would entail.

Continuing the motif set up by Osborne and Richardson's original advertisement, the *Daily Express* presented Tushingham under the headline 'Found: The ugly girl (once she was the hind legs of a donkey)' with a low-angle photograph captioned 'ugly enough' (her brother's words of encouragement to her), while the *Sunday Pictorial* placed an unflattering wide-angle lens shot of her on its front page, captioned 'The ugliest girl in the world'.[14] Even those articles covering this new discovery more sympathetically refused to pull their punches in presenting her as plain and completely lacking in glamour or allure: 'Rita Tushingham is a nineteen-year-old girl with crooked teeth, rough hair and a plain nose on her face', began a piece by Marjorie Proops in which she disclosed that at the premiere of *A Taste of Honey*, the star would be 'wearing an off-the-peg blue chiffon dress, chosen carefully by Rita and me to disguise her biggish hips and smallish bust. For Rita is nothing like the dream version of a film star.'[15] Opinions on her appearance, and physical attractiveness or otherwise, coloured everything. Even while her film debut in *A Taste of Honey* was being acclaimed by reviewers and she was hailed as 'an exciting new piece of feminine talent', it was still thought necessary to couch that praise with trepidation about how shockingly unglamorous she was: 'Rita's no honey', the *Daily Mirror*'s review was titled, 'but this film tastes of success'.[16] Even in the more highbrow *Sight and Sound*, the same strategy applied: 'Rita Tushingham beautifully embodies the role. Beautifully is perhaps hardly the word.'[17] What seems incredible now is how resilient the young star proved herself when faced with such derogatory coverage of her physical appearance, managing to maintain enough self-esteem to look at those calling her an ugly unknown 'and think "I'm just as good looking as them"'.[18]

Perhaps the endless commentary on Rita Tushingham's unorthodox looks for a film star is unsurprising, given what Arthur Marwick says about 'the new explicitness about beauty' that began to take hold during the 1960s, with 'the whole pop, fashion, leisure, public relations world pervaded by an atmosphere which put a premium on a good appearance'.[19] Marwick discusses how this affected the reception of Barbra Streisand as a female star with a different kind of look in the mid-1960s, and surmises that 'the old dishonesties, the old confusions between talent, or other qualities, and mere physical appearance, were disappearing. If someone was actually ugly, it was now more acceptable simply to say so':

> The point is the openness and, in a sense, honesty. What most commentators were saying was that because of the talent, and the personality, the looks began to cease to matter. But all the time a distinction was being made between Streisand's immense and indisputable talent and her looks. No longer was it an essential convention that one must pretend to find the successful star also supremely beautiful.[20]

But this seems altogether too simplistic an understanding of beauty on Marwick's part that fails to account for the genuine physical attractiveness of Streisand not merely because of 'compensatory' talent as a performer but in her own right due to her slim figure, strong aquiline profile, and large, blue, almond-shaped eyes. Although Marwick argues for the ahistorical immutability of beauty, his understanding of what constitutes beauty seems not to span a very wide physiognomic (or ethnic) range. It refuses to admit the possibility of the *jolie laide*, that helpful French phrase referring to an attractive feminine appearance that sits at the intersection between beauty and ugliness, given Francis Bacon's dictum that 'there is no excellent beauty that hath not some strangeness in the proportion'.

It is a concept of beauty that refuses to accept that some faces may be 'growers', more beguiling and fascinating in the longer term than the merely pretty precisely because of their slightly more idiosyncratic attractions. All of this applies equally well to Rita Tushingham, like Streisand an unconventional beauty.

Film historian Marcia Landy recalls Tushingham being 'as popular and appealing as the more glamorous Julie Christie' among her male acquaintances in the 1960s.[21] Novelist Kingsley Amis, temporarily acting as the *The Guardian*'s film reviewer, confessed himself enamored with her 'fairly dear little face' in *Girl with Green Eyes* (1964).[22] Clearly, alongside her detractors, Tushingham had her admirers and advocates, including her Woodfall patrons, with Tony Richardson extolling her 'star magic' and John Osborne, in a much repeated statement, firmly asserting that Tushingham had 'more expression and beauty when she crooks her little finger than most of those damned starlets will ever have – even if they waggle their oversized bosoms and bottoms from here to eternity'.[23]

If Tushingham's looks were generally summarised by journalists and reviewers as 'ugly duckling' or 'plain Jane', the exception to that unflattering rule was the extensive admiration expressed for her wide luminescent eyes that recurs throughout press coverage of the star from her initial discovery onwards.[24] 'I'm being haunted by a pair of eyes', declared Patricia Lewis in the *Daily Express* in 1961, eulogising 'their moist just-woken-up look and their extraordinary depth', and noting that 'they're going to make Miss Tushingham a star at 19'.[25] The anonymous reviewer of *A Taste of Honey* in *The Times* described the actress as having 'the face of an ordinary schoolgirl that is seemingly without make-up but is illuminated by a wonderful pair of eyes'.[26] Donald Zec of the *Daily Mirror* stopped the chatty jocular flow of his 1961 profile of the young star to remark: 'She has the largest, loveliest eyes I have ever looked into.'[27] In another feature for the *Daily Mirror* in 1962, the star admitted they were the feature she was most proud of: 'I get a kick out of hearing people praise my eyes.'[28] In her publicity photographs, throughout the 1960s and beyond, her eyes are the physiognomic feature that are emphasised above all else. David Bailey's 1965 black-and-white photograph of the star, published in US *Vogue*, was accompanied by explanatory text praising 'her astonishing eyes looped with eyeliner'.[29] As colour photography became more commonplace, the hue as well as the size of her eyes was more frequently invoked and remarked upon, one excellent example being the arresting cover for *Observer Magazine*, 11 July 1965, a tight colour close-up in which her large wide kohl-rimmed blue eyes stare directly out at the viewer and dominate the photographic image. Their blueness was seen as uncanny, and redolent

Figure 4.1 The 'astonishing eyes' of Rita Tushingham, playing Kate in *Girl with Green Eyes* (1964).

of a glamour that contrasted with the more ordinary aspects of her star persona. They were 'super-colossal' and as blue as 'an aerial view of twin Beverly Hills swimming pools'[30] for one writer, while another remarked: 'Whoever compared Rita Tushingham's eyes with stewed prunes was ignoring how blue they are.'[31]

As Peter Lewis commented towards the end of the decade, 'the severe fringe and the big startled eyes swiveling underneath' became the hallmarks of her star image.[32] In that respect the Tush look anticipated and corresponded very closely to changing emphases in beauty and make-up popularised in the 1960s, especially the new mod-influenced supremacy of eyes over lips as facial focal points, with pale lipstick providing a counterpoint to heavy dark eyeliner and spiky mascara or false eyelashes, a fashionable saucer-eyed look exemplified by the models Twiggy and Penelope Tree. Startling close-ups on Tushingham's expressive eyes appear across the range of films she made but they feature especially prominently in *A Taste of Honey*, giving us access to the wistfulness and loneliness beneath Jo's defensively cheeky façade, and in her brief scenes in *Doctor Zhivago*, when her character relives the trauma of childhood abandonment. *Girl with Green Eyes* makes clear the ocular emphasis in the characterisation of its Irish heroine (and black-and-white photography enabled Tushingham to disguise the true-blue shade of her eyes). In it, her character Kate is described as having the 'wide hungry eyes of a lemur' and being 'a fawn from the bogs', her large eyes interpreted as a sign of fragile animality. This metaphor continues and intensifies further in *The Trap* (1966) in which Tushingham's character Eve, rendered mute by childhood trauma, is sold off as bride to the uncivilised fur trapper La Bete (Oliver Reed) and abducted to his remote log cabin. Eve's vulnerability is conveyed through her kinship with imperiled animals (she's described as having 'eyes like trapped rabbit'), and the moment when she is forced to shoot a deer for food or face the starvation of both herself and La Bete is a moment of confrontation between two wide-eyed innocent creatures. Tushingham's entirely non-verbal performance in the film places an additional burden on her face, especially her eyes, to convey her deepest feelings. It is a challenge to which she rises with aplomb, and having said in 1965 that her 'ambition' was 'to make silent pictures', her Lilian Gish-like wide-eyed waif abandoned in the wilds in *The Trap* probably comes closest.[33]

'Her Father is a Liverpool Grocer': Class and Region in the Tushingham Persona

One rather bizarre tactic for making sense of or validating Tushingham's 'unusual' looks was to note a supposed resemblance to Princess Margaret. First mentioned in the press by Patricia Lewis in September 1961, 'being likened to Princess Margaret' had soon become such a recurrent discursive feature of Tushingham's stardom that by the end of that year it was being referred to as 'the most disagreeable aspect of her success'.[34] According to the *Daily Express*, the comparisons drawn between the two women 'so intrigued the Princess that it has led to a most unusual episode' when they met backstage at the Royal Court – where Tushingham was appearing in *The Knack* – accompanied by Margaret's husband Anthony Armstrong-Jones, Lord Snowden, who asked the actress 'if she would stand side by side with the princess while he checked the similarities':

> 'We just stood there side by side, grinning' she tells me. 'He said the mouth was very alike and also the eyes. Then he said it was *definitely* our mouths that were the same. I looked so dirty' – it had been one of those squalid plays – 'and she looked so beautiful that I felt worried.'[35]

Even after this attempt at a definitive appraisal from the husband of one of the parties, the comparison between the two continued for some time after, with an article from 1965 still asking 'Well, do YOU think I look like Princess Margaret?', illustrated persuasively by adjacent pictures of the two women, noting that their eyes were 'nearly identical' while their lips had 'similar delicate curls'.[36] Twenty years later, the resemblance was still being recalled.[37] It is difficult to know what to make of the emphasis placed on this rather tenuous celebrity lookalike pairing of a Liverpudlian actress and the reigning monarch's younger sister in the 1960s. Perhaps the aim was to make a case for Tushingham's attractiveness by drawing a regal comparison, or to suggest the emergence of a classless society in which aristocratic and demotic looks may converge. Either way, class was the defining issue.

Indeed, alongside the continual discussion of her looks, the other topic of recurrent fascination surrounding Rita Tushingham was her class provenance and regional background, both read as indicators of her 'ordinariness' and her 'authenticity'. Being a girl from the provinces played a major role in the narrative created around her discovery for *A Taste of Honey* and provided extra piquancy to her transition from obscurity to stardom, as we can see in Proops' 1961 piece:

> Her father is a Liverpool grocer. A charming, ordinary girl – but tomorrow night Rita will be a film star . . . sometimes dreams DO come true. The homely girl next door CAN wake up one day to find the fame she's dreamed about is within her reach. Carry on dreaming, girls. It happened to Rita Tushingham. It could happen to you.[38]

Here Proops presents 'Rita of Liverpool' as an aspirational role model to other ultra-ordinary young women everywhere, although the film in which she made her name plays quite deliberately on the interplay between the ordinary and extraordinary, with Jo reminding her friend Geoffrey that her 'usual self is a very unusual self . . . I'm an extraordinary person!'[39]

She was extraordinary in the film world at that time for her lack of the usual trappings of stardom, so unlike a normal film star in appearance or manner that she and her co-star Dora Bryan were refused admittance to the Cannes gala at which they were due to be honoured.[40] As a press release for *A Taste of Honey* pointed out, 'She has a face as improbable in films as her name.'[41] Unlike Jean Kent, Diana Dors or many other stars, British or otherwise, Rita Tushingham retained her original name despite suggestions it was unwieldy or unglamorous. 'I suppose you will change her name. Tushingham isn't exactly a star name, is it?' asked the reporter in the very first article announcing her casting in *A Taste of Honey*. 'She will stay Rita Tushingham,' insisted Tony Richardson. 'This is 1960 and we are filming a play about life and loneliness and reality.'[42] Tushingham's plain ordinary name thus became as much a statement of realist intent and divergence from previous models of what it meant to be a film starlet as her unconventional looks. They suggested a forthright refusal of the usual fripperies of film stardom, something borne out in a profile piece for the film's press book, '"Tush" goes to the top', which laid great emphasis on the fact that the young star 'uses minimum make-up and dresses simply' and 'has no pretensions'.[43] In interviews she set out her professionalism, 'like any other working girl who wants to be good at her job' and made clear how she differed from 'those "starry" stars [who] are convinced that diamonds are a girl's best friend. I think a girl's best friend is her job.'[44]

All of these qualities – of being un-starry, forthright, candid, ordinary – coalesced around Tushingham's northern-ness, which was seen as the seat of her unpretentious common sense, as demonstrated in this excerpt from another press book, for *Girl with Green Eyes*:

> Rita isn't the film star type. 'What should one conform to?' she asks. 'Should I, because I'm "starred" in a film, act like a ruddy nit – high living and a bosom full of airs and graces. I can't do that. Don't want to. Maybe if I wanted to break away from my background – my family and the people I've lived with and know so well in Liverpool, I'd do it.'[45]

Describing the arrival of this new discovery for the *Daily Mirror* in 1961, star journalist Donald Zec went to town on the North-of-England culinary and meteorological clichés, calling Tushingham 'a Lancashire hot-pot', 'as salty, breezy and bracing as the wind over Morecambe Bay . . . very much my cup of winkles', and, adopting an unspecified northern accent, proclaimed 'Toosh' a 'reet larky bit of stooff'.[46] Off-screen as well as on it, she enacted the role of the little Northern girl being met with incomprehension in the capital:

> There was a hint of defiance when Rita Tushingham, the star of the film of *A Taste of Honey*, said at the film's launching party that she was a Liverpudlian. Her audience – a well-poised woman grasping a cocktail glass as though it were a gladiolus – gave a knowing smile and said: 'In that case you had just the right accent for a film about the North Country.' It was useless for the young Liverpudlian film star to explain the difference between Salford and Manchester – Shelagh Delaney's hunting-ground – and Liverpool. To the knowing smile they were all one, part of that wilderness known as 'The North Country.' . . . *A Taste of Honey* clearly has a lot of missionary work to do yet.[47]

Of course, within a few years, Liverpool would be definitively established as a distinctive place with a very specific identity, courtesy of The Beatles. But at this point, 'Tush' was part of an advance party of general Northern-ness, along with fellow Woodfall discoveries Albert Finney and Tom Courtenay, Salford and Hull born respectively but pretending to be from Nottingham for the purposes of *Saturday Night and Sunday Morning* (1960) and *The Loneliness of the Long Distance Runner* (1962). But, according to one article on the new breed of British stars, while it was 'Finney's comings and goings' that 'filled hundreds of column inches', it was 'Rita

Tushingham's face' that did the same for her, indicating how the fault lines of gender defined and divided the reception of male and female discoveries.[48] Despite Tom Courtenay being at least as unconventional-looking a film star as Tushingham, his looks never seem to have been subjected to quite the same level of forensic scrutiny as his female peer.[49]

Tush Gets the Knack: Sex and Swinging Satire

One writer commented in 1962 when Rita was cast in her next film *The Leather Boys*, that 'many were doubtful if Wardour Street would continue to employ a girl who so shatters the picture of the conventional leading lady'.[50] This was partly true, and Tushingham's career faced an impasse after her award-winning film debut, and she feared becoming a one-off novelty, as she recalled: 'I didn't work for five months. Which is typical in England. They don't use their actresses. Once someone's been discovered they want to keep on discovering.'[51] Instead she appeared on stage, touring in the original Ann Jellicoe play of *The Knack* in 1961 and 1962.[52] The critics admired her performance there – and she would subsequently star in the film version directed by Richard Lester – but she had poor reviews for her performance as Hermia in Tony Richardson's New Wave-inflected Royal Court production of *A Midsummer Night's Dream* in 1962, as did the rest of a stellar cast including Corin Redgrave, Nicol Williamson, Colin Blakely, David Warner, Lynn Redgrave, and Samantha Eggar – all accused of poor verse speaking. The British film exhibition crisis of 1963 that created a bottleneck of British films awaiting release then meant that *The Leather Boys* (1963) and her next film *A Place to Go* (1963), were delayed until 1964, keeping her off cinema screens for several years.[53] But both films appearing in quick succession, followed by *Girl with Green Eyes*, resulted in a sudden gush of Tush in 1964 with a run of films that helped her to win the Variety Club Film Actress award for that year, making good on the promising newcomer award they had given her in 1961.

These film roles during the early to mid-1960s were interesting not only in showing the actress's range, able to play Cockney and Irish girls as well as perky Northerners, but also in the way they mediated ideas around the sexually active young woman, a key cultural figure in the 1960s. While Jo in *A Taste of Honey* is making her first foray into sexual experience with a combination of trepidation and pleasure ('Don't do that.' 'Why not?' 'Because I like it.'), the young Londoners she plays in *The Leather Boys* and *A Place to Go* are both more sexually forthright and, interestingly, are never in doubt about their own physical attractiveness. Mutual sexual desire is what draws her character Dot and her boyfriend Reg (Colin

Campbell) together into a hasty teenage marriage that proves completely incompatible beyond their honeymoon and quickly disintegrates into arguments and infidelity, and is further discombobulated by the homo-erotic dynamic between Reg and best friend Pete (Dudley Sutton). In *A Place to Go* unmarried couple Cat and Ricky (Mike Sarne) consummate their love affair in bombsite ruins that are the only place they can go to get the requisite privacy. But there's no shyness or shame around the sex, and Cat mockingly bawls out across the street, 'Do you want to make love to me, Ricky?' to tease him. Sarne commented in the press on the film's raci-ness: 'There's some fantastic kissing. The film won't get a "U" certificate I can tell you! Rita is a very playful girl.'[54] The young couple's relationship is combative but sexually charged, as proven when she bites his lip when they first kiss ('That'll teach you, I'm not that easy') or when they have a water fight in a laundry house.

Neither Dot nor Cat are seeking the respectability traditionally seen as women's motivation for marriage; they're more combative than some of the other more compliant or victimised women of the New Wave like 'stolid, pudding Ingrid' in *A Kind of Loving* (1962).[55] For Dot, marriage is a means to a sexually motivated end and she rejects the domestic require-ments it entails such as housework, household budgeting, and making her husband a hot dinner. Cat initially rejects Ricky's proposal of mar-riage as an unnecessary encumbrance: 'Get married? What, and end up like me mum? Or your mum? Bedraggled old housewives.' In their lively self-possessed sexuality, whatever their other character flaws, Dot and Cat seem to anticipate the 'spitfire-ish lively, shrewish vivacity' that would later be associated with the working-class women of *Up the Junction*, although neither character is shown having to deal with unplanned preg-nancy like the Battersea women in Nell Dunn, Tony Garnett, and Ken Loach's ground-breaking television drama.[56]

By way of contrast to such sexually confident young women, Kate in *Girl with Green Eyes* and Nancy in *The Knack* are both virgins for whom the process of gaining sexual experience is fraught with complications. For Kate, these not only derive from her tentative shy nature (compared with her much more confident best friend Baba) but also from the sexual repressions inculcated by Irish Catholicism and her patriarchal family who come hunting for her older lover Eugene (Peter Finch) with a shotgun when they find out Kate's moved in with him. The young woman's infatu-ation with the sophisticated émigré writer is suggested in several close-ups of Eugene shot from Kate's point of view as she surveys his ear and jawline, the 'distinguished' greying hair at the temples, and his long-fingered expressive hands holding a cigarette when they first meet in a café. The emergence of a new kind of sexual contract is suggested in Kate living with Eugene despite not being married to him, a more provisional agreement that hinges on an updated version of the marriage vow: 'With this ring I thee bed and board for such time as you remain kind and reasonable.' It is not the case that Eugene merely exploits Kate; Kate also gains from the experience, admiring herself in a new shift dress, hair up in a smart chignon hairstyle, sipping champagne, and asking delightedly, 'Do I look like a woman with a past?' Eugene is her stepping stone first out of what she characterises as rural misery and loneliness, and finally on to a new life in exile in London where, she says, 'I go to school at night, meet different people, different men' (it's remarkably similar to the ending of the 2009 film *An Education*, about another young woman's getting of wisdom). But breaking through into adult life is a bruising process, perfectly encapsulated by Tushingham's heartfelt performance of heartbreak. John Russell Taylor in *The Times* liked the way her character's sobs seemed to come from deep down in her stomach, as though her whole body was in pain.[57]

The complications of emergent female sexuality are all the more pronounced in *The Knack*. It appears that Tolen (Ray Brooks) has 'the knack' for attracting women, while his housemate Colin (Michael Crawford) definitely doesn't, but these sexual certainties are thrown into disarray upon the arrival of a new female tenant in their shared house, Nancy, played by Tushingham. Tolen's aggressive attempts at seduction – not because he desires Nancy but more to prove a point to Colin – come unstuck when he's accused, loudly and repeatedly, of rape. The manner in which the rape accusation is treated comically is discomfiting to contemporary eyes, particularly the scenes in which Colin urges Tolen to make good Nancy's 'fantasy' and rape her, or when Nancy boasts that Colin was the one who raped her 'marvellous super'. But allowing for the context of its time and its generic context as surreal comedy, the film's examination of sexual power dynamics on the cusp of the permissive society is fascinatingly handled. Nancy's provincial innocence becomes the vehicle for her invincibility rather than her victimisation; she does the equivalent of the guileless little boy pointing out the emperor's nakedness in the fairy-tale. The stuttering dialogue reveals her ambivalent feelings towards Tolen, half-attracted, half-repelled: 'Mr Tight Trousers. Just you don't better come near me, d'you hear? Just you don't better come near me. Come near me, Mr Tight Slacks. Come near me, come near me, come near me, come near me, come, come' [she faints]. But by resisting rather than acquiescing to Tolen's charm, Nancy ultimately emasculates him and divests him of his previously all-conquering potency. Her decision to choose the sexu-

Figure 4.2 'Rita is a honey!': Tushingham as Nancy in *The Knack . . . and How to Get It* (1965).

ally reticent clownish Colin as her sexual partner instead undercuts the misogynist assurance of Tolen's previous statements that women are 'not individuals' and 'man must dominate'.

Although 'the knack' referred to in the film's title was Tolen's ability to seduce women, the phrase was mobilised in publicity paratexts to apply to Tushingham herself. She became 'the girl with the knack' as her new geometrical bob hairstyle and kohl-rimmed eyes emphasised her transformation from 'ugly duckling' into fashionable young woman.[58] Fashion designer Gerald McCann recalled that when trendy milliner George Malyard made Rita Tushingham a peaked hat and 'put a photograph of her wearing it in his window, sales went wild', indicating her status as fashion leader.[59] The notable young women's magazine of the sixties, *Honey*, which Nancy is seen reading on the coach down to London, even did a promotional tie-up with *The Knack* entitled 'Rita is a honey!', suggesting how far she had moved into the purview of sixties chic through her 'elfish charm': 'Nobody would say she's got the face that would launch a thousand ships or that she is one of the screen's major heart throbs. But everyone who knows her and has seen her will tell you she's got something which is just as vibrant.'[60] Another sign of her growing star appeal was her appearance in the list of the six most popular young female players in American trade paper *Box Office* in early 1966, the only non-US woman to make the list.[61]

After her forays into epic period drama in *Doctor Zhivago* and *The Trap*, Tushingham returned to *The Knack*'s motif of the modern girl seeking her

fortune in London with 1967's *Smashing Time*. This satire on the swinging London phenomenon saw her paired for the second time – the first
was in *Girl with Green Eyes* – with Lynn Redgrave, another actress who
found herself saddled with the 'ugly duckling' label.[62] Once again they
played physically and temperamentally contrasting best friends, Yvonne
(Redgrave) and Brenda (Tushingham), looking for adventure in the big
city, their heads full of magazine hyperbole about the delights of swinging
London. After an unpromising start finding work as waitresses and nightclub hostesses, both Yvonne and Brenda scale the heights of sixties society,
literally in the case of the big celebratory party for Yvonne's latest pop
record held at the top of the Post Office Tower (now the BT Tower). Yvonne
buys her way to pop fame on the proceeds of a cash prize from a television
stunt show while Brenda is spotted in second-hand clothes (hastily bought
after falling in a puddle) by cool photographer Tom Wabe (Michael York)
who proclaims her the new 'face of the sixties'. Brenda then becomes the
poster girl for 'Gauche' beauty products, and appears in a television commercial for 'Direct Action' eau de toilette: scriptwriter George Melly's dig
at sixties 'radical chic'. The period's boutique culture also comes in for a
savaging, when Brenda gets a job in the trendy shop Too Much owned by
rich girl Charlotte Brillig (Anna Quayle) and Brenda makes the mistake of
demanding that the beautiful people don't just hang out there but actually
buy something. As we've seen, this idea of the guileless northerner pricking
metropolitan pomposity also carried through into Tushingham's off-screen
image, with interviews describing her slipping into 'a mock-posh voice' or
'a plummy fake-deb voice' to create an ironic distance between herself and
the '"po-faced" things'[63] she was sometimes forced to talk about, particularly questions about her appearance: 'We asked Miss Tushingham what
colour she would call her hair. "Mouse", she told us. "It's just brown, I
guess. With haylaits"' [highlights].[64] The tone is not that far removed from
one of her sharpest moments in *The Knack*, when she repeats the posh shop
assistant's patronising patter along with him when he tries it on his next
customer: 'I must please you, and I think I can.'

Alongside its satirical take on empty-headed sixties neophilia, *Smashing
Time* also mobilises a much more old-fashioned form of comedy, silent
movie slapstick, with prolonged dialogue-free ketchup-and-custard-pie
fight sequences; indeed, Michael Billington felt that the film's mixture of
'slapstick with satire' left it looking 'as if the *Carry On* team had decided to
remake *Darling*'.[65] But Billington, along with several other reviewers, also
had positive things to say about the teaming of Tushingham and Redgrave
and even compared them to Laurel and Hardy, a flattering observation
with which director Desmond Davis happily concurred:

Some of the feeling and atmosphere of those old films must be present. Laurel and Hardy were innocents and the girls are innocents. They are sort of Candides in a wicked world and really they only remain totally unscathed in the end because they are innocents.[66]

Tushingham's talent for verbal comedy, demonstrated by her mastery of Shelagh Delaney's acerbic Mancunian mother–daughter cross-talk in *A Taste of Honey*, was accompanied by an equal talent for physical comedy that she showed off in *Smashing Time* but also *The Knack*, with its scenes of her character silently struggling with disobedient luggage lockers or faking pregnancy by shoving her bag under her coat in order to cross the road safely. One reviewer felt that there was 'more than a touch of Chaplin' in Tushingham's performance in *Girl with Green Eyes* that made it possible to 'picture her in the final fade-out, walking down a country lane with her back to the camera, her shoulders squared, and defiantly swinging a little cane'.[67] But her biggest silent movie influence was Buster Keaton, with journalist Peter Lewis noticing the 'enormous picture on the wall of her idol, Buster Keaton, Stoneface' when he interviewed Tushingham at her home in 1969.[68] When she was given the chances, she was able to use her equally distinctive, big-eyed, deadpan physiognomy for modern comedic purposes. She certainly does a very proficient slow wipe of custard pie from her eyes, Oliver Hardy style, in one of the big food fight scenes in *Smashing Time*.

Waif Astray? Moving into the Late Sixties and Seventies

Tushingham worked mainly in comedy for the rest of the decade, being cast in roles that tapped into current social trends. In Merchant Ivory Productions's *The Guru* (1969), she was a hippy chick in India seeking a guru to teach her the sitar and hanging out with pop star Tom Pickle (Michael York). In the same year, she played a groovy, bewigged safe-cracker assisting Marcello Mastroianni in comedy heist movie *Diamonds for Breakfast* (1968), although of this latter film, Penelope Mortimer expressed her wish that 'someone would give Miss Tushingham something worthy of her talents, and stop forcing her to make a fool of herself' while *Monthly Film Bulletin* complained about 'the combination of Liverpudlian kookiness and romantic initiative with which the script burdens her'. [69] She was also Penelope, the unfortunate young woman who finds herself seventeen-months-pregnant in the surreal post-apocalyptic comedy by Spike Milligan and John Antrobus, directed by Richard Lester, *The Bed-Sitting Room* (1969). Tushingham deftly navigated the film's hairpin bends between Goon-ish comedy and the horror of a world decimated by nuclear winter and is given one of the film's most touching monologues, spoken to her sleeping lover as she goes through his good points: 'He's like a sheet of white paper. I haven't seen a sheet of white paper for years I could draw a face on! And I'll say this for him, he's always here . . . he's straight, flat, stupid as the sun . . . and there's nobody else.'

After this foray into a post-apocalyptic future, a project set in the past had been mooted as Tushingham's next project, with the star set to appear in an adaptation of Jane Eyre that would have seen her playing the plain heroine opposite James Mason's Mr Rochester.[70] This project, to be produced by Mason, sadly failed to materialise; the rather-too-unambiguously pretty Susannah York played Jane Eyre opposite George C. Scott's Rochester in 1970 instead.[71] Hoping to make another period adaptation, a new film version of R. D. Blackmore's eighteenth-century-set Lorna Doone, Tushingham set up a production company called Movie Makers Ltd, together with director Desmond Davis (who had directed her in Girl with Green Eyes and Smashing Time).[72] But this project also failed to go ahead. It seemed that the star had limited luck when it came to historical settings. She wanted to do them partly because, she said to Photoplay, 'a woman can look a lot more feminine in period costume than in a dolly dress'.[73] Even when cast in a lavish historical epic such as Doctor Zhivago, she ruefully recalled, 'Everyone had lovely costumes but I was in a boilersuit and Wellingtons!'[74]

Over the course of the 1960s, responses to Rita Tushingham had changed markedly in light of much broader cultural revisions around female identity and appearance, and what constituted a suitable film-star face and body. She had gone from being 'the ugly girl' in 1961 to 'the girl with the knack' in 1965, although even by that point there was still no consensus on how her looks should be interpreted and understood. Within the space of a week in 1965, the Daily Mirror published a reader's letter that expressed frustration with 'seeing flawless beauties on TV who can't act. I would rather see more "ugly ducklings" like Rita Tushingham', while the paper's TV listings conversely described the star as 'young and attractive'.[75] Sometimes a compromise was reached by acknowledging the protean qualities of her appearance, as 'an ugly duckling who can look truly beautiful'.[76] The actress herself adopted a tactic of anticipating uncomplimentary comments about her appearance, as in her self-description as 'having a figure like an ironing board, hair like a mop and a face that a plastic surgeon could make his life's work' (although the same article in which these comments appear then goes on to suggest that she is doing herself 'far less than justice, for with her huge eyes and mobile mouth she has considerable waifish attraction').[77]

By *Smashing Time* in 1967, it no longer seemed outlandish that this big-eyed, blunt-fringed, vintage-wearing girl could be proclaimed 'the face of the sixties', as her character finds herself labelled in a newspaper headline in this film: a fully fledged swan rather than an ugly duckling. Indeed, by the beginning of the 1970s, a spate of articles looked back with disbelief at the (mis)categorisation of Tushingham as anything other than beautiful: 'Was Rita Tushingham ever all that ugly?', asked the *Evening Standard* in 1970. 'One remembers the big headlines of the early 1960s – "Found: the ugly girl" – They called her the plain Jane of British films. Then you look at her again. Could she really have been ugly? Or is it just that our ideas of ugliness have changed?'[78] And again in the same paper in 1971: 'It is difficult to understand how anyone once called her an ugly duckling . . . the truth is she is a strikingly beautiful girl.'[79] And again in the *TV Times* in 1973: 'It seems even odder, looking at this very lovely and vital young woman, that she should ever have been called the "ugly duckling" of British films. Obviously, tastes in looks as well as lifestyles have changed.'[80] A revolution in perceptions of feminine beauty, it is suggested, had taken place between the early 1960s and the early 1970s, enabling Rita Tushingham to move from outlandish novelty to mainstream female star. But this was not the case across the board. Her casting as another girl called Brenda, yet another Northerner coming down to London, in Hammer's *Straight on till Morning* (1972) was described in an advertisement for ABC cinemas as 'Rita Tushingham playing the role she is so good at: the ugly duckling'.[81] As one reviewer noted, 'Poor Tush looks frumpier than ever in this picture', playing a girl who, according to its press book, 'compensates for her ugliness and lack of love by living in her own world of fantasy princes and romantic princesses'.[82]

As producer Michael Carreras elaborated, *Straight On till Morning*'s Brenda was 'faced with the loneliness and eventual terror in the "jungle" that is life in any big city today'.[83] By the 1970s, it seemed that London was no longer a site of swinging liberation but a place of mortal danger where hopeful young girls newly arrived in the city were more likely to be taken in by baby-faced psychopaths than sympathetic schoolteachers. Brenda is only safe from the murderer because she does not conform to the comely availability of his usual victims and is only jeopardised when she attempts to do so by giving herself a make-over with a back-combed bouffant wig, heavy make-up, and a frilly high-necked blouse, an extraordinary moment of grotesque feminine masquerade. *Straight On till Morning* is an odd saraband for the sixties, and a rather nasty closing down of the utopian possibilities suggested by Tushingham's ingénue persona during that decade: an equivalent to Altamont in comparison to *The Knack*'s optimistic Woodstock. Perhaps

Tushingham's 1974 BBC sitcom, *No Strings*, written by Carla Lane, may be seen as a more amiable conclusion to the London flat-sharing trope that recurred throughout her early career, in which her hippy-ish poet ends up comically cohabiting with Keith Barron's uptight vet.

Conclusion

As Tushingham had suggested of that previous period of unemployment she had endured in the early 1960s, it could be very difficult to move from being a new discovery into getting the kind of regular work required to build a sustainable career beyond that award-winning debut, especially when regarded as such an unconventional embodiment of what a female film star could or should be. But the diversification of her career beyond its New Wave beginning into a range of genres, including epics, comedies, and romances, showed that it was possible to achieve stardom against the odds. According to Eileen Atkins, she was also hugely important in giving hope to actresses who felt that they fell short of the 'accepted prettiness' formerly required of film stars.[84]

If it proved harder for Tushingham to sustain that film career in Britain during the 1970s, then that had a lot to do with the country's impoverished film production base at that time, as well as personal decisions about prioritising her family over acting: she had her first daughter Dodonna in 1964 and her second Aisha in 1971, and relocated to Cornwall with her family.[85] But the partial stalling of Rita Tushingham's career beyond the 1960s perhaps also had something to do with her inextricable association with that decade's 'youthquake', as Sally Vincent has suggested: 'Few actresses, appealing in extreme youth, are allowed to grow up gracefully. Tushingham didn't have a prayer . . . She conveyed such luminosity, such brave vulnerability, she somehow impacted herself like a fly in amber.'[86] She was fixed in the Sixties, whether she wanted to be or not.

Eventually moving abroad to live with her second husband, cinematographer Ousama Rawi (the couple married in 1981), Tushingham made numerous films abroad during the 1970s and 1980s and was, 'she says with a slightly arch irony, *very* big in Germany for a while'.[87] Her major British comeback in the 1980s came with a role in the hugely popular BBC sitcom *Bread* in 1988, again written by Carla Lane, which placed the actress firmly back in Liverpudlian territory. This was also true of her role in the Beryl Bainbridge adaptation, *An Awfully Big Adventure* (1995), while *Resurrected* (1989) and *Under the Skin* (1997) both forged intertextual links to the British New Wave by casting Tushingham as key matriarchal figures. She was equally effective in a more supernatural vein in Nicolas

Roeg's unsettling *Puffball* (2007), and has continued to work fairly prolifically across a range of British film and television. Today, she also gives her name to the 'Rita Tushingham community centre' occasionally alluded to in *Coronation Street* (1960–), the soap opera with the same Salford provenance as *A Taste of Honey*, thus returning her persona right back to its Northern roots. Unlike her 1960s near-contemporaries Julie Christie, Susannah York, or Vanessa Redgrave, Tushingham would never have been seen as an English Rose, and this imposed certain limitations on the kinds of roles in which she was cast, even in her heyday. But there were definite advantages in being 'a reet larky bit of stoof' instead, and becoming the wide-eyed, courageous young heroine who perhaps best exemplified the new look and new horizons of the 1960s.

Notes

1. Peter Howell, 'The rise of the British actress', *Photoplay*, December 1966, p. 23.
2. Arthur Marwick, *The Sixties: Social and Cultural Transformation in Britain, France, Italy and the United States, 1958–74* (Oxford: Oxford University Press, 1998), p. 472.
3. Press book for *Fahrenheit 451*, BFI Library.
4. Quoted in Howell, 'The rise of the British actress', p. 40.
5. Tim Pulleine, 'A look back', *Films and Filming*, November 1986, p. 18.
6. Anonymous, 'People are talking about . . .', *Vogue* (US edition), November 1965, p. 152.
7. Sally Vincent, 'The honey trap', *The Guardian* (*Weekend* magazine), 22 March 1997, p. 42.
8. Christine Geraghty, 'Women and 60s British cinema: The development of the "Darling" girl', in Robert Murphy (ed.), *The British Cinema Book*, third edition (London: BFI Palgrave, 2009), p. 315.
9. Vincent, 'The honey trap', p. 42.
10. Alexander Chancellor, 'Whatever happened to the likely lass?', *The Sunday Telegraph Magazine*, 25 April 1999, p. 28.
11. Unlabelled article, *The Sunday Times*, 24 September 1961. Press cuttings file on Rita Tushingham, BFI Library.
12. Peter Evans, 'John Osborne seeking ugly girl for taste of honey', *Daily Express*, 2 March 1960, p. 5.
13. The story is recounted in Vincent, 'The honey trap', p. 40.
14. Peter Evans, 'Found: The ugly girl', *Daily Express*, 27 April 1960, p. 12. *Sunday Pictorial* treatment quoted in Vincent, 'The honey trap', p. 42.
15. Marjorie Proops, 'Honey for the bread and butter girl', *Daily Mirror*, 13 September 1961, p. 11.
16. Dick Richards, 'Rita's no honey – but this film tastes of success', *Daily Mirror*, 15 September 1961, p. 19.

17. George Stonier, 'A taste of honey', *Sight and Sound*, autumn 1961, p. 196.
18. Rita Tushingham in post-screening discussion of *A Taste of Honey* at BFI Southbank, 20 November 2011. Discussion archived online at http://www. bfi.org.uk/films-tv-people/4fc75e8178546
19. Marwick, *The Sixties*, p. 427, p. 430.
20. Ibid., pp. 422–3.
21. Marcia Landy, 'The other side of paradise: British cinema from an American perspective', in Justine Ashby and Andrew Higson (eds), *British Cinema, Past and Present* (London: Routledge, 2000), p. 72.
22. Kingsley Amis, 'Films', *The Guardian*, 19 April 1964, p. 25.
23. Evans, 'Found: The ugly girl', p. 12.
24. A. H. Weiler, 'A taste of honey', *The New York Times*, 1 May 1962, p. 15.
25. Patricia Lewis, 'Wide eyed appeal – in Tush's violet gaze', *Daily Express* 7 September 1961, p. 10.
26. Anonymous, 'Film virtues in A Taste of Honey', *The Times*, 13 September 1961.
27. Donald Zec, 'The odd girls out', *Daily Mirror*, 25 October 1961, p. 15.
28. Marjorie Proops, 'Why are you vain?', *Daily Mirror*, 11 April 1962, p. 18.
29. Anonymous, 'People are talking about . . .', p. 152.
30. Victor Davis, 'The Arab eye-opener on Golan Heights – Rita', *Daily Express*, 15 August 1974, p. 8.
31. Stewart Wavell, 'The girl with blue eyes', *The Guardian*, 26 May 1984, p. 9.
32. Peter Lewis, 'Romantic Rita, the girl with 11 rings on her fingers', *Daily Mail*, 7 April 1969. Press cuttings file on Rita Tushingham, BFI Library.
33. John Gale, 'The girl with the knack', *Observer Magazine*, 11 July 1965, p. 7.
34. Lewis, 'Wide eyed appeal – in Tush's violet gaze', p. 10. *The Sunday Times*, 24 September 1961. Press cuttings file on Rita Tushingham, BFI Library.
35. William Hickey, 'Actress falls in for Tony's "twin" parade', *Daily Express*, 5 June 1962, p. 3; emphasis in the original.
36. 'Well, do YOU think I look like Princess Margaret?', *TV World*, 10 April 1965. Taken from http://ritatushingham.com
37. Wavell, 'The girl with blue eyes', p. 9.
38. Proops, 'Honey for the bread and butter girl', p. 11; emphasis in the original.
39. Ibid.
40. She recalled Cannes being where she first encountered sophisticated new foodstuffs like whitebait and artichokes in Paul Carrol, 'Wish you were here', *Premiere*, June 1994, p. 52.
41. Press release in press cuttings file *A Taste of Honey*, BFI Library.
42. Evans, 'Found: The ugly girl', p. 12.
43. Exhibitors' campaign manual for *A Taste of Honey*, BFI Library.
44. Proops, 'Honey for the bread and butter girl', p. 11.
45. Press book for *Girl with Green Eyes*, BFI Library.
46. Zec, 'The odd girls out', p. 15.

47. Anonymous, 'From the north', *The Guardian*, 13 September 1961, p. 8.
48. Ian Johnson, 'The reluctant stars', *Films and Filming*, May 1962, p. 24.
49. Another emergent male star of the 1960s, Oliver Reed, reflected on his own 'Neolithic' looks as having a different kind of charm from the traditional male idol, and saw his own stardom in the wider context of 'this era of Courtenays and Finneys and the mill boys and miners who came from all over the world and had new appeal'. Anonymous, 'Eyes and ears: Photoplay's gossip section', *Photoplay*, September 1966, p. 6.
50. Anonymous, 'Rita's new rival: a motorcycle', *Evening Standard*, 13 July 1962.
51. Gale, 'The girl with the knack', p. 6.
52. While performing in the play, she experienced at first hand the consequences of its controversial references to rape: 'I heard flap-flap-flap-flap-flap, and thought, "What's that? It's not applause". It was all the seats going up as they walked out.' Ibid., p. 6.
53. See Terence Kelly, *A Competitive Cinema* (London: Institute of Economic Affairs, 1966), p. 35.
54. Judith Simons, 'Sarne regrets', *Daily Express*, 8 March 1963, p. 8.
55. Robert Murphy, *Sixties British Cinema* (London: BFI, 1992), p. 83.
56. Graham Clarke, 'A Place to Go', *Kine Weekly*, 2 April 1964, p. 10.
57. Anonymous [John Russell Taylor], 'A sad little Irish love story', *The Times*, 14 May 1964, p. 8.
58. Gale, 'The girl with the knack', p. 4.
59. Gerald McCann quoted in Iain R. Webb, *Foale and Tuffin: The Sixties. A Decade in Fashion* (London: ACC, 2009), p. 99.
60. Press book for *The Knack*, BFI Library.
61. Anonymous, 'The ten most popular young players of 65', *Box Office*, 28 February 1966, p. 77.
62. In her best-known role in *Georgy Girl* (1966), Lynn Redgrave was described by one US reviewer as 'an ugly duckling of a girl who never gets even close to becoming a swan', drawing on the film's intense internal debates about whether or not her character can ever be beautiful. Michael Stern, 'Angry-young-man fairy tale', *The New York Times*, 18 October 1966, p. 48.
63. Anonymous, 'People are talking about . . .', p. 152.
64. Gale, 'The girl with the knack', p. 4.
65. Michael Billington, 'Satire on modern life', *The Times*, 27 December 1967, p. 12.
66. Davis cited in Derek Todd, 'Paramount produces a peg to hang "swinging London"', *Kine Weekly*, 20 May 1967, p. 12.
67. Anonymous, 'A sad little Irish love story', p. 8.
68. Lewis, 'Romantic Rita, the girl with 11 rings on her fingers'. She cites Keaton as inspiration in an interview in the *Straight on till Morning* press book, too. Years later she also picked *The Navigator* (1924) as her all-time favourite film. 'Cine File', *The Guardian*, 9 May 1997, p. 8.
69. Penelope Mortimer, 'Charley as exhibit A', *The Observer*, 10 November 1968,

p. 24. Anonymous, 'Diamonds for breakfast', *Monthly Film Bulletin*, 1 January 1968, p. 200.

70. Project is mentioned in Tony Toon, 'Me and the guru', *Photoplay*, October 1969, p. 20.

71. Project was announced in *Variety*, 5 April 1967, p. 4. A further report described it as being prepared to film in Ireland with a budget of $1 million. *Variety*, 10 December 1969, p. 35.

72. See *Variety*, 5 August 1970, p. 15.

73. Ian Brown, 'Tushingham', *Photoplay*, April 1968, p. 8. At one point, she had even been slated to star in Woodfall's *Tom Jones* (1963) alongside Albert Finney, but this did not come to pass. See Anonymous, 'Has London had it?', *The Guardian*, 26 October 1962, p. 10.

74. McFarlane, *Autobiography of British Cinema*, p. 579.

75. Anonymous, 'Viewpoint: Your angle on events', *Daily Mirror*, 29 March 1965, p. 14. Ken Irwin, 'Tonight's view', *Daily Mirror*, 8 April 1965, p. 18.

76. Gale, 'The girl with the knack', p. 4.

77. Brown, 'Tushingham', p. 8.

78. *Evening Standard*, 18 March 1970. Press cuttings file on Rita Tushingham, BFI Library.

79. Sydney Edwards, *Evening Standard*, 29 October 1971. Press cuttings file on Rita Tushingham, BFI Library.

80. Knowles, 'The girl with concern in her eyes'.

81. Advertisement in *Daily Express*, 1 July 1972, p. 14.

82. Arthur Thirkell, 'Pretty tough on Tush', *Daily Mirror*, 7 July 1972, p. 20. Despite all the hyperbole about her misrecognised beauty, the swan reverted to being described as 'saucer-eyed ugly duckling' in the 'William Hickey' column in the *Daily Express*, 14 March 1973, p. 14. *Straight on till Morning* press book, BFI Library. Tushingham would appear in another fable based on a children's story shortly after: *Red Riding Hood* for ITV's 'Armchair Theatre' strand, first broadcast 9 October 1973.

83. *Straight On till Morning* press book, BFI Library.

84. Colvin, 'Mystery moves', p. 17.

85. The press book for *Straight on till Morning* included an article entitled 'Meet the Two Tushinghams' that conceptualised the actress's work–life balance in terms of a dual self: 'She is an actress of enormous talent. And she is a devoted wife and mother of two daughters . . . Talking to her, one realises very quickly that Rita Tushingham and Mrs Bicknell are two people – not so very different but two separate identities.'

86. Vincent, 'The honey trap', p. 42.

87. Ibid.; emphasis in the original.

CHAPTER 5

'A Constant Threat':
Glenda Jackson and the Challenges
of Seventies Stardom

Just as the sixties were ending and harbingers of the coming decade were being sought, an American studio executive selected Glenda Jackson as 'the face of the 70s'.[1] The star seemed to represent a new mood in British female stardom. As Alexander Walker argued in his survey of British cinema from the period, whereas a star like Julie Christie 'had given a characteristic burnish to the sixties', the figure who best represented the frame of mind of 1970s British cinema was Jackson, whose 'articulate, pragmatic, rebarbative nature seemed in tune with the raw new decade'.[2] Jackson had first risen to prominence as a screen actor in the final years of the 1960s, having already built a formidable reputation on stage. She then went on to sustain a highly prolific film career throughout the 1970s, an especially remarkable achievement given that it took place during one of the least financially stable periods in British cinema's history, as precipitously declining audience numbers and the withdrawal of American funding from a national industry that had become reliant upon it resulted in falling levels of production. To be a star 'in Britain's current film climate', one journalist noted in 1977, you had to be 'strong, determined and realistic because if not, you will fall by the wayside'.[3] The wayside may have been the fate of many actresses at that time but Glenda Jackson managed to confound the general rule by being very much a British female star *of* the 1970s, one whose film career took off on the cusp of that beleaguered decade and whose greatest success would take place within it.

From 1969 onwards, the year of her first Oscar-winning starring role in *Women in Love*, Glenda Jackson achieved the rare feat of building a female star career and combining her awards success with significant international bankability. The second of her two Best Actress Oscars came for her comedy role in *A Touch of Class* (1973), and in between those two Academy Awards came a British Academy of Film and Television Arts (BAFTA) Award for her performance in *Sunday Bloody Sunday* (1971), and an unprecedented two Emmy Awards for her regal starring role in the television series *Elizabeth R* (1971). One of Jackson's primary assets was that she was venerated as a representative of a great British theatrical acting tradition and, rather like Maggie Smith at about the same time and Judi Dench and Helen Mirren more recently, this meant that she functioned as prime 'award bait'. Explaining why she'd been cast as legendary actress Sarah Bernhardt in *The Incredible Sarah* (1976), director Richard Fleischer explained that 'Sarah was the greatest actress of her day and Glenda Jackson is the greatest today'.[4] For Melvin Frank, the director of *A Touch of Class*, she was 'the most magnificent acting instrument of our time', and he made a link between her acting prowess and the epitome of British quality precision engineering when he remarked that directing her was 'like taking the controls of a new Rolls-Royce, gliding effortlessly, smoothly'.[5]

In 1971 Jackson became the sixth most popular star at the British box office.[6] She also appeared in *Box Office*'s list of the top ten female stars in US cinemas for 1972, 1973, 1975, and 1978, among the company of Jane Fonda, Barbra Streisand, Ali MacGraw, Faye Dunaway, and Diane Keaton, and more often than not was the only British woman in such company.[7] This star status gave her a certain amount of financial leverage, as she noted later in the decade. 'I'm certainly not bankable in the way that, say, Barbra Streisand is. But your name can help a small project,' she said, citing the example of *Stevie* (1978): 'When I said I would commit to it, the money was forthcoming. Mind you, it was a very *small* amount of money.'[8]

But it says something about Jackson's ability to embody the pessimistic zeitgeist of the 1970s that even when she was at the height of her popularity in 1972, she felt that her success was already on the wane: 'There is simply no point in waiting around to start going downhill. I believe every actress has a peak, and my heyday is already past.'[9] But in any case, film stardom wasn't such a great accolade for Jackson who described it as 'totally contrived' and distanced herself from it: 'I don't think of myself in this way – at all. I find it really amusing to see the way in which the press are always pushing me. The whole star thing is really something which they create themselves, and as much for themselves as anybody.'[10] She firmly refuted her own supposed star appeal – 'There's nothing so personally intriguing about me that someone would drag themselves out on a rainy night to see my movies,' she said – and was 'totally unsentimental' about the Oscars she received that, as John Heilpurn argued in 1975, 'don't seem to matter a damn to her'.[11] She had already snubbed, perhaps slightly ostentatiously, the glamorous trappings of theatrical stardom in the 1960s, happily admitting to wearing 'a £2 cotton frock from M&S' to attend a party thrown by

Jackie Kennedy in honour of the Royal Shakespeare Company's US tour.[12] Jackson seemed to have little regard for promotional niceties, admitting ahead of the film's release that she thought her performance in *Bequest to the Nation* (1973) was 'as bad . . . as I ever have been, certainly as far as overacting goes. Somehow when we started I thought it was going to be all right but it turned to ashes in my mouth.'[13] Such unusual levels of candour incurred the wrath of her producer Hal Wallis: 'Glenda, sweetheart,' ran a cable from him, 'will you please stop saying unkind things or no-one will go to see the movie'.[14] At times she almost seemed to be sending up and subverting her movies from within, as with Pauline Kael's observation of *The Romantic Englishwoman* (1975) that the actress was carrying 'no-nonsense precision to the point of brutality; she doesn't just speak her lines – she flicks them out, disgustedly'.[15] Kael's review tallies with Sue Harper's comments on a quality of disavowal being the keynote female performances in 1970s British cinema: a refusal to play things straight and sincere but to deploy instead devices such as irony, detachment, or parody to put up a boundary between performer and role.[16] This certainly fits many of the performances Jackson gave on-screen as well as the presentation of her off-screen self.

Jackson carried disavowal to its ultimate extreme by querying the usefulness of her entire profession, frequently stating her desire to do something more socially beneficial instead: 'I feel quite silly at the moment, when all I can do is open bazaars or fetes. I really want to become involved more directly, maybe on a voluntary basis.'[17] Despite these comments being dismissed by Alexander Walker as nothing more than a 'fetishistic disowning of her own fame', Jackson was eventually as good as her word and she left the acting profession altogether to take up a new career in politics in the early 1990s.[18] That decision to abandon the vicissitudes and trivialities of screen and stage was of a piece with the star persona she had built up in the preceding years, of being a formidable woman with the 'hauteur of a high priestess' and 'an authentically abrasive quality'.[19] In fact, 'abrasive' was an adjective to which critics and reviewers frequently turned in an attempt to conjure Jackson's distinctive personality, as though its evocation of roughness, hardness, and even an edge of aggression, best represented this new kind of female (anti)star.[20] Her sex appeal, wrote one critic, was not seductively enticing but had instead 'the sulking quality of a sleeping volcano, a constant threat'.[21] It was this challenging, threatening side, even in her comedies, that made her something quite new and unlike any other female star working in British cinema at that time, as well as the perfect star for a decade generally seen as riven with discontent.[22]

A Touch of Class Embodiment: Hands, Face, Voice, Body

Jackson's frequent playing of monarchs and other aristocratic roles belied her rather more humble origins in working-class Merseyside, eldest daughter of a bricklayer and a cleaner. Although she went to a girls' grammar school, being a member of the first generation to benefit from the Education Act of 1944, Jackson left aged fifteen to take up a job at Boots the chemists, eventually working her way up to the cosmetics counter, but also trying her hand at amateur dramatics in her spare time. Encouraged to apply to drama school by a friend who thought she had the potential to go professional, Glenda Jackson wrote to the only one she had heard of, the Royal Academy of Dramatic Art (RADA), and after a successful audition, won a place and the scholarship that enabled her to take it up. However, upon graduating in 1957, just one year after Albert Finney (Jackson's *exact* contemporary, both of them born on 9 May 1936), she was warned to expect unemployment since she was 'too young for the sort of parts they thought would suit me – like 43-year-old chars'.[23] The new working-class realism in theatre, film, and television that enabled someone like Finney to escape the kind of reductive supporting casting that may have been his lot a few years before and soar to fame as the bullish, pint-sinking hero of *Saturday Night and Sunday Morning* (1960) didn't seem to benefit Jackson in quite the same way. She made a very brief appearance perched on a piano at a party in *This Sporting Life* (1963) but it wasn't the British New Wave cinema that gave Jackson her opportunity to break into cinema; perhaps there was room for only one Merseyside girl with un-starry looks at the time, and Rita Tushingham had already won that mantle. Instead it was Jackson's adoption by the Royal Shakespeare Company (RSC) under Peter Brook in 1964 that proved her watershed moment. The RSC enabled her to move beyond the patronising working-class stage roles that RADA had warned her lay in store (if she was lucky) and instead she became a linchpin of its experiments in the 'theatre of cruelty'. Two of these productions were eventually adapted for film: *The Persecution and Assassination of Jean-Paul Marat as Performed by the Inmates of the Asylum of Charenton under the Direction of the Marquis de Sade,* known as the *Marat/Sade* for short (1967), in which Jackson played an asylum inmate playing the assassin Charlotte Corday, and *Tell Me Lies* (1968), based on Brook's anti-Vietnam production *US* in which Jackson was entrusted with the Thanatos-heavy closing monologue inviting bombs to rain down on London. It was through the auspices of the big-screen versions of those celebrated stage productions that Jackson accidentally began a career as a film actor.

This professional move was not something she had anticipated when first starting out as an actress because 'in England at any rate, film actresses were blonde and pretty – and I was neither of those'.[24] In some ways, her suspicions were entirely justified: 'You'll never sell her to the Rank Organisation', observed one agent who saw Jackson on stage while he was talent-spotting at RADA.[25] As Margaret Hinxman later observed, 'those raw-boned features and angular proportions would never have been considered leading lady material' in previous decades.[26] Although Jackson's 'discovery' happened towards the end of the 1960s, her press treatment ended up being remarkably similar to Tushingham's when she had first been described as 'the ugly girl' in the early 1960s even though one may have thought that things had changed over that decade and new types of look had become acceptable. Jackson was ungallantly described by journalist Donald Zec in 1970 as 'sallow faced, with razor-lopped hair resembling an argument between streaky bacon and a shredding machine', and more likely to launch 'a couple of Gravesend dredgers' than a thousand ships.[27] For Victor Davis in 1969, she was no 'glamour girl, not exactly your archetypal dolly' but instead 'a worn-looking mother of an eight-month-old son . . . no starlet doing a handstand in her mini'.[28]

Glenda Jackson's physiognomy and physical appearance were often written about in terms that invoked her class background, as though her social provenance was written indelibly on her body. For instance, Alexander Walker described her looks as more indebted to 'elbow-grease than facials', indirectly alluding to her mother's cleaning job perhaps, while he discerns the inheritance of her father in her large strong hands.[29] This particular physical feature was also remarked upon by John Heilpurn, describing them as 'large and worn: worker's hands, rough from cleaning the house perhaps or washing dishes'– more references to abrasion – while another critic thought Jackson's 'large, capable hands' looked like they had 'done more than their fair share of spud-bashing'.[30] Peter Evans linked Jackson's face to her class background even more decisively in this profile from 1970:

> At first sight, it is a factory face, more gargoyle than coquette. The sort of face you once saw travelling third-class in northern towns. A face worn like a pale battle scar from the old days of class warfare. There is sadness in it and hardness and all of the 33 years it has taken to build.[31]

Not only were her labouring hands a giveaway, but class was apparently written all over on her proletarian 'factory face', which acted as a kind of throwback to previous class conflict. But the very fact that a woman with this appearance could become a film star was then read as an indication of far-reaching social mobility.[32] Although probably just intended as a cruel slur on her looks, the description of her 'thin, apprehensive, Northern, white face' looking 'like Tom Courtenay in drag' inadvertently pointed to her kinship with the ground-breaking male actors from working-class origins who had become stars.[33] However, it proved far harder for the press to accept a female star who sometimes looked pale, sad, or hard.

But as with Tushingham before her, the jury was out on Jackson's looks. Her appearance was hard to pin down, according to journalist Catherine Stott: 'a face which, while not actually anonymous, can change so much from one day to the next, from one emotion to another, to be barely recognisable'.[34] Alexander Walker suggests that Jackson evaded conventional categorisation, being 'neither glamour symbol, not yet strident drudge', and director Ken Russell, who worked with Jackson numerous times, concurred with this assessment: 'Sometimes she looks plain ugly, sometimes just plain and then sometimes the most beautiful creature one has ever seen.'[35] Despite being 'Tom Courtenay in drag' for one writer, the style mavens of *Harpers* magazine begged to differ with this view and felt that Jackson was worthy of inclusion in their list of the world's most beautiful women, due to her high cheekbones and bewitching feline eyes.[36] Jackson herself contended that it was all a matter of performance skill: 'Anyone can *act* being beautiful with sufficient conviction to convince the people watching.'[37] Given these ambiguities around the way she looked, it is little wonder that her most famous line relating to her personal attractiveness – 'beauty like what I have got' – came in hilariously ungrammatical form in the parodic context of her appearance as Cleopatra on *The Morecambe and Wise Show* in 1971.

Glenda Jackson's look was clearly something new. But in terms of her persona, how she sounded was at least as important. Described tellingly as '*that* familiar voice' by one of her biographers, Jackson's low-pitched clear and sharp enunciation flies in the face of the general trend identified by James Naremore for film actors' voices to be 'less elitist, closer to speech on the street', although it fits much more readily into a British theatrical vocal tradition.[38] Jackson's performative voice is rather patrician-sounding, with the absence of a regional accent suggesting an altogether different class background from the one supposedly written on her hands and face, or at least its alteration through careful vocal training (although a friend from her amateur dramatic days remembers it already being 'very loud, very deep, very strong and resonant' even when she was a teenager).[39] Basically unchanging from role to role, with no Meryl Streep-esque mastery of diverse accents, Jackson's voice is instantly identifiable and, according to Pauline Kael, 'as easy to imitate as Bette Davis'.[40] Crueller critics may

Figure 5.1 Beauty like what she has got: Glenda Jackson as Gudrun in
Women in Love (1969).

have compared it to 'someone trying to make herself heard on a bad telephone' and seen its oratorical qualities as part of a tendency for over-acting, but its emphatic forcefulness could also be seen as a strength.[41] As noted by Kael in relation to *The Romantic Englishwoman*, it cannot do blurry feminine indecisiveness, but it can be very effective when 'flicking out lines' contemptuously.[42] When it is matched with the right role, such as Queen Elizabeth I, its dry clarity goes a long way in suggesting the gravity of a character. The voice can also be employed for comic purposes, as with her rolling elongation of the word 'struck' when she is upbraiding George Segal's crass American sexual slang 'struck out' in *A Touch of Class*, or her hilarious declamatory approach to the terrible lines she's been given by Ernie Wise when playing Cleopatra to his Mark Antony. More gently modulated, its resolve imbues Stevie Smith's statement 'I loved my aunt' in *Stevie* not only with warmth but substance.

But beyond even her hands, face, or voice, it was Jackson's body and her willingness to display it that was perhaps the single most extensively commented-upon aspect of her stardom in the early part of the 1970s, even earning her the title 'Britain's first lady of flesh'.[43] Jackson's earlier theatrical work with Peter Brook had been, David Nathan suggests, 'the first time a serious actress had fully disrobed in a serious cause in public', and she carried this fearless dedication to her art into her cinema work with nude scenes in *Negatives* (1968), *Women in Love*, *The Music Lovers* (1970), *Sunday Bloody Sunday*, and *The Romantic Englishwoman*.[44] This attracted some sarcastic commentary; one 1970 headline is indicative of the overall tone: 'I took off my clothes for reasons that were deeply intellectual'.[45] A 'fascination with sexuality and with the body', as Andrew Higson suggests, 'pervaded most aspects of 1970s cinema', ranging from highbrow productions taking advantage of fewer censorship constraints than ever before, through to what Leon Hunt calls the 'permissive populism' of more lowbrow modes, particularly the sexploitation cycle.[46] Glenda Jackson represented the former category just as neatly as Mary Millington exemplified the latter.[47]

Despite confessing to being slightly bemused at 'getting all these scripts with nude scenes [when] I've got varicose veins, piano legs and no tits', Jackson nonetheless became a high-end sex symbol, hailed as 'the intellectual's Raquel Welch' and greeting this news with a disbelieving, 'How lovely! How bloody weird!'[48] She was seen to possess some of the sexual frankness of continental European stars, with director Silvio Narizzano describing her as 'the only British actress who can compare with Simone Signoret and Jeanne Moreau' in her unembellished mature sexuality.[49] To some, her face may have been un-coquettishly plain and 'third-class' but elsewhere it was described as 'so erotically explicit it could almost be a diagram for an advanced sex education class'.[50] In fact, her lack of conventional film-star allure became a guarantor of her greater erotic authenticity, as 'a down-to-earth actress' who was 'palpably a part of real life as we know it'.[51] The press even seized upon Jackson's previous job working on the chemist's 'bilious attack and laxatives counter' as indicative of her robustly unromantic approach to the body and its manifold embarrassments.[52]

The 'Man within Oneself' and the 'Star as Feminist'

Her handshake with George Segal to seal the deal in agreeing to have an affair in *A Touch of Class* spoke of a no-nonsense liberated sexuality. But for every representation of Jackson's sexuality as a pragmatic, purely physical entity, there were others that rendered her eroticism as something more dangerous – the 'constant threat' of a volcanic explosion waiting to happen, or combative and even animalistic in its 'undiluted paw and claw passions'.[53] This idea of Jackson as a threatening figure was sometimes expressed in terms of her propensity for 'ball-breaking' or an even more extreme form of genital attack, according to Donald Zec: 'I've heard it said of her: "she can castrate you with her eyes"' – quite a trick.[54] In *Negatives* she subjects Peter McInery's character to cruel sexual taunts, telling him, 'You look ludicrous when you make love, do you know that? . . . I find you hilarious.' Likewise, Oliver Reed's Gerald in *Women in Love* is trapped with Jackson's Gudrun in a dark and damaging relationship that must conclude with the death of one or both of them. There are strong suggestions of *vagina dentata* in that film, replete with shots foregrounding Jackson's mouth, sometimes bearing sharp gritted teeth, described in the press as 'designed for crunching up bones'.[55] Or, alternatively, her mouth is wide open in mocking Medusan laughter or strange rapture, as with the disorienting sequence after frightening away Gerald's cattle, in which her accusation of non-ownership is markedly oral: 'They're not yours, you haven't swallowed them.'

The threat of all-engulfing orifices continues in Jackson's subsequent film with Ken Russell, *The Music Lovers*, with a similar focus on Jackson's mouth: eating; swigging champagne; bloody, and shot in extreme close-up after a violent sexual encounter; laughing hysterically as her character Nina succumbs to madness. But the ultimate expression of castration anxiety comes in that film's honeymoon sequence on the train, in which the sexually frustrated Nina attempts to seduce a revolted Tchaikovsky, with the feverishly rocking camera drawn inexorably up into the ensnaring and perilous-looking wire hoops of her crinoline skirt. The scene's climactic display of the completely naked orgasmic female body somehow confounds the male gaze; as Sue Harper suggests, it is 'the reverse of erotic' rather than its fulfilment.[56]

Such representations are not limited to Jackson's films with Ken Russell alone, striking though they are. Her version of Emma Hamilton in *Bequest to the Nation*, whatever Jackson felt about its failings as a performance, is certainly iconoclastic. In its vulgarity and aggression, showing Emma swigging back alcohol and laughing derisively at her ageing lover, it differs markedly from Vivien Leigh's daintier version in *That Hamilton Woman* (1941). Jackson's comedy performances also have intimations of the 'constant threat' she poses: even in her sketch with Morecambe and Wise, she is a vampily dominant Cleopatra declaring that 'all men are fools', while George Segal suffers the figurative emasculation of a paralysing back spasm on the brink of making love to her in *A Touch of Class*. One widely used publicity still for that film shows Jackson brandishing a large knife, ostensibly for chopping vegetables but the symbolism is vivid. One of the most quoted comments about the actress came from her husband Roy Hodges, who said, 'If she'd gone into politics she'd be Prime Minister, if she'd gone into crime, she'd be Jack the Ripper,' aligning his soon-to-be-ex-wife not only with female eminence in traditionally male preserves but also with one of the world's most infamous knife-wielders.[57]

Jackson herself frequently spoke up for finding 'the man within oneself', urging women 'to develop their own "masculine" qualities of independence, pride, courage and open sexuality'.[58] Perhaps it was this mobilisation of male qualities, Alexander Walker suggested, that disquieted some men, 'for they sense the male spirit inside the undoubtedly female container'.[59] She played archetypal feminine stage roles such as Hedda Gabler and Cleopatra not 'doused in femininity' but as a 'cross, barking person' and a 'tough, crop-haired' woman respectively.[60] Her emphatically unswoony Ophelia in the RSC's 1965 *Hamlet* was hailed by Penelope Gilliat as 'Ophelia, Prince of Stratford' for managing to effect 'a modern blurring of the sexual boundaries' and even outshining David Warner's Dane.[61] This displacement of the male lead is something Jackson achieves several times in her films, revolting against potential marginalisation as muse or helpmeet in *The Music Lovers* and *A Bequest to the Nation* to become the dominant figure in each film. A close-up of *her* emotionally hollow face, as Nina is finally claimed by the lunatic asylum, provides the former film's harrowing final image, not the face of Tchaikovsky, its ostensible protagonist.

Vivid images of androgyny and bisexuality were infused throughout early 1970s British popular culture, particularly courtesy of pop stars like David Bowie and Marc Bolan, and a great many of Glenda Jackson's screen performances from around that period also partook in this atmosphere of gender ambiguity and performativity: dressing up as Ethel Le Neve opposite Peter McEnery's impersonation of Doctor Crippen in *Negatives*; doing a campy pantomime of Tchaikovsky's wife at the behest of the gay artist Loerke in *Women in Love* (the role she would essay in earnest in *The Music Lovers*); transforming herself into a living icon as the monarch in *Elizabeth R*; obsessively and murderously role-playing as one of the sister servants in Jean Genet's *The Maids* (1974), a play originally intended to be played entirely by male actors in drag.[62] Jackson seemed ideally suited too to depicting the new kind of sexual plurality in the air, with *Sunday Bloody Sunday* setting the tone for this particular strand in her career. In it, Jackson played Alex, a divorcée in her thirties who is in a relationship with Bob (Murray Head), a younger bisexual man who is simultaneously in a relationship with a middle-aged doctor, Daniel (Peter Finch): the awkward overlaps in their interpersonal connections are neatly suggested by their shared use of a telephone answering service. Trying to break free from monogamous commitment but still feeling the lure of it nonetheless, struggling to conceal her jealousy when Bob disappears off to see his other lover, Jackson's Alex exemplified what *Vogue*'s critic called 'the terrors of becoming a liberated woman'.[63] Her life is lived provisionally – making instant coffee from the hot tap rather than boiling a kettle, the furniture in her flat covered in dustsheets – in a way that no longer seems swinging but desperate. The old bourgeois certainties have been replaced, as Paul Newland suggests, by 'loneliness and anxiety at best, and alienation and despair at worst', the characters' predicaments in the film mirroring the wider crises of British society in the early 1970s.[64] The very first line of dialogue in the film, 'Now tell me if you feel anything at all?' – Daniel's words to a patient during a consultation – seems to apply more broadly to an exhausted, numb nation all out of swing. The King's Road, Chelsea, is no longer the thoroughfare of carefree hedonism, it's where the heroin addicts go to get their medically necessary fix from the all-night pharmacy. A news bulletin playing on Daniel's car radio informs us that Britain is facing its 'most serious economic crisis since the war', with industrial action imminent and mass unemployment looming. Even Alex's job as careers counsellor refers to this 'state of emergency' (to use Dominic Sandbrook's phrase describing early seventies Britain), as her task is to try to get work for newly redundant middle managers, an endeavour that is doomed to failure. She sleeps with one of them as a kind of recompense but her true object of desire remains the elusive Bob whose body she can fleetingly ogle as he showers but who will never fully commit to her (even if that is what she wants, which is by no means certain).

The ground-breaking sexual multiplicity presented in *Sunday Bloody Sunday* could also be found in a lesser-known film that Jackson made the following year, the wartime drama *The Triple Echo* (1972) in which she plays a remote rural smallholder harbouring an army deserter who then becomes her lover.[65] When the man disguises himself as her sister to avoid capture, both 'women' then come to the attention of a saturnine sergeant who happens to be stationed nearby, played by Oliver Reed. While the development of the relationship between the two men offered the film's main instance of 'gender trouble', Pauline Kael also noticed how Jackson's 'androgynous performance' as the mannish woman in love with a womanly man gave the film 'an extra dimension of sexual ambiguity'.[66]

Given all this association with masculinity and emasculation, it is instructive to think about the rise with Glenda Jackson in parallel with the contemporaneous rise of the Women's Liberation movement in the 1970s. Sometimes the connections were made explicit, as when her character in *A Touch of Class* was clearly seen reading Germaine Greer's best-selling 1970 polemic *The Female Eunuch* in bed. Off-screen, too, Jackson expressed her resistance to chauvinistic ideas of women's limited capabilities, and at the 1972 Women of the Year lunch, also attended by such female notables as Princess Anne, singer Lulu, tennis player Virginia Wade, feminist writer Jill Tweedie, and morality campaigner Mary Whitehouse, the actress gave a speech denouncing media images of women that reduced them to 'long hair, propensity for wearing pink, large bosom, and maddening giggle. Thoughtless on every subject but as her time is devoted to determining the values of washing-up liquids, can you wonder?'[67] A few years later, she also spoke out against the film industry's reductive attitudes to women:

> The story is always told from the man's point of view. The woman is always The Wife or, these days, The Mistress. Or The Mother. I don't like the idea that I have to be either decorative or motherly, that all heroines are supposed to be pretty.[68]

She couldn't go along with a passively written female role even if she tried, as proven by *The Romantic Englishwoman*, in which she completely undermined the film's patronising concept of the heroine as 'a woman who's unaware of her own emotions and has never had a clear thought in her life', in Pauline Kael's scathing assessment.[69]

Although it was frequently the object of dismissive mockery, 'Women's Lib' made an enormous and lasting impact on gender politics, helping to effect what feminist writer Beatrix Campbell described as 'real changes in women's expectations at work, in their personal lives, that can't really be recorded and measured statistically'.[70] Despite that difficulty Campbell identifies in gauging exactly how second-wave feminism changed perceptions of women, we may use the social barometer of celebrity to measure its progress. Film stars, as Richard Dyer has suggested, 'enact ways of making sense of the experience of being a person' in any given time, place, and situation, and like her 1970s contemporaries Jane Fonda and Barbra Streisand, Glenda Jackson 'made sense of the experience' of being a woman in the 1970s by presenting a very topical persona in terms of her associations with female independence and rebellion.[71] She was, to

Figure 5.2 Star as feminist: Glenda Jackson as Vicky, reading Germaine Greer on a dirty weekend, in the rom-com *A Touch of Class* (1972).

borrow Andrew Britton's phrase (first coined with Katharine Hepburn in mind), a striking example of the 'star as feminist', infiltrating the cultural mainstream.[72]

Nostalgia and Radicalism

Despite being hailed by Pauline Kael as a 'staccato' and 'wrenchingly modern' female star, Glenda Jackson actually played more historical roles than she did contemporary ones in the 1970s.[73] And even her roles in modern-day settings sometimes had a nostalgic tinge, harking back to the 'golden age' of Hollywood film. Jackson was described as 'a star in the same sort of mould as the Hollywood greats, an achievement which the film industry believed was no longer attainable', and appeared to be the modern equivalent of the redoubtable women stars who had flourished in the 1930s and 1940s.[74] Even as far back as *Women in Love*, critics had drawn parallels between Jackson and Katharine Hepburn, with one review describing the new star as 'burst[ing] upon the screen like a young, sturdier version' of Hepburn, 'with all of her animal magnetism'.[75] The similarities are clear: both slightly unconventional looking stars, russet haired with high cheekbones and angular features, potentially androgynous in appearance at times, each with distinctive voices, and both similarly sharp and self-possessed.

This parallel became even more noticeable after Jackson had appeared in *A Touch of Class*. Its sparring romance between London-based divorced fashion designer Vicky (played by Jackson) and visiting (married) American businessman Steve (George Segal) was deliberately reminiscent of the classical Hollywood romantic comedy in which two very different but equally matched protagonists enact the battle of the sexes and reach a loving rapprochement. Segal and Jackson's double act, compared variously to Katharine Hepburn and Spencer Tracy or Myrna Loy and William Powell, juxtaposed his brash American wise guy with her 'cold-assed supercilious Englishwoman' (as Jackson describes herself in the film), creating a sparky couple with 'complementary chemistry'.[76] *A Touch of Class* did such impressive box-office that it motivated Jackson and Segal's repeat-teaming in *Lost and Found* (1979), and the logic of pitting Jackson's supercilious Englishwoman against an all-American rough diamond also lay behind her pairing with Walter Matthau in the rom-com *House Calls* (1978), a teaming then repeated in the espionage caper *Hopscotch* (1980).

Acknowledging their Hollywood antecedents, these films often feature the physical rough-and-tumble associated with screwball comedy, with farcical situations involving sudden lumbar seizures, malfunctioning cars, combative games of golf and crockery smashing (*A Touch of Class*), medical jaw restraints and physical contortions to keep one foot on the floor (*House Calls*), and repeatedly broken limbs set in plaster or traction (*Lost and Found*). They also all make use of the genre's verbal badinage, albeit updated for a more permissive age. And although *A Touch of Class* concluded on a bittersweet note with the end of the couple's affair, *House Calls* closed on a more upbeat (and generically typical) public declaration of love followed by wrangling badinage about how long the trial period for the couple's romantic reunion should be: 'We'll try it for one week.' 'A week? How about a month?' 'Two weeks.' 'Three?' 'Two.'

For Jackson, a keen picturegoer as a child, 'all the great Hollywood stars' to whom she was being compared 'were virtually myth figures', whose presence had enlivened her early life.[77] She particularly admired Bette Davis, Joan Crawford, and Marlene Dietrich for 'the arrant rubbish they transformed, not just into something acceptable but even into something you believed'.[78] This admiration ended up being mutual, at least in Bette Davis's case: when she presented Jackson with the New York Critics Award for her work in *Women in Love*, Davis said she felt rather like Margo, the character she'd played in *All About Eve* (1950), handing over the trophy to her younger rival.[79] But it wasn't merely the self-possessed glamour of the Hollywood stars that Jackson admired, it was also their moments of radicalism, and here again Bette Davis figured as Jackson's benchmark of female achievement:

> If women are ever shown to have problems in a film, they are always *emotional* problems. What about the other problems, the other issues that women face every day of their lives? I haven't seen a woman take a stand on a moral issue in a film for about twenty years, not since Bette Davis played that librarian in *Storm Centre*.[80]

Moving into the late 1970s, it seemed that Jackson was increasingly keen to make films that engaged with the full range of female experience and not just their emotional or romantic lives. In order to get these kinds of projects off the ground, Jackson had capitalised on her relative commercial clout to form a production company with writer-producer Robert Enders, Bowden Productions and, in an arrangement with Brut Productions (which had produced *A Touch of Class*), Bowden made a film of Trevor Nunn's production of Ibsen's *Hedda Gabler*, shortened to *Hedda* (1975), *Stevie,* based on Hugh Whitemore's play about the English poet Stevie Smith, and *Nasty Habits* (1977), based on Muriel Spark's transposition of the Watergate scandal to a nunnery in *The Abbess of Crewe,* with Jackson playing the Nixon role in its film adaptation. Brut Productions also backed Jackson's *The Class of Miss MacMichael* (1978) centred on a London schoolteacher who is trying to turn around the lives of her delinquent teenage pupils in face of opposition from the school's reactionary headmaster, played by Oliver Reed (her third teaming with the actor).

Jackson received the Variety Club of Great Britain Best Actress Award in 1978 for her trio of performances in *The Class of Miss MacMichael*, *Stevie*, and *House Calls*. But as she had long predicted, interesting roles were getting harder to come by, as for many actresses in middle age. Already in her early thirties when she first became a film star, Jackson had long been aware of the intersecting effects of ageism and sexism in the film business:

> You don't get offered the young heroine parts in films – not that I've ever been a glamorous figure anyway – and there's a very long way to go before you can play the part of the old lady. It's a period in a woman's life for which very few good parts are written, and if I were to carry on acting, I can only see the offers getting less and less interesting. It's so different for the men in this business. They get all the wonderful parts written for a mature age, and we are just left out of it.[81]

Bowden's attempt to make a biopic of British scientist Rosalind Franklin in the early 1980s sadly came to nothing, although other television biopics did provide Jackson with the opportunity to flex her acting muscles and gain more awards in the 1980s, most notably playing the Oscar-winning actress who recovered from a debilitating stroke in the TV movie *The Patricia Neal Story* (1981).[82] Her films *Return of the Soldier* (1982) and *Turtle Diary* (1985) represented the subtle low-key pleasures of British middlebrow arthouse cinema, the latter being a product of United British Artists, a production consortium set up in 1982 in which Jackson was a founder member alongside Richard Johnson (the originator of the idea), Albert Finney, John Hurt, Diana Rigg, Maggie Smith, and director Peter Wood.[83] Other film roles in the Film on Four productions *Giro City* (1982) and *Business as Usual* (1988) returned to the 'Bette Davis in *Storm Centre*' ideal of making films centred on women taking a moral stand, as Jackson played a reporter battling censorship and a politicised shop manageress in them respectively. But the world of party politics, which promised the possibility for effecting real societal change (or at least trying to) had become a more urgent vocational calling than acting by the end of the 1980s, and a whole new career beckoned.

Conclusion: Politics and Back Again

Jackson was selected as the Labour candidate for the Hampstead and Highgate constituency and was elected as their MP in 1992. In entering the House of Commons, some said that she was merely exchanging one form of theatre for another: if that was the case, Jackson responded, then it was 'remarkably under-rehearsed, the lighting is appalling, and the acoustic is even worse.'[84]

Although her husband had once suggested that she could have been the first female Prime Minister, by the time Jackson finally entered Parliament someone else had got there first by some distance: Margaret Thatcher had been elected leader of her party in 1975 and became Conservative Prime Minister in 1979. Her policies came to define the decade that followed and Jackson recalled being so angry at Thatcher's infamous statement that there was 'no such thing as society' that upon hearing of it she walked straight into a closed French window and nearly broke her nose.[85] So determined was she to do something to oust Thatcher, she later reflected, that entering politics seemed more a matter of duty than choice:

> I could not stand what was happening to my country. Anything I could have done, that was legal, that would have got Margaret Thatcher out, I was prepared to do. There was no 'Oh, I'm tired of acting, I want to do something else.' I mean the country was going to THE DOGS![86]

Her enmity towards Thatcher did not diminish over time and, in April 2013, on the occasion of the former Prime Minister's death, Jackson swam against the general tide of tributes paid in the House of Commons to take the opportunity instead to denounce Thatcher's credo, which she defined as 'sharp elbows, sharp knees' and no concern extended to those who suffered in such Darwinian competition. Thatcher's claims to be a pioneer for women were likewise swatted away: 'The first Prime Minister of female gender, OK. But a woman? Not on my terms.' It was interesting to see someone who had so often had her own femininity as a star questioned then deploy the language of gender essentialism to impugn Thatcher. But Jackson's speech, the only one of its kind in the Commons that day, gave eloquent voice to those sections of British society who wished to bury Thatcher, not praise her – the same people who downloaded the song 'Ding Dong, the Witch is Dead' to make sure it came top of that week's UK music chart. The clip of her denunciation of Thatcher and her legacy went viral online, something that happened again the following year with another impromptu but powerfully scathing attack on Iain Duncan Smith whose reign at the Department for Work and Pensions (DWP) had, she argued, 'plunged thousands and thousands of our fellow citizens into the most abject penury', while he floated 'on his self-appointed sanctity'.[87]

The rhetorical command that Jackson displayed during these moments prompted commentators to recollect her stellar acting career, and to draw parallels between the different kinds of performance demanded by life in the theatre and life in parliament: 'Standing up in the Commons and giving speeches requires skilful oratory and presentation,' theatre critic David Benedict observed, so it was 'not a million miles away from the stage'.[88] Since Jackson had by then announced her intention to step down as an MP in 2015, there was some speculation about whether she would return to acting upon her retirement from the Commons, and she duly took her first acting role in more than thirty years in an Emile Zola radio adaptation for the BBC in 2015. Then, in early 2016, it was announced that she would be taking on the lead role in a gender-blind Old Vic production of *King Lear*, to be directed by Deborah Warner, enabling her to take on one of the great Shakespearean roles and reassume her position as one of the *grande dames* of the British acting establishment. But Jackson's re-embrace of the stage did not necessitate the blunting of her sharper critical edges, as these comments from 2015 on gender equality in theatre suggest:

> Where have been the remarkable new plays which have women as the driving engine as opposed to the adjunct for what is always, and inevitably, a male engine-driver? That hasn't changed. That is what is deeply, deeply depressing. It was exactly the same when I was still earning my living in the theatre – and I have seen no improvement in that area at all . . . Why don't creative people find women interesting?[89]

One may add: Who would dare to find Glenda Jackson uninteresting? Upon her return to acting, it appears that her abrasive persona still reverberates with 'the sharp, feminist note' she first struck back in the 1960s and 1970s.[90] Although there are numerous actresses of her generation flourishing in contemporary theatre, film, and television – Judi Dench, Maggie Smith, and Vanessa Redgrave among them – it is heartening to see that there is still room to accommodate the 'constant threat' posed by Glenda Jackson.

Notes

1. Barry Norman, 'The face of the 70s', *Daily Mail*, 2 April 1970. Press cuttings file on Glenda Jackson, BFI Library.
2. Alexander Walker, *National Heroes: British Cinema in the Seventies and Eighties* (London: Orion, 2005), p. 18. Christie's and Jackson's career paths converged several decades later when they appeared together in *The Return of the Soldier* (1982). Producer Simon Relph noted a certain professional impasse between them, despite their mutual respect: 'Julie and Glenda get on, but just. Basically they challenge one another. Julie thinks Glenda is more of an actress than she is, and Glenda thinks Julie is more of a star than she is. They admire those qualities in each other, but it's still a bridge to cross.' Ian

Woodward, *Glenda Jackson: A Study in Fire and Ice* (London: Coronet, 1986), pp. 268–9.

3. James Cameron-Wilson, 'The class of Miss Jackson', *What's On in London*, 2 December 1977. Press cuttings file on Glenda Jackson, BFI Library.

4. Quoted in Woodward, *Glenda Jackson*, p. 190.

5. Frank cited in David Castell, 'All heroines are supposed to be pretty', *Films Illustrated*, March 1979, p. 261.

6. See Peter Waymark, 'Richard Burton top draw in British cinemas', *The Times*, 30 December 1971, p. 2.

7. She took tenth place in the women's list in 'All-American favorites of 1972', *Box Office*, 9 July 1973, p. 19. That rose to fourth place in 1973's list, and twenty-first place overall in the top twenty-five money-making stars, in 'All-American favorites of 1973', *Box Office*, 12 August 1974, p. 19. She reached eighth position in the women's top ten in 'All-American favorites of 1975', *Box Office*, 20 September 1976, p. 19, and then tenth place for 1977. 'Diane Keaton and Al Pacino top box office 1977 star poll', *Box Office*, 22 May 1978, p. 3.

8. Castell, 'All heroines are supposed to be pretty', p. 260; emphasis in the original.

9. John Williams, 'Glenda Jackson: Why I'll give up acting', *Films Illustrated*, August 1972, p. 17.

10. Ibid.

11. Woodward, *Glenda Jackson*, p. 12, and John Heilpern, 'The magic of Glenda May', *The Observer*, 13 July 1975, p. 17.

12. Catherine Stott, 'Gudrun and Glenda', *The Guardian*, 28 November 1969, p. 9.

13. Sheridan Morley, 'A rather funny lady', *The Guardian*, 11 April 1973, p. 11.

14. Quoted in Woodward, *Glenda Jackson*, p. 141.

15. Pauline Kael, *When the Lights Go Down* (London and Boston: Marion Boyars, 1980), p. 94.

16. Harper, 'The British women's picture', p. 134.

17. Williams, 'Glenda Jackson: Why I'll give up acting', p. 17.

18. Walker, *National Heroes*, p. 24.

19. Janice Warman, 'My Brilliant Career: Glenda Jackson, Labour MP', *The Guardian* (careers section), 13 April 1996, p. 2. Eric Braun, 'The decade of change', *Films and Filming*, December 1973, p. 35.

20. Brian McFarlane and David Thomson both use the word to describe the actress in their encyclopaedia entries on her. McFarlane (ed.), *Encyclopedia of British Film*, p. 339, and Thomson, *A Biographical Dictionary of Film*, p. 368.

21. Unspecified co-star quoted in Peter Evans, 'I took my clothes off for reasons that were deeply intellectual', *People*, 12 April 1970. Press cuttings file on Glenda Jackson, BFI Library.

22. Just the titles of the histories of Britain in the 1970s suggest this ambiance: Philip Whitehead, *The Writing on the Wall: Britain in the Seventies* (London:

Michael Joseph, 1985); Alwyn W. Turner, *Crisis? What Crisis? Britain in the 1970s* (London: Aurum, 2008); Andy Beckett, *When the Lights Went Out: Britain in the Seventies* (London: Faber & Faber, 2010); and Dominic Sandbrook, *State of Emergency: Britain 1970–74* (London: Penguin, 2011).

23. Jackson cited in Norman, 'The face of the 70s'.

24. Gordon Gow, 'One-take Jackson', *Films and Filming*, January 1977, p. 13.

25. David Nathan, *Glenda Jackson* (Tunbridge Wells: Spellmount, 1984), p. 17.

26. Margaret Hinxman, untitled article, *The Sunday Telegraph*, 8 April 1973. Press cuttings file on Glenda Jackson, BFI Library.

27. Donald Zec, 'She was only a builder's daughter', *Daily Mirror*, 18 August 1970. Press cuttings file on Glenda Jackson, BFI Library.

28. Victor Davis, 'Glenda, putting Oscars firmly in their place', *Daily Express*, 4 December 1969, p. 17.

29. Alexander Walker, untitled article, *Evening Standard*, 18 April 1978. Press cuttings file on Glenda Jackson, BFI Library.

30. Heilpern, 'The magic of Glenda May', p. 17, and critic quoted in Woodward, *Glenda Jackson*, p. 89.

31. Evans, 'I took off my clothes for reasons that were deeply intellectual'.

32. The class discourse surrounding Jackson continued into the 1980s, with one journalist observing that in her dressing room at the Duke of York theatre 'while the gift-wrapped bottles of champagne remain unopened, a four pack of stout has two bottles missing', interpreting this as evidence that Jackson had 'stuck to her working-class tastes'. Unlabelled article, *Sunday Express*, 22 April 1984, p. 3. Press cuttings file on Glenda Jackson, BFI Library.

33. Kenneth Eastaugh, untitled article, *The Sun*, 30 December 1970. Press cuttings file on Glenda Jackson, BFI Library.

34. Stott, 'Gudrun and Glenda', p. 9.

35. Walker, *National Heroes*, p. 19, and Russell quoted in Woodward, *Glenda Jackson*, p. 291.

36. Her inclusion in the list of the world's most beautiful women in *Harpers* is mentioned in Stott, 'Gudrun and Glenda', p. 9, and Norman, 'The face of the 70s'.

37. Davis, 'Glenda, putting Oscars firmly in their place'; emphasis in the original.

38. Woodward, *Glenda Jackson*, p. 17. Naremore, *Acting in the Cinema*, p. 47; emphasis in the original.

39. Woodward, *Glenda Jackson*, p. 37. Although she was once described in an early press interview as sniffing 'in her flat, Northern way'. Davis, 'Glenda, putting Oscars firmly in their place', p. 17.

40. Pauline Kael, *Reeling* (New York: Warner Books, 1977), p. 300.

41. Nathan, *Glenda Jackson*, p. 36. John Ellis also cites Jackson as an example of 'overacting', typical of a kind of star who makes explicit that they 'are there as actor, saying "Look at me, I can perform."' John Ellis, *Visible Fictions* (London: Routledge and Kegan Paul, 1982) p. 105.

42. I discuss this in more detail in relation to a scene in which Jackson's character

Elizabeth confronts her novelist husband Lewis (Michael Caine) in 'Staccato and wrenchingly modern: Reflections on the 1970s stardom of Glenda Jackson', in Paul Newland (ed.), *Don't Look Now: British Cinema in the 1970s* (Bristol: Intellect Press, 2010), pp. 43–53.

43. William Hall, 'The naked truth about Glenda', *Evening News*, 19 January 1971. Press cuttings file on Glenda Jackson, BFI Library.

44. Nathan, *Glenda Jackson*, p. 28.

45. Evans, 'I took off my clothes for reasons that were deeply intellectual'.

46. Andrew Higson, 'A diversity of film practices: Renewing British cinema in the 1970s', in Bart Moore-Gilbert (ed.), *The Arts in the 1970s: Cultural Closure?* (London: Routledge, 1994), p. 233. Leon Hunt, *British Low Culture: From Safari Suits to Sexploitation* (London: Routledge, 1998), p. 2.

47. The sexploitation stardom of Mary Millington is discussed in Petley, 'There's something about Mary . . .', pp. 203–17. Sue Harper's discussion of Joan Collins, who also appeared in softcore films like *The Stud* (1978) and *The Bitch* (1979), is also relevant here. Harper, 'The British women's picture'.

48. Nathan, *Glenda Jackson*, p. 17. Raquel Welch comparison mentioned in Evans, 'I took off my clothes for reasons that were deeply intellectual', and in Heilpurn, 'The magic of Glenda May', p. 17. Jackson's response cited in Norman, 'The face of the 70s'.

49. Iain F. McAsh, 'A touch of another class', *Films Illustrated*, February 1978, p. 224. Her co-star Oliver Reed put it more plainly: 'Glenda is a very sexy bird'. Quoted in Woodward, *Glenda Jackson*, p. 224.

50. Evans, 'I took off my clothes for reasons that were deeply intellectual'.

51. Gow, 'One-take Jackson', p. 15.

52 Zec, 'She was only a builder's daughter'.

53. Eastaugh, untitled article.

54. Walker, *National Heroes*, p. 20. Donald Zec, untitled article, *Daily Mirror*, 16 February 1979. Press cuttings file on Glenda Jackson, BFI Library.

55. Norman, 'The face of the 70s'.

56. Harper, 'The British women's picture', p. 135.

57. Walker, *National Heroes*, p. 19.

58. Woodward, *Glenda Jackson*, p. 225.

59 Walker, untitled article.

60 Clare Colvin, 'As you like it or not', *Drama*, 1 April 1986, p. 12.

61. Penelope Gilliat, 'Ophelia, Prince of Stratford', *The Observer*, 22 August 1965, p. 19.

62. She later reanimated Sarah Bernhardt's triumphant performance as Joan of Arc, in male dress, in *The Incredible Sarah* (1976) and played a well-being campaigner rumoured to be transsexual in Robert Altman's satire *HealtH* (1980).

63. Anonymous, 'People are talking about: The unsettling reign of Glenda Jackson', *Vogue* (US edition), April 1971, p. 158.

64. Paul Newland, *British Films of the 1970s* (Manchester: Manchester University Press, 2013), p. 9.

65. Television director Michael Apted's debut feature, *The Triple Echo* (based on a novella by H. E. Bates), was done 'for very little money in six weeks to prove you could make a quality film in England for a limited budget', according to Jackson. Cameron-Wilson, 'The class of Miss Jackson'.

66. Kael, *Reeling*, p. 299.

67. Anonymous, 'Women sure of role in life', *The Guardian*, 10 October 1972, p. 8.

68. Jackson cited in Castell, 'All heroines are supposed to be pretty', p. 262.

69. Kael, *When the Lights Go Down*, p. 94. Jackson later reflected that she did not enjoy working with its director Joseph Losey who she found 'very much anti-female [with] something very misogynistic about him'. McFarlane, *Autobiography of British Cinema*, p. 317.

70. Cited in Whitehead, *The Writing on the Wall*, p. 321.

71. Dyer, *Heavenly Bodies*, p. 17.

72. Andrew Britton, *Katharine Hepburn: Star as Feminist* (London: Studio Vista, 1995). Jackson's most recent biographer also describes her as 'a passionate feminist'. Christopher Bryant, *Glenda Jackson: The Biography* (London: HarperCollins, 1999), p. 95.

73. Kael, *When the Lights Go Down*, p. 205.

74. Williams, 'Glenda Jackson: Why I'll give up acting', p. 17.

75. Quoted in Woodward, *Glenda Jackson*, p. 100.

76. McAsh, 'Lost and found', p. 412.

77. Gow, 'One-take Jackson', p. 13.

78. Ibid., p. 15.

79. Woodward, *Glenda Jackson*, p. 295. Like Davis, Jackson would also play Queen Elizabeth I twice and shave her hairline to do so. Jackson also stated her agreement with Davis's statement that she was sick of apologising for being intelligent. Joseph McBride, 'Glenda Jackson wins Oscars but still can't pick her scripts', *Variety*, 30 April 1975, p. 30.

80. Castell, 'All heroines are supposed to be pretty', p. 262; emphasis in the original.

81. Jackson cited in Williams, 'Glenda Jackson: Why I'll give up acting', p. 17.

82. Woodward, *Glenda Jackson*, p. 265. In the Patricia Neal film, she played opposite Dirk Bogarde who before meeting Jackson referred to her pejoratively as 'Glenda Sludge' but after admiring her professional skill and becoming firm friends with her was moved to dedicate his fourth volume of autobiography, *Backcloth*, to her 'with love'. John Coldstream (ed.), *Ever, Dirk: The Bogarde Letters* (London: Hachette, 2011), p. 25. Dirk Bogarde, *Backcloth* (London: Penguin, 1987).

83. Peter Noble, 'Top British talent in co-op venture', *Screen International*, 18 December 1982, p. 31. United British Artists' first film was *Champions* (1983). The company folded in the early 1990s.

84. Matt Trueman, 'Glenda Jackson says MPs wouldn't cut it in the theatre world', *The Guardian*, 22 January 2013. https://www.theguardian.com/stage/2013/jan/22/glenda-jackson-mps-theatre

85. Warman, 'My brilliant career: Glenda Jackson, Labour MP', p. 2.
86. Ginny Dougary, 'The lady is for turning', *Radio Times*, 21 November 2015, p. 120; emphasis in the original.
87. Smith cited in Siraj Datoo, 'People are going absolutely crazy for this clip of an MP attacking Iain Duncan Smith', *Buzzfeed*, 4 July 2014. https://www. buzzfeed.com/sirajdatoo/iain-duncan-smith-would-like-to-think-he-can-walk-on-water?utm_term=.hcWO88k7g#.ugNEmm7wD
88. Nick Clark, 'Glenda Jackson returns to stage', *The Independent*, 12 February 2016. http://www.independent.co.uk/arts-entertainment/theatre-dance/news/glenda-jackson-returns-to-stage-as-king-lear-in-gender-blind-production-at-old-vic-a6870956.html
89. Dalya Alberge, 'Glenda Jackson laments continuing lack of key acting roles for women', *The Observer*, 12 September 2015. https://www.theguardian.com/stage/2015/sep/12/glenda-jackson-equality-nothings-changed-women-stage-roles
90. Walker, untitled article.

CHAPTER 6

'From Schoolgirl to Stardom': The Discovery and Development of Helena Bonham Carter and Emily Lloyd in the 1980s and 1990s

The early 1980s is remembered as a moment of renaissance for British cinema, exemplified by screenwriter Colin Welland's repurposing of Paul Revere's proclamation 'The British are coming!' as he picked up one of the four Oscars awarded to *Chariots of Fire* (1981), including Best Picture.[1] And yet this night of British triumph on the international stage obscured the deeper problems facing UK film at that time. As John Hill points out, 1981 had seen the lowest rate of production since 1914, while admissions to British cinemas were plummeting towards the eventual all-time low of under 54 million recorded in 1984, just before the introduction of the multiplex helped to spur a gradual revival.[2] It was unsurprising therefore that the ballyhoo of 1985's 'British Film Year' was widely mocked as hollow rhetoric, only drawing attention to the problems facing British film production and exhibition, including a notable lack of government support. Given the initiative's attempt to get audiences into British cinemas, it was perhaps ironic that at about this time the most compelling signs of sustainable life for British film had little to do with traditional cinema but were almost entirely indebted to television, and in particular Channel Four's 'Film on Four' strand that reinvigorated indigenous filmmaking by creating a regular demand for content and offering a new funding infrastructure.[3]

Looking back from the vantage point of its tenth anniversary in 1993, Channel Four screened a season of what it described as 'the most popular and successful Film on Fours' from the past decade.[4] Unsurprisingly, the season featured the landmark film *My Beautiful Laundrette* (1985), which not only brought bracing new writing on sex, ethnicity, and identity from Hanif Kureishi but also acted as a catalyst for more widespread theatrical distribution of television films following its attention-grabbing screening at the Edinburgh Film Festival.[5] Bold, original, and unapologetically contemporary, *My Beautiful Laundrette* soon acquired a totemic status, becoming 'the "archetypal" Film on Four', according to John Hill.[6] It was also one of the films cited by Professor Norman Stone in his thundering polemical critique of 1980s British cinema: 'The rain pours down; skin-heads beat people up; there are race riots; there are drug fixes in squalid corners'; according to Stone it was 'all very depressing and no doubt meant to be'.[7] But as Kureishi made clear, this was part of *My Beautiful Laundrette*'s aim as 'a British film for British Film Year': to provide a bold unflinching account of the state of the nation in 1985.[8]

These two ostensibly different landmark films associated with moments of renaissance in 1980s British film, the historical sporting epic *Chariots of Fire* in 1981 and the urban and cutting-edge *My Beautiful Laundrette* in 1985 share two common features: an ambivalence towards Thatcherite ideologies (much more than their simplified respective reputations as flag-waver and protest film suggest) and a near-exclusive narrative focus on masculinity, and homosocial male relationships. While both films depict sympathetically various sisters, girlfriends, and other female relations, women remain marginal in both texts, in which the primary focus falls on men and their interactions with one another. But to suggest that the 1980s British film renaissance was an all-male affair would be misleading. Drilling down further into British film production beyond these two major touchstones enables a more nuanced picture of its gender politics to emerge. As Hill suggests, perhaps the teenage comedy *Gregory's Girl* (1980) with its various characters seeking to break free of 'conventional social roles and identities (especially those of gender)', should be seen as equally indicative of British cinema's onward direction as *Chariots of Fire*.[9] Likewise, *My Beautiful Laundrette* was released in many cinemas in a double bill with the complementary but far more female-focused anti-Thatcherite *Letter to Brezhnev* (1985), showing that the 1980s British cinema of social critique was not an exclusively masculine preserve either. Furthermore, it is worth noting that upon its first television showing, *My Beautiful Laundrette* did not achieve the top viewing figures for that season of Film on Four; that accolade went instead to the Julie Walters-led female ensemble comedy *She'll Be Wearing Pink Pyjamas* (1984), a less celebrated title today but its popularity at the time providing confirmation of a significant female presence in 1980s British film.[10]

This chapter explores how female stars slotted into a British film renaissance that sometimes appeared to be a very masculine affair but that sometimes offered opportunities for female stories to be powerfully told. More specifically, it examines how two teenage discoveries, Helena Bonham Carter and Emily Lloyd, were handled during this decade, how their youth and novelty value were exploited and how their careers diverged in significant ways.

The Film on Four tenth anniversary season featured another key British film of 1985 featured alongside the 'archetypal' *My Beautiful Laundrette*: Merchant Ivory's E. M. Forster adaptation *A Room with a View* (1985), which represented a quite different tendency in British filmmaking, one that met with Norman Stone's approval. It too was a game-changer, with its worldwide box-office take in excess of $68 million inaugurating a renewed cycle of costume-drama production subsequently labelled 'heritage film' by Andrew Higson and others.[11] Where the likes of *My Beautiful Laundrette* and *Letter to Brezhnev* were read in terms of social engagement and realism (in spite of clear markers of fantasy and fable), *A Room with a View* and others that followed from the Merchant Ivory team were slated for wilfully ignoring the difficulties of the present and escaping into a romantic arcadia. For leftist cultural critics such as Cairns Craig and Tana Wollen, drawing on the work of heritage critics such as Patrick Wright and Robert Hewison, these films were guilty of endorsing a conservative (not to mention Conservative) upper-middle-class vision of the national past.[12]

But despite *My Beautiful Laundrette* and *A Room with a View* being frequently deployed as each other's 'counter-example', symbolising two very distinct and opposing pathways taken by 1980s British filmmaking, the two films do of course have something in common: Daniel Day-Lewis, who features respectively as butch skinhead Johnny and etiolated aesthete Cecil Vyse. His actorly skill in embodying two highly divergent masculine types so convincingly was much commented upon at the time, particularly in the US where both films premiered in the same week in March 1986.[13] The praise for Day-Lewis's versatility across *My Beautiful Laundrette* and *A Room with a View* was matched by the acclaim accorded to a number of older character actors in supporting roles in both films, including Saeed Jaffrey, Roshan Seth, Maggie Smith, Judi Dench, and Denholm Elliott. But what was less readily acknowledged in the critical commentary on *A Room with a View* specifically was the emergence of a new female star in the shape of Helena Bonham Carter playing its blossoming ingénue Lucy Honeychurch. If we follow Alison Light's lead in reading the film primarily as romance, then its main narrative focus is the romantic dilemma faced by its young heroine, played by Bonham Carter.[14] And as the heritage cycle subsequently burgeoned, she would be the actress whose name was associated more than any other with this mode of filmmaking, attaining the status according to Andrew Higson of being '*the* quintessential heritage star'.[15]

Discovered one year previously to play the tragic title role in Trevor Nunn's *Lady Jane* (which ended up being released after *A Room with a View*), Bonham Carter soon developed an on-screen image 'of extraordinary consistency' inextricably linked to period film.[16] In addition to her debut and *A Room with a View*, she also had roles in the next six years in three further films from Merchant Ivory Productions, sizeable in *Where Angels Fear to Tread* (1991) and *Howards End* (1992) and a brief appearance in *Maurice* (1987), as well as starring in the Barbara Cartland period romance *A Hazard of Hearts* (1987) and Franco Zeffirelli's *Hamlet* (1990). While many other actors at this time specialised in period drama of similar ilk – Higson offers the examples of Rupert Graves and James Wilby among others – it is telling that Helena Bonham Carter is the only actor specifically named in the *The Guardian*'s snide mock-recipe for making a costume drama, with '1 Helena Bonham Carter (or own-brand equivalent)' featuring as a key ingredient alongside '1 classic text, 1 large tub whimsy' and '2 gross frocks'.[17] Her name alone began to function as shorthand for a certain kind of British film, with one review of *Howards End* efficiently summarising the heritage cycle as 'an Edwardian nirvana where Helena Bonham Carter is always tripping through the grass in a long frock'.[18] Similarly, Patrick Wright summed up what he saw as heritage culture's unfortunate stranglehold over representations of British identity simply in terms of 'Helena Bonham Carter working overtime', trusting his readers to recognise instantly her synecdochic status.[19] Bonham Carter even referred to this in her self-ascription in the late nineties as 'me, Mrs Merchant Ivory mascot' and effectively 'a genre unto myself. If a period film opens and I'm not in it, the critics write "And the Helena Bonham Carter role is played by . . ." Period movies are my destiny.'[20] Bonham Carter could ruefully send up her heritage stardom but others were more cutting in their critique of the actress and all that she was deemed to represent: Hanif Kureishi suggested that in 1991 all you needed to make a British film 'was to travesty an old book, throw in some ugly frocks and point your camera at Helena Bonham Carter's miserable pout'.[21] Comments such as Kureishi's seem to bear out journalist Sarah Gristwood's point that 'Merchant-Ivory's well-born protégée seems emblematic of so much we dislike about ourselves', or at least dislike about British society.[22] The critical animus directed at heritage film, astutely summarised by Claire Monk as an 'entanglement of political criticisms with a gut-level cultural-aesthetic aversion' often seems to slip into a language of scarcely cloaked gynophobia and misogyny, then applied seamlessly to its symbolic feminine figurehead Bonham Carter.[23]

While someone like Daniel Day-Lewis was not defined by his appearance in a Merchant Ivory film such as *A Room with a View* and indeed was highly praised for his skill in being able to traverse genres, Helena

Bonham Carter, at least in the earlier stages of her career, was both defined and damned by her association with period film, in spite of also working across other genres. Since the late 1990s, she has developed a considerably more nuanced public image as an actor, with her Oscar-nominated performance in *The Wings of the Dove* (1997), another period film albeit one in a dark register, her appearance as the damaged therapy-group addict Marla in *Fight Club* (1999), and her convincingly simian Ari in *Planet of the Apes* (2001) all being important touchstones in the development of a more varied career and complex persona. Now she is probably at least as well-known for playing the evil Bellatrix Lestrange in the Harry Potter films or as the muse of her ex-partner Tim Burton with whom she made many films as she is for being the 'corset queen' of British period drama, although historical roles still feature strongly in her repertoire, evident from recent films such as *The King's Speech* (2010) and *Suffragette* (2015). But the discussion in this chapter focuses on that earlier phase of her career from the mid-1980s to mid-1990s.

Helena Bonham Carter was not the only noteworthy teen female discovery in 1980s British film: Emily Lloyd, the sixteen-year-old star of *Wish You Were Here* (1987) – yet another Film on Four – was an equally impactful young debutante. Both actresses were presented as exciting new discoveries, and their meteoric ascents from schoolgirl obscurity to cinema fame were emphasised in coverage of their careers: 'From school productions to a title role of a prestigious new film. That, with just one television role en route, has been the success story of 18-year-old Helena Bonham Carter', reported the *Evening Standard* in 1984, while *Just Seventeen* magazine's cover line in December 1987 presented 'the rise and rise of Emily Lloyd – from schoolgirl to movie star in under a year'.[24] Bonham Carter and Lloyd had both been chosen from large cohorts of more experienced hopefuls, and each had been judged perfect for their respective roles that had seemed impossible to be satisfactorily filled until the right charismatic individual turned up. 'I was looking for a precociously intelligent, sensually provocative, childishly innocent, aristocratically assured 15-year-old', said Trevor Nunn of the role of Lady Jane Grey: 'I thought the task was impossible until she walked in.'[25] Emily Lloyd was deemed 'perfect' for rebellious Lynda in *Wish You Were Here*, loved by the camera from her first screen test according to both writer-director David Leland and editor George Akers, and thus selected 'to become Britain's newest film star'.[26] Although Emily Lloyd was also making a debut in a period role, it seemed that the closer historical proximity of its post-war setting and the fact that she was playing such a rebellious character helped to avoid any moribund heritage preconceptions of the kind that would dog Bonham Carter's early career. After *Wish You Were Here*'s hugely successful Cannes premiere, Lloyd found herself the subject of remarkable press hyperbole and industry clamour. 'The whole world is falling in love with Emily Lloyd' said screenwriter Nora Ephron of the actress's subsequent Hollywood debut in *Cookie* (1989).[27] She was hailed in the press as a rare discovery: 'It isn't often that Britain gets its own star. Young, sexy, jumping out of the screen. The genuinely international sort.'[28] But such elevated expectations would prove difficult to fulfil and Lloyd describes her personal trajectory succinctly in the subtitle of her autobiography: 'I was the golden girl of British cinema . . . then my life fell to pieces.'[29] Emily Lloyd's initial build-up as a potentially world-conquering star gave way to increasingly ambivalent media commentary as her career path didn't map out as hoped. Meanwhile, Helena Bonham Carter's initially less applauded arrival as a new British female star ultimately resulted in a more enduring screen career. The reasons for the differing fates of Lloyd and Bonham Carter are complex and various. This chapter explores some of the differences, as well as the parallels and overlaps, between their personae and careers in their formative years as actresses, seeking to delineate how these two young 'golden girls' of 1980s British cinema – to use Lloyd's phrase – travelled along different pathways to arrive at quite different destinations as they moved into the 1990s and beyond, but also what that may tell us about gendered stardom in British cinema over that period, in which renaissance frequently seemed to figure in masculine terms, from *Chariots of Fire* and *My Beautiful Laundrette* to *Trainspotting* (1996) and *The Full Monty* (1997).

Sulky Scion: Introducing Helena Bonham Carter

It seems entirely indicative of her emergent star persona that Helena Bonham Carter first made an impact by appearing in *Tatler*, the glossy magazine of choice for English high society, in a colour photospread in the April 1984 issue on 'girls who look "out of time"' which depicted her as a dreamily gorgeous pre-Raphaelite maiden. The same issue's feature on the production of *Another Country* (1984), complete with photos of its floppy-haired, firm-jawed male stars Rupert Everett, Cary Elwes, and Colin Firth, all playing public schoolboys, said something about the changing temper of the times and the triumphant return of unrepentant poshness after its eclipse during the socially mobile 1960s and 1970s – an aristocratic aesthetic spearheaded by the television adaptation of *Brideshead Revisited* in 1981. Clearly, something was in the air. The surprise publishing sensation of the early 1980s had been Ann Barr and Peter York's *Sloane Ranger*

Handbook (1982), which used Princess Diana as its cover girl and meticulously outlined the rules and rituals of the English upper classes, intended to be gently satirical but adopted by some as a lifestyle template. In such a milieu, as one writer noted, magazines like *Tatler* had become the place to spot future stars and 'essential reading for movie makers these days!'[30] This was borne out when Bonham Carter was called to audition for Trevor Nunn for the role of Lady Jane Grey in his forthcoming film (despite having virtually no acting experience) on the strength of her picture in that magazine.[31]

Nunn auditioned many actresses but was drawn to Helena Bonham Carter because of what he called her 'natural intelligence and natural aristocracy; she is the scion of a great English family'.[32] Breeding mattered, it seemed, with Bonham Carter not merely *looking* the part but having the genuine upper-class provenance required to play a queen, with ancestors including Prime Minister Herbert Asquith (her great-grandfather) and Liberal peer Lady Violet Bonham Carter (her grandmother). Although claiming to be 'conscious of the family tradition' and having 'positive pride in the family name', the actress also admitted being irritated by her 'aristocratic forbears' being 'lovingly chronicled in publicity notes' for *Lady Jane* and subsequent films.[33] She felt it perpetuated a 'silly fallacy that I've got where I am because of my name': 'My genealogy is always mentioned in every article about me,' she grumbled in 1987.[34] Her familial heritage played a pivotal role in forging her star persona, with her perceived poshness very much in her favour at this time: as *The Guardian* teasingly suggested, the actress's 'USP' (Unique Selling Point) was the fact she was 'genuine double barrelled'.[35]

Just as with *Lady Jane*, she was cast in her international breakthrough role of Lucy Honeychurch in *A Room with a View* because of a certain aristocratic equanimity about getting or not getting the role. As director James Ivory recalled: 'She came in for a reading and she just sort of came in and scowled and flung herself on the couch . . . Even though she didn't have much experience and she'd never been in a drama school and so on, I thought I'd try it.'[36] Producer Ishmail Merchant concurred: 'Normally actors try to oversell themselves. None of that was there with Helena. She was slumped on the sofa. There was an innocence and charm and haughtiness. I was drawn towards that.'[37] These discovery stories, repeated in the press during the production and release of both *Lady Jane* and *A Room with a View* across 1985 and 1986, fixed an image of Helena Bonham Carter as 'a natural' – 'unformed, and yet herself' in Ivory's words – but someone who refused to beguile in auditions and even had to be pursued by Trevor Nunn for the role of Jane Grey after she had disappeared on holiday.[38] 'On occasion', one journalist suggested, she could 'sound rather churlish about the middle-aged men who have pleaded with her to become a star.'[39] But it is possible to see this as a quite reasonable reaction to the enormity of suddenly achieving fame while still a teenager, which she later reflected had thrown her completely '"off balance"': it 'came too quickly, too easily. It meant making career decisions earlier' like whether or not to go to university.[40]

Although *Lady Jane* had been completed first, it premiered after *A Room with a View*, which far outstripped it in popularity and reach. *A Room with a View* did spectacularly well on the US repertory cinema circuit, most strikingly so in New York where a box-office take of about $1million a week 'from one screen alone' were understandably deemed 'pretty good going for an art-house adaptation of a fairly obscure English novel, and a film, moreover, which only cost £2.4m to make'.[41] *Lady Jane* proved a slower-burning success both in the UK and the US, gaining a stronger following via home video (on which *A Room with a View* would also do very well) where it topped the British rental charts 'just two weeks after its release' and then later gaining an enthusiastic viewership via cable television screenings: as Bonham Carter recalled, 'They started playing it every few hours on HBO. Now I get all these teenage girls who just go mad for it because she's a perfect heroine – smart, and dead at 15.'[42] Both films – in effect a kind of 'twin debut' for the young star – were granted the royal seal of approval at their British premieres by being attended by members of the royal family, the Queen Mother (whom Bonham Carter would later play in *The King's Speech*) at *A Room with a View*, and Prince Charles and Princess Diana at *Lady Jane* (one newspaper reporting that Diana sobbed throughout this tale of a tragic young woman's sacrifice on the altar of monarchical power, which seems rather more meaningful with the benefit of hindsight).[43] Playing royals and being watched approvingly by members of the royal family seemed to create a halo effect for *Lady Jane*'s two young stars, Bonham Carter and Cary Elwes, the *jeunesse doree* of British film, with one reviewer suggesting that with their beauty, good fortune, and high birth: 'Off-screen as well as on, they are truly the royal children.'[44]

Although reviewer Derek Malcolm had spoken of Bonham Carter's 'extraordinarily vivid physical presence' in *Lady Jane*, other critics were much more guarded about her abilities.[45] Despite Molly Haskell's review of *A Room with a View* for US *Vogue* being titled 'Why I love Lucy', she had actually identified Bonham Carter as one of the weaker elements of what she saw as an otherwise impeccable production.[46] Other critics, such as pop-culture tyro Toby Young, were even harsher:

[H]er range of expression was limited to looking either cross or bored. Yet she was on screen over 50 per cent of the time. A good deal of the tension in the book stems from Lucy Honeychurch's struggle to overcome her sexual repression. Helena Bonham Carter had to struggle to hold her head up straight . . . it's difficult to be swept by the romance of the story when the lead actress has no neck.[47]

This seems a little unfair. To adopt Andrew Higson's phrasing, in certain quarters Helena Bonham Carter was 'the wrong sort' of film star for critics with a demotic allegiance to blockbuster cinema to ever admit to liking. Instead, she was held up as an example of all that was deemed to be wrong with insipid middlebrow British culture and its deluded admirers, as demonstrated in Young's full review and Hanif Kureishi's comments about Helena Bonham Carter's miserable pout quoted earlier. Performing her synecdochic function, she became a scapegoat for much broader cultural tendencies beyond the control of any one actress.

One may surmise that these criticisms of her acting may have stung all the more because Bonham Carter had already been gripped by the fear while making *A Room with a View* that she wasn't able to measure up to her vastly more experienced co-stars, describing herself as 'cringing permanently. It's this massive exposure, thinking that all these people are seeing you at your worst.'[48] 'I felt I was in deep water and unable to swim,' she said a few years later of the experience.[49] Indeed, the 'no neck' jibe appears to have affected her so strongly that she undertook posture training to correct the flaw that had been identified, reportedly gaining two inches in height.[50] But in some respects her inadequacies, real or imagined, and a certain degree of adolescent awkwardness and truculence, were entirely congruent with both her roles in *Lady Jane* and *A Room with a View*. Contrary to the more romanticised visions of Bonham Carter as submissive English ingénue, in neither film is she presented as shrinking violet or fragile rose, and instead her heroines contain a bracing element of sulky bad temper (cross and bored, as Toby Young suggests), lashing out at her relations when they frustrate or enervate her. Particularly as Lucy Honeychurch, Bonham Carter's screen presence is more glowering and scowling than simpering and submissive. As she later reflected on this stage of her career: 'I wasn't Mrs Demure. I saw *A Room with a View* again not long ago, and went "Fucking hell!" I was such an angry little thing, stomping around. I certainly wasn't delicate.'[51]

Cultivating a Rose

Bonham Carter's other major asset, besides her ancestry and all the self-assurance it connoted, was her striking appearance, loving descriptions of which filled numerous column inches, and that someone like Toby Young was consciously writing against in his jibes at her 'no neck' appearance. As in her original ultra-romantic *Tatler* spread, her looks were frequently seen as being pre-modern or 'out of time'.

> Helena Bonham Carter possesses the kind of features that inspire clichés: luxuriant brown hair, wide-set almond eyes, a lovely heart-shaped face, little bow lips – a face that belongs on a cameo. There is something undeniably old-fashioned about her, nostalgic, even wistful.[52]

From her earliest publicity and press coverage, she was consistently placed in the 'English rose' category and, although variously positioned as Victorian, Edwardian, Holbein-esque, or pre-Raphaelite, always presented as a face redolent of the English past who looked best in period dress: 'like a small, sleek, glorious mouse, all buttoned-up in silk and lace and velvet'.[53] Ironically, this heritage look, the very fact she seemed old-fashioned, also saw her hailed as the height of contemporary fashionability, dubbed 'The Face of '86' by numerous fashion publications, including *Vogue*.[54] But, just as she rejected continual references to her ancestry, Bonham Carter also made clear she found 'this business of looks', as she called it, to be 'a problem'.[55] One journalist found when interviewing her in 1986, 'She doesn't like being known as The Face [and] she doesn't want to be a film star; she wants to be a good, if not a great, actress'; comments that echo Lucy's protestations to Cecil in *A Room with a View* that she doesn't want to be aestheticised and put on display like a beautiful object.[56] From the outset of her career, Bonham Carter made a point of saying that she did not want to 'be conspicuous or act the starlet': 'I'm told I should cultivate a sexier, more glamorous image – mainly by my family and agent. It's "Put your hair up, girl. Show a bit of leg!" If I did that, I'd lose a part of myself.'[57]

As is often the case with young female celebrities, an unseemly fascination with the transition from girlhood to womanhood is in evidence, always seen in highly sexualised terms, and Helena Bonham Carter is no exception: Robert Kilroy-Silk's 1988 interview with the actress in which he pries into whether she currently has a lover provides a good example of this kind of prurient intrusive interest in a young woman's sexual development.[58] Arguably the question of sex and sexual experience was all the more fraught for a star like Bonham Carter emerging in the mid-1980s

Figure 6.1 Heritage ingénue 'all buttoned up': Helena Bonham Carter as Lucy Honeychurch in *A Room with a View* (1985).

at about the time of the acquired immune deficiency syndrome (AIDS) crisis and concomitant moral panic about promiscuity. In some respects, it seems entirely fitting for the period that Bonham Carter should first make her name in two chaste costume dramas where sex occurs only within marriage and that she should proudly describe herself as 'quite celibate' in her private life.[59] She went on to play the heroine in the 1987 Barbara Cartland mini-series *A Hazard of Hearts* in which she gained the virginal stamp of approval from the romantic novelist herself: 'She has an aura of innocence and purity that cannot be acted – it can only come from within.'[60] But this kind of comment, intended as complementary, could easily become a millstone around the neck of someone aspiring to play different kinds of roles, as Bonham Carter suggested in 1992: 'I am not a virgin though even my agent, who took me on when I was 17, has carried on thinking I am. I was sort of frozen at that age and people equated me with my roles.'[61]

In relation to these matters of maturation, one long-standing recurrent trope in Helena Bonham Carter's press coverage was the fact that she was still living at home with her parents in Golders Green. One comment from 1986 that she was 'still just a little girl at heart [who] lives with her mum and dad – and she hasn't got a boyfriend' emphasised her innocence by noting that she was yet to attain what were constructed as twin markers of maturity: heterosexual coupledom and her own home.[62] As time went on, press concern about her extended adolescence grew, often expressed in sardonic terms – as with the suggestion that her '28 years on Planet Earth have been spent living at home with Mum and Dad, and lacing up corsets for Merchant and Ivory', and nothing more.[63] Never mind that the family home was sufficiently capacious to provide her with more than enough independent living space or that she may have wanted to remain close to her parents, particularly her severely disabled father; instead, leaving home was continually invoked as a necessary objective and the star's refusal to do so increasingly pathologised. A later article with the heartfelt confessional title 'I have to try living on my own' represented it as the actress's defining personal dilemma.[64]And keen though the press were for Bonham Carter to be in a relationship, there was adverse commentary when she was seen to have 'stolen' Kenneth Branagh from her *Howards End* co-star Emma Thompson in the mid-1990s.

Questions around whether or not Bonham Carter had 'grown up' were also mediated through commentary on her off-duty choice of clothes, frequently deemed insufficiently smart or inappropriately scruffy. Her garb of 'vast outsize man's woollen pullover, thermal underwear against the piercing wind on location and a T-shirt which proclaimed "I didn't get this far on looks alone"' while making *Lady Jane* may have been initially interpreted as simply wearing whatever was necessary to keep warm, but it soon became clear that this higgledy-piggledy look was not mere expediency but the cultivation of a particular kind of rebellious anti-fashion stance viewed by her detractors as the sumptuary equivalent of a teenage sulk.[65] Sometimes she drew on the subculture of goth, typified by the 'brown top hat, thick shroud of purple sweatshirt, striped tights, black nail polish and bright green baseball boots' that she wore to the UK premiere of *A Room with a View* in 1986, an outfit that journalist Catherine Bennett thought 'looked calculated to dismay'.[66] At other times, the rebellion was enacted by wearing ill-matched, baggy garments inside out 'so that you can see the seams and the label', making her 'a *vision*', as one journalist rather sarcastically put it.[67] It became a press commonplace to see her described as 'dressed like a ragbag' or in 'her usual hotpotch of Orphan-Annie-meets-Oxfam gladrags'.[68] Partly inspired by her admiration of Diane Keaton's masculine style in *Annie Hall* (1977), Bonham Carter inflected the look in specifically English ways, and in spite of her irritation at being perpetually defined in relation to her family inheritance, it was quite literally written on her body through the 'jumble of Chaplinesque clothes' borrowed from the family wardrobe that she chose to wear: 'her grandfather's brown waistcoat, her father's grey socks, her grandmother's black clogs – and her own baggy trousers and braces'.[69]

For some commentators, Bonham Carter's deliberately un-starry appearance began to take on a neurotic tinge, a suspicion that reached its apotheosis with Lynn Barber's comments in 1997:

Why does she do it? What is the problem? Why can't she ever find a frock that fits? Why can't she have cardigans that button up? Or sleeves that stop at her wrists? Why does she have to keep twitching and hitching these gormless garments? If she finds clothes so difficult to manage, couldn't she just wear a Babygro? We all appreciate she doesn't want to be mistaken for a sex object, but there's a yawning gap between looking like Pamela Anderson and looking like a Victorian orphan.[70]

Denying the actress any agency in her clothing choices, Barber instead polices her appearance and reads her clothes as expressions of self-loathing and self-infantilisation, therefore proposing stretchy all-in-one baby clothes as a punitive solution to the problem. Bonham Carter's outré clothing choices were not seen as expressions of her free will, as they would later be (she made the *Vanity Fair best*-dressed list in 2010, fronted the Fall 2011 campaign for designer Marc Jacobs, and was acclaimed as a 'style original' on the cover of UK *Vogue* in July 2013) but more as symptoms of arrested development, and a refusal to grow up into 'proper' womanhood.[71] In particular, her refusal to wear 'grown-up' high-heeled shoes, and to favour masculinised flat shoes even on the red carpet was continually commented on. Her tentative foray into (low-heeled, black suede) heels from Pied à Terre was considered noteworthy enough to be a major discussion point in a 1991 interview: 'My new shoes have made a huge difference to how I feel and walk.'[72]

Although she first made an impact in the 1980s, it was in about the early 1990s that Helena Bonham Carter's status as 'quintessential heritage star' became firmly consolidated, not least by her appearance in 1992's *Howards End*, another Merchant Ivory period drama. As Andrew Higson notes, the film used her face, looking out while in a clinch with Samuel West (whose face is obscured), as the 'key promotional image' for its marketing campaign.[73] The names of Emma Thompson, Anthony Hopkins, and Vanessa Redgrave may be prominently featured, but not their faces. One could arguably place *Howards End* within Martin Shingler's categorisation of the star vehicle as 'a film designed to exploit the popularity of a particular performer by accommodating their established "type" and both reworking and advancing aspects of their previous work that had already proven popular with an audience, providing a delicate balance between novelty (originality) and familiarity (repetition)'.[74] If we follow Higson in seeing the heritage film as a 'reworking of the classical woman's film' then, as with the original cycle of films, female stardom is absolutely crucial to its promotional process.[75] *Howards End*'s marketing as a 'middlebrow, crossover product' hinged quite centrally on the star presence of Helena Bonham Carter, denoting and promising certain kinds of viewing pleasures to certain kinds of audience, just as the strong brand identity of a woman's picture star like Joan Crawford had done in the 1930s and 1940s.[76] She may have played a rebellious and often angry young woman, representative of 'the current of passion running through the film', but the fact that she was literally the poster girl for Merchant Ivory had the effect of fixing Bonham Carter in public discourse as 'all-purpose Edwardian ingénue' – regardless of the complexities of the film in which she starred, her image boiling down to 'Englishness. Poshness. Innocence. Sexual awakening. Usually a combination of the above.'[77] Despite having taken a number of contemporary roles – like bulimic party girl Lady Minerva Munday in the comedy *Getting It Right* (1989) or Don Johnson's drug-addicted doctor girlfriend in a couple of episodes of the hugely popular US television series *Miami Vice* in 1987– these were seen as marginal aberrations to her heritage-dominated persona.[78]

The primary way in which Bonham Carter's association with period drama was articulated was through the representational trope of wearing a corset, repeated constantly across press coverage of the star for more than a decade and going beyond lazy journalistic cliché to take on an almost obsessive dimension. It began as early as 1987. 'Helena Bonham Carter still has some girdles to overcome' punned Nigel Dempster in an article from that year with the groan-worthy title 'Of corsets Helena', which then lasciviously noted that Helena would 'be crammed into restraining corsetry to cover her ample bosom for the filming of Hazard of Hearts'.[79] A few years later, it had clearly become an entrenched association, with a 1991 article entitled 'Rebel without a corset' quoting Bonham Carter suggesting that 'people must think I put a corset on every morning when I wake up at home in Golders Green'.[80] By the mid-1990s the hysterically overdetermined repetition was clearly beginning to pall more and more: 'I like to remind people I exist out of a corset', the actress stated in 1994, while in 1996 the protest became a more straightforward 'I hate corsets!'[81] It had become such a well-worn cliché that Bonham Carter was able to anticipate its journalistic use to describe her edgier role in *Margaret's Museum* (1995): '"shedding the corsets", she says, not bothering to stifle a yawn.'[82] And yet still it held firm as the primary way of referring to her image, not least because of its continuing convenience for pun-making subeditors: 'Corset still makes sense' and 'Par for the corset' ran typical examples.[83] By this point, the corset trope became a further form of synecdoche, and just as the British period drama could be collapsed into a mere mention of its representative star Helena Bonham Carter, so the corset could in turn be used as shorthand to represent her heritage-imbued persona. She had become the 'corset queen': 'Period movies are my destiny,' she stated in 1998. 'I should have a few ribs taken out, because I'll be in a corset for the rest of my life.'[84] The trope proved so pervasive and defining, the actress even incorporated it into her name: 'No matter what I do, I'll still be Helena Corset Carter.'[85]

Elaborate or unusual costuming is often one of the key attractions of period film – its near-synonym 'costume drama' suggests as much – and as Christine Geraghty points out, the genre invites us 'to a performance in which characters, far from looking natural and at ease, are dressed up in elaborate and sometimes uncomfortable-looking costumes which often limit their physical movement'.[86] A fascination with what these unfamiliar costumes do to the body is expressed in continual questions about how it feels to be corseted, what physical effects it may have, particularly the pain of the chest and abdomen being compressed.[87] But for all its association with certain kinds of period authenticity, the fact remains that the corset is also an item of clothing with highly fetishistic connotations, simultaneously encasing the body, hence its association with repression, but also displaying an idealised tiny-waisted feminine physique to best advantage, emphasising sexual difference. Despite usually being hidden, it is an item of underwear that draws attention to itself and is engaged in a continual dialectic between done up and undone. Its tightness also inevitably, irresistibly, prompted thoughts about the release offered by unlacing and loosening the stays, again often in a sexual context, and as recent scholarship has rediscovered, the tight lacing of corsets could be used to induce sexual arousal in the wearer.[88] The sheer density and richness of the corset's sexual associations may suggest another reason why it was so frequently invoked in discussions of a young female star who otherwise did not offer herself up as an object of the male gaze. The corset's association with encasement or imprisonment also made it a particularly apt metaphor for the heritage typecasting to which Bonham Carter was apparently subject, with her recurrent experience of being 'caged in corsets, layered in petticoats' acting as a literal expression of 'the period-drama straitjacket' in which she found herself trapped.[89] Conversely, getting a chance to play other kinds of character in more contemporary settings was always conceptualised as escaping the grip of corsetry: 'Out of her corsets and into California' was how one magazine covered her career journey in 1999, suggesting an opposition between modern Hollywood and the old-fashioned trappings of old-world femininity.[90]

While the corset trope became the dominant feature of any profile of Bonham Carter, the idea of the actress as an 'English Rose' ran a close second.[91] An appellation that has been applied to many other English female stars, the English Rose label crystallises a nationally specific feminine ideal. Its application to a star described as 'the quintessential English face' and 'a role model for British women' makes sense.[92] But despite her porcelain pale complexion, in most other ways Bonham Carter departed from the usual fair-haired typology of the rose, and she convincingly argued that really she 'was *never* an English rose. I've got my mum's dark looks. She's Spanish-French.'[93] Noting this irony, another interviewer observed that 'she doesn't even look English' and described her as more Mediterranean in appearance.[94] In spite of this, the English Rose epithet did map perfectly on to her frequent portrayal of Englishwomen from the past who seemed to embody more decorous traditions of femininity, and so it stuck regardless of her arguably more hybridised appearance.

Bonham Carter's reputation as an English Rose was also undoubtedly the prime motivation behind her adoption by Yardley in 1993 to front a major relaunch of its cosmetics and fragrance lines, allegedly for a six-figure sum. Although it had used modish figures like Jean Shrimpton and Twiggy to advertise its products back in the 1960s, Yardley had latterly tended to market itself in quite traditional ways that harked back to the company's origins in the eighteenth century, and 'cultivated an image of its model customer as the archetypal English rose'.[95] But while this image worked very well for its older customer base, by the 1990s there were concerns that Yardley's associations with 'greying grannies and lavender water' were off-putting for younger women.[96] Hence their decision to choose a new poster girl who could appeal to younger customers while simultaneously not overly alienating its traditional customer demographic. As a spokeswoman for the company explained: 'We wanted someone who was intelligent and articulate and looked it. Somebody quintessentially English and the reverse of a bimbo – a modern young woman with ideas of her own.'[97]

Helena Bonham Carter seemed like an ideal choice to meet all these demands. However, as many commentators noted at the time, there was no small irony in using an actress best known 'for her portrayal of corset-wearing Victorian and Edwardian types' as the pivotal figure in Yardley's attempt to rejuvenate itself as a fresh, up-to-date brand.[98] But perhaps more crucial to the re-brand's ultimate failure was Bonham Carter's ill-disguised indifference towards cosmetics that even saw her admitting at Yardley's big re-launch event that she wasn't sure why she had been chosen to front the campaign since she was 'not really into make-up'. The company attempted to draw on connotations of prestige and quality acting associated with the star in their ads, with 'Complete Performance' foundation sold with the slogan 'The classic face. The ultimate performance', but there was no recovery from the campaign's inauspicious start. The actress was dropped by the company the following year to the mutual relief of both parties (they went for the more obvious choice of supermodel Linda Evangelista next instead). Perhaps Yardley should have been more careful in their research: it was unlikely that a star who had stated a preference for 'looking a bit ill and wasted: pale skin, lips pallid or bloodstained, the dark rings under the eyes kept in' could ever be easily pressed into service as brand ambassador for a classic cosmetics firm.[99] As *Harpers and Queen*'s beauty editor Newby Hands reflected on the whole debacle: 'They thought they were getting an English rose but in fact they were getting an English eccentric.'[100]

The Yardley affair also provides a useful demonstration of how tastes had changed and heritage was becoming a derogated currency in comparison with youthful innovation by the mid-1990s. New Labour's renaming of the Department of Heritage (itself a 1980s invention) as the Department for Culture, Media & Sport upon their landslide election victory in 1997 indicated the shift in mood, and implemented the vision of Britain previously set out by Tony Blair as 'a young country' rather than one always 'resting on past glories', hoping to usher in an era of 'Cool Britannia' (and partially succeeding).[101] The heritage film genre that had propelled Bonham Carter to stardom in the 1980s was itself mutating and adapting, becoming something more appropriately described as 'post-heritage' or even 'anti-heritage', with the likes of Michael Winterbottom's *Jude* (1996) and Shekar Kapur's *Elizabeth* (1998) representing a new defiantly un-pretty mood in British historical filmmaking. Symbolically, Bonham Carter cut off her long, luxuriant wavy hair around this period, as though signalling a break with her past persona. The *Daily Mail* reported that she was 'tired of playing the "English Rose with the hair" in frock flicks . . . So now the tresses have been trimmed to reveal a new, gamine look with the actress planning to play the modern woman'.[102] Although, as Bonham Carter subsequently suggested, it wasn't that easy to dissociate herself from her established image by means of a haircut alone: 'Even when I cut my hair off, they just stick it back on again. They've got it in a box next door.'[103]

In the 1990s, Bonham Carter benefited from diversifying her career beyond period dramas, turning up in Woody Allen's comedy *Mighty Aphrodite* (1995), and then speaking perfect French as a young fashion designer in the Parisian-set *Portraits Chinois* (1996), and playing a bohemian young mum with a reasonably convincing Scottish accent in the Edinburgh-set *Women Talking Dirty* (1999). She also made forays into the products of the new 'post-heritage' approach to historical films. *Mary Shelley's Frankenstein* (1994), which attempted to yoke literary fidelity to *grand guignol* horror, yielded mixed results, although Bonham Carter's

Figure 6.2 Beyond period dramas: Helena Bonham Carter playing bohemian Cora in modern-day Edinburgh in *Women Talking Dirty* (1999).

feisty Elizabeth, murdered and then reanimated as the monster's bride, marked a significant departure from her previous costume roles. But her most notable 'post-heritage' film role came as the calculating desperate anti-heroine of the Henry James adaptation *The Wings of the Dove* (1997), resplendent in flowing jewel-toned Paul Poiret-inspired gowns (and with not a corset in sight because of the decision to shift the novel's original 1904 setting to the cusp of modernity in 1910–11 instead, thus entailing new kinds of women's fashion). And it wasn't just her clothed appearance that was different in this period film. Although Bonham Carter had done several discreet or fleeting nude scenes by this point, one commentator suggested that her uncharacteristic 'full-frontal nude scene' in *The Wings of the Dove* (which 'would have made the prudish [Henry] James pop his pince-nez') was a marker of her ability to do 'a period role with a modern attitude' and move on from Merchant Ivory purdah.[104] *The Wings of the Dove* was also important in marking a change in the critical respect accorded to her acting abilities, with the role earning her an Oscar nomination, that traditional touchstone for international recognition. Playing a villainess in a darker-toned period drama acted as the gateway to a more diverse and internationalised future career. Having said in 1989 that she 'hate[d] this public image of me, pirouetting in Victorian nighties ... I want to shock everyone. To say "No, I'm not this one-dimensional 19th-century person you think I am",' Helena Bonham Carter was able to evade such reductive pigeonholing and play increasingly varied roles in films set in both past and present as her career progressed into the 1990s and

2000s.[105] No longer solely a heritage star, she could now lace up or set aside the corsets as and when required without having to be defined by them.

'Emily, We Love You': Discovering Emily Lloyd

Compared to the more muted reception initially accorded to Helena Bonham Carter back in the 1980s, Emily Lloyd's arrival was subject to quite extraordinary levels of breathless enthusiasm. Her performance in *Wish You Were Here* became one of the sensations of the 1987 Cannes Film Festival and she and the film received a five-minute standing ovation. The French press christened her '*mignonne* (adorable) and *la petite allumeuse Anglaise* (the little English flirt)' and, in the words of critic Benedict Nightingale, 'Cannes elected itself her oyster.'[106] A plane trailing the message 'Emily, We Love You' circled over the Riviera, while down on the ground the new star-in-the-making found herself mobbed by 'talent spotters and celebrity hunters' alike.[107] Among Lloyd's hectic schedule of interviews and photo calls, she was chosen to present a posy to Princess Diana, an honour seen as the cherry on an already rather impressive multi-tiered cake. 'A 16-year-old schoolgirl returns to the classroom today, head filled with memories of champagne, strawberries and sunshine, theatrical knights and royal princes', ran the *Daily Mirror*'s romanticised coverage of Lloyd's remarkable week at the film festival, deeming her story 'the Cannes fairytale that so rarely happens'.[108] But the dream of overnight acclaim had certainly come true for Lloyd, even if its suddenness had left the young starlet feeling slightly dazed and confused. 'I knew the film was going to be good but I didn't dream I'd be the talk of Cannes,' *The Mail on Sunday* reported Lloyd as saying. 'I couldn't believe it was all happening to me. I felt as if I was walking around in a big bubble.'[109] And, in a question that would gather more resonance with hindsight, 'I'm only 16 and I wonder where I am going from here?'[110]

However, at this point, any qualms or doubts were pushed to the side-lines and it seemed that Emily Lloyd was able to magically combine the impact of Diana Dors' attention-grabbing appearances as blonde bombshell at Cannes with Rita Tushingham's aura of freshness and novelty when she picked up the festival's best actress award for her debut film in 1962. Alexander Walker's glowing review of Lloyd's performance in *Wish You Were Here* made clear that he regarded her as a rare discovery and placed her in an impressive female star pantheon:

> She's done something I've seen happen so rarely in films that I count it in single figures. Julie Christie did it swinging insouciantly down the street in *Billy Liar*, Julie

Walters did it again much later on, stomping independently over the college cobbles to 'better herself'" in *Educating Rita*. Just by inhabiting a role, not playing it, by using instinct not training, by relying on natural looks not make-up, by projecting an inner verve and not just dialogue, in short simply by being there, these players serve notice as soon as they appear onscreen that they're here to stay.[111]

However, Walker's suggestion that the power of Lloyd's performance may have stemmed from instinctive inhabitation of her role rather than actorly skill reverberated across many subsequent appraisals of Lloyd, several of which voiced the suspicion that 'perhaps the reason she was so convincing is that she was simply playing herself'.[112] Asked an awkward question in an interview, she responded with her character Lynda's favourite riposte, 'Up your bum!', prompting the interviewer to ask, 'So is Emily like Lynda?'[113] Another profile forged the same connection between actress and role: 'Emily is quite the rogueish imp who may, like Lynda Mansell, stand up in a crowd and shout "Up your bum!"[114] Whereas Bonham Carter found herself defined in terms of period femininity around this time, exemplified by the continual references to corset-wearing, Lloyd's emergent persona hinged on her off-screen self being indistinguishable from Lynda, the rebellious wild child who just happened to be in post-war period dress. Either way, both young women were understood in terms of their screen roles, often in quite restrictive ways.

Figure 6.3 Rebellious wild child in post-war period dress: Emily Lloyd as Lynda in *Wish You Were Here* (1987).

Like a number of other British films of the 1980s, including *Dance with a Stranger* (1985), *Prick Up Your Ears* (1987), and *Scandal* (1989), *Wish You Were Here* returned to Britain's post-war past with the 1950s being an era of special fascination. In deliberate contradiction of Thatcherite constructions of the 1950s as the last settled era before the unwanted upheavals of 1960s permissiveness, these films painted it as a deeply repressive period. They focused their attention on misfits and rebels who were, as John Hill put it, 'in protest against the drabness and conformity of the society around them', from Ruth Ellis to Joe Orton, Christine Keeler to Cynthia Payne (whose early life provided the inspiration for Lynda in *Wish You Were Here*).[115] In repudiating Conservative visions of the (supposedly) thriftier, more dutiful 1950s, *Wish You Were Here* and other films of the same retro ilk had a particular political resonance. They suggested that the good old days being nostalgically longed for and wistfully invoked weren't actually that great, and moreover that they were particularly repressive for women who found themselves at odds with the consensus on appropriate feminine behaviour. *Wish You Were Here*'s Lynda is justifiably 'bloody bored' and desperate for *something* to liven up suffocating small-town English existence in the 1950s. The image of her ceaselessly riding her bike around town is powerfully expressive of her wish for mobility and freedom. Avidly curious about sex and gaining sexual experience, she refuses to kowtow to patriarchal hypocrisy, whether represented by her father, her psychiatrist, or her older lover. Although her ultimate redemption through motherhood may be seen as following a traditional script of femininity, her irrepressible rebellious energy is the film's most memorable feature, flashing her legs at the boys, skipping around in the backyard shouting, 'Up your bum!', calling a psychiatrist a 'dirty old bugger', climbing on the table in a staid tearoom to ask the clientele, 'Hands up all those who like willies? I do!' For Lloyd, Lynda was 'a hero . . . too intelligent for the times she lived in. She couldn't put it into words, it was just a feeling she had that all the people around her were too suppressed and rigid . . . She saw through people.'[116]

Having played such a compelling character so convincingly in her debut film to such acclaim, it was difficult to know what Lloyd's next move would be. As director David Leland suggested, 'How do you follow a performance like that when you're 16 years old?'[117] There was certainly no shortage of hyperbole and hope surrounding this new British star discovery. Declared variously not only as a new Julie Christie or Julie Walters by Alexander Walker, but also the most exciting debuting young starlet since Carroll Baker in *Baby Doll* (1956), 'the new Brigitte Bardot' (in fact 'the new every other female megastar apart from Lassie') and as someone causing the biggest stir in Hollywood since Marilyn Monroe

posed over New York subway grating.[118] It was true that Lloyd had generated a rare buzz, with numerous Hollywood studios and agents all engaged
in extravagant bidding wars to woo her to their side, sensing her potential
for international stardom. One company offered 'an extremely valuable
gold watch engraved "Wish you were here"' and upon her arrival in LA,
it was reported, she was met by 'drivers of limousines sent by rival agencies vying to take her wherever she wanted to go'.[119] It was reported in one
paper that a 'man from the mighty CAA agency, which has the likes of Paul
Newman and Robert Redford on its books, offered to buy her a racehorse',
prompting Lloyd's mum to suggest that it may be hard to accommodate a
horse in their Islington maisonette.[120] Press coverage of this unanticipated
Hollywood clamour took the characteristic British tone of being dismissive of such overwrought silliness while simultaneously expressing barely
concealed delight at a British girl being seen as a hot star property.

The mention of the maisonette hints at an important distinction between
the way that Helena Bonham Carter and Emily Lloyd were written about
as young stars of the 1980s. While Bonham Carter was discussed in terms
of aristocratic provenance in her early press coverage, the opposite was
true for Lloyd who was presented instead as the epitome of an ordinary
sixteen-year-old girl, attending 'a north London comprehensive', living
in 'her mum's small, simple maisonette in North London' (with no room
for stables), 'almost aggressively unstarlike in her cheap black t-shirt and
leggings', and with a 'voice and manner' like that 'of any lively London
schoolgirl'.[121] Lloyd was reportedly delighted to earn a small amount of
money while making *Wish You Were Here* because, she said, in comparison
with the wages she 'used to get working in a shoe shop on a Saturday, it
was a fortune'.[122] Although Lloyd actually did have some famous fore-
bears that may have disrupted the picture of absolute ordinariness, the
fact that they were the actors Charles and Roger Lloyd-Pack, the latter
(her father) best known for playing Trigger in the popular sitcom *Only
Fools and Horses*, made this more easily recuperated into a demotic image
than Bonham Carter's prime ministerial ancestors. But, as this family
background suggested, Lloyd was hardly a completely average schoolgirl,
having also attended the celebrated Italia Conti stage school in addition
to a number of other private and state schools, even if she hadn't found
any of them a particularly rewarding experience. Her social provenance
was interestingly mixed, combining both middle-class and working-class
elements. Her father had found fame playing a working-class character
but was middle class himself. Her mother originally came from a more
working-class background but had previously worked as Harold Pinter's
secretary, a position with considerable cultural capital. But it was simpler

to ignore these nuances and present Lloyd rising from total obscurity into meteoric mega-stardom instead.

Preserving a sense of ordinary normality served a further purpose for Lloyd, for whom hanging on to her identity as a 'curly-haired, slightly tomboyish, streetwise girl who goes to discos, has what she calls crushes on actors but no boyfriend, and goes shopping in old sweaters and jeans with her old schoolfriends' was an act of self-preservation – what Lloyd called 'a sort of survival kit' for times of duress.[123] Her *Wish You Were Here* director David Leland spotted this tactic in action, in a poignant observation on the losses entailed in achieving fame: 'At one point she used to talk a lot about still being Emily Lloyd. About going out with her roller skates and Walkman in Islington. But that's something she can't do anymore.'[124] Lloyd's frequently professed love of going 'to the park for a kick-around with a soccer ball' or roller-skating down the street also underlined her youth and proximity to childhood.[125] One profile of the young star from 1987 set the scene by describing the paraphernalia of childhood visible throughout her home:

> The rollerskates in the hall are a hint, but the ET doll and teddy bears scattered round her bedroom are a giveaway. Emily Lloyd, the tall, tanned, leggy 16–year-old Londoner whose film debut has made her the hottest girl in town, is still a kid at heart.[126]

Although Lloyd had obviously relished the opportunity to play Lynda in *Wish You Were Here*, she also expressed disquiet at her queasy labelling as 'Lolita 1988' and impatience with the way that stories about teenage girls always had to be presented in terms of what she archly referred to in a funny voice as their 'sexual awakening', asking, 'Why can't they make a film where girls do what boys do?'[127] "I'm a tomboy not a sex-pot,' she stated in another interview, adding elsewhere that she'd like to play 'Indiana Jones the Second, jumping from building to building, or jumping off a moving train, or having a fight on top of a train. That'd be great.'[128] When she was asked to play Mandy Rice-Davies in *Scandal* (1989) she turned it down for being too akin to Lynda in both its period setting and its emphasis on sex.[129]

Instead, Lloyd saw America as her destiny, partly because she was being courted so persuasively by Hollywood in contrast to a paucity of opportunities for a young actress in Britain: 'So few films get made over here and how many of them have good scripts and good parts for a girl my age?'[130] But as with many British stars who have relocated to Hollywood, Lloyd was forced into a slightly defensive position about that decision: 'I'm not turning my back on Britain. I want to go home and do more films there and do some theatre. But I feel I've got to take my chances while they're around. You never know how long it's going to last.'[131] She envisaged America as a place for liberated self-expression: 'My character suits the environment here. You can get away with doing crazy things. If you go to the park and start singing you'd get locked up at home but here they are more likely to join in.'[132] She continued:

> [Americans are] so much more open-minded and optimistic, and they've got lots of go, they know how to enjoy themselves more than we do. What's especially great about Americans is that none of them wants to grow up . . . I'd like to move there and be a kid for the rest of my life.[133]

Lloyd spoke the transatlantic dialect of contemporary youth, a girl whose enthusiasm for US popular culture was evident in the clothes she wore, like her 'Batman baseball cap' or her 'spangled black t-shirt that reads BEACH CALIFORNIA'.[134] Her ability to do well in the US was helped enormously by her natural aptitude for mimicking accents, which opened up a much broader range of potential roles. It enabled her to play a Brooklyn mobster's daughter in *Cookie*, directed by Susan Seidelman and written by Nora Ephron who had intended the role for 'someone like Emily Lloyd but American' but then realised they could cast the real thing if Lloyd was willing to perfect her Brooklyn-ese through voice coaching.[135]

She was equally impressive in her adoption of a Southern American accent for *In Country* (1989), in which she plays a teenage girl who wants to find out more about her father who died in Vietnam before she was born, and was judged 'astonishing in the film's leading role' by critic Roger Ebert: 'she masters not only the Kentucky accent but the whole feeling of Sam: her gawkiness, her energy, the power of her curiosity.'[136] Lloyd had beaten all the 'hot' young American actresses who'd been desperate for the role, including Winona Ryder, and at that point in the late 1980s, as one writer observed, it was 'the fate of all young film actresses to be compared to Emily Lloyd'.[137] Norman Jewison, who directed her in *In Country*, felt that she had an 'innocence' and a 'glow' comparable to Judy Garland and came across 'as a true teenager. Compared with other actresses of her approximate age, she is a downright kid. [She] emanates the vibes of a dancer on *American Bandstand*.'[138] In her lack of sophistication, Lloyd was seen as authentically teenage, as suggested by a 1988 fashion feature in US *Vogue* that described her as 'delightfully adolescent: she talks at 45 rpm, pops her knuckles, nibbles her nails, and hones apocryphal tales'.[139] Whereas Bonham Carter's *Tatler* spread presented her as a dreamy nostalgic vision from the past, Lloyd's spread in *Vogue* had her decked out in ultra-contemporary flouncy little skirts, black and white polka dots, crazy fruit-laden hats, and jeans appliqued with flowers, while the photographer had her jumping in the air and pulling funny faces for the camera.[140] Where Bonham Carter at about the same age had described herself as 'so highly responsible, I'm prematurely mature', Lloyd revelled in her youthfulness and named her ideal role as Peter Pan: 'I never want to grow up. Who does?'[141]

The press characterised Lloyd as a girl whose 'energy level could fuel Concorde' and for whom 'bubbly is a tame description'.[142] Indeed, meteorological and volcanic metaphors seemed in order to describe such high energy levels:

> She burst into the lobby of the Brighton Apartments in Atlantic City like a tornado with nowhere to go. The elderly residents relaxing in the lobby didn't know what to make of the skinny ball of fire with the Cockney accent . . . finally she sits. Even then it's like trying to bottle a mini-volcano. She chats, she stands, she mugs, she jumps up and down.[143]

'Hurricane Emily' was presented as a force of nature, just like her character Lynda from *Wish You Were Here*.[144] But as Lynda had been met with a gaze that was half-admiring, half-diagnostic, so press coverage of Lloyd worried over the unsustainability of such hyperactive effervescence. Where it was supposed arrested development that elicited concern in Helena Bonham Carter's case, Lloyd's problem was perceived as prodigious over-development as this unchaperoned teenager experienced too much of adult life too soon and became a 'wild child', as this 1987 article implies:

> It's two in the morning and I've just danced a mean rumba with British starlet Emily Lloyd. Clearly it is late and Emily should be in bed. She's only 16, sweet 16, but she knows her own mind. 'I just want to dance the night away', she screamed as I left the dance floor at the Café de Paris the other night.[145]

Similarly, while standing at the bar in a posh Manhattan nightclub in 1988, Lloyd resembled 'a kid ordering ice creams from a van in the street, jumping up and down excitedly every time a waitress looks her way', according to journalist Simon Mills.[146] He also noted her habit of taking a water pistol to nightclubs and surreptitiously squirting unsuspecting fellow clubbers, more like comic character Minnie the Minx than the usual aspiring Hollywood player.[147]

Would the young star follow the typical script of child and teen stars and burn herself out? Recounting her first moments of fame at Cannes, one reporter noted how when she arrived at a party, 'all hell broke loose. Suddenly the flies pounced on the jam-pot and she switched to autopilot like a true pro. She kicked her legs for the battery of flash-bulbs.' However, the labour of stardom exacted payment and 'behind the carefully made-up eyes lay the glassiness of exhaustion'.[148] In her autobiography, Lloyd describes working days that 'started at 8am and sometimes didn't finish until midnight and consisted of a seemingly never-ending run of television appearances, press lunches and more interviews'.[149] She feared her teenage years were being eaten up by relentless 'make-up sessions, lawyers' lunches, business meetings and status symbols lumped together under the general heading of "bullshit"'[150] and struggled with the power dynamics of her meetings with Hollywood executives:

> And all the time you're supposed to be a real laser beam, I'm thinking, what are they getting out of this and what am I getting out of this and I'm getting really confused, and thinking either they like me for what I am or it's because they can see dollar signs. And I think it's the dollar signs.[151]

Not for the first time, Hollywood was being presented as the altar on which youthful exuberance was sacrificed in pursuit of profit. 'Sometimes you feel like a lump of meat surrounded by ravens,' Lloyd said in 1988.[152] The metaphor of predator and prey was also the one chosen by David Leland to describe the aftermath of Lloyd's Cannes success: 'I could see the sharks coming out of the deep water, heading right towards her.'[153] Behaving like a cartoon tomboy, armed with water pistol, could be seen as an understandable reaction to the precocious maturity being forced upon the young actress as a 'hot property' with lots of capital riding on her ongoing success. Her childhood paraphernalia of roller skates and ET dolls and teddies had been replaced by hotel rooms in a less innocent state of 'self-inflicted devastation': 'She wades around the room up to her Reeboks in stray film scripts, bouquets of thirsty flowers and piles of unanswered telephone messages.'[154] The messy room and the practical jokes perhaps spoke to a deeper sense of loss that the teenager was attempting to remedy: 'I really miss being a kid and just being able to be stupid and not have responsibility,' she lamented in an interview in 1989.[155] Or maybe one inevitably reads this into her situation with the benefit of hindsight, knowing about Lloyd's subsequent struggles with serious mental illness, including depression and obsessive compulsive disorder (OCD), which she documents frankly in her autobiography. But even at the time, voices of concern were raised about whether she had 'the personality to handle the exposure that flows from such success', fitting her into well-worn cultural mythology about stardom being a curse merely disguised as a blessing that eventually drives its recipients mad.[156]

But it was in Britain rather than in Hollywood that Lloyd's first major breakdown, by her account, occurred. She had accepted the female lead in *Chicago Joe and the Showgirl* (1990), based on the real 'cleft chin' murder case of the 1940s that Orwell had written about in his essay 'The decline of the English murder'. Lloyd's role as Betty Jones was like a nastier re-tread of Lynda in *Wish You Were Here*, another austerity misfit but this time one whose anti-social behaviour became genuinely dangerous rather than mildly uproarious. Betty, a stripper desperate for excitement and fame, teams up with a G. I. deserter (played by Kiefer Sutherland) and they embark on a delusional crime spree pretending to be a gangland kingpin and his moll. The film's sexual scenes, about which *The Sun* expressed its usual prurient indignation ('Emily Lloyd will shock her fans with her most sexually explicit film yet. The girl who shot to fame at 15 . . . has slid into SOFT PORN'), were more troubling for their linkage of arousal and violence, with Lloyd improvising her character sniffing one victim's blood before having sex with her partner in crime.[157] Betty gets the same uncontrollable giggles as Lynda had when she was rather farcically losing her virginity to a bus conductor but Betty's laughter accompanies a different first – her first experience of murder – and is a sign of her psychopathic tendencies.

Figure 6.4 Dangerous and delusional: Lloyd as wannabee gangster's moll Betty in *Chicago Joe and the Showgirl* (1990).

Lloyd's father Roger Lloyd-Pack expressed his worries publicly about the harsh treatment his daughter was receiving during such a harrowing production:

> She isn't getting enough sleep because she is being worked too hard. She is very, very tired. Film people are pretty ruthless. They are not concerned with what's going on in their actors' lives, just with their own budgets and deadlines . . . I'm worried she is not being allowed to live a normal teenage life.[158]

His fears were not unfounded. The combination of making a mentally arduous and unpleasant film with a director Lloyd recalled as deeply unsympathetic, as well as simultaneously dealing with the reawakening of previously suppressed memories of childhood sexual abuse, along with ongoing 'feelings of self-doubt and flagging self-confidence', all culminated in what Lloyd called 'a lethal cocktail of emotions' that led her to attempt suicide.[159]

Lloyd recovered enough to complete the film, and experienced better times on her next two American productions, the low-budget *Scorchers* (1991) and the high-profile family saga *A River Runs through It* (1992), but her ongoing mental health problems, exacerbated by physical and mental exhaustion, recurred periodically, resulting in periods of time spent recuperating in clinics in the UK and US. Her description of her inner torment around this time is chastening bleak:

> Sometimes, when I was alone with only my thoughts for company I yearned for someone to have a gun so I could put it to my head and pull the trigger. I didn't want to die. I just wanted to end the pain inside my head, kill the person inside there that was making my life a misery.[160]

For all that Lloyd's fragility was a product of personal childhood trauma, Hollywood's power structures also played their part in exacerbating her unhappiness. She had been offered a major role in *Mermaids* (1990), which Lasse Hallstrom was slated to direct, but was later bumped off it at Cher's behest and replaced with Winona Ryder who Cher thought looked more plausible as her daughter: 'You don't look genetically like me,' Cher allegedly told Lloyd, to which Lloyd had supposedly replied, perhaps unwisely, 'Well, you don't look genetically like you.'[161] Rightfully angry at Orion for reneging on their contract with her after she had turned down other work to take the role, Lloyd threatened legal action. They then offered a six-figure out-of-court settlement to cover her loss of earnings. A victory for Lloyd perhaps but a pyrrhic one: as several commentators noted at the time, you sued a studio at your peril, especially if you were young, female, and newly arrived in town: 'British stars like Bob Hoskins and Anthony

Hopkins could get away with suing a studio. They had a long pedigree. But this *girl*?'[162] As *Premiere* journalist Jane Preston put it: 'While many saw her stance against movie executive games as being extraordinarily brave, there were those who shook their heads in disbelief, thinking she had committed professional suicide.'[163] Nonetheless, Lloyd still got auditions and won some good roles, proving the industry's received wisdom to be slightly flawed, but arguably she never recovered her peak 'golden girl' status to quite the same extent thereafter.

She had ridden out the publicity generated by her conflicts with Peter Falk while filming *Cookie* (he had supposedly slapped her face in a temper about the way she was playing a particular scene, and she slapped him back, but somehow this reflected less well on her than it did on him), and got over the *Mermaids* debacle, but the problems Lloyd experienced on two further productions in short succession dealt her reputation a more serious blow. After shooting had begun on Woody Allen's *Husbands and Wives* (1992), she was replaced with Juliette Lewis, a decision that Lloyd respected and understood since she felt the role in which she was cast was one she couldn't play convincingly anyway. Harder to bounce back from was her sacking from *Tank Girl* (1995), for which she'd been seen as perfect casting as its riotous eponymous action heroine but from which she was unceremoniously dumped in favour of Lori Petty in a dispute with director Rachel Talalay over the character's haircut. Word got around that Lloyd had refused to shave her hair off, and although she denied that this had ever been the case, the disagreement and her subsequent sacking didn't help her growing reputation as trouble, with her career becoming 'more noted for the films she *didn't* make than for those she did'.[164] As one writer suggested, adapting Oscar Wilde for the occasion, 'to lose one role may be considered misfortune, to lose two might be coincidence, but to lose three is downright careless'.[165] Tabloid stories (of dubious veracity) about her wild antics also had an impact, as she later reflected when trying to resurrect her British career with a smaller role in *When Saturday Comes* (1996): 'Not only do the lies affect your private life, it also affects your career [when] directors and producers pick it up and think, "Oh, that Emily Lloyd's unstable, she's difficult, she's going to have a nervous breakdown, better forget about her."'[166] Lloyd voiced these concerns about her future employability in the March 1996 issue of *Premiere* magazine. Ewan McGregor as Renton in *Trainspotting* graced its cover, representing the latest British film renaissance, but what an indictment of its gender politics that the British cinema revival of the 1990s could only find a minor place for someone as talented and vital as Lloyd, shunting her into a supporting role as Sean Bean's girlfriend in a run-of-the-mill film about football.

The mid-1990s had also seen the growth of 'lad culture', with unapologetically unreconstructed hetero-masculinity, reified by a thin coating of irony, being celebrated across popular culture. Its flagship conduit was the lad's magazine, with the movement's ethos neatly summarised by the tagline for one of the market leaders *Loaded*, for 'men who should know better'. One of the most popular features in 'lads mags' were their pin-up pictures showing young starlets from various entertainment industries in titillating poses and varying states of undress. In the post-feminist climate of the time, this was promoted as empowering for women rather than sexist, and Mike Soutar, editor of *FHM* magazine, noted how the photoshoots were 'fashionable at the moment. Very few women turn it down. The famous want to be flattered. They want to be seen as sexy.'[167] As a young female star with a career to resurrect and a film to promote, Emily Lloyd participated in this trend, appearing as the cover girl for the higher-end men's magazine *GQ* in February 1996, wearing a see-through top, white trousers unbuttoned low on the hip, with her hands clasping (and covering) her breasts under the rather creepy cover line 'Emily Lloyd: She's a big girl now'. Perhaps more surprisingly, the hitherto less sexualised Helena Bonham Carter, who had previously talked about there being 'too much emphasis on the sexuality of actresses', now joined in with the lad-mag photoshoot phenomenon.[168] Wearing black lace underwear, she appeared on the cover of both the US and UK versions of *Maxim* magazine in August and September 2001 respectively, with the cover lines 'Go ape!' (tying in with the release of *Planet of the Apes*) and 'Gosh!', the British variation reflecting both the ultra-Englishness of Bonham Carter's established persona as well as how her appearance as pin-up girl indicated a surprising change of direction.

The fact that both Bonham Carter and Lloyd's very different careers nonetheless converged around this locus of representation suggests something of its dominance over the way that young female stars were understood and presented in media culture at this time: as fully paid-up post-feminists celebrating their sexiness by displaying their bodies for an implied male gaze, in spite of their previously stated wishes to be tomboyish, to wear scruffy rather than sexy clothes, to be appreciated for their acting not merely their looks. The 'choice' agenda of 1990s post-feminism didn't seem to encompass a genuine choice to remain fully clothed while promoting a film.

Conclusion: A Tale of Two Careers

Helena Bonham Carter and Emily Lloyd's discovery and development in the 1980s and 1990s provides a fascinating comparative case study for understanding the complexities of class and gender in British cinema at this time. Both 'chosen from hundreds of young hopefuls to become Britain's newest film star', Lloyd and Bonham Carter's careers and personae were constructed along different lines, although sometimes there were points of convergence.[169] Beyond the formative moments of their initial establishment as stars, their careers also took different paths. As we have seen, Bonham Carter was fortunate enough to evade her rigid persona of perpetually 'pouting under parasols' and was able to navigate her way to an illustrious career, as a highly respected and regularly cast British actress working on both sides of the Atlantic.[170] Lloyd, in spite of a debut that created an extraordinary buzz followed by further critical acclaim for her subsequent roles (particularly *In Country*), found it much harder to move on from the white heat of initial discovery. 'Can we please talk about something else apart from my past?', she requested in an interview in 1996. 'Can't we discuss the present?'[171] But more recently, Lloyd appears to have become more reconciled to how she is remembered for her debut film more than any other: 'I will always be the teenager in the pink dress shouting "up yer bum"', as she put it in the conclusion to her autobiography.[172] Her career became haunted by its 'spectral CV of might-have-beens', not only including the films she'd been hired for and then dismissed from but also those she'd turned down in the process, including Julia Roberts' role in *Pretty Woman* (1990) and Uma Thurman's in *Pulp Fiction* (1994).[173] In both cases, one wonders what may have happened to Lloyd had she been able to play either of these career-defining roles and then enjoyed the massive boost they would in all likelihood have provided. But perhaps her mental equilibrium would only have been unsettled further by reaching those stratospheric levels of A-list fame, the kind of stardom she got momentarily close to but never fully attained. Her rueful awareness of the gap between the glorious future that had been predicted for her and what she actually ended up doing – finding her way through 'the labyrinth of my mental illness' and coming to terms with a less high-flying life – sits at the centre of her fine, funny 2013 memoir. It's a long way from gold watches and limos and planes flying your name over Cannes to the more modest pleasures of volunteering 'at a residential old people's home' in Hackney, 'making cups of tea and playing games, such as "What's the Time Mr Wolf?"' ('Sadly, however, my squeaky shoes meant it was always dinnertime for me.' Lloyd added. 'They taught me a thing or two.').[174] Lloyd seems fully alive to the absurdity of it all, and also just glad to be alive, with no rancour about what may have been. While expressing a tentative wish to revive her acting career in the future, she recognises that this would not be on the same grand scale as before and could not be at the expense of her psychological well-being: 'I realise I may never once again soar so high as I did in the early part of my career. But that's okay. Maybe this time my wings might not get singed.'[175] Lloyd's story may fit with well-worn cultural scripts about Hollywood's all-consuming cruelty as well as the cultural logic of retreatism, as outlined by Diane Negra, whereby various narratives 'prove' women are happiest when they rein in their ambitions and decide to abandon worldly goals in favour of domesticity, and of course Lloyd's story is yet another sad tale of unfulfilled British female star potential.[176] But given her long, hard struggle to gain a modicum of stability and happiness, who could blame her for staying earthbound and eyeing the skies sceptically – a female Icarus who had a lucky escape.

Notes

1. The following year seemed to consolidate that particular moment of British film renaissance with Richard Attenborough's *Gandhi* (1982) harvesting eight Oscars, including Best Picture, Best Director and Best Actor.
2. John Hill, *British Cinema in the 1980s* (Oxford: Clarendon, 1999), p. 48, p. 31.
3. See Hill, *British Cinema in the 1980s*, pp. 53–70, and work arising from the Arts and Humanities Research Council (AHRC)-funded project 'Channel Four and British film culture', including the 2014 special issue of the *Journal of British Cinema and Television*, Vol. 11, No. 4, co-edited by Paul McDonald and Justin Smith.
4. Press release quoted in Laura Mayne, 'Assessing cultural impact: Film4, canon formation and forgotten films', *Journal of British Cinema and Television*, Vol. 11, No. 4, 2014, p. 472.
5. This history is tracked comprehensively in Christine Geraghty, *My Beautiful Laundrette* (London: I. B. Tauris, 2005).
6. Hill, *British Cinema in the 1980s*, p. 56.
7. Norman Stone, 'Through a lens darkly', *The Sunday Times* (Review), 10 January 1988, pp. 1–2.
8. Kureishi quoted in Geraghty, *My Beautiful Laundrette*, p. 10.
9. Hill, *British Cinema in the 1980s*, p. 243.
10. Geraghty, *My Beautiful Laundrette*, p. 16. Justine Ashby has discussed *Pink Pyjamas* as part of a cycle of women's films from this decade, in 'It's been emotional: Reassessing the contemporary British woman's film', in Bell and Williams (eds), *British Women's Cinema*, pp. 153–69.
11. Andrew Higson, *English Heritage, English Cinema: Costume Drama since 1980* (Oxford: Oxford University Press, 2003), p. 93. On the debates around heritage cinema, see also Sheldon Hall, 'The wrong sort of cinema: Refashioning the heritage film debate', in Robert Murphy (ed.), *The British Cinema Book*, third edition (London: BFI, 2009), pp. 46–56; Claire

Monk, 'The British heritage film debate revisited', in Claire Monk and Amy Sargeant (eds), *British Historical Cinema* (London: Routledge, 2002), pp. 176–98; and Hill's summary in chapter 4 of *British Cinema in the 1980s*.

12. For examples of this discourse, see Higson, *English Heritage, English Cinema*, pp. 70–1.
13. Geraghty, *My Beautiful Laundrette*, p. 15.
14. Alison Light, 'Englishness', *Sight and Sound*, March 1991, p. 63.
15. Higson, *English Heritage, English Cinema*, p. 31; emphasis in the original.
16. Michael Church, 'Out of Edwardiana', *The Observer*, 6 December 1992, p. 53.
17. David Bennun, 'Costume drama', *The Guardian* (G2), 7 February 1997, p. 23.
18. Review of *Howards End* quoted in Higson, *English Heritage, English Cinema*, p. 184.
19. Patrick Wright, 'Wrapped in the tatters of the flag', *The Guardian*, 31 December 1994, p. 25.
20. James Rampton, 'Corset still makes sense', *The Independent* (Guide), 10 January 1998, p. 4. Anonymous, 'Helena Bonham Carter', *Film Review Special #24*, 1998, p. 28.
21. Higson, *English Heritage, English Cinema*, pp. 30–1. Hanif Kureishi, 'London's killing off its film-makers', *The Guardian*, 16 October 1991, p. 23.
22. Sarah Gristwood, 'Get Carter', *The Guardian* (G2), 4 October 1996, p. 11.
23. Claire Monk, 'The British heritage film debate revisited', p. 180.
24. Lynda Murdin, 'Helena's royal road to success', *Evening Standard*, 28 September 1984, p. 8. *Just Seventeen*, 2 December 1987, p. 1.
25. Catherine Bennett, 'From schoolgirl to stardom', *The Sunday Telegraph Magazine*, 30 March 1986, p. 36.
26. Morven Kinlay, 'Star is born at sweet 16!', *Daily Express*, 1 October 1986, p. 3.
27. Davis, 'Sign please! Hollywood's in a fizz for Emily', p. 19.
28. Sarah Gristwood, 'Wish you were her?', *Daily Mail* (Femail), 15 April 1989, p. 9.
29. Emily Lloyd, *Wish I Was There: I was the Golden Girl of British Cinema . . . Then my Life Fell to Pieces* (London: John Blake, 2014).
30. Unlabelled article, *Girl About Town*, 2 June 1986, p. 19. Press cuttings file on Helena Bonham Carter, BFI Library.
31. Francesca Simon, 'Lady Jane's leading kids', *Vogue* (US edition), February 1986, p. 92.
32. David Lewin, 'The girl they made a queen', *The Mail on Sunday* (*You* magazine), 10 March 1985, pp. 19–20.
33. Ibid., p. 20.
34. Bennett, 'From schoolgirl to stardom', p. 36. Michael Cable, 'Heart to heart with Helena', *Sunday Express Magazine*, 14 June 1987, p. 20.
35. Anonymous, 'Pass notes: Helena Bonham Carter', *The Guardian (G2)*, 19

August 1993, p. 3. Questions of class continued to dog Bonham Carter's career, and her (rather naïve) claim that '[i]f you're not pretty and you're working class, you have an easier time in terms of people's attitudes to you' (Gristwood, 'Get Carter', p. 11) was met with a curt dismissal from actress Kathy Burke in the letters page of *Time Out*: 'As a lifelong member of the nonpretty working classes I would like to say to Helena Bonham Carter (wholly pledged member of the very pretty upper and middle classes): shut up you stupid c***.' Cited in John Dugdale, 'Feuds Corner', *The Sunday Times* (Review), 20 October 1996, p. 16.

36. James Ivory, quoted in Toby Young, 'The snob value of ivory', *The Guardian*, 2 April 1992, p. 25.
37. Chris Mundy, 'Helena Grows Up', *Premiere*, November 1994, p. 89.
38. Bennett, 'From schoolgirl to stardom', p. 36.
39. Ibid., p. 32.
40. Robert Kilroy-Silk, 'I prefer older men, I can manipulate them', *Today*, 5 November 1988, p. 23.
41. Simon Banner, 'Three of a kind', *The Guardian*, 10 April 1986, p. 13.
42. Sarah Bond, 'Whatever happened to Lady Jane?', *Daily Express*, 1 January 1987, p. 9. Martha Frankel, 'California dreaming', *Movieline*, December/ January 1999, p. 67.
43. Bond, 'Whatever happened to Lady Jane?', p. 9.
44. Louise Tanner, 'Helena Bonham Carter and Cary Elwes', *Films in Review*, April 1986, p. 214.
45. Derek Malcolm, 'An innocent on mean streets', *The Guardian*, 29 May 1986, p. 11.
46. Molly Haskell, 'Why I love Lucy', *Vogue* (US edition), March 1986, p. 70.
47. Young, 'The snob value of ivory', p. 25.
48. Bennett, 'From schoolgirl to stardom', p. 36.
49. Jane Langdon-Davies, 'Thoroughly modern vapours', *What's On in London*, 4 March 1992, p. 4. In another interview, she said: 'I spent most of that film in a fury with myself.' Church, 'Out of Edwardiana', p. 53.
50. Ibid.
51. Bonham Carter cited in Mark Salisbury, 'Helena Bonham Carter', *Total Film*, January 2002, p. 36.
52. Nina Darnton, 'From school to stardom: A teenager's lark for Helena Bonham Carter', *The New York Times* (Review section), 2 March 1986, p. 17.
53. Marshall, 'I can be loud-mouthed, even cocky but I'm not a little madam', p. 9.
54. Anne Williamson, 'Sweet Lady Jane', *Sunday Mirror*, 25 May 1986, p. 20. *Interview* magazine noted that 'both Vogue and Tatler magazines were smitten enough to nominate Bonham Carter as their new face of the 80s.' Anonymous, 'Helena Bonham Carter', *Interview*, March 1986, p. 29.
55. Martin, 'Fame is a pain in the neck for Lady Jane Grey', p. 13.

56. Marshall, 'I can be loud-mouthed, even cocky but I'm not a little madam', p. 9.
57. Beverley D'Silva, 'Private emotions lie hidden in a very public body', *The Sunday Times* (Style), 15 October 1989, p. 5.
58. Kilroy-Silk, 'I prefer older men, I can manipulate them', p. 22.
59. Phrase appears in both Hadley, 'Queen Helena's keeping her head', p. 28, and Cable, 'Heart to heart with Helena', p. 20.
60. Ibid.
61 Corinna Honan, 'My long-distance romance with Warren Beatty', *Daily Mail*, 23 April 1992, p. 7.
62. Williamson, 'Sweet Lady Jane', p. 20.
63. Mundy, 'Helena grows up', p. 87.
64. Cassandra Jardine, 'I have to try living on my own', *The Daily Telegraph*, 21 April 1997, p. 15.
65. Lewin, 'The girl they made a queen', p. 19.
66. Bennett, 'From schoolgirl to stardom', p. 32.
67. Marshall, 'I can be loud-mouthed, even cocky but I'm not a little madam', p. 9; emphasis in the original.
68. Ibid. and Honan, 'My long-distance romance with Warren Beatty', *Daily Mail*, p. 7.
69. Martin, 'Fame is a pain in the neck for Lady Jane Grey', p. 13.
70. Barber, 'Couldn't she just wear a babygro?', p. 5.
71. Anonymous, 'The 2010 international best-dressed list', *Vanity Fair*, September 2010. http://www.vanityfair.com/style/photos/2010/09/the-2010-international-best-dressed-list; Dhani Mau, 'Helena Bonham Carter models in Marc Jacobs Fall ad campaign'. *Fashionista*, 9 June 2011, http://fashionista.com/2011/06/helena-bonham-carter-stars-in-marc-jacobs-fall-ad-campaign; 'Helena Bonham Carter: a style original', *Vogue* (UK edition), July 2013, p. 1.
72. Bonham Carter cited in Beverley D'Silva, 'Goody new shoes', *Sunday Express Magazine*, 21 April 1991, pp. 13–14. Bonham Carter obviously branched out and bought another pair, because an interview from the following year made a point of noting her 'peculiar shoes – cream-coloured lace-up ankle boots with little heels'. Langdon-Davies, 'Thoroughly modern vapours', p. 4.
73. Higson, *English Heritage, English Cinema*, p. 163.
74. Shingler, *Star Studies*, pp. 111–12.
75. Higson, *English Heritage, English Cinema*, p. 25.
76. Ibid., p. 192.
77. Anonymous, 'Pass notes: Helena Bonham Carter', p. 3.
78. On how she came to be in *Miami Vice*, Bonham Carter has said: 'They called and asked if I would do it and I said "sure". It was the hippest show in America, so I thought why not?' Frankel, 'California dreaming', p. 67. But still only twenty at the time, Bonham Carter was not only too young to have

been a qualified doctor, but she looked it too, which created problems for her plausibility. Moreover, in bedroom scenes, she recalled that she 'looked like one of those Victorian photographs of a child – semi-pornographic. They were horrified. Don, particularly, because it made him look like a paedophile. We got on very well and kept laughing about how we were a completely incongruous pair', the tough Miami cop and 'this midget from England who looks sort of 19th Century'. Bond, 'Whatever happened to Lady Jane?', p. 9.

79. Nigel Dempster, 'Of corsets Helena', *Daily Mail*, 21 April 1987, p. 17.

80. Bonham Carter cited in David Lewin, 'Rebel without a corset', *Daily Mail*, 14 March 1991, p. 7.

81. Andrew Duncan, 'I like to remind people I exist out of a corset', *Radio Times*, 1 January 1994, p. 24. Anonymous, 'Spotlight: Helena Bonham Carter', *Radio Times*, 13 July 1996, p. 7.

82. Jardine, 'I have to try living on my own', p. 15.

83. Rampton, 'Corset still makes sense', p. 4. Andrew Duncan, 'Par for the corset', *Radio Times*, 11 October 2003, pp. 26–9.

84. Cited in Salisbury, 'Helena Bonham Carter', p. 36.

85. Ibid.

86. Geraghty, 'Crossing over: Performing as a lady and a dame', p. 44.

87. Bonham Carter discusses suffering from 'inevitable indigestion' as a result of wearing corsetry for screen roles and being 'convinced that the corsets she wore as Lucy Honeychurch exacerbated her varicose veins (she had the veins removed shortly afterwards)'. Anonymous, 'Ten things every Helena Bonham Carter fan ought to know', *Radio Times*, 17 January 1998, p. 43.

88. Valerie Steele, *The Corset: A Cultural History* (Boston: Yale University Press, 2001).

89. Anonymous, 'The Victorian', *Vanity Fair*, April 1998, p. 171. Andrew Pulver, 'What's all the fuss about Helena Bonham Carter', *The Guardian* (G2), 24 September 1999, p. 12.

90. Frankel, 'California dreaming', p. 63. It is worth noting that this obsessively repeated metaphor of the corset does not only apply to Bonham Carter but to a whole range of 1990s English actresses, including Kate Winslet: the twenty-fourth *Film Review* star supplement listed Kate Winslet as the ninth most significant international star in 1998 because 'get her in a corset and the girl's a winner' (p. 50). Similarly, Kate Beckinsale in the same special issue spoke of being linked with similarly nineteenth-century accoutrements as a result of appearing in 'quaint costume dramas': 'for a while there people sort of assumed that I used a chamber pot, wore bloomers, and always had both feet on the floor!' (p. 93).

91. A few examples of this recurrent English Rose labelling include Steve Walker, 'A thorny new role for an English rose', *The Mail on Sunday*, 30 August 1992, p. 13; Anonymous, 'The fresh face of the 90s', *The Mail on Sunday* (*You* magazine), 10 April 1994, p. 54; Mundy, 'Helena grows up', p. 87; Baz Bamigboye, 'Helena cuts the costume parts to play modern

Miss', *Daily Mail*, 16 February 1996, p. 43; Stephen Rebello, 'Lady Jane', *Movieline*, December/January 1999, p. 22.

92. Church, 'Out of Edwardiana', p. 53, and how Bonham Carter was described at the Yardley launch, as reported in 'Pass notes: Helena Bonham Carter', p. 3.

93. Bonham Carter cited in Salisbury, 'Helena Bonham Carter', p. 36; emphasis in the original.

94. Sean Thomas, untitled article, *Evening Standard Magazine*, 23 December 1993, p. 8. Press cuttings file on Helena Bonham Carter, BFI Library.

95. Diana Hutchinson, 'Why me?', *Daily Mail*, 18 August 1993, p. 3.

96. Anonymous, 'Look who's making-up with Helena', *Daily Mail*, 28 July 1993, p. 21.

97. Hutchinson, 'Why me?', p. 3.

98. Anonymous, 'Look who's making-up with Helena', p. 21.

99. D'Silva, 'Goody new shoes', p. 16.

100. Claire Roberts, 'Face facts Elizabeth', *Evening Standard*, 14 March 1995, p. 47.

101. Tony Blair, *New Britain: My Vision of a Young Country* (London: Fourth Estate, 1996), p. 65.

102. Bamigboye, 'Helena cuts the costume parts to play modern Miss', p. 43.

103. Cited in Rampton, 'Corset still makes sense', p. 4.

104. Anonymous, 'The Victorian', p. 171.

105. D'Silva, 'Private emotions lie hidden in a very public body', p. 5. The same desire to shatter preconceptions is also in evidence in these remarks from a few years later: 'everyone seems to think I'm very ladylike. That I'm very cultured and intelligent. I drink a lot of diet coke and belch. I've been known to use the F-word. I've told a few dirty jokes.' *Film Review Special #24*, 1998, p. 28.

106. Jeff Ferry, 'See Emily play', *Sunday Express Magazine*, 22 November 1987, p. 26. Benedict Nightingale, 'Britain's Emily Lloyd: sweet 16 and a smash', *The New York Times* (Review section), 19 July 1987, p. 21.

107. Ibid.

108. Hilary Bonner, 'School daze', *Daily Mirror*, 1 June 1987, p. 23.

109. Jo Weedon, 'Wish you were her?', *The Mail on Sunday* (*You* magazine), 28 June 1987, p. 34.

110. Andrew Moncur, 'Happy to be there', *The Guardian*, 16 May 1987, p. 36.

111. Nightingale, 'Britain's Emily Lloyd: Sweet 16 and a smash', p. 21.

112. Daniela Soave, 'Advantage Miss Lloyd', *The Sunday Telegraph* (*7 Days* magazine), 14 January 1990, p. 15.

113. Ferry, 'See Emily play', p. 26.

114. Jim Varriale, 'Emily Lloyd: Little Miss Moxie', *Vogue* (US edition), February 1988, pp. 372–7.

115. Hill, *British Cinema in the 1980s*, p. 127. For more on this cycle of 1980s films, see Phil Powrie, 'On the threshold between past and present: "Alternative

heritage"', in Justine Ashby and Andrew Higson (eds), *British Cinema, Past and Present* (London: Routledge, 2000), pp. 316–26. In spite of their often scrupulously authentic recreations of their period settings (and sometimes being critiqued for being just as much 'art-directed to within an inch of their lives' as the heritage cycle), these films have been seen as taking a less elitist and more historically interrogative approach to the national past, sometimes labelled 'alternative' heritage or 'retro film'. Claire Monk, *Heritage Film Audiences* (Edinburgh: Edinburgh University Press, 2011), p. 16.

116. Ferry, 'See Emily play', p. 26. Although in another interview, her take on the character was slightly different: 'She's just a sad, lonely girl who swears a lot and uses sex to get attention because her father doesn't really love her.' Weedon, 'Wish you were her?', p. 34.

117. Leland cited in Nightingale, 'Britain's Emily Lloyd: Sweet 16 and a smash', p. 21.

118. David Lewin, 'Hottest cookie in town', *Daily Mail*, 8 March 1988, p. 7.

119. Anonymous, 'Wish you were on our books, Emily', *Today*, 22 August 1987, p. 11.

120. Ibid.

121. Ferry, 'See Emily play', p. 26. Mary Riddell, 'Miss Knockout', *Daily Mirror*, 6 May 1988, p. 18. Nightingale, 'Britain's Emily Lloyd: Sweet 16 and a smash', p. 21.

122. Weedon, 'Wish you were her?', p. 32.

123. Baz Bamigboye, 'Funny girl's balancing act', *Daily Mail*, 13 June 1988, p. 24. Riddell, 'Miss Knockout', p. 18.

124. Sarah Gristwood, 'Emily changes her spots', *TV Times*, 10 February 1990, p. 4.

125. Benedict Nightingale, 'The Americanization of Emily', *The New York Times* (Review section), 20 August 1989, p. 23.

126. Weedon, 'Wish you were her?', p. 32.

127. Lloyd cited in Lewin, 'Hottest cookie in town', p. 7. Ferry, 'See Emily play', p. 29.

128. Weedon, 'Wish you were her?', p. 34. Nightingale, 'Britain's Emily Lloyd: Sweet 16 and a smash', p. 21.

129. Michael Owen, 'From here to America', *Evening Standard*, 4 November 1988, p. 22.

130. Ibid.

131. Anonymous, 'So glad to be here', *Evening Standard*, 15 January 1988, p. 24.

132. Ibid.

133. Nightingale, 'Britain's Emily Lloyd: Sweet 16 and a smash', p. 32.

134. Nightingale, 'The Americanization of Emily', p. 23. Neal Karle, 'Is America ready for a star like Emily Lloyd?', *Rolling Stone*, 5 October 1989, p. 95.

135. Ibid.

136. Roger Ebert, 'In country', originally published 29 September 1989. Archived at http://www.rogerebert.com/reviews/in-country-1989

137. Untitled article, *The Sunday Telegraph* (*7 Days* magazine), 5 November 1989, p. 9. Press cuttings file on Emily Lloyd, BFI Library.
138. Karle, 'Is America ready for a star like Emily Lloyd?', p. 97.
139. Varriale, 'Emily Lloyd: Little Miss Moxie', p. 373.
140. Ibid. Lloyd recalls how Annie Leibowitz had her running in and out of New York traffic to convey a sense of energy in another photoshoot around the same time. Lloyd, *Wish I Was There*, p. 88.
141. Tanner, 'Helena Bonham Carter and Cary Elwes', p. 214. Varriale, 'Emily Lloyd: Little Miss Moxie', p. 374.
142. Unlabelled article, *Today*, 4 December 1987, p. 31. Press cuttings file on Emily Lloyd, BFI Library.
143. Davis, 'Sign please! Hollywood's in a fizz for Emily', p. 19. A possible cocaine habit was inferred as one reason for her endless effervescence although one of her friends defended her from this accusation: 'People think she's on drugs but that's just her personality.' Richard Pendlebury, 'What went wrong with the world of Emily Lloyd?', *Daily Mail*, 7 July 1997, p. 23. Lloyd herself admitted to dabbling in drug use later on in Hollywood but insisted that despite 'speculation that my troubles have been down to drug addiction', she actually had more trouble with 'the legal drugs that were prescribed to [her] over the years' in order to help control her depression and bi-polar disorder. Lloyd, *Wish I Was There*, pp. 139–40.
144. Nightingale, 'The Americanization of Emily', p. 1.
145. Baz Bamigboye, '"Wild" Emily's a sweet 16', *Daily Mail*, 19 September 1987, p. 7.
146. Simon Mills, 'Tough kooky!', *Sky*, June 1988, p. 9.
147. The water pistol habit was also noted in Riddell, 'Miss Knockout', p. 18.
148. Unlabelled article, *Today*, 4 December 1987, p. 31. Press cuttings file on Emily Lloyd, BFI Library.
149. Lloyd, *Wish I Was There*, pp. 66–7.
150. David Quantick, 'The knuckleduster hits Hollywood', *NME*, 28 November 1987, p. 26.
151. Ibid.
152. Riddell, 'Miss Knockout', p. 18.
153. Gristwood, 'Emily changes her spots', p. 4.
154. Mills, 'Tough kooky!', p. 7.
155. Drew MacKenzie, 'Am I growing up too fast?', *Daily Mirror*, 10 December 1989, p. 24.
156. Gristwood, 'Emily changes her spots', p. 4.
157. Anonymous, 'Lloyd's lust', *The Sun*, 22 March 1990, p. 26.
158. Chris Hitchin, 'Ruthless routine broke lonely Emily, says dad', *Today*, 17 August 1989, p. 18.
159. Lloyd, *Wish I Was There*, p. 116.
160. Ibid., p. 132.
161. Ibid., p. 109.

162. Sue Russell, 'Redford rescued me from my Hollywood nightmare', *The Mail on Sunday*, 17 January 1993, p. 35; emphasis in the original.
163. Jane Preston, 'Wish you were her', *Premiere*, March 1996, p. 46.
164. Ibid., p. 43; emphasis in the original.
165. Untitled article, *Time Out*, 22 June 1994, p. 67. Press cuttings file on Emily Lloyd, BFI Library.
166. Preston, 'Wish you were her', p. 43.
167. Quoted in Roger Tredre, 'A spate of undress', *The Guardian* (G2), 14 January 1996, p. 9.
168. Hadley, 'Queen Helena's keeping her head', p. 28.
169. Kinlay, 'Star is born at sweet 16!', p. 3.
170. Church, 'Out of Edwardiana', p. 53.
171. Emma Cook, 'Look back in horror', *The Guardian* (G2), 12 November 1996, p. 6.
172. Lloyd, *Wish I Was There*, p. 268.
173. Andrew Billen, 'The Billen interview: Emily Lloyd', *The Observer Magazine*, 4 February 1996, p. 6.
174. Lloyd, *Wish I Was There*, p. 265.
175. Ibid., p. 268.
176. Diane Negra, *What a Girl Wants? Fantasizing the Reclamation of Self in Postfeminism* (London: Routledge, 2009).

CHAPTER 7

National Treasure: Judi Dench and Older Female Stardom into the 2000s

There are not many major female film stars over sixty, and fewer still are 'newcomers' at that age, but Judi Dench is an exception to those general rules, having become an important figure in films after receiving an Oscar nomination for her performance in *Mrs Brown* (1997) at the age of sixty-three. Of course, Dench's acting career had begun decades earlier. A doctor's daughter from York, she had trained at the Central School of Speech and Drama in the mid-1950s and joined the Old Vic in 1957. She then went on to develop an enduring and especially rewarding recurrent association with the Royal Shakespeare Company (RSC) stretching from 1961 to the present day, one major highlight being her Lady Macbeth opposite Ian McKellen in the RSC's 1976 production. In lighter vein she had also been a celebrated Sally Bowles in the first UK production of the musical *Cabaret* in 1968, with the distinctive 'sob-catch' in her voice prompting the theatre to display a sign explaining 'Miss Dench does not have a cold, that is her normal voice'.[1] Dench had also done some very distinguished television work early in her career, most notably as the rebellious daughter of the family in John Hopkins' four-part drama *Talking to a Stranger* (1966). A few decades later, Stephen Frears made excellent use of her in the television films *Going Gently* (1981) and *Saigon – Year of the Cat* (1983), especially relishing 'the bits in between' the dialogue when he could 'just photograph the light on her face' and felt the actress had 'real cinematic qualities. She reminds me slightly of Celia Johnson.'[2] But despite the high esteem in which she was held as a screen presence by someone like Frears, not everyone shared his view. Dench had been told by a film producer back in 1959 that she had every single thing wrong with her face during an audition, which left her lastingly wary of seeking work in that particular medium (although she nearly got the lead in *A Taste of Honey* but, as she put it, 'Rita Tushingham just pipped me'[3]). Nonetheless Dench still won a BAFTA Most Promising Newcomer to Leading Film Roles Award for one of her rare early film performances, as a young mother at the end of her tether in *Four in the Morning* (1965) and in the same year she was also a sympathetic screen presence as the girl who falls for a cat burglar in *He Who Rides a Tiger* (1965). But this early promise would not be fully realised until much later in her career. Between 1965 and 1995, the main focus of her attention and efforts lay elsewhere, predominantly in theatre, as represented by her impressive awards tally of three *Evening Standard* awards and four Olivier awards as best stage actress accrued over that thirty-year period. Beyond occasional appearances and more minor roles (like the lady novelist in *A Room with a View*), her next really significant foray into the cinema would come with her arrival as the new 'M', 007's boss, in the James Bond film *Goldeneye* (1995), accusing 007 of being a 'sexist, misogynist dinosaur'. Dench's M progressively acquired more screen time and greater narrative importance in the films, culminating in her last one, *Skyfall* (2012), in which she was central to its oedipal dynamic as good/bad mother to both Bond (Daniel Craig) and his antagonist Silva (Javier Bardem).

Mrs Brown, the film about Queen Victoria's widowhood and romantic friendship with John Brown (Billy Connolly) which had acted as Dench's belated calling card for a major-league film career, was originally intended as a television film for the BBC. But its theatrical distribution rights were acquired by Miramax on the basis of Harvey Weinstein's belief that this was 'a movie' with the potential to do well in the US arthouse sector. Weinstein's hunch was vindicated by the $13 million plus it went on to gross, helped along the way by Dench's Oscar nomination for which Weinstein had lobbied hard. 'It is thanks to him that I've got a film career,' Dench has said of Weinstein, and even went to the extent of getting a fake tattoo of his name on her buttock to demonstrate her gratitude: 'It's quite difficult to embarrass Harvey, but I did! I've never seen a man more embarrassed and I've never let him forget it!'[4] The status conveyed by having first been Oscar-nominated, and then Oscar-winning the following year for another regal role, Elizabeth I in *Shakespeare in Love* (1998), conspired to give Dench's film career, previously just a minor tributary, a huge boost in exposure and leverage. Weinstein, first via Miramax and then the Weinstein Company, has distributed four out of the five further films for which Dench has been nominated as Best Actress to date: *Chocolat* (2000), *Iris* (2001), *Mrs Henderson Presents* (2005), and *Philomena* (2013) – Fox Searchlight distributed *Notes on a Scandal* (2006). He has been a crucial ally and advocate of Dench's acting abilities, positioning her as 'the consummate actress of her day. When you think of great acting there are two names at the top of the list: Meryl Streep and Judi Dench. It's been a privilege for me to have made seven movies with Judi. I have gone out of my way to make sure that there were parts written for her.'[5] Having such a powerful friend in Hollywood has undoubtedly served her well.

On the strength of Dench's late-blooming international film stardom, on top of a long and illustrious stage and television career, the actress has become enshrined as a 'national treasure', seen to embody the best of Britain: 'Railings should be built around her so that all may admire her in an orderly and respectful fashion,' Stephen Fry has suggested, in comments that recall earlier comparisons of Diana Dors to various state monuments.[6] Dench's on-screen performance of Queen Victoria and Queen Elizabeth I, and her off-screen status as a Dame of the British Empire, coalesce perfectly, making her a figure of semi-monarchical significance. Director John Madden believes that 'in a lot of people's eyes she is the equivalent of the queen' while critic Michael Coveney suspects that 'the British public would probably vote for her as their queen in an open election'.[7] In fact she came second only to Queen Elizabeth II in a 2002 poll to determine who was 'the most respected and liked public figure in Britain'.[8] But the quasi-monarchical 'national treasure' label is one that Dench herself rejects: 'I don't like that very much, I'm afraid. That sounds pretty dusty to me. It's Alan Bennett and I behind glass in some forgotten old cupboard.'[9] Comedienne Tracey Ullman presented a more subversive version of Dench's national treasure status in her 2016 comedy show, showing the actress (uncannily impersonated by Ullman) behaving appallingly and using her 'national treasure' status as a form of diplomatic immunity or magic charm to prove her innocence. Of course she couldn't be shoplifting those bottles of wine from the convenience store or vandalising hotel toilets, she's Dame Judi Dench.

From comments such as Harvey Weinstein's quoted above, valorising Dench's professional excellence, it is clear how Judi Dench's persona could be seen to correspond very closely with Christine Geraghty's category of the 'star as performer', a film star who is 'defined by work' and usually 'associated with the high cultural values of theatrical performance, even when that performance takes place in film or television'.[10] Industry insiders like Weinstein as well as her fans celebrate Dench for her outstanding acting abilities. Like a number of other stage-trained British actors, she has been able to adapt her style of performance to work equally effectively on-screen, which has facilitated her late blooming as a film star. 'Acting is not the things you say, it's the things you don't say. It's like in watercolour – it's what you leave out that's most important,' she has suggested; comments that recall Richard Dyer's identification of understatement as the keystone of powerful British screen performance.[11] The emotive power of this understated approach reverberates through Dench's screen performances, particularly (in my view) in the films *Iris, Notes on a Scandal*, and *Philomena*. However, this chapter will not focus on the specificities of Dench's acting performances, and will take somewhat for granted her much-vaunted abilities as an actress. Instead, it will focus on how Dench fulfils another of Geraghty's categories: the 'star as celebrity'. Although Dench's acting prowess goes a long way in constituting her persona, it is not the whole story of how she is understood as a public figure. Her recurrent presence in popular culture – whether as a 'national treasure', as someone analogous to the Queen, as chat-show guest, newspaper and magazine interviewee, or an object of comic parody – suggest her extratextual cultural currency beyond stage or screen roles alone. There's an interesting comparison to be made with Dame Maggie Smith, who has herself enjoyed a late career boost through starring roles in films such as *The Best Exotic Marigold Hotel* (2011) and *Quartet* (2012) but most prominently through her celebrated role as the Dowager Countess in the popular television series *Downton Abbey* (2010–15). That character's acid asides spawned an online meme cult (as documented by Stefania Marghitu), but it is important to note that Smith's online celebrity is not as herself but *in character* as the countess.[12] Smith seems much more confined to the 'star as performer' category, and in spite of her stylish off-screen appearance, she does not seem to function as a celebrity in quite the same way as Judi Dench.[13] This chapter will consider the various ways in which Dame Judi Dench's persona as an older female star mediates issues around age and ageing and how Dench is not only a celebrated actress and 'national treasure' but also a figure of major significance in modelling 'good' female ageing, a territory still riddled with pitfalls borne of both misogyny and gerontophobia.

Graceful Ageing or Grey Abandon

Richard Dyer once suggested that 'we're fascinated by stars because they enact ways of making sense of the experience of being a person', and older female stars and celebrities can certainly help to 'make sense' of the experience of ageing.[14] They offer guidance on how to navigate the challenging territory of ageing appropriately as a woman, caught between the rock and the hard place of either inappropriately trying to preserve youth beyond its 'natural' tenure (sometimes through surgical intervention) or alternatively succumbing too readily to the ravages of age by 'letting oneself go'. That there should be such a thirst for positive images of ageing is unsurprising, given current Western demography. The populous baby-boom generation entering the early stages of old age, boosting the economic power of the 'grey pound', has created an unprecedented new desire for visibility in age. Judi Dench's later-life movie stardom is of a piece with the broader growth in British and American films centred on older protagonists, notable examples of the trend including *Something's Gotta Give* (2003), *Calendar Girls* (2003), *Ladies in Lavender* (2004), *It's Complicated* (2010), *Song for Marion* (2012), *45 Years* (2015), *Grandma* (2015), *Mr. Holmes* (2015) and the *RED* and *The Expendables* action franchises (2010 onwards). *The Best Exotic Marigold Hotel* of 2011, starring both Dench and Maggie Smith as well as Bill Nighy, Penelope Wilton, and Celia Imrie, was seen by industry commentators as especially 'game-changing', with a worldwide box-office take of about $137 million. It 'dynamited a door that had long been padlocked to aged actors: bankable, above-the-title stardom' and inspired a 2015 sequel that took in the region of a further $86 million.[15]

In being an older star actress, Judi Dench fitted in with what *Entertainment Weekly* called 'Hollywood's hottest new trend' for 2015: its burgeoning gerontophilia. *The Best Exotic Marigold Hotel*'s address to a sixty-plus demographic who are 'willing to reach into their wallets for movies that speak to them' and moreover 'account for 13 percent of all tickets sold in North America, a fairly large slice of the pie' may have been one of the strongest contributory factors to the enormous profits it generated. For similar reasons, in the last few years Jane Fonda, Charlotte Rampling, and Helen Mirren have been chosen to front major cosmetics advertising campaigns while in their sixties and seventies. Nowadays, as Jermyn and Holmes suggest, 'the older woman celebrity need not fade away into invisibility but instead may still embody style and desirability'.[16] Contrary to previous industry wisdom, using older stars and models is no longer off-putting but aspirational.

It is impossible to go any further in this discussion of older female stardom without pausing to consider another British Dame, Helen Mirren, who like Dench also won an Oscar for playing a monarch – in *The Queen* (2006) – and who has also enjoyed an unexpected later-career boost as a film star after being previously more strongly associated with prestigious stage and television work. The highly prominent international success of both Dench and Mirren says something about older women's new cultural visibility, and the growing cultural advocacy for post-middle-age life being just as dynamic and fulfilling as the years that came before. As Helen Mirren remarks in her 2015 L'Oréal advertising campaign: 'Age is just a number!' However, despite their numerous similarities, Mirren and Dench present rather different forms of celebrity embodiment. They are more than ten years apart in age (at the time of writing, Mirren is seventy while Dench is eighty-one) and Mirren's public image is much more obviously entangled with discourses of sexuality than Dench's. As scholars Sadie Wearing and Kirsty Fairclough-Isaacs have noted, Mirren is 'framed as explicitly desirable', perpetually typed as 'hot Helen', and when her 'bikini body' was captured by a paparazzi photographer in 2008, her remarkably nubile figure became a media cause célèbre. [17] On the strength of incidents like this and her numerous very glamorous red-carpet appearances (far more than for the roles she actually plays on film), Mirren has become ubiquitous as a model of 'remarkably lovely' exceptional ageing, managing to be both sexy and 'graceful', and has become a central figure in the growing corpus of scholarship on media representations of older women.[18] By comparison, Dench presents an image that is more gamine than bombshell image, exemplified by her trademark pixie haircut. In contrast to Mirren's 'transgressive, exceptional' sexual allure represented by her preternaturally youthful physique, Dench could be seen as embodying a more physically ordinary version of femininity.[19] Fellow actress Minnie Driver's comment in 2002 about Dench being 'very small, round, middle-aged' may have been interpreted as unsisterly critique but it does suggest something of Dench's more quotidian un-starry physicality (as well as tallying with Dench's own remarks that she was 'a menopausal dwarf' when she played Cleopatra on stage in her fifties).[20] This may be one reason for Dench having garnered less academic commentary around questions of female ageing thus far in comparison with Mirren.[21] But Dench's ordinariness is arguably the source of her power, as a more readily attainable ideal of the 'graceful ager', to use Dolan and Tincknell's phrase, who is still able to negotiate the tricky terrain of female ageing with apparently effortless aplomb.[22]

Having crossed the threshold age of eighty, Judi Dench may be seen as moving beyond the so-called 'third age' and towards the gerontological category of the 'fourth age', into what sociologist Julia Twigg describes as 'the more challenging territory of deep old age'.[23] But even prior to her landmark eightieth birthday in December 2014, Dench had directly addressed, both in her on-screen appearances and in her off-screen publicity, some of the challenges endemic to ageing. A number of her roles deal either indirectly or more directly with the losses or aftermath of widowhood, as in *Mrs Brown*, *As Time Goes By* (1992–2005), *The Last of the Blonde Bombshells* (2000), *Mrs Henderson Presents*, *The Best Exotic Marigold Hotel*, and *Esio Trot* (2015), and Dench herself was sadly widowed in 2001 after a long and happy partnership with actor Michael Williams, with whom she had frequently co-starred. A number of other films starring Dench present ageing in terms of decline, decrepitude, and irrecoverable loss. The biopic *Iris* focuses on Iris Murdoch's harrowing one-way journey into dementia, contrasting the bright eloquent young writer with the numbness of the older and much diminished iteration. Both *Ladies in Lavender* and *Notes on a Scandal* deal movingly with the unreciprocated sexual desire for younger people felt by the characters played by Dench. Even in films that generally have a lighter tone, there are moments of tension centred on ageing as loss, as critic Whitney Pastorek discerns in a short scene from *Mrs Henderson Presents*:

> [T]here is a moment when Dame Judi Dench stands before her mirror, clad in a loosely tied dressing gown, and performs a short, sultry, entirely unabashed fan dance in the darkness of her bedroom. When the dance ends, she stares into the glass – her gown slipping from one pale shoulder – and her blue eyes burn with heartbreak. She is ravishing, and it's almost too painfully private to watch.[24]

The waning of nubile youth and subsequent enforced movement into desexualised old age are presented as an arduous voyage that takes its emotional toll, echoing Bette Davis's famous remark about old age being no place for sissies.[25] Beyond her screen roles, Judi Dench has also spoken out publicly about her own struggles with loss of sight caused by age-related macular degeneration and, in broader terms, what she sees as the failings of care for the elderly in contemporary Britain, borne of a deep-seated gerontophobia: 'We're not good at dealing with old age in this country. We shove people in a room and leave them sitting round a television.'[26] Indeed, the whole premise of *The Best Exotic Marigold Hotel* is that the labour of caring for older people could be outsourced to the Indian subcontinent, in parallel with call-centre work (although the only character in

Figure 7.1 Unreciprocated desire in old age: Judi Dench as Ursula in *Ladies in Lavender* (2004).

the ensemble who really requires extensive care is Maggie Smith's Muriel who is recovering from a hip-replacement operation).

Although ageing entails loss, it can also provide new opportunities. The trauma of bereavement that features in a number of Dench's screen roles is often linked to a kind of rebirth. This includes taking on new professional roles, as in *Mrs Henderson Presents* in which her character takes over a theatre, or *The Best Exotic Marigold Hotel* in which she plays a woman who has never had a paid job before but becomes a cultural consultant for an Indian call centre. Although not a widow, Dench's Matty Jenkyns in *Cranford* (2007–9) also starts a business in later life and gains a new vitality from it. Widowhood also enables new romantic entanglements for the characters she plays, such as the one with Bill Nighy's character in *The Best Exotic Marigold Hotel*, or with Billy Connolly's Scottish ghillie in *Mrs Brown*. Dench's on-screen roles communicate a vision of the older female protagonist as, to use Jermyn's formulation, 'active, vital, still passionate about life and new experiences'.[27] As one character remarks of sex in *The Best Exotic Marigold Hotel* (although the comment applies to aspects of life beyond sex too): 'it's never over.' This continual thirst for new challenges tallies with Dench's own approach to life, as outlined in interviews: 'I'm not prepared to stop doing things. If I can't do one thing then I'll have a go at another,' a credo presented as 'a legend's sparky wisdom' from which we could all learn.[28]

In spite of the challenging aspects of ageing to which Dench's screen roles often allude, the longevity of her acting career and its sudden stratospheric success in a new medium, offers a powerful counter-narrative of positive ageing. Rather than old age seeming to represent a dwindling of one's powers as so often suggested, particularly of post-menopausal women, Judi Dench suggests the possibility of later life as a period of unparalleled success, capitalising on the accumulated wisdom and skill that come from years of life experience. Eva Krainitzki suggests that Dench's late-flowering and ongoing success as a film star 'fabulously subverts commonsensical notions of an actress's life course'; as the narration for a recent television documentary on Dench insisted, 'she just gets better and better'.[29] Some commentators have even suggested that her looks have improved with age, which has 'endowed her with the kind of imperious beauty that she perhaps once lacked'.[30]

But interestingly this idea of welcoming and enjoying the experience of ageing is something the star herself problematises and sometimes actively repudiates in interviews: 'I don't embrace ageing, I think it's hideous . . . I don't let the word "old" happen in my house.'[31] This rhetoric of transcending age by ignoring it features in other interviews with Dench and echoes the 'just a number' slogan in Mirren's L'Oréal advert: 'Age is a number. It's something imposed on you . . . You are only as old as you feel. It's not to do with age; it's something to do with inside. It's the engine.'[32] In such remarks, we can see how chronological age is being superseded by a more subjective approach, corresponding with Sadie Wearing's observations on how ageing in post-feminist culture frequently entails 'a fantasy of escaping (or evading) time', or of maintaining a state of perpetual girlhood despite one's biological age.[33] In light of this, it is interesting to note how Judi Dench's publicity often details the star's engagement with activities more readily associated with younger demographics. She has talked about her love of the Facetime app on her iPhone, while her knowledge of texting acronyms like 'YOLO' provides the title for an article on her in *Good Housekeeping* magazine: 'You don't have to tell me what YOLO means!'[34] In that same article, the star reports that she is considering getting a permanent tattoo, in addition to her fake Harvey Weinstein one, and her temporary crystal neck tattoo of the 007 logo for the *Skyfall* premiere.[35] On her seventieth birthday, she bought herself a speedy sports car to roar along the roads and 'play her Bond greatest hits CD at full volume and make the pensioners stare'.[36] It is significant that several of these youthful activities are linked with her appearance in the Bond films; arguably her connection with this franchise has kept her in close association with (youth-orientated) contemporary action cinema unlike many of her other acclaimed film roles that tend more towards the arthouse end of the market and an older audience.

Dench delighted in being shown how to smoke a joint convincingly for her role in Sally Potter's film *Rage* (2009), and enthusiastically took up drinking Starbucks' Caramel Macchiatos and riding a micro-scooter while filming *The Shipping News* in 2001 – all activities and pursuits more readily associated, however erroneously, with younger people.[37] Even when she does adopt a hobby that is seen as more culturally befitting of an older woman, it is presented as having a surprising twist, as actor Matthew Macfadyen observed of Dench on the set of *Pride and Prejudice* (2005):

> She makes these like needlework embroideries on set in the tedium of filming . . . but they are all: 'You Are a Cunt'. And she gives them as presents. And it's Dame Judi Dench. And she is doing this beautifully, intricate, ornate [work]. You kind of see the work materializing as the shoot goes on. Like: 'You Are a Fucking Shit'.[38]

Given the fact that the British Board of Film Classification (BBFC) receives more complaints when Judi Dench swears in a film than any other star, one wonders what those complainants would make of her love of obscene embroidery.[39] But revelations like these correspond with recurrent comments in profiles and biographies about Dench's unruly sense of humour, as do her participatory appearances on cheeky comedic chat shows such as *The Graham Norton Show* (2007–). They forge some unexpected connections between her ostensibly sedate celebrity image and the raucous sweary 'ladette' culture associated with certain versions of post-feminism, in the same way as Tracey Ullman's caricature does in comedic form.[40] Far less subject to the criticisms faced by younger women who adopt such behaviours, Dench's privileged position in terms of seniority, class identity, and professional status enables her to use culturally loaded signifiers like tattoos and swearing to complicate the stuffy reputation commonly bestowed upon theatrical dames. Instead of compromising her damely dignity, they arguably provide a fuller sense of a well-rounded individual running counter to the usual (rather restrictive) cultural logic of what is appropriate for women over sixty. Despite being 'enthroned as a "national treasure"', for critic Michael Coveney she is 'in reality the naughty girl at the back of the class'.[41] Dench's co-star in *Mrs Brown*, Billy Connolly, has suggested 'how tiresome she finds the doily-and-serviette crowd. You know, those English twittering f***ing women – they think she's one of them, and she isn't': a rebuttal of any possible staidness about Dench's personality that nonetheless problematically hinges on her juxtaposition with a broader denigration of older English femininity and of the star's own fan base.[42]

In an intriguing coda, Judi Dench even became an inadvertent participant in British youth culture when her surname was adopted as an acclamatory adjective by the rapper Lethal Bizzle, a phenomenon met with understandably bemused broadsheet commentary.[43] When Dench was interviewed for Greg James's BBC Radio 1 show in October 2012 – a remarkable event in itself, given the station's generally youth-oriented tone – she agreed to pose in Bizzle's 'Stay Dench' merchandise, striking a pose in a baseball cap emblazoned with her unexpectedly repurposed surname. Her approval, in turn, galvanised sales of Bizzle's clothing line, as the rapper later recounted:

'I pulled over to the side of the road when she came on the radio and she really smashed it. When she started saying in her posh voice that her grandchildren wore T-shirts saying "Denchgang" on them it had me in stitches. I'll send her a Christmas card and send her whole family some Denchgang stuff'.

Speaking about his sales since Judi Dench wore the cap, he said: 'They have gone mental. I'll wake up and I'll get random sales at 3am from Australia. We've been talking to Selfridges for a while but the reaction from Judi hurried up the deal. They took loads of caps. They were like, "We can't ignore this". It sealed the deal'.[44]

It may have started off as coincidence that Bizzle's synonym for 'cool' happened to be the same as the surname of one of Britain's foremost actresses (and the source of much 'culture clash' hilarity in the press). But the way in which that random connection then developed and flourished provides further evidence of Dench's engagement with youth and youthfulness, as well as consolidating her status as a 'good sport' who doesn't take herself too seriously – perhaps one of the highest accolades in British culture.

'Judi Dench: Style Icon'

Central to her embodiment of 'graceful ageing', Judi Dench's style of dress, hairstyle, and make-up have been the subject of extensive laudatory commentary in the press and in online fora. Tellingly, the star features regularly in the UK *Daily Mail*, in both its print and online iterations, a newspaper that has been recognised as an important site of debates around contemporary female identity, due to both its appeal to women readers as well as its frequently paradoxical strictures around what constitutes 'acceptable' femininity. As Diane Railton and Paul Watson point out, it offers 'a blueprint for how to grow old(er) and how to be old(er) as a woman as well as a set of guidelines for how to put this into practice [and] frequently identifies and celebrates "role models" for the older woman, figures in the public eye who are deemed to have aged well', among them Joan Collins, Twiggy, Jerry Hall, and the inevitable Helen Mirren.[45] And yet, as Railton and Watson note, this newspaper regulates successful ageing in terms that are so narrow and so self-contradictory as to border on the uninhabitable:

> So, women should diet, but do so 'sensibly'; exercise, but 'in moderation'; dye greying hair, but to a 'natural' shade; wear make-up, but not appear 'gaudy'; look 'sexy', but not act sexually. Indeed, the watchwords of attractive older femininity are apparently decorum, poise, elegance and grace.[46]

It is noteworthy, therefore, that Dench is held up by the *Daily Mail* as an exponent of successful older femininity, balancing perfectly those contradictory demands. For example, a picture of her red-carpet appearance in a long dress with split skirt at the 2013 Venice Film Festival was captioned 'Elegant: The distinguished actress shows her younger counterparts how to flash the flesh and still maintain dignity', invoking unspecified inelegant younger women flashing too much flesh in order to boost Dench's prestige by comparison, in a 'slut-shaming' move typical of the *Mail*'s commentary.[47]

Despite not having fashion model provenance like the aforementioned Twiggy and Jerry Hall, nor being a 'well-maintained' former sex symbol like Joan Collins, Judi Dench has nonetheless managed to achieve the status of style icon, named as such in a Pinterest page devoted to her look ('Judi Dench, style icon'). Fashion bloggers have eulogised her prescient sense of style ('she rocked the pixie long before Anne Hathaway', according to one of them), *The Guardian*'s fashion team have named her as one of the most stylish over-fifties, and *Elle* magazine has acclaimed her 'timeless glamour', admiring how she has 'perfected the art of red carpet dressing later, rather than earlier, in life. We learned everything we know about dress coats from her.'[48] Having presented her with a lifetime achievement award in 2011, *Harper's Bazaar*'s fashion and beauty editor Avril Graham has lavished further praise on Dench's personal taste more recently as 'never froufrou. She possesses an innate elegance, but is comfortable and is a touch bohemian.'[49] Noting that the star 'does not have (and never has had) a designated stylist,' Graham concluded: 'Let's be real here: this is a lady of a certain age and an actress who is about her craft. She doesn't need a style agenda.'[50] Stylishness is thus constructed as being best served by not being attended to over-assiduously, and 'effortless' style depends upon an apparent lack of contrivance, a concern with higher matters.

This belies the degree of effort and, it is worth stating, money that goes into the maintenance of such 'casual' elegance. Avril Graham's commentary on Dench reveals how far designer brands underpin the star's glamorous appearance, with mention of 'a Donna Karan black v-neck gown', a 'relaxed black Eileen Fisher ensemble', 'a dusty blue kurta and white trousers by the Linen Press (an English company that operates out of a former Cumbrian farmhouse)' and 'Indian designers Abu Jani and Sandeep Khosla [who] have a shop on Beauchamp Place right around the corner from Harrods'.[51] Dench's look may appear artless but its air of bohemianism conceals the expenditure that makes it much harder to emulate than it may initially appear.

This was demonstrated when one *The Daily Telegraph* reader wrote to the newspaper's fashion editor Hilary Alexander, planning a mother-of-the-bride (MOB) outfit and using Dench as a possible role model:

> I feel a special effort is called for and so have been investigating the MOB possibilities in magazines and on the net. Most are awful! I realise I am 60 and not as slim as I once was, but I do not want to look either frumpy or shiny! What I would really like is something akin to the jewelled/beaded coats which Dame Judi Dench has worn to many film premieres.[52]

Dench figures here as a template for the average-sized older woman who wants to be glamorous (not 'frumpy') while avoiding gaudiness (or being too 'shiny'). The advice that follows is revealing:

> Judi Dench's coats are indeed like something from 1,001 Nights – but they are expensive . . . the cost for off-the-peg coats is between £1,500 and £6,000. For made-to-measure sharwanis, as they are called, try Daminis, Green Street . . . £2000 for the more detailed . . . A cheaper alternative, worth exploring, is one of the devoré (burnt-out) velvet coats from Hampstead Bazaar, St Christopher's Place, London . . . in velvet with metallic gold thread, £175; matching scarf, £45.[53]

Even the cheapest option listed here is expensive, with the top-of-the-range coats worn by the star herself costing significantly more, thereby making the emulation of that look on a regular basis economically impossible for many women. As Joanne Garde-Hansen has observed, 'reinvention of the aging self may be costly and unsustainable', and Dench's much-admired signature hairstyle ('Judi Dench haircut' is one of the most popular internet search terms associated with her name), despite its artless casual appearance, is perfected through the kind of precision cutting and carefully applied sparkly silver and ash blonde highlights that do not come cheap.[54]

Surgical interventions and invasive cosmetic procedures are often seen as the true battleground of female ageing in the public eye, and Judi Dench is often praised for her mature acceptance of the wrinkles and lines that 'natural ageing' brings. The courage of this stance is not to be taken lightly, given the cultural pressure on older women in the public eye to 'refresh' their appearance periodically. It seems like a mixture of pride and trepidation that motivated Dench to write in her diary on the eve of the 1998 Academy Awards: '<u>Countdown to the Oscars!</u> Or will I be the only unlifted face in Hollywood?'[55] Making it in Hollywood 'unlifted' and over sixty, Dench acts as a powerful endorsement of the ageing woman's continuing 'radiance' (a word often applied to the star) and a repudiation of the idea that an acceptable embodiment of older femininity necessarily entails medicalised intervention. Indeed, some commentators have explicitly juxtaposed what they see as more generous European approaches to women's ageing with the dynamic of denial that they conflate with the American attitude:

> [O]ne cannot enjoy the abundant offerings of our current film and TV landscape without noticing the distinct differences between the faces of our counterparts across the various ponds and the sinewy, panicked faces over here. Watching *Downton Abbey* with Maggie Smith's delightfully craggy face and the aging – and ageless – women who make up both the upstairs and 'down'; *Broadchurch* with Olivia Colman's

unglamorous and oh-so-human and weary eyes; *The Bletchley Circle* with its 'four ordinary women' (truly); Dame Judi Dench in . . . anything . . . The gritty offerings of pretty much every other country that casts actors and actresses who look like real people with *un*perfect faces and bodies who, therefore, truly represent the *un*perfect audiences watching them. Here in the States? We have men and women who clearly hate their faces so much that when any hint of age makes itself known, it's cut away like so much loathsome debris. Perfection is the goal; age is the cancer.[56]

But this celebration of age 'acceptance' should perhaps be tempered with an awareness of the cultural capital possessed by the likes of Judi Dench that makes this rejection of artificial rejuvenation not only possible but much more acceptable. Dench candidly acknowledges the appeal of erasing the ravages of age: 'I'd love to go right now and come back with completely smooth skin . . . it's not that I don't mind the lines, because I do, but just not enough to do anything.'[57] However, she then goes on to imply that a combination of being 'squeamish' and of not wanting to compromise her ability to act, and indeed her niche in the industry, may have prevented her: 'My agent would go barmy. I'd do myself out of the parts for old people.'[58] And the star's rejection of the quick, easy rejuvenation of surgery or cosmetic fillers does not preclude her ability to benefit from the less culturally derogated youth-giving properties of an expensive hairstyle and bespoke tailoring. Those watchwords of appropriate ageing identified by Railton and Watson – 'decorum, poise, elegance and grace' – and the avoidance of anything overly sexy or 'gaudy', have obvious connotations of class, with a strong bias towards a subtlety of self-presentation implicitly understood to be middle class.[59] As Jermyn suggests of Jane Fonda, '"successful" ageing is explicitly tied to her consumerism and use of the right products', and despite Judi Dench's somewhat different star image, there are obvious connections to be made to Dench's own highly 'classed' star image, her purchase of the correct accoutrements, and what is widely regarded as her graceful negotiation of ageing.[60]

Conclusion: 'The Sense of a Future'

Judi Dench's on-screen and off-screen appearances are usually quite distinct from each other, with the actress most frequently appearing either in period dress (*Ladies in Lavender, Pride and Prejudice, Cranford*) or in more dowdy contemporary guise (*Notes on a Scandal, Philomena*) in contrast with her more glamorous 'red carpet' appearances or her casual elegance 'off duty'. Mike Goodridge noted the disparity between Dench in character as Barbara in *Notes on a Scandal* – 'the actress has never looked so grim, all dark nylon suits and sensible shoes' – and how glamorous Dench looked

Figure 7.2 Elegant ageing in flowing scarves: Judi Dench as Evelyn Greenslade in
The Best Exotic Marigold Hotel (2011).

off-screen: 'Smart, in a green linen suit with her trademark short, grey haircut and topaz jewellery adorning neck and fingers, she's as sophisticated as Barbara is drab.'[61] Her on- and off-screen images converge in the perfectly tailored suits she wears in the Bond films or the all-black fashion garb of *Rage,* but there's an even greater degree of convergence in *The Best Exotic Marigold Hotel*, in which her character Evelyn Greenslade wears clothes that are virtually indistinguishable from the actress's own signature wardrobe of tunics and loose trousers, accessorised with draped patterned scarves, and the same gamine cropped hairstyle.

As discussed earlier, *The Best Exotic Marigold Hotel* is directly concerned with the indignities and difficulties of old age experienced by its ensemble of characters as well as reflecting upon (while also shoring up) India's magical status as a realm in which the British are able to 'find themselves'. Evelyn begins the first film newly widowed, closeted, and befuddled by aspects of modern life ('Is wireless the same as broadband and what on earth does that have to do with Wi-Fi?') before reinventing herself as a foreign traveller, adventurer, blogger, and financially independent woman with a fulfilling job. In its final sequences, her fond friendship with Douglas (Bill Nighy) tentatively blossoms into romance and the closing shots of the film visually link the triumphantly reunited young couple riding on their motorbike, Dev Patel's Sonny up front while Tena Desae's Sunaina clings on to him riding pillion, and the older couple who strike exactly the same pose on their own motorbike, eliding any distinctions along the lines of age: romance is romance, regardless of how old the couple may be. Nighy's cobalt blue and white patterned shirt contrasts beautifully with Dench's flowing turmeric and saffron tunic and scarf, as their bike zips along the busy street. The overall impression of this moment is very much akin to what Jermyn discerns in certain moments in *Something's Gotta Give*, 'which, however clumsily, give subjectivity, visibility and the sense of a *future* to these older women'.[62]

For all the class-bound impediments to any simple notion of identification with Dench, such a vibrant portrayal of an older woman *still* remains a relative rarity despite the evident thirst for such a thing: for instance, a 2011 UK Film Council survey found that 69 per cent of women aged 50–75 felt that their group was significantly under-represented.[63] This may have been the reason why this film struck such a chord, and made such a profit, receiving the ultimate endorsement of bankability in the shape of a sequel. Things are beginning to change in terms of age's figuration in cinema and Judi Dench is one of the 'patron saints' of that tentative representational shift, whether playing the increasingly central M in the Bond films leading up to *Skyfall*, or a woman on a quest whose situation dominates and defines the narrative, as in *Philomena*, or an older romantic lead, as in *The Best Exotic Marigold Hotel* films. In an essay on representations of older women, Rosy Martin asked about where we may 'look for images of "average" middle-aged or older women when the media concentrate upon a heroine/victim dichotomy showing older women as either super-fit marathon runners or shivering in lonely pensioner poverty, whilst radical make-over, under-the-knife, prime-time entertainment reinforces the desirability of looking ten years younger'.[64] I would suggest that something resembling the kind of middle ground sought by Martin may be found in the celebrity persona of Dame Judi Dench, doing the utopian work of stardom identified by Richard Dyer of magically resolving societal contradictions. Both aspirational and down-to-earth, 'real' and glamorous, regal and raucous, Dench's star persona acknowledges the physical, mental, and social changes of old age while managing to disavow the conventional wisdom that it necessarily entails dilapidation and a 'process of dispossession'.[65] Although the apparent resolutions Dench's star persona offers to that series of feminine contradictions are, of course, largely illusory, it would feel ungenerous to do anything other than agree with one blogger's assessment of Dench's remarkable achievement not only as a great actress but as an important older female celebrity: 'Pretty badass, don't you think?'[66] While 'the figure of the ageing woman star remains a heavily contested site', as Jermyn suggests, Judi Dench's ability to incarnate age and power in female form, 'exuding authority and confidence [so] that she doesn't so much walk into a room as sweep through it', may be what makes her a true national treasure.[67]

Notes

1. Alan Franks, 'Mother courage', *The Times Magazine*, 19 November 2005, p. 48.
2. Gerald Jacobs, *Judi Dench: A Great Deal of Laughter* (London: Weidenfeld and Nicolson, 1985), p. 138. Dench also appeared in the popular sitcoms *A Fine Romance* (1981–4) and *As Time Goes By* (1992–2005), another indication of her performative range.
3. Jacobs, *Judi Dench*, p. 119.
4. Dench cited in Scott Feinberg, 'And now, a word with the queen', *The Hollywood Reporter*, 28 February 2014, p. 60.
5. Weinsein cited in ibid.
6. Kira Cochrane, 'Does nobody ever believe anything I do?', *The Guardian* (Weekend), 12 September 2009, p. 21. Other selected examples of Dench's description as national treasure include Michael Coveney, 'Queen Judi', *The Independent*, 9 December 2004, p. 12, and Michael Billington, 'Please god, not retirement', *The Guardian*, 12 September 2005, p. 22.
7. Madden cited in Matt Wolf, 'Interview', *The Sunday Telegraph* (Review), 30 November 2003, p. 3. Coveney, 'Queen Judi', p. 12.
8. Chloe Fox, 'Do not go gentle', *Telegraph Magazine*, 3 February 2007, p. 37.
9. Cochrane, 'Does nobody ever believe anything I do?', p. 21. In another 2009 interview, she instructed the journalist, 'Please stop using that phrase . . . And it is your mission to make sure everyone else does too.' Tim Teeman, 'Judi twinned with punch', *The Times (Times 2)*, 11 December 2009, p. 3.
10. Christine Geraghty, 'Re-examining stardom: Questions of texts, bodies and performance', in Christine Gledhill and Linda Williams (eds), *Reinventing Film Studies* (London: Arnold, 2000), p. 188.
11. Alex Lewin, 'Judi Dench', *Premiere*, December 1999, p. 46. Richard Dyer, 'Feeling English', *Sight and Sound*, March 1994, p. 16.
12. Stefania Marghitu, 'Violet, Dowager Countess of one-liners: Maggie Smith in *Downton Abbey* and internet stardom', unpublished paper presented at Exploring British Film and Television Stardom conference, Queen Mary, University of London, 2 November 2013. It is worth noting that Tracey Ullman's impersonation of Maggie Smith for the same series mentioned earlier hinges on the actress's versatility and her professional self, not her off-screen behaviour as with her take on Dench.
13. Interesting to note that Michael Coveney sees Dench and Maggie Smith as claimants for the title of 'greatest living British actress' along with a third actress, Vanessa Redgrave, whose persona is significantly complicated by her off-screen political activities and allegiances. Coveney, 'Queen Judi', p. 12.
14. Dyer, *Heavenly Bodies*, p. 17.
15. Keith Staskiewicz, 'Is 70 the new 30?', *Entertainment Weekly*, 14 August 2015, p. 22.
16. Deborah Jermyn and Su Holmes (eds), 'Introduction', in *Women, Celebrity*

and Cultures of Ageing: Freeze Frame (London: Palgrave Macmillan, 2015), p. 4.

17. Wearing, 'Exemplary or exceptional embodiment? Discourses of aging in the case of Helen Mirren and *Calendar Girls*', p. 149. Fairclough-Isaacs, 'Mature Meryl and Hot Helen', pp. 140–54. Anonymous, 'Helen Mirren the bikini queen reigns supreme at 63', *Mail Online*, 21 July 2008. http://www.mailon sunday.co.uk/tvshowbiz/article-1035510/Helen-Mirren-bikini-queen-reig ns-supreme-63.html.

18. The phrase 'remarkably lovely' comes from Bim Adewumni, 'The crush: Helen Mirren', *The Guardian* (Weekend), 1 November 2014, p. 6. Mirren's exceptional ageing is also discussed in Josie Dolan, '*The Queen*, aging femininity, and the recuperation of the monarchy', in Aagje Swinnen and John A. Stotesbury (eds), *Aging, Performance and Stardom: Doing Age on the Stage of Consumerist Culture* (Zurich and Berlin: LIT Verlag, 2012), pp. 39–53.

19. However, Dench is far from being an asexual figure, given her playing of Sally Bowles in *Cabaret*, her nude scenes in the television drama *Langrishe Go Down* (1978) and her *Esio Trot* (2015) co-star Dustin Hoffman's comments about her powerful allure, reported in Abid Rahman, 'Dustin Hoffman: Judi Dench is a "scrumptious-looking woman"', *The Hollywood Reporter*, 26 November 2014. http://www.hollywoodreporter.com/news/ dustin-hoffman-judi-dench-is-752443

20. Christa D'Souza, 'Leave the dame alone, Minnie', *The Daily Telegraph*, 24 January 2002, p. 23.

21. The exceptions to the general rule of Dench being neglected in favour of focusing on Mirren are Eve Krainitzki, 'Judi Dench's age-inappropriateness and the role of M: Challenging normative temporality', *Journal of Aging Studies*, Vol. 29, April 2014, pp. 32–40; Melanie Williams, 'The best exotic graceful ager: Dame Judi Dench and older female celebrity' in Jermyn and Holmes (eds), *Women, Celebrity and Cultures of Ageing*, pp. 146–61; and discussion of Dench's tenure as M in Lisa Funnell (ed.), *For His Eyes Only: The Women of James Bond* (London: Wallflower Press, 2015).

22. Josephine Dolan and Estella Tincknell (eds), *Aging Femininities: Troubling Representations* (Cambridge: Cambridge Scholars Press, 2012), p. xi.

23. Quoted in Deborah Jermyn, 'Introduction: "Get a life, ladies. Your old one is not coming back": Ageing, ageism and the lifespan of female celebrity', *Celebrity Studies*, Vol. 3, No. 2, 2012, p. 2.

24. Whitney Pastorek, 'Judi Dench', *Entertainment Weekly*, 10 February 2006, p. 36.

25. Quoted in Martin Shingler, 'Bette Davis: acting and not acting her age', in Jermyn and Holmes (eds), *Women, Celebrity and Cultures of Ageing*, p. 54.

26 Dench cited in Anonymous, 'Meet the very British cast of The Best Exotic Marigold Hotel', *Radio Times Online*, 24 February 2012. http://www.radio times.com/news/2012-02-24/meet-the-very-british-cast-of-the-best-exotic -marigold-hotel.

27. Jermyn, 'Introduction: "Get a life, ladies. Your old one is not coming back"', p. 1.
28. Simon Perry, 'Judi Dench: What I know now', *People*, 16 March 2015, p. 93.
29. Krainitzki, 'Judi Dench's age-inappropriateness and the role of M', p. 32. *Talking Pictures (Judi Dench)*, BBC Television, 13 December 2014.
30. Fox, 'Do not go gentle', p. 37.
31. Becky Freeth, 'Now THIS is why Dame Judi Dench is nothing short of awesome', *Marie Claire*, 9 December 2013. http://www.marieclaire.co.uk/blogs/545057/now-this-is-why-dame-judi-dench-is-nothing-short-of-awesome.html.
32. Abid Rahman, 'Judi Dench is tired of people saying she is too old to act', *The Hollywood Reporter*, 12 November 2014. http://www.hollywoodreporter.com/news/judi-dench-is-tired-people-748698.
33. Sadie Wearing, 'Subjects of rejuvenation: Aging in postfeminist culture', in Yvonne Tasker and Diane Negra (eds), *Interrogating Postfeminism: Gender and the Politics of Popular Culture* (Durham, NC: Duke University Press, 2007), p. 278.
34. Feinberg, 'And now, a word with the queen', p. 60. Joanne Finney, 'You don't have to tell me what YOLO means!', *Good Housekeeping*, March 2015, pp. 22–6. Therefore, what Bryan Appleyard says of her character in *Philomena* applies equally to the actress: 'Far from being an unsophisticated old lady, she is worldly and fully aware of modern ways.' Brian Appleyard, 'What Philomena is really about', *Huffington Post*, 9 March 2014. http://www.huffingtonpost.com/bryan-appleyard/what-philomena-is-really_b_4555773.html.
35. Finney, 'You don't have to tell me what YOLO means!', pp. 22–6.
36. Fox, 'Do not go gentle', p. 37.
37. John Miller, *Judi Dench: With a Crack in her Voice* (London: Orion, 2003), p. 323.
38. Yagana Shah, '5 things we love about Judi Dench on her 80th birthday', *Huffington Post*, 5 August 2014. http://www.huffingtonpost.com/2014/12/08/judi-dench-birthday_n_6277764.html. The playwright David Hare was the recipient of a cushion with the words 'fuck em fuck em fuck em fuck em' (Dench's motto in relation to unkind critics) daintily embroidered on it, according to Billington, 'Please god, not retirement', p. 22. Other recipients of similar gifts have included Nigel Havers, Anna Massey and Stephen Frears. Jacobs, *Judi Dench*, p. 151.
39. Cochrane, 'Does nobody ever believe anything I do?', p. 21.
40. Carolyn Jackson and Penny Tinkler, '"Ladettes" and "Modern Girls": "Troublesome" young femininities', *Sociological Review*, Vol. 55, No. 2, 2007, pp. 251–72.
41. Coveney, 'Queen Judi', p. 12. See also Richard Eyre's comment that 'there's a kind of roguishness, a larkiness to her, that's irresistible. There is forever a twinkle in her eye.' 'Richard Eyre on Judi Dench', *The Times* (Times 2), 2 February 2006, p. 15.

42. Franks, 'Mother courage', p. 52.
43. Sam Wolfson, 'Judi Dench: A new street icon?', *The Guardian*, 6 December 2011. http://www.theguardian.com/culture/shortcuts/2011/dec/06/judi-dench-street-icon. This had been partly pre-empted by the revelation that macho US star Vin Diesel was an unlikely Dench fan, to the extent of having a part specially written for her so that she could star in his action vehicle *The Chronicles of Riddick* (2004).
44. Tom Eames, 'Lethal Bizzle thanks Judi Dench for sales of clothing brand', *Digital Spy*, 11 December 2012. http://www.digitalspy.co.uk/showbiz/news/a444466/lethal-bizzle-thanks-judi-dench-for-sales-of-clothing-brand.html#~p59Z3FaqxjGKdW.
45. Diane Railton and Paul Watson, '"She's so vein": Madonna and the drag of aging', in Josie Dolan and Estella Tincknell (eds), *Aging Femininities: Troubling representations* (Cambridge: Cambridge Scholars Press, 2012), p. 199.
46. Ibid., p. 200.
47. Anonymous, 'Still stunning at 78! Dame Judi Dench wows at Venice Film Festival in elegant ivory gown . . . as she shows how to elegantly flash a leg', *Mail Online*, 1 September 2013. http://www.dailymail.co.uk/tvshowbiz/article-2408128/Dame-Judi-Dench-wows-Venice-Film-Festival-elegant-ivory-gown--shows-elegantly-flash-leg.html.
48. Amanda McGowan, 'Judi Dench style evolution: She rocked the Pixie long before Anne Hathaway', *Huffington Post*, 7 December 2012. http://www.huffingtonpost.com/2012/12/06/judi-dench-photos-2012_n_2251608.html. Jess Cartner-Morley, 'The 50 best-dressed over-50s – in pictures', *The Guardian*, 29 March 2013. http://www.theguardian.com/fashion/gallery/2013/mar/29/50-best-dressed-over-50s. Leisa Millar, 'Timeless glamour', *Elle UK*, 23 May 2014. http://www.elleuk.com/fashion/celebrity-style/timeless-glamour-fashion-icons-joan-collins-judi-dench-jane-fonda#image=6.
49. Bee Shapiro, 'Judi Dench of "Philomena": In real life, dressing the part', *The New York Times*, 20 December 2013. http://www.nytimes.com/2013/12/22/fashion/Judi-Dench-Philomena-Red-Carpet-Fashion-.html?_r=2&.
50. Graham cited in ibid.
51. Ibid.
52. Hilary Alexander, 'Ask Hilary: Where can I find a Judi Dench evening coat?', *The Daily Telegraph*, 23 August 2010. http://fashion.telegraph.co.uk/article/TMG7954089/Ask-Hilary-Where-can-I-find-a-Judi-Dench-evening-coat.html.
53. Ibid. The particular difficulties for older women in finding flattering clothes that are pleasurable to wear is outlined in Pamela Church Gibson, 'No-one expects me anywhere: Invisible women, ageing and the fashion industry', in Stella Bruzzi and Pamela Church Gibson (eds), *Fashion Cultures* (London: Routledge, 2000), pp. 79–89.

54. Joanne Garde-Hansen, 'The hip-op generation: Re-presenting the ageing female body in Saga Magazine' in Josie Dolan and Estella Tincknell (eds), *Aging Femininities: Troubling Representations* (Cambridge: Cambridge Scholars Press, 2012), p. 163.

55. Quoted in Miller, *Judi Dench: With a Crack in her Voice*, p. 292; emphasis in the original.

56. Lorraine Devon Wilke, 'Why American women hate their faces and what they could learn from the Brits', *Huffington Post*, 4 March 2014. http://www.huff ingtonpost.com/lorraine-devon-wilke/why-american-women-hate-their-fac es_b_4897336.html; emphasis in the original.

57. Dench cited in Finney, 'You don't have to tell me what YOLO means!', p. 26.

58. Ibid.

59. See Beverly Skeggs, *Class, Self, Culture* (London: Routledge, 2003).

60. Jermyn, 'Introduction: "Get a life, ladies. Your old one is not coming back"', p. 2.

61. Mike Goodridge, 'It's a bitch of a role for Dame Judi', *Evening Standard*, 5 October 2006, p. 34.

62. Deborah Jermyn, '"Glorious, glamourous and that old standby, amorous": The late blossoming of Diane Keaton's romantic comedy career', *Celebrity Studies*, Vol. 3, No. 1, 2012, p. 48; emphasis in the original.

63. Ibid.

64. Rosy Martin, 'Outrageous agers: Performativity and transgression: Take one', in Josie Dolan and Estella Tincknell (eds), *Aging Femininities: Troubling Representations* (Cambridge: Cambridge Scholars Press, 2012), p. 99.

65. Kathleen Woodward, *Aging and its Discontents: Freud and Other Fictions* (Bloomington: Indiana University Press, 1991), p. 149.

66. McGowan, 'Judi Dench style evolution'.

67. Jermyn, '"Glorious, glamourous and that old standby, amorous"', p. 49. Unlabelled article, *Daily Mail* (*Weekend* magazine), 24 May 2008, p. 7. Press cuttings file on Judi Dench, BFI Library.

CHAPTER 8

Conclusion: The Unbearable Whiteness of Being (a Female British Star)

In 1997, just as Judi Dench was gaining a major star profile via *Mrs Brown*, Helena Bonham Carter was receiving acclaim for her career-changing role in *The Wings of the Dove*, and Kate Winslet was completing the block-buster *Titanic* (1997) that would make her globally famous by the end of the year, a controversy arose that would reveal a great deal about the unspoken gatekeeping processes for British film stardom. For the Cannes Film Festival's fiftieth anniversary year, the industry body British Screen had organised a deputation of fifty young 'rising British stars' to be flown over to mark the occasion. It included Winslet, as well as Anna Friel, Natascha McElhone, and Lena Headey among its female contingent. But Marianne Jean-Baptiste, an Oscar nominee earlier that year for *Secrets and Lies* (1996), and the first black British woman (and only the second black Briton) to be nominated, was not invited to join the group. While Emily Watson and Kristin Scott Thomas, the other eligible British Oscar nominees that year, had been included, Jean-Baptiste had not. Nor were any other black or Asian actors of either sex. The actress decided to speak out about her feelings at this egregious exclusion:

> It's been getting to me. I had got a bit down when I saw some of the celebrities in Cannes because I thought it would be good to be there. Then when I was told that British Screen had invited a group of young actors out to celebrate the 50th anniversary, I just burst into tears because I thought this is so unfair. It was a snub.
>
> What more do they want? Maybe I should have done a soap. It is a shame on Britain. I see myself as British and I want to be celebrated by Britain. It's difficult to know how to react when something like this happens. Sometimes you think maybe I should keep quiet. I don't want to sound like someone who has a chip on their shoulder. But if you keep quiet nothing will ever change and nothing will ever be done about it.[1]

Jean-Baptiste's brave disclosure of her disappointment and anger at not being considered a worthy rising star to represent Britain at Cannes raised serious questions about the exclusionary whiteness of the British film industry. It laid bare a situation that was rarely so explicitly demonstrated: that even in late twentieth-century Britain, in a supposedly modern multi-cultural society, British film stardom still seemed to be conceived in wholly white terms. British Screen chair Simon Perry's weak response – 'There were people who in terms of credits had the edge. Everybody has their pet omission' – singularly failed to acknowledge the obvious double standard at work in the selection criteria for who could and couldn't be considered a 'rising star'. Oscar nominations counted for nothing in the face of this cognitive block.

When thinking over the difficulties and prejudices faced by many of the stars detailed in this book's preceding chapters – the lack of opportunities to demonstrate their talent or even just to get work, the criticism of their looks, the way they were disregarded as they grew older – it is vital to recall that the obstacles faced by Black, Asian and minority ethnic (BAME) British actresses have been more numerous and harder to surmount. They did not only have to contend with an industry that frequently lurched from crisis to crisis and was not always very effective in its development and deployment of female talent but also with there being virtually no opportunities for them to be able to forge any kind of meaningful career, let alone attain stardom. Diana Dors, Rita Tushingham, and Emily Lloyd did at least all have their moment in the sun at Cannes, regardless of whatever transpired next for them – something that Marianne Jean-Baptiste was denied.

Looking back over the period in time covered by this book, and even during the decades before, the same stories of marginalisation of non-white actresses echo down the years, revealing new depths of thwarted or unrealised female potential. There is the charismatic and radiant Elisabeth Welch, the American-born singer and performer who settled in Britain in the 1930s and co-starred with Paul Robeson in *Song of Freedom* (1936) and *Big Fella* (1937) but otherwise, as Stephen Bourne notes, 'was given little to do in British films other than sing songs in cabaret or nightclub sequences' and who would later say of her career, 'I was in films, but I wasn't a "star".'[2] The breathtakingly beautiful Merle Oberon *was* a star of both British and Hollywood films in the 1930s and 1940s, mentored and supported by her husband Alexander Korda, but in order to achieve that success she had to deny her Anglo-Indian heritage and concoct a fake ultra-white upbringing in Tasmania as the daughter of an aristocratic colonial family (and, according to some reports, pretend her mother was actually her Indian servant).[3] Fearful that her 'exotic' looks may give the game away, Oberon made use of skin-bleaching cosmetics and a special light was even devised with her in mind, nicknamed 'the Obie', which had the effect of making skin appear lighter.[4] Thirty years on, similar problems around ethnicity and exclusion manifested themselves. Despite the wishes of director Carol Reed, he was not able to cast Shirley Bassey as Nancy in *Oliver!* (1968) because Columbia Studios feared such a casting choice 'would alienate filmgoers in the American South' (it would take until 2007 for Sophie Okonedo to play the role as a black woman in a BBC adaptation of Dickens' novel).[5] Singers like Bassey or Cleo Laine provided important input into films but it was through their memorable rendering of theme tunes rather than as on-screen performers that they did it. It seems remiss that the evident star potential that Glenna Forster-Jones demonstrated in *Joanna* (1968) and *Leo the Last* (1970) went undeveloped. The same is true of Cassie McFarlane, despite winning the *Evening Standard* British Film Award for Best Newcomer for *Burning an Illusion* (1981). In 1992, the chair of Equity's Afro-Asian committee Louis Mahoney said Cathy Tyson 'should be getting lots of leading roles' after her BAFTA and Golden Globe-nominated debut in *Mona Lisa* (1986) 'but you don't see much of her'.[6] But, as Tyson discussed in an interview in 1987, her opportunities in film had been highly circumscribed: 'Woman equals bed-scene equals nakedness equals beaten up equals raped or whatever. It's so exploitative within the framework of the business. You just get used to reading things like this.'[7] The fact that British-born Thandie Newton got her first break in an Australian film, *Flirting* (1991), and then felt she had to go to Hollywood to build her career is as big an indictment of British cinema's inability to recognise and nurture obvious star potential as the story about Audrey Hepburn that I cited in the introduction to this book.[8] One wonders how many other talents have been squandered, how many more careers have been stymied, and how much this has in turn impoverished British film culture. That comment on Cathy Tyson, 'you don't see much of her', could be applied to entire generations of potential BAME stars. It seems to have been a particular problem with British cinema. Other areas of British entertainment have been rather more amenable to a BAME female presence with British pop music, television, and even fashion modelling all creating black female stars at about this time. Ironically, the biggest non-white British female star at the UK box-office in the 1990s was Melanie Brown, on the strength of her single film appearance as part of the Spice Girls pop group in *Spice World* (1997).

Male BAME British actors have of course faced many similar obstacles to becoming a star: Idris Elba famously had to go to the US and play an American character in *The Wire* (2002–4) in order to advance his previously stagnating career, and his was not an isolated case. But arguably their female counterparts have struggled for recognition even more due to being, as Lola Young put it, 'doubly inscribed with Otherness, as black and female'. [9] In the few British media texts attempting to engage seriously with black experience and identity in the 1970s and 1980s, Young found that 'black men's experience and attitudes [were] foregrounded and elaborated' while 'black women are even less developed than their white counterparts. It is as if there is a repertoire of images and stereotypes of white femininity on which to draw but little which charts black female subjectivity.'[10]

Marianne Jean-Baptiste felt that one of the obstacles to a fuller BAME presence in British films was 'the old men running the industry' having a tendency to focus on the past rather than reflecting present-day ethnic diversity: 'They've got to come to terms with the fact that Britain is no longer a totally white place where people ride horses, wear long frocks and drink tea. The national dish is no longer fish and chips, it's curry.'[11] Of course, historical settings need not entail BAME absence or marginalisation, as Amma Asante's Georgian-set *Belle* (2013) proved so eloquently. But it has often been the case that a kind of aversive racism has been in operation, as Lola Young suggests, where British cinema has frequently sought 'refuge in period pieces where, presumably in ignorance, white writers and directors still seem unable to grasp the point that black people have been living in this country, undergoing a full spectrum of emotional experiences, for several hundred years'.[12] So while period drama has been seen as a generic field that, as prime exponent Helena Bonham Carter put it, offers 'good parts for women' in a national cinema where they are sometimes scant and, as Geraghty notes, enables actresses to showcase their performative skills, this route has been blocked for BAME actresses, thus creating further barriers to their ascent to stardom.[13]

I would also suggest that the stranglehold of the 'English rose' ideal in relation to British femininity, often connected to a nostalgic vision of the past, has also played a crucial role in the exclusion of BAME women from stardom, becoming another example of the 'repressive nostalgia' that Patrick Wright identified as a keynote of British culture.[14] Looking over the retinue of British female star discoveries in the twenty years that have elapsed since Jean-Baptiste's non-invitation to Cannes – Kate, Keira, Carey, Emma, Emily, Rosamund, Felicity, Lily – one is struck by a sense of narrowly reiterative white middle-class femininity that may be intuited even from the similarities between their names, with the chromatic resonance of that final name in the list summing up much of the unacknowledged but emphatic whiteness of British female stardom.[15] Richard Dyer talked about the need for 'whiteness to be made strange', for its constructed-ness as an identity to be recognised rather than going along with its assumptions of hegemony, for us 'to see the specificity of whiteness, even when the text itself is not trying to show it to you, doesn't even know that it is there to be shown'.[16] And few things point to the 'strangeness' of whiteness quite so much as the obsessively repetitive feminine typology celebrated by the mechanisms of British star-making. Older ideas about what kinds of femininity are prized, rooted in colonial ideology, extend their long tendrils into the present day and still define our contemporary hierarchies of value. The nomenclature of English rose, which has been variously invoked in relation to all the stars mentioned above, is far from being a neutral descriptive term; one does not have to dig very deep to find its imperial antecedence. For instance, Deborah Kerr's ascription as 'everything Englishmen mean when they become lyrical about roses' goes hand in hand with the idea that she is 'so English you'd send a gunboat at her slightest distress', recalling colonial myths centred on the protection and rescue of fragile white women.[17] As Young points out, colonial discourse idealised 'the middle class European woman' and made her symbolise 'control of self, of sex, of Others'.[18] In terms of racial and gendered hierarchies, as Dyer suggests, 'to be a lady is to be as white as it gets'.[19] The obverse of this elevation of white femininity was the denigration of black femininity and its insistent construction as Other, lacking in the self-control and sexual probity the pure white woman was meant to exemplify. Whiteness, as Cornel West suggests, 'is a politically constructed category parasitic on "Blackness"', the Other upon which it depends and against which it defines itself.[20] One can see this in the construction of Deborah Kerr's persona as a white female British star, which hinges on a dialectic between what Deleyto defines as 'her spirituality, her moral fortitude and her imperial righteousness', associated with whiteness, and its opposite, her 'surrender, whether real or metaphorical, to various forms of carnality and desire', associated with blackness.[21] The construction of blackness as structuring absence in the white femininities reified by British film stardom does not only impact upon white stars of course; it also defines the difficulties faced in non-white femininities being seen as viable for stardom. As Dyer has demonstrated in *White*, the aesthetic assumptions of cinematography are that the subject is white and the 'interactions of film stock, lighting and make up' have the specific and intentional 'effect of privileging the white performer', something that is especially true of visual constructions of white women as glowing and angelic, 'bathed in and permeated by light'.[22] By comparison, as Young points out, 'the valorisation of the beauty of the female star' has not applied in the same way to women of colour, who 'have not been subject to overvaluation in the same sense' because 'images of white European women as the standard of beauty are pervasive'.[23]

There is a fascinating hint at some of these bifurcations within stardom along ethnic lines in a throwaway comment made by film critic Sukhdev Sandhu while reviewing *Pride and Prejudice* (2005), that he thought its star Keira Knightley had been 'the second-best actress (and the second prettiest) in *Bend It Like Beckham*', implicitly ranking Parminder Nagra, the main star of that earlier film, higher than Knightley.[24] While one may want to take issue with a male critic rating the relative attractiveness of two women, Sandhu's comments do draw attention to the unspoken value judgements within British stardom and how Knightley and Nagra have experienced quite different career trajectories since co-starring in that film, possibly on the basis of an invidious privileging of white over BAME femininity. Despite both being equally beautiful and talented, it was Knightley who was then chosen to star as the feisty heroine of the Disney blockbuster *Pirates of the Caribbean: The Curse of the Black Pearl* (2003) and its subsequent sequels, who then became the face of Chanel's Coco Mademoiselle perfume and appeared in a lavish high-budget series of commercials for it, who gained critical acclaim and award nominations for her work in prestige period dramas such as *Pride and Prejudice, Atonement* (2007) and *The Duchess* (2008), and who became the only British star of either sex to appear in *Forbes* magazine's list of the top-ten highest-earning stars in Hollywood in 2008, coming second only to Cameron Diaz in the women's list.[25] Knightley's career in films seemed to be fast-tracked to the big time. By comparison, Nagra's film career didn't quite take flight in the same way, and aside from a best friend role in *Ella Enchanted* (2004), her destiny was US television instead and specifically a leading role in the medical drama *ER* from 2003 to 2009.[26] Nagra has also had a very success-ful career by any estimation after her 'discovery' in *Bend It Like Beckham* but it is still possible to interpret the differences between Knightley and Nagra's careers as being entangled in some way with that idea that some femininities are more worthy of the full movie star treatment than others, and that the major faultline in this comparative case study is ethnicity. Of course, body shape may also be seen as a factor here, with Keira Knightley exemplifying an exceptionally thin contemporary ideal (often assumed to be the result of an eating disorder) while Nagra's slenderness is more 'normal' in appearance. But thinness and whiteness interconnect to make Knightley a perfect candidate for radiant white stardom, expressive of that sublime self-control seen as the apotheosis of idealised femininity from women in nineteenth-century imperial discourse to the 'thin white women' used almost without exception in contemporary advertising.[27]

Moving into television, as Parminder Nagra did, seems to have been the most fruitful route for a number of BAME British actresses, taking

Figure 8.1 Two stars of tomorrow, two different destinies: Parminder Nagra and Keira Knightley in *Bend It Like Beckham* (2002).

advantage of a bigger boom in American shows employing Brits. After making a memorable film debut as the sister among a cohort of brothers in the British comedy *East Is East* (1999) and demonstrating plenty of star quality, Archie Panjabi only became a fully fledged star through the auspices of American quality television and her role in *The Good Wife* (2009–15).[28] And this was also the route that Marianne Jean-Baptiste took to advance her career, gaining particular success with her long-running lead role in the series *Without a Trace* (2002–9) for which she adopted an American accent and persona, as have many other British actors working in Hollywood. Of course, there is no inherent problem with British actors taking advantage of the opportunities offered by American television but in the case of BAME actors, this has often felt like more of a forced migration than a free choice, something that came about due to a paucity of leading roles available in Britain. As Jean-Baptiste made clear, just prior to her stateside relocation: 'I'm unemployed here [in the UK]. I want to work so I'm going where the work is. I want to work here because it's what I know. But what am I supposed to do?'[29]

Twenty years on from Jean-Baptiste's Cannes exclusion, how much has changed? As we have seen so many times before with white female stars as well, the problem is not necessarily with the discovery of talent but in knowing how to develop it, and in actors being able to make the transition from promising newcomer to someone with a sustainable career and perhaps even star status. But being in a continual state of 'becoming' is a particularly entrenched problem for BAME black actors, as actress

Carmen Munroe has reflected of her own continually re-starting career in television and film: 'I felt I did a good job, we all did, and then we were dropped and forgotten, and then every time we were given another opportunity, we felt we were being "discovered" again. We had to play catch up. Every job that I did I was "discovered".'[30] Writer/Actress Zawe Ashton was nominated for a British Independent Film Award as 'Most Promising Newcomer' for her performance in *Dreams of a Life* (2011) while Gugu Mbatha-Raw, the star of *Belle*, won a BAFTA Rising Star Award in 2015, winning in a category with the same nomenclature as the deputation that excluded Marianne Jean-Baptiste from Cannes. In 2015, director Michael Caton-Jones called BAFTA Breakthrough Brit winner Letitia Wright 'the most exciting young screen acting talent that I've had the pleasure of working with since Leonardo DiCaprio', but will this young black actress get the same chances as him to explore and exploit fully that talent, let alone gain anything resembling his level of fame? Will Ashton or Mbatha-Raw get the chance to deliver on their 'promise'?[31] Agents like Femi Oguns of the Identity Agency group have been proactive in promoting British BAME talent, aiming to overturn the longstanding under-representation of BAME actors on British screens (as Oguns notes, 'Fourteen per cent of the population is BAME but only five per cent of talent on screen is').[32] Oguns was instrumental in John Boyega being auditioned for and cast as Finn in *Star Wars: The Force Awakens*, indicative of his strategy as an agent to get the performers he represents into mainstream big-budget Hollywood films and not only in niche 'specialist' productions.

A similar strategy has worked for raising the profile of black British actresses Thandie Newton, who appeared as Tom Cruise's love interest in *Mission: Impossible II* (2000), and more recently Naomie Harris, who has not only appeared opposite the aforementioned Keira Knightley in the blockbuster *Pirates of the Caribbean* films *Dead Man's Chest* (2006) and *At World's End* (2007) but has also become the re-imagined Moneypenny in the James Bond films *Skyfall* and *Spectre* (2015). Harris's Eve Moneypenny is a former field agent and presented as a 'Bond woman' rather than a Bond girl, 007's equal, and an entrusted confidante rather than an eternally waiting fiancée, or a brief fling (the fate of most Bond girls). Although there is the danger that Moneypenny merely becomes a feminised version of the perpetual black 'buddy' role, always ancillary rather than the star of the show, the fact that Harris's Moneypenny is self-possessed, capable, incredibly glamorous and has a significant narrative function, does suggest some new possibilities for the casting of BAME actresses in star roles in British films. Playing Moneypenny may not have done much for Lois Maxwell's career back in the 1960s but one

Figure 8.2 Something new? Naomie Harris as 'Bond woman' Eve Moneypenny in *Skyfall* (2012).

hopes that the new Moneypenny will not prove a repetitive dead end for Harris.

But while some advances seem to be made in widening the scope of British stardom, other things seem to regress. Julie Walters, from a working-class Liverpudlian background (not a million miles away from Rita Tushingham or Glenda Jackson in that respect) has spoken in recent years of the increasing re-embourgeoisement of the British acting profession:

> [W]here do kids start out? They have to pay a lot to go to drama school, then hope they get straight into television or film. But working-class kids can't afford that. I was lucky – I had a grant. You can't get a grant to go to drama school now. Soon the only actors are going to be privileged kids whose parents can afford to send them to drama school. That's not right. It feels like we are going backwards.[33]

Class and the class-connected social capital of connections play an important part in deciding who does or doesn't make the grade for potential stardom. This description of the career trajectory of Emily Blunt, conveyed in a 2015 interview, is enlightening in this respect:

> While studying in the sixth form at Hurtwood House, a boarding school in Surrey, she took part in a student production that went up to the Edinburgh festival fringe . . . one of the drama teachers at the school was Adrian Rawlins, a professional actor (he plays Harry Potter's dad in the movie franchise), who persuaded his agent, Roger Charteris, to attend the school performance in Edinburgh. Rawlins told him to look out for Blunt, and Charteris signed the teenager shortly afterwards.'[34]

This account presents the young actress's entry into professional acting in terms quite different from, say, Lana Turner's archetypal drugstore discovery. Yes, the young woman's perceived 'star quality' is still important, and, yes, it hinges on a certain amount of luck and happenstance, of being in the right place at the right time. But it is crucially facilitated by structures of class privilege unavailable to most people: the sixth-form drama production going to Edinburgh, the teacher being a well-connected professional actor, the agent being willing to attend a glorified school play. This is not to deny for a moment Blunt's beauty, or talent, or charisma, all of which are considerable. But it does demonstrate some of the ways in which the acting profession, and indeed many other professions, have become almost impregnably middle class, even upper middle class, because members of those social classes are the only ones with the necessary capital – cultural and financial – to surmount all the obstacles in their way. This has often been discussed in relation to the rise of Etonian Eddie Redmayne and Harrovian Benedict Cumberbatch but, as we can see from Blunt and others, it is just as much of a problem when it comes to the increasingly narrow tranche of society from which female acting talent is drawn in the UK. The odd working-class discovery may get in – Katie Jarvis, spotted arguing with her boyfriend at Tilbury railway station by director Andrea Arnold and then cast in *Fish Tank* (2009), or Samantha Morton and Vicky McClure discovered by the Nottingham-based Central Junior Television Workshop, or Gemma Arterton, a rare example of an actress with an 'English Rose'-inflected image who has a working-class background – but generally the accelerating gentrification of British cinema stardom is a noticeable phenomenon.

The general adherence to the middle-class, slender, young 'English rose' template for British female stardom does not only damage those who find themselves excluded from it for various reasons; it also creates a punishingly reductive ideal even for those stars who meet the entry criteria. The hate directed towards Keira Knightley for being too thin, too pouty, having too prominent a jaw, or being a wooden actress, surely have something to do with this.[35] As Sean Redmond has suggested, in the course of a discussion of Kate Winslet, 'one can see how limiting, potentially lifeless, it must be to be an idealised white star':

> Idealised white stars have to be heterosexual rather than bisexual or homosexual; monogamous rather than polygamous; glamorous but not excessively so; expensive but not 'cheap'; bronzed but not brown/dark; muscle but not flab; thin/slender and never fat; muscular but not too masculine; (natural) light but not neon; reproductive but not sexual; desirable but not available; available but pure.[36]

As Redmond recounts, Winslet revolted against these endless restrictions by refusing to conform, for a time at least, to the enforced ideal of ultra-slenderness as well as flouting some of the cultural expectations around the 'English rose' mythology by adopting a rowdy, tomboyish persona, 'called "Combat Kate" due to her predilection for rolling cigarettes and wearing motorcycle boots' despite 'looking[ing] like a cream puff', according to *Vanity Fair* in 1998 – rather like Helena Bonham Carter using her scruffiness as a form of defence.[37] Actresses Sophie Ward and Saffron Burrows contradicted the compulsory heterosexuality associated with the 'English rose' designation and their careers arguably suffered as a result. More recently, Emma Watson has tried to revolt against the 'rose-tinted' constraints of British stardom through her publicly vocalised serious commitment to gender equality, taking a year out of filmmaking in order to advance her feminist activities and striking up a friendship and 'mutual girl crush' with black feminist bell hooks.[38]

Perhaps the most perfect contemporary incarnation of the English rose type is Rosamund Pike. Interviewing her in 2009 over afternoon tea, Lynn Barber found herself intoxicated by Pike's apparent perfection:

> [She] offers tea in delicate antique china cups and invites me to look round her extremely pretty Kensington mews flat. There is a lovely wisteria outside, forming great swags of flowers around the window – it feels like being in a treetop bower . . . She is even prettier in the flesh than on film, wearing harem pants and a soft floral blouse that sometimes flops sideways to give glimpses of her breasts. The whole effect – the flat, the cake, the tea, the wisteria, this lovely porcelain girl – is utterly feminine and exquisite.[39]

But even this absolute epitome of the English rose, with everything to gain from embodying it, rejects this 'label that hangs like a millstone round her slender, Grace Kelly neck', according to a 2010 profile in the *Daily Mail*:

> [S]he is a picture of unselfconscious elegance, positively radiating the sort of money-can't-buy class that most actresses would kill for. But when I say as much, her exasperation is palpable. 'I'm not an English rose at all,' she says.
> 'Or maybe I'm an English rose with . . .'
> 'Thorns?' I interject.
> 'Oh no,' her eyes widen in well-bred dismay. 'A rose with bruised petals – not emotional bruises, but flaws; I get into scrapes too often for perfection.'[40]

The endless linguistic redefinition of what being a rose may mean and what features it may encompass is testimony to the trickiness of satisfactorily living within it. However, Pike's role as the anti-heroine in *Gone Girl* (2014) showed the possibilities to deconstruct its ladylike mythos from within just as surely as James Stewart subverted expectations that he would be an all-American good guy in *Vertigo* (1958). Moreover, Pike's characterisation in that film points towards the performed nature of *all* identities, including gendered ones: a lesson of even greater importance as the very basis of the cisgender category of 'female' becomes increasingly queried (and queered) by trans identities.

This book has charted some of the major changes that have occurred in the construction of British star femininities from 1940 to 2015, but it has also found some important elements of continuity. One of these has regrettably been its 'unbearable whiteness of being', although it looks as though some long overdue traction is being gained in this area at last and British cinema is finally becoming a more diverse place. But another key continuity has been British cinema's ability – in the right circumstances – to encompass and sustain a variety of stardoms and to provide vivid and sometimes transgressive images of femininity that enter the cultural bloodstream of their eras. The creation of more women stars, and further questions around their personae, shows no sign of abating.

Notes

1. Dan Glaister, 'Oscar actress hits out at "old men" of British film industry', *The Guardian*, 15 May 1997. https://www.theguardian.com/film/1997/may/15/news.danglaister
2. Stephen Bourne, *Black in the British Frame: Black People in British Film and Television 1896–1996* (London: Cassell, 1998), p. 74.
3. Angela Woollacott, *Race and the Modern Exotic: Three 'Australian' Women on Global Display* (Clayton: Monash University Press, 2011). Several major British female stars were born and/or brought up in India, including Margaret Lockwood, Googie Withers, and Julie Christie.
4. Macnab, *Searching for Stars*, p. 66.
5. Robert F. Moss, *The Films of Carol Reed* (New York: Columbia University Press, 1987), p. 251.
6. Susan Young, 'Battle over BBC series role offers hope for end to black type-casting', *The Observer*, 9 February 1992, p. 3.
7. Tyson quoted in Karen Alexander, 'Fatal beauties: Black women in Hollywood', in Gledhill (ed.), *Stardom*, p. 52.
8. Newton gave a particularly eloquent and moving Technology, Entertainment, Design (TED) talk on the difficulties she faced growing up as a 'visible nobody' in rural England and how her experiences as a child had defined her adult understanding of selfhood. Thandie Newton, 'Embracing otherness, embracing myself', *TED Global*, July 2011. https://www.ted.com/talks/thandie_newton_embracing_otherness_embracing_myself
9. Lola Young, *Fear of the Dark: 'Race', Gender and Sexuality in the Cinema* (London: Routledge, 1996), p. 178
10. Ibid., p. 165.
11. Glaister, 'Oscar actress hits out at "old men" of British film industry'. This

view was shared by black actress Carmen Munroe who said in 1996 that she felt 'disheartened every time I look at the screen and see something like *Pride and Prejudice* or *Sense and Sensibility* that will exclude minority ethnic artists'. Quoted in Stephen Bourne, 'Secrets and lies: Black histories and British historical films', in Monk and Sargeant (eds), *British Historical Cinema*, p. 47.

12. Young, *Fear of the Dark*, p. 26.
13. Rampton, 'Corset still makes sense', p. 4. Geraghty, 'Crossing over: Performing as a lady and a dame', p. 46.
14. Patrick Wright, *On Living in an Old Country: The National Past in Contemporary Britain* (London: Verso, 1985), p. 1.
15. I refer to Kate Winslet (and Kate Beckinsale), Keira Knightley, Carey Mulligan, Emma Watson, Emily Blunt, Rosamund Pike, Felicity Jones, and Lily James.
16. Richard Dyer, *White* (London: Routledge, 1997), p. 10, pp. 13–14.
17. Quoted by Deleyto, 'The nun's story: Femininity and Englishness in the films of Deborah Kerr', p. 122.
18. Young, *Fear of the Dark*, p. 47.
19. Dyer, *White*, p. 57.
20. West quoted in Young, *Fear of the Dark*, p. 181. West's work also corresponds with Edward Said's influential work on othering in orientalist discourses.
21. Deleyto, 'The nun's story: Femininity and Englishness in the films of Deborah Kerr', p. 124.
22. Dyer, *White*, p. 91, p. 101, p. 122.
23. Young, *Fear of the Dark*, p. 16, p. 44.
24. Sukhdev Sandhu, 'A jolly romp to nowhere', *The Daily Telegraph*, 16 September 2005. http://www.telegraph.co.uk/culture/film/3646583/A-jolly-romp-to-nowhere.html
25. Catherine Elsworth, 'Keira Knightley is highest earning British Hollywood star on Forbes list', *The Daily Telegraph*, 24 July 2008. http://www.telegraph.co.uk/news/celebritynews/2455107/Keira-Knightley-is-highest-earning-British-Hollywood-star-on-Forbes-list.html For more on the entanglement of celebrity culture, including film stardom, with fashion, see Pamela Church Gibson, *Fashion and Celebrity Culture* (London: Bloomsbury, 2012).
26. Nagra had appeared in two innovative Channel Four productions in between, both Shakespeare adaptations: *Twelfth Night* (2003) alongside Chiwetel Ejiofor, and *Second Generation* (2003), inspired by *King Lear*. Although not huge ratings winners, both were critical successes and testified to Channel Four's emphasis on representing diversity in their programming.
27. See Sean Redmond, 'Thin white women in advertising: Deathly corporeality', *Journal of Consumer Culture*, Vol. 3, No. 2, 2003, pp. 170–90.
28. Panjabi had supporting roles in a number of high-profile British-US films, including *A Mighty Heart* (2007) and *The Constant Gardener* (2005), and in the British television series *Life on Mars* (2006–7), but no starring role aside

from playing the lead in Channel Four's critically esteemed drama about post-9/11 Islamophobia, *Yasmin* (2004).

29. Glaister, 'Oscar actress hits out at "old men" of British film industry'.
30. Interview with Carmen Munroe, quoted in Bourne, *Black in the British Frame*, p. 171.
31. Caton-Jones also said of Wright: 'I've not felt like this about someone since Leonardo. I've had plenty of really good actors, but I just go on my instinct. My instinct is she can be as big as she wants.' Dalya Alberge, 'Letitia Wright, Britain's newest rising screen star, says black actors need more positive roles', *The Observer*, 5 April 2015. https://www.theguardian.com/film/2015/apr/05/letitia-wright-britains-rising-screen-star-michael-caton-jones-leonardo-dicaprio
32. Adam Sherwin, 'Femi Oguns: Agent whose black British actors are causing waves across Hollywood on racism in the industry', *The Independent*, 3 January 2016. http://www.The Independent.co.uk/arts-entertainment/films/features/femi-oguns-agent-whose-black-british-actors-are-causing-waves-across-hollywood-on-racism-in-the-a6795056.html
33. Warren Manger, 'Julie Walters: Working class kids can't afford drama school – soon only posh kids will be actors', *Daily Mirror*, 5 December 2014. http://www.mirror.co.uk/tv/tv-news/julie-walters-working-class-kids-4750761
34. Emma Brockes, 'To be perfectly blunt', *The Guardian (Weekend)*, 3 January 2015, p. 19.
35. On the phenomenon of 'Keira hating', see David Sexton, 'What is it about Keira Knightley that gets people all riled up?' *Evening Standard*, 13 November 2014. http://www.standard.co.uk/lifestyle/london-life/what-is-it-about-keira-knightley-that-gets-people-all-riled-up-9857879.html. The message that Knightley herself says she has taken from much of her press coverage is 'you're a shit actress and you're anorexic, and people hate you'. Celia Walden, 'Girl most likely', *Glamour*, November 2014, p. 272. On the middle point, Knightley successfully sued the *Daily Mail* for libel in 2007 and donated the damages to the eating disorder charity BEAT. 'Knightley wins weight libel claim', *BBC News*, 24 May 2007. http://news.bbc.co.uk/1/hi/entertainment/6687109.stm.
36. Redmond, 'The whiteness of stars: Looking at Kate Winslet's unruly white body', p. 268.
37. 'The Hollywood Issue', *Vanity Fair*, April 1998, p. 138. Winslet suggests another archetype of English femininity in operation that is a modification of and/or a departure from the ladylike rose: the more physically voluptuous, sexually available 'wench'. It is possible to discern the presence of this type in the modern-day barmaid eulogised in H. V. Morton's *In Search of England* (London: Methuen, 1927) as a 'buxom wench with a face like a ripe pippin and a waist made for the arm of an eighteenth century gallant' (p. 187). It is another nostalgic vision of femininity but one with different erotic and class connotations, and may be a useful type to think of in relation to a number

of female British stars including Jean Kent, Diana Dors, and Emily Lloyd as well as someone like *Carry On* star Barbara Windsor, and a whole raft of British pin-up girls from the 1940s onwards.

38. bell hooks and Emma Watson, 'In conversation', *Paper*, 18 February 2016. http://www.papermag.com/emma-watson-bell-hooks-conversation-16098 93784.html . Although, in this respect, Watson actually fits into a long line of politically committed British actresses undertaking activism of various kinds, including Julie Christie, Vanessa Redgrave, Susannah York, Glenda Jackson, and Emma Thompson.

39. Lynn Barber, 'I don't sleep around, if that's what you mean . . . Would you like some more cake?', *The Observer*, 24 May 2009. https://www.theguard ian.com/stage/2009/may/24/rosamund-pike-actress-interview.

40. Judith Woods, 'Rosamund Pike: From reluctant English rose to Britain's new screen queen', *Daily Mail*, 24 September 2010. http://www.dailymail. co.uk/home/you/article-1311882/Rosamund-Pike-From-reluctant-English -rose-Britains-new-screen-queen.html

Bibliography

Information on page numbers, author, and article title is sometimes absent from the documentation included in the BFI Library's press cuttings files, and this is reflected in the partial information listed in several of the references below.

BFI Library press cuttings files and pressbooks (press cuttings often do not contain information about page numbers and sometimes authors and article titles are also absent, hence the partial information in some of the items listed in the references and bibliography)
BFI Special Collections
Mass Observation Archive

Anonymous, 'Britain's bad girl', undated press release for *The Loves of Joanna Godden* (1947). BFI Library press cuttings file for Jean Kent.

Anonymous, 'In a world of Kardashians', *Know Your Meme*, undated. http://knowyourmeme.com/memes/in-a-world-of-kardashians (last accessed 31 May 2016).

Anonymous, 'Q&A with Rita Tushingham for *A Taste of Honey*', *BFI website*, undated. http://www.bfi.org.uk/films-tv-people/4fc75e8178546 (last accessed 31 May 2016).

Anonymous, undated press cutting in scrapbook, box 3, Jean Kent Collection, BFI Special Collections.

Anonymous, 'Letters from our readers: English beauty v. Hollywood glamour', *Picturegoer*, 28 July 1934, p. 30.

Anonymous, 'Star campaigns being launched in London', *Showmen's Trade Review*, 7 July 1945, p. 17.

Anonymous, 'A new star made in Britain', *Picture Post*, 24 November 1945, pp. 26–8.

Anonymous, 'Caravan', *Motion Picture Herald* (product digest section), 4 May 1946, p. 2,971.

Anonymous, 'Letters from our readers: More glamour', *Picturegoer*, 31 August 1946, p. 14.

Anonymous, 'What the picture did for us', *Motion Picture Herald*, 15 February 1947, p. 52.

Anonymous, unlabelled article, *Daily Mail*, 8 April 1947. Press cuttings file on Ann Todd, BFI Library.

Anonymous, 'The man within', *Showman's Trade Review*, 12 April 1947, p. 19.

Anonymous, 'The stars you pay to see!', *Picturegoer*, 17 January 1948, p. 3.

Anonymous, 'British Technicolor drama will appeal', *Film Bulletin*, 2 February 1948, p. 8.

Anonymous, *Daily Mail*, 30 April 1948. Press cuttings file on Jean Kent, BFI Library.

Anonymous, advertisement for *The Smugglers* (US title for *The Man Within*), *Showman's Trade Review*, July–September 1948, p. 2.

Anonymous, *Daily Mirror*, 12 August 1949. Press cuttings file on *Trottie True*, BFI Library.

Anonymous, *Sunday Dispatch*, 14 August 1949. Press cuttings file on *Trottie True*, BFI Library.

Anonymous, 'Young stars shine brighter than ever', *Picturegoer*, 15 October 1949, p. 5.

Anonymous, unlabelled review, *Daily Express*, 4 September 1950. Press cuttings file on *The Woman in Question*, BFI Library.

Anonymous, *Daily Graphic*, 5 October 1950. Press cuttings file on *The Woman in Question*, BFI Library.

Anonymous, 'Success of British Films', *The Times*, 29 December 1950, p. 4.

Anonymous, 'Diana's swapped!', *Picturegoer*, 8 December 1951, p. 5.

Anonymous, 'Stars who fill the cinemas: Anna Neagle's distinction', *Manchester Guardian*, 28 December 1951, p. 6.

Anonymous, 'Golden Slipper Diana Dors goes to court in a Rolls', *Daily Express*, 25 July 1953, p. 5.

Anonymous, advertisement for *Tit-Bits*, *Daily Mirror*, 20 October 1953, p. 12.

Anonymous, *Daily Sketch*, 6 January 1954. Press cuttings file on Jean Kent, BFI Library.

Anonymous, '3-D book found not obscene', *Manchester Guardian*, 5 October 1954, p. 3.

Anonymous, 'Artistes (Income Tax)', *Hansard*, 28 October 1954, vol. 531, cc. 2124–6.

Anonymous, 'How does Diana Dors draw £50 a week tax free?', *Daily Express*, 29 October 1954, p. 5.

Anonymous, '"It's not true" says Miss Dors', *Manchester Guardian*, 29 October 1954, p. 1.

Anonymous, 'It took courage to look like this', *Picturegoer*, 26 March 1955, p. 14.

Anonymous, '3 Ds are the tops!', *Daily Mirror*, 29 December 1955, p. 9.

Anonymous, 'Diana – propaganda pin-up', *Daily Express*, 27 February 1956, p. 1.

Anonymous, unlabelled article, *Daily Mail*, 9 May 1956. Press cuttings file on Diana Dors, BFI Library.

Anonymous, 'Letters: Don't slam Dors', *Daily Mirror*, 14 June 1956, p. 2.

Anonymous, 'Diana steals front page from Marilyn', *Daily Mirror*, 17 July 1956, p. 1.

Anonymous, Cartoon by Cummings, *Daily Express*, 18 July 1956, p. 6.

Anonymous, 'See! I dunnit . . .!', *Daily Express*, 18 July 1956, p. 3.

Anonymous, 'Well? WAS she pushed – OR did she fall?', *Daily Express*, 21 August 1956, p. 3.

Anonymous, 'Escapers club', *The Times*, 27 August 1956, p. 9.

Anonymous, 'Go home, Diana! – and take Mr Dors with you!', *New York Enquirer*, 1 September 1956, p. 1.

Anonymous, 'Behind the scenes at the Windmill', *Sunday Dispatch*, 6 January 1957. Press cutting in scrapbook, box 3, Jean Kent Collection, BFI Special Collections.

Anonymous, 'News of the north-west', *Manchester Guardian*, 21 March 1957, p. 14.

Anonymous, 'Miss Diana Dors at Finsbury Park: Upholding celebrity's mask', *The Times*, 7 October 1958, p. 5.

Anonymous, 'Diana Dors wants damages from RKO', *Variety*, 18 February 1959, p. 10.

Anonymous, Unlabelled article, *Daily Mail*, 4 September 1959. Press cuttings file on Jean Kent, BFI Library.

Anonymous, Unlabelled article, *Sunday Graphic*, 20 September 1959. Press cuttings file on Jean Kent, BFI Library.

Anonymous, 'Government supports press bill', *The Guardian*, 6 February 1960, p. 2.

Anonymous, 'Diana Dors gets balm', *Variety*, 13 July 1960, p. 8.

Anonymous, 'Film virtues in A Taste of Honey', *The Times*, 13 September 1961, p. 14.

Anonymous, 'From the north', *The Guardian*, 13 September 1961, p. 8.

Anonymous, *The Sunday Times*, 24 September 1961. Press cuttings file on Rita Tushingham, BFI Library.

Anonymous, 'The padded waif', *Time*, 8 June 1962. Press cuttings file on Rita Tushingham, BFI Library.

Anonymous, 'Rita's new rival: a motorcycle', *Evening Standard*, 13 July 1962. Press cuttings file on Rita Tushingham, BFI Library.

Anonymous, 'Has London had it?', *The Guardian*, 26 October 1962, p. 10.

Anonymous [John Russell Taylor], 'A sad little Irish love story', *The Times*, 14 May 1964, p. 8.

Anonymous, 'Viewpoint: Your angle on events', *Daily Mirror*, 29 March 1965, p. 14.

Anonymous, 'Well, do YOU think I look like Princess Margaret?', TV World, 10 April 1965. Taken from 'Credits and photos – 1964–66', *Rita Tushingham Home Page*. http://ritatushingham.com/1964.htm (last accessed 31 May 2016).

Anonymous, 'People are talking about . . .', *Vogue* (US edition), November 1965, p. 152.

Anonymous, 'The ten most popular young players of 65', *Box Office*, 28 February 1966, p. 77.

Anonymous, 'James Mason, producer: Will re-do "Jane Eyre" with Tushingham, Leighton', *Variety*, 5 April 1967, p. 4.

Anonymous, 'Diamonds for Breakfast', *Monthly Film Bulletin*, 1 January 1968, p. 200.

Anonymous, 'Mason preps "Jane Eyre" as $1-mil Eire locationer', *Variety*, 10 December 1969, p. 35.

Anonymous, *People*, 12 April 1970. Press cuttings file on Glenda Jackson, BFI Library.

Anonymous, *Evening Standard*, 18 March 1970. Press cuttings file on Rita Tushingham, BFI Library.

Anonymous, 'Rita Tushingham and Davies form film co.', *Variety*, 5 August 1970, p. 15.

Anonymous, 'People are talking about: The unsettling reign of Glenda Jackson', *Vogue* (US edition), April 1971, p. 158.

Anonymous, Advertisement for *Straight On Till Morning* at ABC cinemas, *Daily Express*, 1 July 1972, p. 14.

Anonymous, 'Women sure of role in life', *The Guardian*, 10 October 1972, p. 8.

Anonymous, 'All-American favorites of 1972', *Box Office*, 9 July 1973, p. 19.

Anonymous, *Evening Standard*, 28 June 1974. Press cuttings file on Diana Dors, BFI Library.

Anonymous, 'All-American favorites of 1975', *Box Office*, 20 September 1976, p. 19.

Anonymous, 'Diana Dors: My stories of the stars – as only I can tell them', *Daily Mirror*, 6 December 1977, p. 1.

Anonymous, 'Diane Keaton and Al Pacino top box office 1977 star poll', *Box Office*, 22 May 1978, p. 3.

Anonymous, 'Diana shows off her all-star cast', *Daily Express*, 25 November 1981, p. 15.

Anonymous, 'Diary', *The Times*, 20 January 1984, p. 10.

Anonymous, unlabelled article, *Girl About Town*, 2 June 1986, p. 19. Press cuttings file on Helena Bonham Carter, BFI Library.

Anonymous, 'Wish you were on our books, Emily', *Today*, 22 August 1987, p. 11.

Anonymous, 'So glad to be here', *Evening Standard*, 15 January 1988, p. 24.

Anonymous, untitled article, *The Sunday Telegraph* (*7 Days* magazine), 5 November 1989, p. 9. Press cuttings file on Emily Lloyd, BFI Library.

Anonymous, 'Lloyd's lust', *The Sun*, 22 March 1990, p. 26.

Anonymous, 'Look who's making-up with Helena', *Daily Mail*, 28 July 1993, p. 21.

Anonymous, 'Pass notes: Helena Bonham Carter', *The Guardian* (G2), 19 August 1993, p. 3.

Anonymous, 'The fresh face of the 90s', *The Mail on Sunday* (*You* magazine), 10 April 1994, p. 54.

Anonymous, 'Spotlight: Helena Bonham Carter', *Radio Times*, 13 July 1996, p. 7.

Anonymous, 'Cine File: Rita Tushingham', *The Guardian* (Friday Review), 9 May 1997, p. 8.

Anonymous, 'Helena Bonham Carter', *Film Review Special*, No. 24, 1998, p. 28.

Anonymous, 'The Victorian', *Vanity Fair*, April 1998, p. 171.

Anonymous, 'Kate Winslet', *Film Review Special: The Young Ones*, No. 24, 1998, p. 50.

Anonymous, 'Ten things every Helena Bonham Carter fan ought to know', *Radio Times*, 17 January 1998, p. 43.

Anonymous, 'The heavenly creature', *Vanity Fair*, April 1998, pp. 138–9.

Anonymous, 'Knightley wins weight libel claim', *BBC News*, 24 May 2007. http://news.bbc.co.uk/1/hi/entertainment/6687109.stm (last accessed 31 May 2016).

Anonymous, unlabelled article, *Daily Mail* (*Weekend* magazine), 24 May 2008, p. 7. Press cuttings file on Judi Dench, BFI Library.

Anonymous, 'Helen Mirren the bikini queen reigns supreme at 63', *Mail Online*, 21 July 2008. http://www.mailonsunday.co.uk/tvshowbiz/article-1035510/Helen-Mirren-bikini-queen-reigns-supreme-63.html (last accessed 31 May 2016).

Anonymous, 'Meet the very British cast of The Best Exotic Marigold Hotel', *Radio Times Online*, 24 February 2012. http://www.radiotimes.com/news/2012-02-24/meet-the-very-british-cast-of-the-best-exotic-marigold-hotel (last accessed 31 May 2016).

Anonymous, 'Still stunning at 78! Dame Judi Dench wows at Venice Film Festival in elegant ivory gown . . . as she shows how to elegantly flash a leg', *Mail Online*, 1 September 2013. http://www.dailymail.co.uk/tvshowbiz/article-2408128/Dame-Judi-Dench-wows-Venice-Film-Festival-elegant-ivory-gown--shows-elegantly-flash-leg.html (last accessed 31 May 2016).

Adewumni, Bim, 'The crush: Helen Mirren', *The Guardian* (Weekend), 1 November 2014, p. 6.

Alberge, Dalya, 'Letitia Wright, Britain's newest rising screen star, says black actors need more positive roles', *The The Observer*, 5 April 2015. https://www.theguardian.com/film/2015/apr/05/letitia-wright-britains-rising-screen-star-michael-caton-jones-leonardo-dicaprio (last accessed 31 May 2016).

Alberge, Dalya, 'Glenda Jackson laments continuing lack of key acting roles for women', *The The Observer*, 12 September 2015. https://www.theguardian.com/stage/2015/sep/12/glenda-jackson-equality-nothings-changed-women-stage-roles (last accessed 31 May 2016).

Alexander, Hilary, 'Ask Hilary: Where can I find a Judi Dench evening coat?', *The Daily Telegraph*, 23 August 2010. http://fashion.telegraph.co.uk/article/TMG7954089/Ask-Hilary-Where-can-I-find-a-Judi-Dench-evening-coat.html (last accessed 31 May 2016).

Alexander, Karen, 'Fatal beauties: Black women in Hollywood', in Christine Gledhill (ed.), *Stardom: Industry of Desire* (London: Routledge, 1991), pp. 45–54.

Amis, Kingsley, 'Films', *The Guardian*, 19 April 1964, p. 25.

Appleyard, Bryan, 'What Philomena is really about', *Huffington Post*, 9 March 2014. http://www.huffingtonpost.com/bryan-appleyard/what-philomena-is-really-_b_4555773.html (last accessed 31 May 2016).

Ascheid, Antje, *Hitler's Heroines: Stardom and Womanhood in Nazi Germany* (Philadelphia: Temple University Press, 1993).

Ash, Niema with Jason Dors-Lake, *Connecting Dors: The Legacy of Diana Dors* (London: Purple INC Press, 2011).

Ashby, Justine, 'It's been emotional: Reassessing the contemporary British woman's film', in Melanie Bell and Melanie Williams (eds), *British Women's Cinema* (London: Routledge, 2009), pp. 153–69.

Aughey, Arthur, *The Politics of Englishness* (Manchester: Manchester University Press, 2007).

Babington, Bruce, 'Queen of British hearts: Margaret Lockwood revisited', in Bruce Babington (ed.), *British Stars and Stardom* (Manchester: Manchester University Press, 2001), pp. 94–107.

Babington, Bruce, *Launder and Gilliat* (Manchester: Manchester University Press, 2002).

Babington, Bruce (ed.), *British Stars and Stardom: From Alma Taylor to Sean Connery* (Manchester: Manchester University Press, 2001).

Bamigboye, Baz, '"Wild" Emily's a sweet 16', *Daily Mail*, 19 September 1987, p. 7.

Bamigboye, Baz, 'Funny girl's balancing act', *Daily Mail*, 13 June 1988, p. 24.

Bamigboye, Baz, 'Helena cuts the costume parts to play modern Miss', *Daily Mail*, 16 February 1996, p. 43.

Banner, Simon, 'Three of a kind', *The Guardian*, 10 April 1986, p. 13.

Barber, John, 'Miss Dors razzles', *Daily Express*, 7 October 1958, p. 7.

Barber, Lynn, 'Couldn't she just wear a babygro?', *Observer Magazine*, 20 April 1997, pp. 5–8.

Barber, Lynn, 'I don't sleep around, if that's what you mean . . . Would you like some more cake?', *The Observer*, 24 May 2009. https://www.theguardian.com/stage/2009/may/24/rosamund-pike-actress-interview (last accessed 31 May 2016).

Barr, Charles, 'Introduction: Amnesia and schizophrenia', in Charles Barr (ed.), *All Our Yesterdays: 90 Years of British Cinema* (London: BFI, 1986), pp. 1–30.

Barr, Charles, *Ealing Studios*, third edition (Berkeley: University of California Press, 1998).

Barr, Ann and York, Peter, *The Official Sloane Ranger Handbook: The First Guide to What Really Matters in Life* (London: Ebury, 1982).

Beckett, Andy, *When the Lights Went Out: Britain in the Seventies* (London: Faber & Faber, 2010).

Bell, Melanie, *Julie Christie* (London: BFI Palgrave, forthcoming).

Bell, Melanie and Melanie Williams, 'The hour of the cuckoo: Reclaiming the

British woman's film', in Melanie Bell and Melanie Williams (eds), *British Women's Cinema* (London: Routledge, 2009), pp. 1–18.

Bennett, Catherine, 'From schoolgirl to stardom', *The Sunday Telegraph Magazine*, 30 March 1986, p. 36.

Bennun, David, 'Costume drama', *The Guardian* (G2), 7 February 1997, p. 23.

Beresford, David, 'Diana Dors dies at 52', *The Guardian*, 5 May 1984, pp. 1–2.

Betts, Ernest, 'Ann Todd: I borrowed clothes . . . shocking!', *Daily Express*, 8 April 1947, p. 3.

Billen, Andrew, 'The Billen interview: Emily Lloyd', *Observer Magazine*, 4 February 1996, p. 6.

Billington, Michael, 'Satire on modern life', *The Times*, 27 December 1967, p. 12

Billington, Michael, 'Please god, not retirement', *The Guardian*, 12 September 2005, p. 22.

Blair, Duncan, 'Glamour as you like it', *Picturegoer*, 25 March 1950, p. 11.

Blair, Tony, *New Britain: My Vision of a Young Country* (London: Fourth Estate, 1996).

Bogarde, Dirk, *Backcloth* (London: Penguin, 1987).

Bond, Sarah, 'Whatever happened to Lady Jane?', *Daily Express*, 1 January 1987, p. 9.

Bonner, Hilary, 'School daze', *Daily Mirror*, 1 June 1987, p. 23.

Bourne, Stephen, *Black in the British Frame: Black People in British Film and Television 1896–1996* (London: Cassell, 1998).

Bourne, Stephen, 'Secrets and lies: Black histories and British historical films', in Claire Monk and Amy Sargeant (eds), *British Historical Cinema* (London: Routledge, 2002), pp. 47–65.

Boxall, Patricia, 'Plump and happy, that's me, says Diana Dors', *People*, 19 April 1970. Press cuttings file on Diana Dors, BFI Library.

Braun, Eric, 'Diana Dors: In her own terms', *Films and Filming*, February 1973, pp. 28–30.

Braun, Eric, 'Rank's young generation', *Films and Filming*, October 1973, pp. 32–40.

Braun, Eric, 'The decade of change', *Films and Filming*, December 1973, pp. 28–40.

Bret, David, *Hurricane in Mink* (London: JR Books, 2010).

Britton, Andrew, *Katharine Hepburn: Star as Feminist* (London: Studio Vista, 1995).

Brockes, Emma, 'To be perfectly blunt', *The Guardian* (Weekend), 3 January 2015, pp. 16–19.

Brown, Ian, 'Tushingham', *Photoplay*, April 1968, p. 8.

Bruley, Sue, *Women in Britain since 1900* (London: Palgrave, 1999).

Bryant, Christopher, *Glenda Jackson: The Biography* (London: HarperCollins, 1999).

Bryden, Ronald, 'The genius of Genet', *The Observer,* 1 February 1970, p. 28.

Burnup, Peter, 'Rank states design to be distributor in America', *Motion Picture Herald*, 28 July 1945, p. 20.

Burrows, Jon, 'Our English Mary Pickford: Alma Taylor and ambivalent British stardom in the 1910s', in Bruce Babington (ed.), *British Stars and Stardom* (Manchester: Manchester University Press, 2001), pp. 29–41.

Burrows, Jon, 'Girls on film: The musical matrices of film stardom in early British cinema', *Screen*, Vol. 44, No. 3, 2003, pp. 314–25.

Burrows, Jon, *Legitimate Cinema: Theatre Stars in Silent British Films, 1908–1918* (Exeter: Exeter University Press, 2003).

Cable, Michael, 'Heart to heart with Helena', *Sunday Express Magazine*, 14 June 1987, p. 20.

Cameron-Wilson, James, 'The class of Miss Jackson', *What's On in London*, 2 December 1977. Press cuttings file on Glenda Jackson, BFI Library.

Candidus, 'Close that Dors!', *Daily Sketch*, 20 July 1956. Press cuttings file on Diana Dors, BFI Library.

Carrol, Paul, 'Wish you were here', *Premiere*, June 1994, p. 52.

Cartner-Morley, Jess, 'The 50 best-dressed over-50s – in pictures', *The Guardian*, 29 March 2013. http://www.theguardian.com/fashion/gallery/2013/mar/29/50-best-dressed-over-50s (last accessed 31 May 2016).

Castell, David, 'All heroines are supposed to be pretty', *Films Illustrated*, March 1979, pp. 260–2.

Chancellor, Alexander, 'Whatever happened to the likely lass?', *The Sunday Telegraph Magazine*, 25 April 1999, pp. 28–30.

Chappell, Connery, 'The voice of the kinemagoer on what every exhibitor wants to know', *Kine Weekly*, 17 April 1947, p. 6.

Church, Michael, 'Out of Edwardiana', *The Observer*, 6 December 1992, p. 53.

Church Gibson, Pamela, 'No-one expects me anywhere: Invisible women, ageing and the fashion industry', in Stella Bruzzi and Pamela Church Gibson (eds), *Fashion Cultures* (London: Routledge, 2000), pp. 79–89.

Church Gibson, Pamela, *Fashion and Celebrity Culture* (London: Bloomsbury, 2012).

Clark, Nick, 'Glenda Jackson returns to stage', *The Independent*, 12 February 2016. http://www.independent.co.uk/arts-entertainment/theatre-dance/news/glenda-jackson-returns-to-stage-as-king-lear-in-gender-blind-production-at-old-vic-a6870956.html (last accessed 31 May 2016).

Clarke, Graham, 'A place to go', *Kine Weekly*, 2 April 1964, p. 10.

Clwyd, Ann, 'The family shiftworkers', *The Guardian*, 22 October 1973, p. 9.

Cochrane, Kira, 'Does nobody ever believe anything I do?', *The Guardian* (Weekend), 12 September 2009, pp. 18–22.

Coldstream, John (ed.), *Ever, Dirk: The Bogarde Letters* (London: Hachette, 2011).

Collier, Lionel, 'Must we have stars?', *Picturegoer*, 6 February 1943, pp. 6–7.

Collier, Lionel, 'Are we making our own stars at last?', *Picturegoer*, 16 October 1943, p. 5.

Collinson, Dawn, 'Liverpool teen Amy Jackson on her new life in Mumbai and becoming an in-demand Bollywood leading lady', *Liverpool Echo*, 25 January 2012. http://www.liverpoolecho.co.uk/news/liverpool-news/liverpool-teen-amy-jackson-new-3355952 (last accessed 31 May 2016).

Colls, Robert and Philip Dodd (eds), *Englishness: Politics and Culture 1880–1920*, second edition (London: Bloomsbury, 2014).

Colvin, Clare, 'Mystery moves', *The Times*, 23 May 1983, p. 17.

Colvin, Clare, 'As you like it or not', *Drama*, 1 April 1986, p. 12.

Cook, Emma, 'Look back in horror', *The Guardian* (G2), 12 November 1996, p. 6.

Cook, Pam, *Fashioning the Nation: Costume and Identity in British Cinema* (London: BFI, 1996).

Cook, Pam, 'The trouble with sex: Diana Dors and the blonde bombshell phenomenon', in Bruce Babington (ed.), *British Stars and Stardom* (Manchester: Manchester University Press, 2001), pp. 167–78

Coveney, Michael, 'Queen Judi', *The Independent*, 9 December 2004, p. 12.

Coxhill, Shelia, 'Letters from our readers: Stay as you are!', *Picturegoer*, 17 March 1945, p. 3.

Crawford, Anne, 'Of course British stars can be glamorous!', *Picturegoer*, 29 January 1949, p. 9.

Curtis, Adam, 'What the fluck!', *BBC Blogs: Adam Curtis*, 5 December 2013. http://www.bbc.co.uk/blogs/adamcurtis/entries/44122901-c2e8-34f5-93e 0-d4402c163966 (last accessed 31 May 2016).

Darnton, Nina, 'From school to stardom: A teenager's lark for Helena Bonham Carter', *The New York Times* (Review section), 2 March 1986, p. 17.

Datoo, Siraj, 'People are going absolutely crazy for this clip of an MP attacking Iain Duncan Smith', *Buzzfeed*, 4 July 2014. https://www.buzzfeed.com/sira jdatoo/iain-duncan-smith-would-like-to-think-he-can-walk-on-water?utm_ term=.hcWO88k7g#.ugNEmm7wD (last accessed 31 May 2016).

Davies, Jack, 'I'll take the mink and the glamour', *Picturegoer*, 11 December 1954, p. 23.

Davies, Russell (ed.), *The Kenneth Williams Diaries* (London: HarperCollins, 1994).

Davis, Ivor, 'Sign please! Hollywood's in a fizz for Emily', *Sunday Express*, 4 September 1988, p. 19.

Davis, Victor, 'Glenda, putting Oscars firmly in their place', *Daily Express*, 4 December 1969, p. 17.

Davis, Victor, 'The Arab eye-opener on Golan Heights – Rita', *Daily Express*, 15 August 1974, p. 8.

DeCordova, Richard, *Picture Personalities: The Emergence of the Star System in America* (Urbana: University of Illinois Press, 1990).

Deleyto, Celestino, 'The nun's story: Femininity and Englishness in the films of Deborah Kerr', in Bruce Babington (ed.), *British Stars and Stardom* (Manchester: Manchester University Press, 2001), pp. 120–31.

Dempster, Nigel, 'Of corsets Helena', *Daily Mail*, 21 April 1987, p. 17.

Dodd, Philip, 'Englishness and the national culture', in Robert Colls and Philip Dodd (eds), *Englishness: Politics and Culture 1880–1920*, second edition (London: Bloomsbury, 2014), pp. 25–52.

Dolan, Josephine and Estella Tincknell (eds), *Aging Femininities: Troubling Representations* (Cambridge: Cambridge Scholars Press, 2012).

Dolan, Josephine and Sarah Street, 'Twenty million people can't be wrong: Anna Neagle and popular British stardom', in Melanie Bell and Melanie Williams (eds), *British Women's Cinema*, (London: Routledge, 2009), pp. 34–48.

Dolan, Josie, '*The Queen*, aging femininity, and the recuperation of the monarchy', in Aagje Swinnen and John A. Stotesbury (eds), *Aging, Performance and Stardom: Doing Age on the Stage of Consumerist Culture* (Zurich and Berlin: LIT Verlag, 2012), pp. 39–53.

Dors, Diana, 'They made me a Good Time Girl', *Picturegoer*, 7 October 1950, pp. 8–9.

Dors, Diana, 'My blonde blunder', *Daily Express*, 13 May 1959, p. 10.

Dors, Diana, *Swingin' Dors* (London: World, 1960).

Dors, Diana, 'I have never been very wise about men', *TV Story*, April 1974, pp. 16–19.

Dors, Diana, *Dors by Diana* (London: Queen Anne, Macdonald Futura, 1981).

Dors, Diana, *Diana Dors' A–Z of Men* (London: Futura, 1984).

Dougary, Ginny, 'The lady is for turning', *Radio Times*, 21 November 2015, p. 120.

Douglas-Home, Robin, 'DD', *Daily Express*, 8 January 1962, p. 4.

Downing, Lisa and Sue Harris (eds), *From Perversion to Purity: The Stardom of Catherine Deneuve* (Manchester: Manchester University Press, 2007).

Drazin, Charles, *The Finest Years: British Cinema of the 1940s* (London: I. B. Tauris, 1998).

D'Silva, Beverley, 'Private emotions lie hidden in a very public body', *The Sunday Times* (Style), 15 October 1989, p. 5.

D'Silva, Beverley, 'Goody new shoes', *Sunday Express Magazine*, 21 April 1991, pp. 13–14.

D'Souza, Christa, 'Leave the dame alone, Minnie', *The Daily Telegraph*, 24 January 2002, p. 23.

Dugdale, John, 'Feuds Corner', *The Sunday Times* (Review), 20 October 1996, p. 16.

Duncan, Andrew, 'I like to remind people I exist out of a corset', *Radio Times*, 1 January 1994, pp. 24–5.

Duncan, Andrew, 'Par for the corset', *Radio Times*, 11 October 2003, pp. 26–9.

Durgnat, Raymond, *Films and Feelings* (London: Faber & Faber, 1967).

Durgnat, Raymond, *A Mirror for England: British Movies from Austerity to Affluence* (London: Faber & Faber, 1971).

Dyer, P. J., 'To find a star', *Picturegoer*, 21 July 1945, pp. 6–7.

Dyer, Richard, *Heavenly Bodies: Film Stars and Society* (Basingstoke: Macmillan, 1986).

Dyer, Richard, 'Four films of Lana Turner', in *Only Entertainment* (London: Routledge, 1992), pp. 79–111.

Dyer, Richard, 'Feeling English', *Sight and Sound,* March 1994, p. 16.

Dyer, Richard, *White* (London: Routledge, 1997).

Dyer, Richard, *Stars,* second edition (London: BFI, 1998).

Eames, Tom, 'Lethal Bizzle thanks Judi Dench for sales of clothing brand', *Digital Spy,* 11 December 2012. http://www.digitalspy.co.uk/showbiz/news/a444466/lethal-bizzle-thanks-judi-dench-for-sales-of-clothing-brand.html#~p59Z3FaqxjGKdW (last accessed 31 May 2016).

Eastaugh, Kenneth, untitled article, *The Sun,* 30 December 1970. Press cuttings file on Glenda Jackson, BFI Library.

Ebert, Roger, 'Review: In country', originally published *Chicago Sun-Times,* 29 September 1989. http://www.rogerebert.com/reviews/in-country-1989 (last accessed 31 May 2016).

Edwards, Anne, 'Woman's point of view', *Daily Express,* 17 October 1949, p. 3.

Edwards, Sydney, *Evening Standard,* 29 October 1971. Press cuttings file on Rita Tushingham, BFI Library.

Egan, Kate, 'A *real* horror star: articulating the extreme authenticity of Ingrid Pitt', in Kate Egan and Sarah Thomas (eds), *Cult Film Stardom* (London: Palgrave, 2013), pp. 212–25.

Ellis, John, *Visible Fictions* (London: Routledge and Kegan Paul, 1982).

Ellis, John, 'The quality film adventure: British critics and the cinema 1942–1948', in Andrew Higson (ed.), *Dissolving Views: Key Writings on British Cinema* (London: Continuum, 1996), pp. 66 –93.

Elsworth, Catherine, 'Keira Knightley is highest earning British Hollywood star on Forbes list', *The Daily Telegraph,* 24 July 2008. http://www.telegraph.co.uk/news/celebritynews/2455107/Keira-Knightley-is-highest-earning-British-Hollywood-star-on-Forbes-list.html (last accessed 31 May 2016).

Evans, Peter, 'To Bardot and Dors: The same questions on going to be a mother', *Daily Express,* 28 November 1959, p. 6.

Evans, Peter, 'John Osborne seeking ugly girl for taste of honey', *Daily Express,* 2 March 1960, p. 5.

Evans, Peter, 'Found: The ugly girl', *Daily Express,* 27 April 1960, p. 12.

Evans, Peter, 'I took my clothes off for reasons that were deeply intellectual', *People,* 12 April 1970.

Eyre, Richard, 'Richard Eyre on Judi Dench', *The Times* (Times 2), 2 February 2006, p. 15.

Fairclough-Isaacs, Kirsty, 'Mature Meryl and Hot Helen: Hollywood, gossip and the "appropriately" ageing actress', in Imelda Whelehan and Joel Gwynne (eds), *Ageing, Popular Culture and Contemporary Feminism: Harleys and Hormones* (London: Palgrave, 2014), pp. 140–54.

Fallows, George, 'Diana's new £2 ticket – on top of her £49,000 debt', *Daily Mirror,* 6 December 1968, p. 27.

Feinberg, Scott, 'And now, a word with the queen', *The Hollywood Reporter*, 28 February 2014, p. 60.

Ferry, Jeff, 'See Emily play', *Sunday Express Magazine*, 22 November 1987, pp. 24–7.

Finney, Joanne, 'You don't have to tell me what YOLO means!', *Good Housekeeping*, March 2015, pp. 22–6.

Fox, Chloe, 'Do not go gentle', *Telegraph Magazine*, 3 February 2007, p. 37.

Frankel, Martha, 'California Dreaming', *Movieline*, December/January 1999, pp. 62–67.

Franks, Alan, 'Mother courage', *The Times Magazine,* 19 November 2005, p. 48.

Freeth, Becky, 'Now THIS is why Dame Judi Dench is nothing short of awesome', *Marie Claire*, 9 December 2013. http://www.marieclaire.co.uk/blogs/545057/now-this-is-why-dame-judi-dench-is-nothing-short-of-aweso me.html (last accessed 31 May 2016).

Funnell, Lisa (ed.), *For His Eyes Only: The Women of James Bond* (London: Wallflower Press, 2015).

Gale, John, 'The girl with the knack', *Observer Magazine*, 11 July 1965, pp. 6–9.

Garde-Hansen, Joanne, 'The hip-op generation: Re-presenting the ageing female body in Saga Magazine', in Josie Dolan and Estella Tincknell (eds), *Aging Femininities: Troubling Representations* (Cambridge: Cambridge Scholars Press, 2012), pp. 161–70.

Gardner, Raymond, 'Powder blue bankrupt', *The Guardian*, 10 February 1978, p. 8.

Geraghty, Christine, 'Diana Dors', in Charles Barr (ed.), *All Our Yesterdays: 90 Years of British Cinema* (London: BFI, 1986), pp. 341–5.

Geraghty, Christine, 'Femininity in the fifties: The new woman and the problem of the female star', in *British Cinema in the Fifties: Gender, Genre and the 'New Look'* (London: Routledge, 2000), pp. 155–74.

Geraghty, Christine, 'Post-war choices and feminine possibilities', in Ulrike Sieglohr (ed.), *Heroines without Heroes: Reconstructing Female and National Identities in European Cinema, 1945–51* (London: Cassell, 2000), pp, 15–32.

Geraghty, Christine, 'Re-examining stardom: Questions of texts, bodies and per-formance', in Christine Gledhill and Linda Williams (eds), *Reinventing Film Studies* (London: Arnold, 2000), pp. 183–201.

Geraghty, Christine, 'Crossing over: Performing as a lady and a dame', *Screen*, Vol. 43, No. 1, spring 2002, pp. 41–56.

Geraghty, Christine, *My Beautiful Laundrette* (London: I. B. Tauris, 2005).

Geraghty, Christine, 'Women and 60s British cinema: The development of the "Darling" girl', in Robert Murphy (ed.), *The British Cinema Book*, third edition (London: BFI Palgrave, 2009), pp. 313–20.

Gilbey, Ryan (ed.), *The Ultimate Film* (London: BFI, 2005).

Gilliat, Penelope, 'Ophelia, Prince of Stratford', *The Observer*, 22 August 1965, p. 19.

Glaister, Dan, 'Oscar actress hits out at "old men" of British film industry', *The*

Guardian, 15 May 1997. https://www.theguardian.com/film/1997/may/15/news.danglaister (last accessed 31 May 2016).

Gledhill, Christine, 'Introduction', in *Stardom: Industry of Desire* (London: Routledge, 1991), pp. xiii–xx.

Gledhill, Christine, *Reframing British Cinema 1918–1928* (London: BFI, 2003).

Gledhill, Christine, 'Reframing women in 1920s British cinema: The case of Violet Hopson and Dinah Shurey', *Journal of British Cinema and Television,* Vol. 4, No. 1, 2008, pp. 1–17.

Gledhill, Christine and Gillian Swanson (eds), *Nationalising Femininity: Culture, Sexuality and Cinema in World War Two Britain* (Manchester: Manchester University Press, 1996).

Good Time Girl, press book, BFI Library.

Goodridge, Mike, 'It's a bitch of a role for Dame Judi', *Evening Standard,* 5 October 2006, p. 34.

Gosling, Kenneth, 'TV-am viewers top million mark', *The Times,* 15 August 1983, p. 3.

Gow, Gordon, 'One-take Jackson', *Films and Filming,* January 1977, p. 13–14.

Graham, Alison, 'Our girls in Hollywood', *Radio Times,* 11 May 1996, pp. 18–19.

Greer, Germaine, *The Female Eunuch* (London: MacGibbon & Kee, 1970).

Grimstead, Ruth, 'Down on the farm with Jean Kent', *Picturegoer,* 6 November 1948, pp. 6–7.

Gristwood, Sarah, 'Wish you were her?', *Daily Mail* (Femail), 15 April 1989, p. 9.

Gristwood, Sarah, 'Emily changes her spots', *TV Times,* 10 February 1990, p. 4.

Gristwood, Sarah, 'Get Carter', *The Guardian* (G2), 4 October 1996, p. 11.

Hadley, Katharine, 'Queen Helena's keeping her head', *Daily Express,* 22 May 1986, p. 28.

Hall, John, 'Dianamite yet', *The Guardian,* 18 March 1970, p. 9.

Hall, Sheldon, 'The wrong sort of cinema: Refashioning the heritage film debate', in Robert Murphy (ed.), *The British Cinema Book,* third edition (London: BFI, 2009), pp. 46–56.

Hall, William, 'The naked truth about Glenda', *Evening News,* 19 January 1971. Press cuttings file on Glenda Jackson, BFI Library.

Hamblett, Charles, 'Kent's heading for a crisis!', *Picturegoer,* 28 October 1950, pp. 12–13.

Harman, Jympson, *Evening News,* 7 April 1947. Press cuttings file on *The Man Within,* BFI Library.

Harper, Sue, 'Historical pleasures: Gainsborough costume melodrama', in Christine Gledhill (ed.), *Home Is Where the Heart Is: Studies in Melodrama and the Woman's Film* (London: BFI, 1987), pp. 167–96.

Harper, Sue, *Picturing the Past: The Rise and Fall of the British Costume Film* (London: BFI, 1994).

Harper, Sue, 'Thinking forward and up: The British films of Conrad Veidt', in Jeffrey Richards (ed.), *The Unknown 1930s* (London: I. B. Tauris, 1998), pp. 121–38.

Harper, Sue, *Women in British Cinema: Mad, Bad and Dangerous to Know* (London: Continuum, 2000).

Harper, Sue, 'The British women's picture: Methodology, agency and performance in the 1970s', in Melanie Bell and Melanie Williams (eds), *British Women's Cinema* (London: Routledge, 2009), pp. 124–37.

Harty, Russell, 'Works outing', *The Observer*, 14 August 1977, p. 26.

Harvey, John, 'She's becoming our top dollar earner', *Reynolds News*, 21 August 1949. Press cuttings file on Jean Kent, BFI Library.

Haskell, Molly, 'Why I love Lucy', *Vogue* (US edition), March 1986, p. 70.

Hayward, Susan, 'Framing national cinemas', in Mette Hjort and Scott MacKenzie (eds), *Cinema and Nation* (London: Routledge, 2000), pp. 88–102.

Hayward, Susan, *Simone Signoret: The Star as Cultural Sign* (London: Continuum, 2004).

Heilpern, John, 'The Magic of Glenda May', *The Observer*, 13 July 1975, p. 17.

Heilpurn, John, 'Empire of the stage', *Vanity Fair*, November 1995, pp. 161–215.

Hickey, William, 'Actress falls in for Tony's "twin" parade', *Daily Express*, 5 June 1962, p. 3.

Higson, Andrew, 'A diversity of film practices: Renewing British cinema in the 1970s', in Bart Moore-Gilbert (ed.), *The Arts in the 1970s: Cultural Closure?* (London: Routledge, 1994), pp. 216–39.

Higson, Andrew, 'Britain's finest contribution to the screen: Flora Robson and character acting', in Bruce Babington (ed.), *British Stars and Stardom* (Manchester: Manchester University Press, 2001), pp. 68–79.

Higson, Andrew, *English Heritage, English Cinema: Costume Drama since 1980* (Oxford: Oxford University Press, 2003).

Hill, Derek, 'A window on Dors', *Films and Filming*, April 1955, p. 10.

Hill, John, *British Cinema in the 1980s* (Oxford: Clarendon, 1999).

Hinxman, Margaret, 'They make me too old, says Jean Kent', *Picturegoer*, 13 November 1954, p. 23.

Hinxman, Margaret, 'The remarkable diary of Diana Dors', *Picturegoer*, 7 May 1955, pp. 14–15.

Hinxman, Margaret, untitled article, *The Sunday Telegraph*, 8 April 1973. Press cuttings file on Glenda Jackson, BFI Library.

Hirschhorn, Clive, 'I'm out in the cold now, says Diana Dors', *Sunday Express*, 15 September 1966, p. 22.

Hirschhorn, Clive, 'Men were my downfall – says Miss Dors', *Sunday Express*, 17 September 1978.

Hitchin, Chris, 'Ruthless routine broke lonely Emily, says dad', *Today*, 17 August 1989, p. 18.

Holden, Anthony, 'Mitfords and Mosleys', *The Sunday Times*, 3 April 1977, p. 32.

Holmes, Su, 'Starring Dyer?: Revisiting star studies and contemporary celebrity culture', *Westminster Papers in Communication and Culture*, Vol. 2, No. 2, 2005, pp. 6–21.

Holmes, Su and Diane Negra (eds), 'Introduction', in Diane Negra and Su Holmes (eds), *In the Limelight and under the Microscope* (London: Continuum, 2001), pp. 1–16.

Holt, Paul, 'Looking at the rushes', *Picturegoer*, 9 July 1949, p. 5.

Honan, Corinna, 'My long-distance romance with Warren Beatty', *Daily Mail*, 23 April 1992, p. 7.

hooks, bell and Emma Watson, 'In conversation', *Paper*, 18 February 2016. http://www.papermag.com/emma-watson-bell-hooks-conversation-1609893784.html (last accessed 31 May 2016).

Hopkins, Harry, *The New Look: A Social History of the Forties and Fifties* (London: Secker and Warburg, 1964).

Horner, Rosalie, 'Dors doing it in style', *Daily Express*, 30 June 1981, p. 23.

Howell, Peter, 'The rise of the British actress', *Photoplay*, December 1966, pp. 22–4, 40.

Hunt, Leon, *British Low Culture: From Safari Suits to Sexploitation* (London: Routledge, 1998).

Hutchins, Shelia, 'Some fruity advice from a domestic Diana Dors', *Daily Express*, 20 December 1973, p. 14.

Hutchinson, Diana, 'Why me?', *Daily Mail*, 18 August 1993, p. 3.

Hutchinson, Tom, 'The rose shows her thorns', *Picturegoer*, 12 November 1955, p. 13.

Irwin, Ken, 'Tonight's view', *Daily Mirror*, 8 April 1965, p. 18.

Jackson, Carolyn and Penny Tinkler, '"Ladettes" and "Modern Girls": "Troublesome" young femininities', *Sociological Review*, Vol. 55, No. 2, 2007, pp. 251–72.

Jacobs, Gerald, *Judi Dench: A Great Deal of Laughter* (London: Weidenfeld and Nicolson, 1985).

Jardine, Cassandra, 'I have to try living on my own', *The Daily Telegraph*, 21 April 1997, p. 15.

Jean Kent International Fan Club newsletter, October 1949. Jean Kent Collection, box 4, BFI Special Collections.

Jermyn, Deborah, '"Glorious, glamourous and that old standby, amorous": The late blossoming of Diane Keaton's romantic comedy career', *Celebrity Studies*, Vol. 3, No. 1, 2012, pp. 37–51.

Jermyn, Deborah, 'Introduction: "Get a life, ladies. Your old one is not coming back": Ageing, ageism and the lifespan of female celebrity', *Celebrity Studies*, Vol. 3, No. 2, 2012, pp. 1–12.

Jermyn, Deborah and Su Holmes (eds), 'Introduction', in *Women, Celebrity and Cultures of Ageing: Freeze Frame* (London: Palgrave Macmillan, 2015) pp. 1–10.

Johnson, Frank, 'Miss Dors listens in on the other wild blonde', *The Times*, 28 January 1983, p. 28.

Johnson, Frank, 'Now we know why he is called the Speaker', *The Times*, 4 February 1983, p. 26.

Johnson, Ian, 'The reluctant stars', *Films and Filming*, May 1962, p. 24.

Just Seventeen, 2 December 1987, p. 1.

Kael, Pauline, *Reeling* (New York: Warner Books, 1977).

Kael, Pauline, *When the Lights Go Down* (London and Boston: Marion Boyars, 1980).

Karle, Neal, 'Is America ready for a star like Emily Lloyd?', *Rolling Stone*, 5 October 1989, p. 95.

Kelly, Terence, *A Competitive Cinema* (London: Institute of Economic Affairs, 1966).

Kent, Jean, 'They make me too old', *Picturegoer*, 13 November 1954, p. 23.

Kilroy-Silk, Robert, 'I prefer older men, I can manipulate them', *Today*, 5 November 1988, pp. 22–3.

King, Barry, 'Embodying the elastic self: The parametrics of contemporary stardom', in Thomas Austin and Martin Barker (eds), *Contemporary Hollywood Stardom* (London: Arnold, 2003), pp. 45–61.

King, Justine, 'Crossing thresholds: The contemporary British woman's film', in Andrew Higson (ed.), *Dissolving Views: Key Writings on British Cinema* (London: Cassell, 1996), pp. 216–31.

Kinlay, Morven, 'Star is born at sweet 16!', *Daily Express*, 1 October 1986, p. 3.

Klevan, Andrew, *Film Performance: From Achievement to Appreciation* (London: Wallflower Press, 2005).

Knowles, Stewart, 'The girl with concern in her eyes', *TV Times*, 4 October 1973. Press cuttings file on Rita Tushingham, BFI Library.

Krainitzki, Eve, 'Judi Dench's age-inappropriateness and the role of M: Challenging normative temporality', *Journal of Aging Studies*, Vol. 29, April 2014, pp. 32–40.

Kuhn, Annette, 'Film stars in 1930s Britain: A case study in modernity and femininity', in Tytti Soila (ed.), *Stellar Encounters: Stardom in Popular European Cinema* (New Barnet: John Libbey, 2009), pp. 180–94.

Kureishi, Hanif, 'London's killing off its film-makers', *The Guardian*, 16 October 1991, p. 23.

Landy, Marcia, 'The other side of paradise: British cinema from an American perspective', in Justine Ashby and Andrew Higson (eds), *British Cinema, Past and Present* (London: Routledge, 2000), pp. 63–79.

Langdon-Davies, Jane, 'Thoroughly modern vapours', *What's On in London*, 4 March 1992, p. 4.

Lambert, John, 'The star-meter', *Daily Express*, 7 December 1956, p. 3.

Lambert, John, 'How's your starometer rating?', *Daily Express*, 19 September 1957, p. 8.

Lant, Antonia, *Blackout: Reinventing Women for Wartime British Cinema* (Princeton: Princeton University Press, 1991).

Lewin, Alex, 'Judi Dench', *Premiere*, December 1999, p. 46.

Lewin, David, 'Diana dares', *Daily Express*, 14 July 1954, p. 3.

Lewin, David, 'The girl they made a queen', *The Mail on Sunday* (*You* magazine), 10 March 1985, pp. 19–20.

Lewin, David, 'Hottest cookie in town', *Daily Mail*, 8 March 1988, p. 7.

Lewin, David, 'Rebel without a corset', *Daily Mail*, 14 March 1991, p. 7.

Lewis, Jane, *Women in Britain since 1945* (Oxford: Wiley-Blackwell, 1992).

Lewis, Patricia, 'Wide eyed appeal – in Tush's violet gaze', *Daily Express*, 7 September 1961, p. 10.

Lewis, Peter, 'Romantic Rita, the girl with 11 rings on her fingers', *Daily Mail*, 7 April 1969. Press cuttings file on Rita Tushingham, BFI Library.

Light, Alison, 'Englishness', *Sight and Sound*, March 1991, p. 63.

Light, Alison, *Forever England: Femininity, Literature and Conservatism between the Wars* (London: Routledge, 1991).

Limpkin, Clive, 'A Boadicea for the 20th century', *The Sunday Times*, 17 January 1982, p. 15.

Lloyd, Emily, *Wish I Was There: I was the Golden Girl of British Cinema . . . Then My Life Fell to Pieces* (London: John Blake, 2014).

Lowry, Suzanne, 'Diana, opening new doors', *The Observer*, 12 February 1978, p. 24.

Lusted, David, 'The glut of personality', in Christine Gledhill (ed.), *Stardom: Industry of Desire* (London: Routledge, 1991), pp. 251–8.

MacColl, Rene, 'Why Diana Dors can blossom like a rose in the desert – this place IS a desert, even if SHE'S no rose!', *Daily Express*, 5 September 1956, p. 6.

Mackay, Alice Jane and Pat Thane, 'The Englishwoman', in Robert Colls and Philip Dodd (eds), *Englishness: Politics and Culture 1880–1920*, second edition (London: Bloomsbury, 2014), pp. 217–54.

MacKenzie, Drew, 'Am I growing up too fast?', *Daily Mirror*, 10 December 1989, p. 24.

Macnab, Geoffrey, *J. Arthur Rank and the British Film Industry* (London: Routledge, 1993).

Macnab, Geoffrey, *Searching for Stars: Screen Acting and Stardom in British Cinema* (London: Cassell, 2000).

McAsh, Iain F., 'A touch of another class', *Films Illustrated*, February 1978, pp. 224–7.

McAsh, Iain F., 'Lost and found', *Films Illustrated*, July 1978, pp. 412–13.

McBride, Joseph, 'Glenda Jackson wins Oscars but still can't pick her scripts', *Variety*, 30 April 1975, p. 30.

McCarthy, Fiona, 'Sweet lives', *The Guardian*, 7 June 1967, p. 6.

McDonald, Paul, 'Star studies', in Joanne Hollows and Mark Jancovich (eds), *Approaches to Popular Film* (Manchester: Manchester University Press, 1995), pp. 79–98.

McDonald, Paul, 'The star system: The production of Hollywood stardom in the post-studio era', in Paul McDonald and Janet Wasko (eds), *The Contemporary Hollywood Film Industry* (Oxford: Blackwell, 2008), pp. 167–81.

McDonald, Paul, *Hollywood Stardom* (Oxford: Wiley-Blackwell, 2013).

McDowell, Felice, 'Clarks "star" advertisements of the 1940s: Classificatory terms and practices of historical interpretation', *Film, Fashion and Consumption*, Vol. 3, No. 3, December 2014, pp. 241–58.

McFarlane, Brian, *An Autobiography of British Cinema* (London: Methuen/BFI, 1997).

McFarlane, Brian (ed.), *Encyclopedia of British Film* (London: Methuen/BFI, 2003).

McFarlane, Brian, 'Ingénues, lovers, wives and mothers: The 1940s career trajectories of Googie Withers and Phyllis Calvert', in Melanie Bell and Melanie Williams (eds), *British Women's Cinema* (London: Routledge, 2009), pp. 62–76.

McGowan, Amanda, 'Judi Dench style evolution: She rocked the Pixie long before Anne Hathaway', *Huffington Post*, 7 December 2012. http://www.huff ingtonpost.com/2012/12/06/judi-dench-photos-2012_n_2251608.html (last accessed 31 May 2016).

Majumdar, Neepa, *Wanted Cultured Ladies Only! Female Stardom and Cinema in India, 1930s–1950s* (Chicago: University of Illinois Press, 2009).

Malcolm, Derek, 'An innocent on mean streets', *The Guardian*, 29 May 1986, p. 11.

Manger, Warren, 'Julie Walters: Working class kids can't afford drama school – soon only posh kids will be actors', *Daily Mirror*, 5 December 2014. http://www.mirror.co.uk/tv/tv-news/julie-walters-working-class-kids-4750761 (last accessed 31 May 2016).

Marghitu, Stefania, 'Violet, Dowager Countess of one-liners: Maggie Smith in *Downton Abbey* and internet stardom', unpublished paper presented at Exploring British Film and Television Stardom conference, Queen Mary University of London, 2 November 2013.

Marshall, P. David, *Celebrity and Power: Fame in Contemporary Culture* (Minneapolis: University of Minnesota Press, 1997).

Marshall, William, 'I can be loud-mouthed, even cocky but I'm not a little madam', *Daily Mirror*, 14 April 1986, p. 9.

Martin, Gill, 'Fame is a pain in the neck for Lady Jane Grey', *Daily Express*, 25 January 1985, p. 13.

Martin, Rosy, 'Outrageous agers: Performativity and transgression: Take one', in Josie Dolan and Estella Tincknell (eds), *Aging Femininities: Troubling Representations* (Cambridge: Cambridge Scholars Press, 2012), pp. 97–112.

Marwick, Arthur, *The Sixties: Social and Cultural Transformation in Britain, France, Italy and the United States, 1958–74* (Oxford: Oxford University Press, 1998).

Mask, Mia, *Divas on Screen: Black Women in American Film* (Chicago: University of Illinois Press, 2009).

Mayer, Annette, *Women in Britain, 1900–2000* (London: Hodder, 2002).

Maynard, John, 'Diana Dors: Girl with three dimensions', *Screenland*, March 1957, pp. 54–5, 67.

Mayne, Judith, *Cinema and Spectatorship* (London: Routledge, 1993).

Mayne, Laura, 'Assessing cultural impact: Film4, canon formation and forgotten films', *Journal of British Cinema and Television*, Vol. 11, No. 4, 2014, pp. 459–80.

Medhurst, Andy, 'Can chaps be pin-ups? The British male film star in the 1950s', *Ten 8*, No. 17, 1985, pp. 3–8.

'The Mike Wallace interview: Diana Dors', ABC network, 9 November 1957, uploaded on to YouTube on 23 January 2016 as 'Diana Dors – Complete Mike Wallace Interview, 1957'. https://www.youtube.com/watch?v=-Eaw29uk1BY (last accessed 31 May 2016).

Millar, Leisa, 'Timeless glamour', *Elle UK*, 23 May 2014. http://www.elleuk.com/fashion/celebrity-style/timeless-glamour-fashion-icons-joan-collins-judi-dench-jane-fonda#image=6 (last accessed 31 May 2016).

Miller, John, *Judi Dench: With a Crack in her Voice* (London: Orion, 2003).

Miller, Ruth, 'Jean Kent has something to say', *Leader*, 15 June 1946, pp. 18–19.

Mills, Simon, 'Tough kooky!', *Sky*, June 1988, pp. 7–10.

Moncur, Andrew, 'Happy to be there', *The Guardian*, 16 May 1987, p. 36.

Monk, Claire, 'The British heritage film debate revisited', in Claire Monk and Amy Sargeant (eds), *British Historical Cinema* (London: Routledge, 2002), pp. 176–98.

Morley, Sheridan, 'A Rather Funny Lady', *The Guardian*, 11 April 1973, p. 11.

Mortimer, Claire, 'Mrs. John Bull: The later life stardom of Margaret Rutherford', in Lucy Bolton and Julie Lobalzo Wright (eds), *Lasting Screen Stars* (London: Palgrave, forthcoming).

Mortimer, Penelope, 'Charley as exhibit A', *The Observer*, 10 November 1968, p. 24.

Morton, H. V., *In Search of England* (London: Methuen, 1927).

Mosley, Leonard, 'One girl – three lives', *Daily Express*, 11 August 1950, p. 4.

Moss, Robert F., *The Films of Carol Reed* (New York: Columbia University Press, 1987).

Mundy, Chris, 'Helena Grows Up', *Premiere*, November 1994, pp. 86–9.

Murdin, Lynda, 'Helena's royal road to success', *Evening Standard*, 28 September 1984, p. 8.

Murphy, Robert, 'Rank's attempt to the American market, 1944–9', in James Curran and Vincent Porter (eds), *British Cinema History* (London: Weidenfeld and Nicolson, 1983), pp. 164–78.

Murphy, Robert, *Sixties British Cinema* (London: BFI, 1992).

Naremore, James, *Acting in the Cinema* (Berkeley: University of California Press, 1990).

Nathan, David, *Glenda Jackson* (Tunbridge Wells: Spellmount, 1984).

Negra, Diane, *Off-White Hollywood: American Culture and Ethnic Female Stardom* (London: Routledge, 2001).

Negra, Diane, *What a Girl Wants? Fantasizing the Reclamation of Self in Postfeminism* (London: Routledge, 2009).

Negra, Diane and Su Holmes (eds), *In the Limelight and under the Microscope: Forms and Functions of Female Celebrity* (London: Continuum, 2011).

Newland, Paul, *British Films of the 1970s* (Manchester: Manchester University Press, 2013).

Newnham, John K., 'Jean enjoys her fame', *Picturegoer*, 23 November 1946, p. 12.

Newnham, John K., 'Progress report on the Charm School', *Picturegoer*, 25 September 1948, pp. 6–7.

News report, ITV Anglia News, 1 July 2011, uploaded on to YouTube on 30 April 2012 as 'Happy 90th birthday Jean Kent'. https://www.youtube.com/watch?v=KSqh31eDEuU (last accessed 31 May 2016).

Newton, Thandie, 'Embracing otherness, embracing myself', *TED Global*, July 2011. https://www.ted.com/talks/thandie_newton_embracing_otherness_embracing_myself (last accessed 31 May 2016).

Nightingale, Benedict, 'Britain's Emily Lloyd: Sweet 16 and a smash', *The New York Times* (Review section), 19 July 1987, pp. 21, 32–3.

Nightingale, Benedict, 'The Americanization of Emily', *The New York Times* (Review section), 20 August 1989, pp. 1, 22–3.

Noble, Peter, 'Top British talent in co-op venture', *Screen International*, 18 December 1982, p. 31.

Norman, Barry, 'The face of the 70s', *Daily Mail*, 2 April 1970.

Ottaway, Robert, 'No one loves a film star who looks forty', *Sunday Graphic*, 3 October 1954. Press cuttings file for Jean Kent, BFI Library.

Owen, Michael, 'From here to America', *Evening Standard*, 4 November 1988, p. 22.

Pastorek, Whitney, 'Judi Dench', *Entertainment Weekly*, 10 February 2006, p. 36.

Pendennis, 'Table talk', *The Observer*, 10 February 1957, p. 6.

Pendlebury, Richard, 'What went wrong with the world of Emily Lloyd?', *Daily Mail*, 7 July 1997, p. 23.

Perry, Simon, 'Judi Dench: What I know now', *People*, 16 March 2015, pp. 92–4.

Petley, Julian, 'There's something about Mary . . .', in Bruce Babington (ed.), *British Stars and Stardom* (Manchester: Manchester University Press, 2001), pp. 205–17.

Pevsner, Nikolaus, *The Englishness of English Art* (London: Architectural Press, 1956).

Plain, Gill, *John Mills and British Cinema: Masculinity, Identity and Nation* (Edinburgh: Edinburgh University Press, 2006)

Player, Ernie, 'Where does your money go?', *Picturegoer*, 27 November 1954, p. 18.

Polley, Naomi, 'My life as Swindon's Diana Dors', BBC Wiltshire, 16 December 2009, http://news.bbc.co.uk/local/wiltshire/hi/people_and_places/newsid_8416000/8416029.stm (last accessed 31 May 2016).

Powrie, Phil, 'On the threshold between past and present: "Alternative heritage"', in Justine Ashby and Andrew Higson (eds), *British Cinema, Past and Present* (London: Routledge, 2000), pp. 316–26.

Preston, Jane, 'Wish you were her', *Premiere*, March 1996, p. 46.

Proops, Marjorie, 'Honey for the bread and butter girl', *Daily Mirror*, 13 September 1961, p. 11.

Proops, Marjorie, 'Why are you vain?', *Daily Mirror*, 11 April 1962, p. 18.

Pulleine, Tim, 'A look back', *Films and Filming*, November 1986, p. 18.

Pulver, Andrew, 'What's all the fuss about Helena Bonham Carter', *The Guardian* (G2), 24 September 1999, p. 12.

Quantick, David, 'The knuckleduster hits Hollywood', *NME*, 28 November 1987, p. 26.

Rahman, Abid, 'Judi Dench is tired of people saying she is too old to act', *The Hollywood Reporter*, 12 November 2014. http://www.hollywoodreporter. com/news/judi-dench-is-tired-people-748698 (last accessed 31 May 2016).

Rahman, Abid, 'Dustin Hoffman: Judi Dench is a "scrumptious-looking woman"', *The Hollywood Reporter*, 26 November 2014. http://www.holly woodreporter.com/news/dustin-hoffman-judi-dench-is-752443 (last accessed 31 May 2016).

Railton, Diane and Paul Watson, '"She's so vein": Madonna and the drag of aging', in Josie Dolan and Estella Tincknell (eds), *Aging Femininities: Troubling Representations* (Cambridge: Cambridge Scholars Press, 2012) pp. 195–206.

Rampton, James, 'Corset still makes sense', *The Independent* (Guide), 10 January 1998, p. 4.

Rebello, Stephen, 'Lady Jane', *Movieline*, December/January 1999, p. 22.

Redmond, Sean, 'The whiteness of stars: Looking at Kate Winslet's unruly white body', in Sean Redmond and Su Holmes (eds), *Stardom and Celebrity: A Reader* (London: Sage, 2007), pp. 263–74.

Redmond, Sean, 'Thin white women in advertising: Deathly corporeality', *Journal of Consumer Culture*, Vol. 3, No. 2, 2003, pp. 170–90.

Redmond, Sean and Su Holmes (eds), 'Introduction', in *Stardom and Celebrity: A Reader* (London: Sage, 2007), pp. 1–12.

Richards, Dick, 'Rita's no honey – but this film tastes of success', *Daily Mirror*, 15 September 1961, p. 19.

Richards, Jeffrey, *The Age of the Dream Palace: Cinema and Society in Britain 1930–1939* (London: Routledge and Kegan Paul, 1984).

Riddell, Mary, 'Miss Knockout', *Daily Mirror*, 6 May 1988, p. 18.

Roberts, Claire, 'Face facts Elizabeth', *Evening Standard*, 14 March 1995, p. 47.

Robb, 'The things they do', *Daily Express*, 10 October 1952, p. 3.

Robinson, Robert, 'Now Jean is out of the doldrums', *Sunday Graphic*, 11 August 1957. Theatre press cuttings, Jean Kent collection, box 1a, BFI Special Collections.

Rook, Jean, 'Larger than life Diana – billowing into a new golden age', *Daily Express*, 12 November 1976, p. 15.

Rumbold, Judy, 'The mullah of Mondo Trasho', *The Guardian*, 10 July 1990, p. 37.

Russell, Sue, 'Redford rescued me from my Hollywood nightmare', *The Mail on Sunday*, 17 January 1993, p. 35.

Salisbury, Mark, 'Helena Bonham Carter', *Total Film*, January 2002, p. 36.

Sampson, Antony, 'Dig that crazy jive, man!', *The Observer*, 16 September 1956, p. 11.

Sandbrook, Dominic, *State of Emergency: Britain 1970–74* (London: Penguin, 2011).

Sandhu, Sukhdev, 'A jolly romp to nowhere', *The Daily Telegraph*, 16 September 2005. http://www.telegraph.co.uk/culture/film/3646583/A-jolly-romp-to-nowhere.html (last accessed 31 May 2016).

Sedgwick, John, 'Cinema-going preferences in Britain in the 1930s', in Jeffrey Richards (ed.), *The Unknown 1930s* (London: I. B. Tauris, 1998), pp. 1–36.

Sedgwick, John, *Popular Filmgoing in 1930s Britain: A Choice of Pleasures* (Exeter: Exeter University Press, 2000).

Sexton, David, 'What is it about Keira Knightley that gets people all riled up?', *Evening Standard*, 13 November 2014. http://www.standard.co.uk/lifestyle/london-life/what-is-it-about-keira-knightley-that-gets-people-all-riled-up-9857879.html (last accessed 31 May 2016).

Shah, Yagana, '5 things we love about Judi Dench on her 80th birthday', *Huffington Post*, 5 August 2014. http://www.huffingtonpost.com/2014/12/08/judi-dench-birthday_n_6277764.html (last accessed 31 May 2016).

Shapiro, Bee, 'Judi Dench of "Philomena": In real life, dressing the part', *The New York Times*, 20 December 2013. http://www.nytimes.com/2013/12/22/fashion/Judi-Dench-Philomena-Red-Carpet-Fashion-.html?_r=2& (last accessed 31 May 2016).

Sherry, Ken, 'I bet this shook the boys', *Picturegoer*, 25 September 1954, p. 12.

Sherwin, Adam, 'Femi Oguns: Agent whose black British actors are causing waves across Hollywood on racism in the industry', *The Independent*, 3 January 2016. http://www.TheIndependent.co.uk/arts-entertainment/films/features/femi-oguns-agent-whose-black-british-actors-are-causing-waves-across-hollywood-on-racism-in-the-a6795056.html (last accessed 31 May 2016).

Shingler, Martin, *Star Studies: A Critical Guide* (London: BFI Palgrave, 2012).

Shingler, Martin, 'Bette Davis: Acting and not acting her age', in Deborah Jermyn and Su Holmes (eds), *Women, Celebrity and Cultures of Ageing* (London: Palgrave Macmillan, 2015), pp. 43–58.

Simon, Francesca, 'Lady Jane's leading kids', *Vogue* (US edition), February 1986, p. 92.

Simons, Judith, 'Sarne regrets', *Daily Express*, 8 March 1963, p. 8.

Skeggs, Beverly, *Class, Self, Culture* (London: Routledge, 2003).

Soave, Daniela, 'Advantage Miss Lloyd', *The Sunday Telegraph* (*7 Days* magazine), 14 January 1990, pp. 15–17.

Sontag, Susan, 'Notes on camp', in *Against Interpretation and Other Essays* (New York: Picador, 1966), pp. 275–92.

Spain, Nancy, 'Diana Dors – that well-known mother', *Daily Express*, 10 February 1960, p. 9.

Spicer, Andrew, *Typical Men: The Representation of Masculinity in Popular British Cinema* (London: I. B. Tauris, 2001).

Spraos, John, *The Decline of the Cinema* (London: Allen & Unwin, 1962).

Stacey, Jackie, *Star Gazing: Hollywood Cinema and Female Spectatorship* (London: Routledge, 1994).

Stacey, Jackie, 'Crossing over with Tilda Swinton – the mistress of "flat affect"', *International Journal of Politics, Culture, and Society*, Vol. 28, No. 3, 2015, pp. 243–71.

Stapleton, John Y., 'Ladies or dames?', *Picturegoer*, 10 November 1945, p. 11.

Staskiewicz, Keith, 'Is 70 the new 30?', *Entertainment Weekly*, 14 August 2015, pp. 22–3.

Steele, Valerie, *The Corset: A Cultural History* (Boston: Yale University Press, 2001).

Stern, Michael, 'Angry-young-man fairy tale', *The New York Times*, 18 October 1966, p. 48.

Stone, Norman, 'Through a lens darkly', *The Sunday Times* (Review), 10 January 1988, pp. 1–2.

Stonier, George, 'A taste of honey', *Sight and Sound*, autumn 1961, p. 196.

Stott, Catherine, 'Gudrun and Glenda', *The Guardian*, 28 November 1969, p. 9.

Strachan, Alan, *Secret Dreams: A Biography of Michael Redgrave* (London: Weidenfeld and Nicholson, 2004).

Straight On till Morning press book, BFI Library.

Street, Sarah, *British National Cinema* (London: Routledge, 1997).

Street, Sarah, *British Cinema in Documents* (London: Routledge, 2000).

Street, Sarah, 'A place of one's own? Margaret Lockwood and British film stardom in the 1940s', in Ulrike Sieglohr (ed.), *Heroines without Heroes: Reconstructing Female and National Identities in European Cinema, 1945–51* (London: Cassell, 2000), pp. 33–46.

Street, Sarah, 'Star trading: The British in 1930s and 1940s Hollywood', in Alastair Philips and Ginette Vincendeau (eds), *Journeys of Desire: European Actors in Hollywood* (London: BFI, 2006), pp. 61–70.

Street, Sarah, 'Margaret Rutherford and comic performance', in I. Q. Hunter and Laraine Porter (eds), *British Comedy Cinema* (London: Routledge, 2012), pp. 89–99.

Swann, Paul, *The Hollywood Feature Film in Postwar Britain* (Kent: Croom Helm, 1987).

Sweet, Matthew, *Shepperton Babylon: The Lost Worlds of British Cinema* (London: Faber & Faber, 2005).

Tanner, Louise, 'Helena Bonham Carter and Cary Elwes', *Films in Review*, April 1986, p. 214.

Teeman, Tim, 'Judi twinned with punch', *The Times (Times 2)*, 11 December 2009, pp. 2–3.

Thirkell, Arthur, 'Pretty tough on Tush', *Daily Mirror*, 7 July 1972, p. 20.

Thomas, Sean, untitled article, *Evening Standard Magazine*, 23 December 1993, p. 8. Press cuttings file on Helena Bonham Carter, BFI Library.

Thomson, David, *A Biographical Dictionary of Film* (London: André Deutsch, 1995).

Thumin, Janet, *Celluloid Sisters: Women and Popular Cinema* (London: Macmillan, 1992).

Tincknell, Estella, 'The nation's matron: Hattie Jacques and British postwar popular culture', *Journal of British Cinema and Television*, Vol. 12, No. 1, 2015, pp. 6–24.

Todd, Derek, 'Paramount produces a peg to hang "swinging London"', *Kine Weekly*, 20 May 1967, p. 12.

Toon, Tony, 'Me and the Guru', *Photoplay*, October 1969, p. 20.

Tredre, Roger, 'A spate of undress', *The Guardian (G2)*, 14 January 1996, p. 9.

Truby, Jeffrey (ed.), *Daily Mail Film Award Annual: British Films of 1947*, London: Winchester Publications.

Truby, Jeffrey (ed.), *The British Film Annual 1949*, London: Winchester Publications.

Trueman, Matt, 'Glenda Jackson says MPs wouldn't cut it in the theatre world', *The Guardian*, 22 January 2013. https://www.theguardian.com/stage/2013/jan/22/glenda-jackson-mps-theatre (last accessed 31 May 2016).

Turner, Alwyn W., *Crisis? What Crisis? Britain in the 1970s* (London: Aurum, 2008).

Turner, Graeme, 'Approaching celebrity studies', *Celebrity Studies*, Vol. 1, No. 1, 2010, pp. 11–20.

Varriale, Jim, 'Emily Lloyd: Little Miss Moxie', *Vogue* (US edition), February 1988, pp. 372–7.

Vincendeau, Ginette, *Stars and Stardom in French Cinema* (London: Continuum, 2000).

Vincendeau, Ginette, *Brigitte Bardot* (London: BFI Palgrave, 2013).

Vincent, Sally, 'The honey trap', *The Guardian (Weekend* magazine), 22 March 1997, pp. 40–6.

Walden, Celia, 'Girl most likely', *Glamour*, November 2014, pp. 270–9.

Walker, Alexander, untitled article, *Evening Standard*, 18 April 1978. Press cutting file on Glenda Jackson, BFI Library.

Walker, Alexander, *National Heroes: British Cinema in the Seventies and Eighties* (London: Orion, 2005).

Walker, Steve, 'A thorny new role for an English rose', *The Mail on Sunday*, 30 August 1992, p. 13.

Ware, John, 'Hard time girl', *Picturegoer*, 20 December 1947, p. 8.

Warman, Janice, 'My brilliant career: Glenda Jackson, Labour MP', *The Guardian* (careers section), 13 April 1996, p. 2.

Wavell, Stewart, 'The girl with blue eyes', *The Guardian*, 26 May 1984, p. 9.

Waymark, Peter, 'Richard Burton top draw in British cinemas', *The Times*, 30 December 1971, p. 2.

Wearing, Sadie, 'Subjects of rejuvenation: Aging in postfeminist culture', in Yvonne Tasker and Diane Negra (eds), *Interrogating Postfeminism: Gender and the Politics of Popular Culture* (Durham, NC: Duke University Press, 2007), pp. 277–310.

Wearing, Sadie, 'Exemplary or exceptional embodiment? Discourses of aging in the case of Helen Mirren and *Calendar Girls*', in Josie Dolan and Estella Tincknell (eds), *Aging Femininities: Troubling Representations* (Cambridge: Cambridge Scholars Press, 2012), pp. 145–60.

Weaver, John, 'A flying fan drops in on Dors', *Daily Express*, 21 April 1958, p. 4.

Webb, Iain R., *Foale and Tuffin: The Sixties. A Decade in Fashion* (London: ACC, 2009).

Weedon, Jo, 'Wish you were her?', *The Mail on Sunday* (*You* magazine), 28 June 1987, pp. 32–4.

Weiler, A. H., 'A taste of honey', *The New York Times*, 1 May 1962, p. 15.

Whewell, Harry, 'Time to kill a few myths', *The Guardian*, 22 January 1966, p. 14.

Whitehall, Richard, 'DD', *Films and Filming*, January 1963, pp. 21–2.

Whitehead, Philip, *The Writing on the Wall: Britain in the Seventies* (London: Michael Joseph, 1985).

Whitley, Reg, 'Why British girls fail to – our men famous, but women disappoint', *Daily Mirror*, 13 April 1934, p. 20.

Whitley, Reg, 'Who are the stars of 1952?', *Daily Mirror*, 20 December 1951, p. 2.

Whitley, Reg, 'Success!', *Daily Mirror*, 8 September 1955, p. 1.

Whitley, Reg, 'Why Diana is banned again', *Daily Mirror*, 31 January 1952, p. 4.

Wilke, Lorraine Devon, 'Why American women hate their faces and what they could learn from the Brits', *Huffington Post*, 4 March 2014. http://www. huffingtonpost.com/lorraine-devon-wilke/why-american-women-hate-their-faces_b_4897336.html (last accessed 31 May 2016).

Williams, John, 'Glenda Jackson: Why I'll give up acting', *Films Illustrated*, August 1972, pp. 16–17.

Williams, Melanie, 'Twilight women of 1950s British cinema', in Robert Murphy (ed.), *The British Cinema Book*, third edition (London: BFI, 2009), pp. 286–95.

Williams, Melanie, *Prisoners of Gender: Women in the Films of J. Lee Thompson* (Berlin: VDM, 2009).

Williams, Melanie, 'Staccato and wrenchingly modern: Reflections on the 1970s stardom of Glenda Jackson', in Paul Newland (ed.), *Don't Look Now: British Cinema in the 1970s* (Bristol: Intellect Press, 2010), pp. 43–53.

Williams, Melanie, 'Entering the paradise of anomalies: Studying female character acting in British cinema', *Screen*, Vol. 52, No. 1, spring 2011, pp. 97–104.

Williams, Melanie and Ellen Wright, 'Betty Grable: An American icon in wartime Britain', *Historical Journal of Film, Radio and Television*, Vol. 31, No. 4, December 2011, pp. 543–59.

Williams, Melanie, 'The best exotic graceful ager: Dame Judi Dench and older female celebrity', in Deborah Jermyn and Su Holmes (eds), *Women, Celebrity and Cultures of Ageing: Freeze Frame* (London: Palgrave Macmillan, 2015), pp. 146–61.

Williams, Michael, *Ivor Novello: Screen Idol* (London: BFI, 2003).

Williamson, Anne, 'Sweet Lady Jane', *Sunday Mirror*, 25 May 1986, p. 20.

Wilson, Cecil, 'Panto will fill the cinema', *Daily Mail*, 26 September 1947.

Wise, Damon, *Come by Sunday: The Fabulous Ruined Life of Diana Dors* (London: Sidgwick and Jackson, 1998).

Wolf, Matt, 'Interview', *The Sunday Telegraph* (Review), 30 November 2003, p. 3.

Wolfson, Sam, 'Judi Dench: A new street icon?', *The Guardian*, 6 December 2011. http://www.theguardian.com/culture/shortcuts/2011/dec/06/judi-dench-street-icon (last accessed 31 May 2016).

The Woman in Question, press book, BFI Library.

Woods, Judith, 'Rosamund Pike: From reluctant English rose to Britain's new screen queen', *Daily Mail*, 24 September 2010. http://www.dailymail.co.uk/home/you/article-1311882/Rosamund-Pike-From-reluctant-English-rose-Britains-new-screen-queen.html (last accessed 31 May 2016).

Woodward, Ian, *Glenda Jackson: A Study in Fire and Ice* (London: Coronet, 1986).

Woodward, Kathleen, *Aging and its Discontents: Freud and Other Fictions* (Bloomington: Indiana University Press, 1991).

Woolf, Virginia, *A Room of One's Own and Three Guineas* (London: Penguin, 1993).

Woollacott, Angela, *Race and the Modern Exotic: Three 'Australian' Women on Global Display* (Clayton: Monash University Press, 2011).

Wright, Patrick, *On Living in an Old Country: The National Past in Contemporary Britain* (London: Verso, 1985).

Wright, Patrick, 'Wrapped in the tatters of the flag', *The Guardian*, 31 December 1994, p. 25.

Wyatt, Woodrow, 'Wake up!', *Daily Mirror*, 4 July 1956, p. 11.

Yield to the Night press book, BFI Library.

Young, Lola, *Fear of the Dark: 'Race', Gender and Sexuality in the Cinema* (London: Routledge, 1996).

Young, Susan, 'Battle over BBC series role offers hope for end to black typecasting', *The Observer*, 9 February 1992, p. 3.

Young, Toby, 'The snob value of ivory', *The Guardian*, 2 April 1992, p. 25.

Zec, Donald, 'At home – with Miss Dors', *Daily Mirror*, 31 May 1954, p. 2.

Zec, Donald, 'The odd girls out', *Daily Mirror*, 25 October 1961, p. 15.

Zec, Donald, 'The old firm', *Daily Mirror*, 3 May 1968, p. 9.

Zec, Donald, 'She was only a builder's daughter', *Daily Mirror*, 18 August 1970. Press cuttings file on Glenda Jackson, BFI Library.

Zec, Donald, untitled article, *Daily Mirror*, 16 February 1979. Press cuttings file on Glenda Jackson, BFI Library.

Zweininger-Bargielowska, Ina (ed.), *Women in Twentieth Century Britain* (London: Routledge, 2001).

Index

Adam and the Ants, 78
All Our Saturdays (1973), 77
Alligator Named Daisy, An (1955), 67
Amazing Mr. Blunden, The (1972), 76
Amis, Kingsley, 93
Andrews, Julie, 21, 88
Another Country (1984), 138
Arterton, Gemma, 11, 203
As Long as They're Happy (1955), 67, 70
As Time Goes By (1992–2005), 178
Ashton, Zawe, 201
Asquith, Anthony, 49–50
Associated British Picture Corporation, 3
Atkins, Eileen, 22, 106
Atonement (2007), 199
Attenborough, Richard, 44, 164n
Awfully Big Adventure, An (1995), 106

Baby Love (1968), 85n
Baker, Carroll, 153
Baker, Stanley, 14
Balfour, Betty, 10
Ball, Lucille, 25
Barber, Lynn, 17, 144–5, 204
Bardot, Brigitte, 11, 68–70, 153
Bassey, Shirley, 196
Beatles, The, 76
Beckinsale, Kate, 21, 168n
Bed-Sitting Room, The (1969), 103
Bees in Paradise (1944), 37, 39
Before I Wake (1954), 51
Belle (2013), 197, 201
Bend It Like Beckham (2002), 199
Bequest to the Nation (1973), 113, 119–20
Best Exotic Marigold Hotel, The (2011),
    176–80, 187–8
Biba, 88
Billy Liar (1963), 89–90, 151
Black, Cilla, 88
Blackman, Honor, 88
Blair, Tony, 149
Blethyn, Brenda, 20

Blunt, Emily, 11, 202–3
Bogarde, Dirk, 51, 67
Bond Street (1948), 45
Bonham Carter, Helena, 1, 19, 20, 23–6,
    133–72, 194, 197, 204
Bonjour Tristesse (1958), 52
Box, Muriel, 44–5
Box, Sydney, 44–5
Boyega, John, 201
Bread, 106
Brideshead Revisited (1981), 138
Brief Encounter (1945), 12
Browning Version, The (1951), 50–1
Bryan, Dora, 96
Burke, Kathy, 166n
Burrows, Saffron, 204
Burton, Richard, 14
Business as Usual (1988), 125

Caffin, Yvonne, 57n
Caine, Michael, 23
Calendar Girls (2003), 177
Calvert, Phyllis, 10, 19, 36, 39–41, 52–3
Cannes Film Festival, 70, 96, 137, 151,
    157–8, 163, 194–5, 200
Caravan (1946), 42–4
Chariots of Fire (1981), 133–4, 138
Cher, 160
Chicago Joe and the Showgirl (1990),
    159–60
Chocolat (2000), 174
Christie, Julie, 5, 19, 23, 75, 89–90, 93,
    107, 111, 127–8n, 151, 153
Class of Miss MacMichael, The (1978),
    124–5
Collier, Lionel, 5
Collins, Joan, 183–4
Connery, Sean, 14, 23
Connolly, Billy, 174, 182
Cookie (1989), 138, 156, 161
Coronation Street (1960–), 107
Courtenay, Tom, 23, 97–8, 116

Cranford (2007–9), 180, 186
Crawford, Anne, 3, 37, 42
Crawford, Joan, 40, 51, 124, 146
Crossroads (1964–88), 53
Cumberbatch, Benedict, 203
Cummins, Peggy, 53

Dam Busters, The (1955), 4
Dance with a Stranger (1985), 153
Danger Route (1967), 75
Darling (1965), 89–90, 102
Davis, Bette, 23, 40, 51, 116, 124–5, 179
Davis, Desmond, 102, 104
Day, Doris, 40
Day-Lewis, Daniel, 135–6
Deep End (1970), 76
Delaney, Shelagh, 90, 97, 103
Dench, Judi, 1, 19–20, 24, 112, 127, 135,
    173–93, 194
Deneuve, Catherine, 2, 11
Diamond City (1949), 59
Diamonds for Breakfast (1968), 103
Diaz, Cameron, 199
Dietrich, Marlene, 40, 124
Doctor Zhivago (1965), 89, 94, 104
Dors, Diana, 1, 16, 19–22, 59–87, 89, 151,
    175, 195
Downton Abbey (2010–15), 176, 185
Dreams of a Life (2011), 201
Driver, Minnie, 178
Duchess, The (2008), 199
Dunaway, Faye, 112
Dyer, Richard, 1, 8, 15, 17, 20, 122, 175–6,
    188, 197–8

East Is East (1999), 200
Eggar, Samantha, 89, 98
Elba, Idris, 196
Elizabeth (1998), 149
Elizabeth R (1971), 112, 120
Ella Enchanted (2004), 199
Elvey, Maurice, 5
Elwes, Cary, 138, 140
E.R. (1994–2009), 199
Esio Trot (2015), 178
Evans, Edith, 20
Evans, Peter, 17, 115

Faithfull, Marianne, 88
Fanny by Gaslight (1944), 38–9, 45
Fields, Gracie, 3, 10–11
Fight Club (1999), 137
Film on Four, 125, 133–5

Finch, Peter, 99, 120
Finney, Albert, 23, 97, 114, 125
Fish Tank (2009), 203
Foale and Tuffin, 88
Fonda, Jane, 112, 122, 177, 186
Forever Amber (1947), 53
Forster-Jones, Glenna, 196
Four in the Morning (1965), 174
Franklin, Rosalind, 125
Friel, Anna, 194
Full Monty, The (1997), 138

Gainsborough Studios, 36–7, 39, 41
Garson, Greer, 12, 21
Getting It Right (1989), 146
Girl with Green Eyes (1964), 93–5, 98–100,
    103
Giro City (1982), 125
Going Gently (1981), 173
Goldeneye (1995), 174
Gone Girl (2014), 204
Good-Time Girl (1948), 45, 49, 59
Good Wife, The (2009–15), 200
Gordon, Noele, 53
Grable, Betty, 21, 41, 48–9, 51, 61
Graham Norton Show, The (2007–), 182
Granger, Stewart, 39, 41–2, 44
Greenwood, Joan, 19
Greer, Germaine, 121
Gregory's Girl (1980), 134
Grip of the Strangler (1958), 37
Guinness, Alec, 5, 51
Guru, The (1969), 103
Gynt, Greta, 38

Haffenden, Elizabeth, 43
Hall, Jerry, 183–4
Hamilton, Dennis, 62–3, 71, 74
Hamlet (1990), 136
Hampshire, Susan, 89
Harper, Sue, 2, 20, 113
Harris, Naomie, 201–2
Hathaway, Anne, 26, 184
Hawkins, Jack, 51, 67
Hayward, Susan, 40
Hayworth, Rita, 40, 48
Hazard of Hearts, A (1987), 136, 143,
    146
He Who Rides a Tiger (1965), 174
Headey, Lena, 194
Hedda (1975), 124
Hepburn, Audrey, 3, 25, 90
Hepburn, Katharine, 23, 123

Her Favourite Husband/The Taming of Dorothy (1950), 49
Heywood, Anne, 4
Hobson, Valerie, 37
Hoggart, Richard, 65
hooks, bell, 204
Hopscotch (1980), 123
House Calls (1978), 123–5
Howards End (1992), 136, 144–6
Hurley, Liz, 6
Husbands and Wives (1992), 161

In Country (1989), 156, 163
Incredible Sarah, The (1976), 112
Iris (2001), 174, 176, 178–9
Is Your Honeymoon Really Necessary? (1953), 63
It's a Grand Life (1953), 64
It's That Man Again (1943), 39

Jackson, Amy, 21
Jackson, Glenda, 1, 20, 23, 111–32, 202
Jarvis, Katie, 203
Jean-Baptiste, Marianne, 194–5, 197, 199, 201
John, Rosamund, 37
Johnson, Celia, 5, 12, 37, 173
Joplin, Janis, 26
Jude (1996), 149

Kael, Pauline, 113, 116, 121–3
Kardashian, Kim, 25–6
Keaton, Buster, 103
Keaton, Diane, 112, 144
Kendall, Kay, 19
Kent, Jean, 1, 20, 21–2, 36–58, 61
Kerr, Deborah, 14–15, 22, 37, 40, 198
Kid for Two Farthings, A (1955), 67–8, 70
King's Speech, The (2010), 137, 140
Knack, The (1965), 90, 100–2
Knightley, Keira, 11, 199, 201, 203
Kureishi, Hanif, 133–4, 136, 141

Ladies in Lavender (2004), 177, 179, 186
Lady Godiva Rides Again (1951), 63, 79
Lady Jane (1985), 135, 139–41, 144
Laine, Cleo, 196
Lake, Alan, 76
Lake, Veronica, 61
Lane, Carla, 106
Last of the Blonde Bombshells, The (2000), 178
Leather Boys, The (1963), 98–9

Leigh, Vivien, 11, 119
Leighton, Margaret, 6
Leland, David, 137, 153, 155, 158
Lethal Bizzle, 182–3
Letter to Brezhnev (1985), 134–5
Liberace, 80
Light, Alison, 12
Lloyd, Emily, 1, 20, 24, 133–72, 195
Lloyd-Pack, Roger, 154, 160
Lock, Stock and Two Smoking Barrels (1998), 4
Lockwood, Margaret, 5, 10–11, 19, 36–8, 40–3, 47, 51–2, 81
Long Haul, The (1957), 73, 74
Lost and Found (1979), 123–4
Loves of Joanna Godden, The (1947), 38, 45
Lulu, 88, 121
Lupino, Ida, 21, 53

Mbatha-Raw, Gugu, 201
McClure, Vicky, 203
MacDonald, Kelly, 14
McElhone, Natasha, 194
McFarlane, Cassie, 196
McGowan, Cathy, 88
MacGraw, Ali, 112
Mackaill, Dorothy, 21
McKenna, Virginia, 19, 73
Madonna of the Seven Moons (1944), 10, 39
Magic Bow, The (1946), 39
Maids, The (1974), 120
Man in Grey, The (1943), 10, 37
Man Within, The (1947), 44
Marat/Sade (1967), 114
Margaret's Museum (1995), 146
Mary Shelley's Frankenstein (1994), 149
Mason, James, 36, 41, 43, 47, 104
Matthau, Walter, 123
Matthews, Jessie, 10, 19
Maurice (1987), 136
Merchant Ivory, 24, 103, 135–6, 139, 144, 146, 150
Mermaids (1990), 160–1
Miami Vice (1984–90), 146
Mighty Aphrodite (1995), 149
Miles, Sarah, 89
Millington, Mary, 19, 118
Mills, Hayley, 88
Mills, John, 51, 67
Mirren, Helen, 11, 19, 24, 112, 177–8, 181, 183
Miss London Ltd. (1943), 39
Mona Lisa (1986), 196

Monroe, Marilyn, 64, 68, 72, 78, 80, 153
More, Kenneth, 51, 67
Moreau, Jeanne, 118
Morecambe and Wise, 116, 119
Morton, Samantha, 203
Mrs Brown (1997), 173–4, 178, 180, 182, 194
Mrs Henderson Presents (2005), 174, 178–80
Munroe, Carmen, 201, 206n
Music Lovers, The (1970), 117, 119, 120
My Beautiful Laundrette (1985), 133–5, 138
My Wife's Lodger (1952), 60

Nagra, Parminder, 199
Napier-Bell, Simon, 61
Nasty Habits (1977), 124
Neagle, Anna, 10, 19, 36, 47, 51, 81
Negatives (1968), 117–18, 120
Newton, Thandie, 196, 201
Nighy, Bill, 177, 180, 187
Night with Mrs Da Tanka, A (1968), 52
No Strings (1974), 106
Notes on a Scandal (2006), 174, 176, 179, 186
Nunn, Trevor, 124, 135, 137, 139

Oberon, Merle, 195–6
Oguns, Femi, 201
Okonedo, Sophie, 196
Oldman, Gary, 5
Oliver Twist (1948), 62
Ormond, Julia, 6

Panjabi, Archie, 200
Paradine Case, The (1947), 8
Patricia Neal Story, The (1981), 125
Philomena (2013), 174, 176, 186, 188
Pickford, Mary, 6
Picturegoer, 3, 5, 8, 17, 41–2
Pike, Rosamund, 204–5
Pitt, Ingrid, 19
Place to Go, A (1963), 98–9
Planet of the Apes (2001), 137, 162
Portraits Chinoise (1996), 149
Poulton, Mabel, 19
Pretty Woman (1990), 163
Price, Dennis, 45
Pride and Prejudice (2005), 181, 186, 199
Prince and the Showgirl, The (1957), 52, 68
Princess Anne, 121
Princess Diana, 25, 138, 140, 151

Princess Margaret, 95–6
Psychobitches (2013–), 68, 80–1
Puffball (2007), 107
Pulp Fiction (1994), 163

Quant, Mary, 88
Queen, The (2006), 177
Queenie's Castle (1970–2), 77

Ragazza Del Palio, La (1957), 73
Rage (2009), 181
Rake's Progress, The (1945), 38, 39
Ramart, Yusuf, 44
Rampling, Charlotte, 24, 177
Rank, J. Arthur, 43, 48
Rank 'Charm School', 23, 62, 115
Rashomon (1950), 49
Redgrave, Lynn, 98, 102
Redgrave, Michael, 50, 67
Redgrave, Vanessa, 23, 89, 107, 127, 145
Redmayne, Eddie, 203
Reed, Oliver, 95, 119, 121, 125
Reluctant Widow, The (1950), 49
Resurrected (1989), 106
Return of the Soldier (1982), 125
Richardson, Tony, 91, 93, 96, 98
Ridley, Daisy, 11
Rigg, Diana, 88, 125
River Runs Through It, A (1992), 160
RKO, 60, 71
Roc, Patricia, 37, 40, 43, 51
Rogers, Ginger, 40
Romantic Englishwoman, The (1975), 113, 117, 122
Room at the Top (1958), 52
Room with a View, A (1985), 24, 135–7, 139–42, 144, 174
Royal Shakespeare Company, 113–14, 120, 173
Russell, Ken, 116, 119
Rutherford, Margaret, 20, 49
Ryder, Winona, 156, 160

Saigon – Year of the Cat (1983), 173
Saturday Night and Sunday Morning (1960), 97, 114
Scandal (1989), 153, 155
Sceptre (2015), 201
Scorchers (1991), 160
Scott Thomas, Kristin, 194
Segal, George, 118–19, 123
Sellers, Peter, 5

Seventh Veil, The (1945), 7
Shakespeare in Love (1998), 174
Shapiro, Helen, 90
Shaw, Sandie, 88
She'll Be Wearing Pink Pyjamas (1984), 134
Sheen, Michael, 5
Shipping News, The (2001), 181
Shop at Sly Corner, The (1946), 62
Shrimpton, Jean, 88, 148
Signoret, Simone, 52, 118
Sim, Alastair, 67
Simmons, Jean, 22, 37
Skyfall (2012), 174, 181, 188, 201
Sleeping Car to Trieste (1948), 45
Smashing Time (1967), 90, 102–3
Smith, Maggie, 24, 112, 125, 127, 135, 176, 185
Smiths, The, 80
So Evil My Love (1948), 8
Something's Gotta Give (2003), 177, 188
Spice Girls, The, 196
Sporting Life, This (1963), 114
Spring in Park Lane (1948), 36
Springfield, Dusty, 88
Stacey, Jackie, 10
Steaming (1985), 79–80
Steele, Barbara, 21
Steiger, Rod, 71
Stevie (1978), 112, 117, 124–5
Stone, Sharon, 6
Straight on till Morning (1972), 105
Streep, Meryl, 116, 174
Streisand, Barbra, 92–3, 112, 122
Suez crisis, 71–3
Suffragette (2015), 137
Sunday Bloody Sunday (1971), 111, 117, 120–1
Swinton, Tilda, 19

Talking to a Stranger (1966), 173
Tank Girl (1995), 161
Taste of Honey, A (1961), 23, 90, 94, 96, 98, 107, 173
Tatler, 138–9, 142, 156
Taylor, Alma, 10, 26
Taylor, Elizabeth, 21, 65
Tell Me Lies (1968), 114
Temple, Shirley, 61
Thatcher, Margaret, 78–9, 126
There's a Girl in My Soup (1970), 76
Thompson, Emma, 6, 144–5
Todd, Ann, 7–10, 37

Todd, Richard, 51, 67
Touch of Class, A (1973), 111, 117–19, 123–4
Town Like Alice, A (1956), 73
Trainspotting (1996), 138, 161
Trap, The (1966), 95
Tread Softly Stranger (1958), 73
Tree, Penelope, 94
Trevor, Claire, 53
Triple Echo, The (1972), 121
Trottie True (1949), 45–6, 48
Turtle Diary (1985), 125
Tushingham, Rita, 1, 20, 22–3, 75, 88–110, 114–15, 151, 173, 195, 202
TVAM (1983–92), 79
Twiggy, 88, 94, 148, 183–4
Two Ronnies, The (1971–87), 78
Two Thousand Women (1944), 39–40
Tynan, Kenneth, 3, 67, 78
Tyson, Cathy, 196

Ullman, Tracey, 175, 182
Under the Skin (1997), 106
Unholy Wife, The (1957), 71

Value for Money (1955), 67, 79
Venice Film Festival, 67, 183

Walker, Alexander, 113, 115, 120, 151–3
Walters, Julie, 151–3, 202
Ward, Sophie, 204
Waterloo Road (1945), 39
Waters, John, 65
Watson, Emily, 194
Watson, Emma, 11, 204
Weak and the Wicked, The (1954), 79
Weinstein, Harvey, 174–5, 181
Weisz, Rachel, 11
Welch, Elisabeth, 195
Welch, Raquel, 118
West, Mae, 6, 48, 67
West 11 (1963), 75
When Saturday Comes (1996), 161
Where Angels Fear to Tread (1991), 136
White, Carol, 88
Whitehouse, Mary, 121
Wicked Lady, The (1945), 36, 39
Windsor, Barbara, 208n
Wings of the Dove, The (1997), 137, 150, 194
Winslet, Kate, 6, 11, 19, 168n, 194, 203–4

Wisdom, Norman, 51, 67
Wish You Were Here (1987), 24, 137,
151–5, 157, 159
Withers, Googie, 19, 37, 38, 42, 52
Withnail and I (1987), 4
Without a Trace (2002–9), 200
Women in Love (1969), 111, 117, 119, 120,
123
Woman in Question, The (1950) 1, 22,
49–50
Women Talking Dirty (1999), 149

Woolf, Virginia, 12
Wright, Letitia, 201

Yardley, 148–9
Yield to the Night (1956), 68–70
York, Susannah, 23, 89, 104, 107
Young, Loretta, 8

Zec, Donald, 17, 65, 93, 97, 115, 118
Zeta-Jones, Catherine, 14
Zulu (1964), 4